ENCOUNTER ON THE GREAT PLAINS

Encounter on the Great Plains

SCANDINAVIAN SETTLERS AND THE DISPOSSESSION OF
DAKOTA INDIANS, 1890–1930

Karen V. Hansen

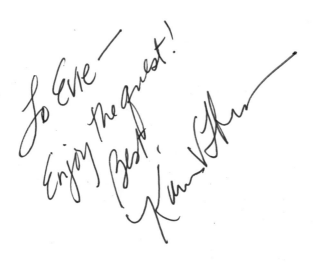

OXFORD
UNIVERSITY PRESS

OXFORD
UNIVERSITY PRESS

Oxford University Press is a department of the University of Oxford.
It furthers the University's objective of excellence in research, scholarship,
and education by publishing worldwide.

Oxford   New York
Auckland   Cape Town   Dar es Salaam   Hong Kong   Karachi
Kuala Lumpur   Madrid   Melbourne   Mexico City   Nairobi
New Delhi   Shanghai   Taipei   Toronto

With offices in
Argentina   Austria   Brazil   Chile   Czech Republic   France   Greece
Guatemala   Hungary   Italy   Japan   Poland   Portugal   Singapore
South Korea   Switzerland   Thailand   Turkey   Ukraine   Vietnam

Oxford is a registered trademark of Oxford University Press
in the UK and certain other countries.

Published in the United States of America by
Oxford University Press
198 Madison Avenue, New York, NY 10016

Library of Congress Cataloging-in-Publication Data
Hansen, Karen V.
Encounter on the Great Plains : Scandinavian Settlers and the Dispossession of Dakota Indians, 1890–1930 /
Karen V. Hansen.
pages cm
Includes bibliographical references and index.
ISBN 978–0–19–974681–1 (hbk. : alk. paper); 978–0–19–062454–5 (pbk. : alk. paper)
1. Scandinavian Americans—North Dakota—Devils Lake Region (Lake)—History.   2. Scandinavian
Americans—Land tenure—North Dakota—Fort Totten Indian Reservation.   3. Indians of North
America—Land tenure—North Dakota—Devils Lake Region (Lake)   4. Spirit Lake Tribe, North
Dakota—History.   5. Indian allotments—North Dakota—Devils Lake Region (Lake)   6. Rural women—
North Dakota—History.   7. Dakota Indians—North Dakota—Interviews.   8. Norwegians—North
Dakota—Interviews.   9. North Dakota—Ethnic relations.   10. Fort Totten Indian Reservation (N.D.)—
History. I. Title. II.   Title: Scandinavian settlers and the dispossession of Dakota Indians, 1890-1930.
F645.S2H35 2013
305.8009784—dc23
2013004849

For Anita and Eva,
undaunted fighters, true friends

Contents

APPENDIXES

Maps (interleaved in text)

Documents (interleaved in text)

Figures

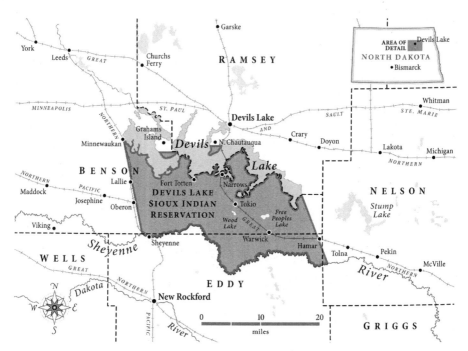

MAP 1 Map of Devils Lake region.

The Spirit Lake Dakota Reservation at the center is bounded by Devils Lake to the north and the Sheyenne River to the south. Map drawn by David Deis.

Preface: The Story Dowser

AS I WAS growing up in Sonoma County, California, my mother would regale me with stories about her childhood on the homestead in Saskatchewan and the move to Alberta in 1932, under the crush of the Great Depression. She gifted me snippets of bold characters and a farm life I found absolutely foreign. She would conjure up vivid portraits of her kindly father, her heroic brothers who fought in World War II, her mother and sisters full of humor and strength, and cousins with a talent for music-making. By the time I was nine, these story sessions were my primary conduit for intimacy with my mother. They connected me to a family past and to those she had wrenchingly left behind. Many of these relatives were still living, but the distance between us made them larger than life. This inheritance of storytelling linked me with a larger history as I sought my own place within the world.

The mythic figures of the Northern Plains sounded so much more appealing than my ordinary relatives at hand. Here we were, bound in a small knot, far away from the resilient web of security and sanity represented by my extended kin as I came to know them through my mother's stories. On late nights, full of emotion, I would ache to reunite with my idealized family. Often, when sent to bed, I would deploy my most irresistible ruse: "Tell me a story." My mother, Esther, granted my inopportune requests. Suffering from immigration's dismembering, the anguish of her thoughtless children's unceasing demands, and her husband's insensitivity, she sought healing through her stories. So my ploy would work. For Esther, telling stories represented vindication and a reunification of her fractured life. Throughout my life I have continued to pester people for stories about my ancestors and those of others, even after I understood the many sources of their resistance.

HISTORICAL MEMORY AND FAMILY STORIES

My own quest has led me to seek to understand my mother and her mother in the context of their times and struggles. I see them as agents of their own destinies, and yet they acted within identifiable, collective patterns in North American history. Both of them are protected by our family mythology, which is at least as powerful as the family itself. The stories inspire honorable behavior, elicit shame, and cloak the ephemeral actions of today with the meaning of yesterday. Inevitably we interpret historical events through the prism of the present.

In my family's legends, my maternal grandmother, Helene Haugen Kanten, stood out as a heroic pioneer (see figure 1). She arrived in North America as a flaxen-haired eleven-year-old and became a sturdy woman, tall for her generation, with steel-grey braids folded atop her head. I was awestruck by her fortitude, which, in my mind, implied strength of character. In the face of ever-present Victorian conceptions of women's frailty, my grandmother's endurance and productivity served as a visible rebuff to the dominant culture. My generation-skipping adoration gave renewed meaning to the Norwegian term for grandmother—*bestemor*, literally, "best mother." She cleared new land three times during her life, raised eight children, and lived to be ninety-one years old. Family lore reports that once, while my grandfather was away on a trip, she even built a barn. I did not see her often enough to have her tell me many stories; my cousins were the lucky ones in that regard. She left me with some gems, however. She would say she was born in Hønefoss, Norway. "Chicken Falls," she would giggle, clasping her hands in front of her mouth in delight as her shoulders jiggled. Hønefoss sounded to me like a town in a children's fable, where traveling carnivals would park before venturing into the big city.

Through my research, I have discovered significant untruths in our family mythology. Hønefoss was not Helene's actual birthplace, but rather the large town in the Ringerike region that others were more likely to know. Many accounts were not merely factually inaccurate, but misleading. For example, we were told that Grandma's father died before she was born. In fact, he died *two years* before she was born. Her biological father was a younger man whom my widowed great-grandmother never married. We were told that my great-aunt Aagodt's first husband died in Norway. Yet, ship passage lists from 1903 reveal that he traveled to North Dakota with Aagodt and their month-old son. He spent the last seventeen years of his short life in the Jamestown Insane Asylum. Whatever wisps of truth accompanied those stories blew by too quickly to capture them. Through her silence about her family history, my grandmother participated actively in the mythmaking about her own past. Selectively "forgetting" her family's history was deliberate; the strategic construction of "ignorance" enabled those after her to hold fast to these misconceptions.[1] In the New World, you can recreate your past—at least until your pesky granddaughter persists in asking questions.

ASKING QUESTIONS

In 1995, I traveled to North Dakota for the first time to piece together the puzzle (see map 1). A town called Devils Lake had been my grandmother's original North American destination. I wanted to find her mother's homestead where she came of age. I wanted to imagine the world as my grandmother had experienced it. Staff at the Fort Totten historic site just south of Devils Lake on the Spirit Lake Dakota Indian Reservation pointed me to one of the remarkable local history keepers— Cherry Wood Monson, a "Pioneer Daughter" descended from white settlers who came to Dakota Territory prior to statehood. Born and raised on the reservation and called to record and recount history, she introduced me to plat maps and led me to my great-grandmother's homestead in Eddy Township.

A plat map records the owners of land within a thirty-six-square-mile town-ship. On the survey grid imposed upon the Northern Plains, every square-mile section was subdivided into quarter sections of 160 acres each. Never having lived in the Midwest, where plat maps are as common as road atlases, I was immediately mesmerized. To my amazement, I discovered that my grandmother and her mother were not the only Norwegians who lived on the Spirit Lake Dakota Reservation. Nor was my great-grandmother the only woman to own land; women's names were sprinkled liberally across the maps. The mosaic of long Dakota names, difficult for my unfamiliar tongue to pronounce, sat adja-cent to the myriad "sons" of Scandinavian origin I remember from my child-hood—the Olsons, Andersons, Carlsons.

My drive across the reservation was full of beauty and surprises, from vast wet-lands and acres of sunflowers with faces turned toward the light, to the rickety Norwegian ski jump erected atop a hill in the early 1930s (see figure 2). Tall green cattails line the abundance of bright blue ponds, called "pot holes" or sloughs by locals, that provide habitat for numerous species of waterfowl—from Canada geese to red-necked grebes and northern shovelers. Driving at dusk often pits a car or truck against flocks of birds crossing from one pond to the next. I regularly found myself braking so as not to hit a swooping bird. The windshield and grill of the car stand as a testament to the abundant insect life that attracts birds and feasts on unsuspecting livestock and humans. In the last twenty years, roads have been rebuilt higher and higher as the water table has been rising and Devils Lake overflows, saturating the earth. The great never-ending flood has washed out highways, turned through ways into dead ends, inundated homes, and rendered thousands of acres on and around the reservation impossible to farm.

As we drove the gravel road wending down to the Sheyenne River, I was struck with wonder at this hilly terrain. This area near the Sheyenne has long been recognized as a magnet for wildlife, and people often come here to hunt for deer. My great-grandmother, Berthe Haugen, took possession of her quarter section in 1905 and built a twelve-by-fourteen-foot home that was just barely standing ninety years later. From this perch at the crest of the hill, right near the northern boundary of her land, she had a magnificent view of the Sheyenne River valley, etched progressively deeper over thousands of years. Clusters of trees sheltered the house, some of the 600 Berthe had planted by the time she took title in 1912. The floors inside the weathered grey wooden structure were broken through in places, evidence of a heavy animal seeking shelter from the elements. Each time I return to the reservation, I am compelled to revisit this spot, a place I think of as my great-grandmother's land even though she sold it seventy-five years ago. How strange that her homestead was on an Indian reservation.

As astonishingly beautiful as the landscape was, nothing was familiar. No formation held markings I recognized. Nothing felt comfortable. In turn, I realized, I was equally foreign to the people who, like Cherry Wood Monson, welcomed me so kindly.

One morning a few years later, as I was interviewing a respected Dakota elder, Agnes Greene, her son arrived to have coffee and inspect me. "Good morning," he said. "Hi, I'm Karen Hansen, visiting from Boston," I replied. "Oh, a stranger, in other words."[2] Yes, I thought to myself, I am a stranger. I talk too fast. I travel thousands of miles with a university grant to pay for my rental car, my hotel, and the expensive equipment I use to record interviews. I recognized the implicit antipathy to people with advanced education and ample resources; as a college professor from a working-class background, that, at least, was familiar.

With good reason, Dakota Indians did not embrace intrusions from white settlers like my great-grandmother, or from supposedly well-intentioned researchers who visited from time to time. Renowned and controversial anthropologist Robert Lowie briefly traveled to the reservation in 1911, where he interviewed leading men of the tribe, and later wrote "Dance Associations of the Eastern Dakota."[3] Native people remained skeptical and resisted European Americans' desire to voyeuristically observe sacred rituals and abscond with mystical powers. Social scientists and photographers, like writers and artists, have sought something in indigenous culture sadly lacking in their own. In the 1920s, the collaboration between Amos E. Oneroad (Sisseton-Wahpeton from Lake Traverse), who was training to be a

Presbyterian minister, and anthropologist Alanson B. Skinner ended catastrophically. In 1925, when, driving near the reservation village of Tokio and collecting artifacts and stories of Sissetons and Wahpetons, their car veered off the muddy road and overturned, killing Skinner instantly. Some locals explained the tragedy as retribution by the spirits for "fooling around with the *wakanwacipi* stuff."[4] Wakanwacipi is a sacred dance that, according to the missionary Stephen R. Riggs, is performed by "the secret society among the Dakotas which purports to be the depository of their sacred mysteries."[5]

Most peoples, whether fragile or robust, experience a tug of war over history and integrity, a tension between trumpeting the news and guarding secrets. As I set out to uncover the human stories and societal truths behind my ancestors' journey across the Atlantic and their new lives in North Dakota, I encountered individuals and groups who are pulled back and forth by this taut rope.

North Dakotans, white as well as Indian, have long expressed distrust of outsiders, profiteers, big business, those who come only to extract natural resources. My field notes from my early visits reflect people's skepticism about my motives. They might hang up when I called, or simply never answer my letters. The resistance paralleled that found by Daniel Mendelsohn, who sought narratives about what had happened to his Polish family before and during the Holocaust. One family member refused to give him an on-the-record interview because, she protested, "I don't want my life in your book."[6] Frustrated, Mendelsohn conceded that "she knew that the minute she allowed me to start telling her stories, they would become my stories."[7] She would lose control, and perhaps in his hand the meaning of her stories would shift.

From North Dakotans' perspective—Dakota and Scandinavian alike—the main thing that gave me legitimacy was my ancestry. My great-grandmother homesteaded here. My grandmother grew up here. As I traveled around the reservation and its environs, people would automatically accept my quest when they learned that I sought to understand my grandmother's life. Like those third-generation children of immigrants who seek histories buried in the Americanization process, I sought to understand my heritage as a means of coming to terms with a history that privileged my family at the expense of Native Americans.

Some people found my questions nettling, bothersome, unsettling. Some greeted me with silence. Others rejected my requests altogether. Like the clamoring grandchildren in Tillie Olsen's story about a life reconsidered, *Tell Me a Riddle,* I would refuse to accept "no" for an answer. Olsen's short story centers on an elderly protagonist, Eva, and her agonizing effort to maintain her personhood as she faces her mortality. Her desire to retreat unhindered into herself and her books after a lifetime of interruptions is greater than her desire to reach out and embrace. "I know no riddles," she protests.[8] But some seek healing in this history: setting the record straight, confronting painful truths, finding catharsis in the telling, and holding on to the promise of reconciliation. Over time others' distrustful stance toward me seemed to shift. Perhaps I lost my acute sensitivity to their skepticism; maybe our interactions changed as I learned more about this place and people got to know me.

DOWSING FOR STORIES

In an oral history recorded for the State Historical Society of North Dakota, second-generation Norwegian American Gurine Moe (b. 1890) told of her husband's rare and valuable talent: he was a water dowser. "He could go out with the willow and wherever…there was water, the willow turned down to the ground." Many on the prairie were called upon to find and tap that scarce, essential resource. Water was harder to find in some places, and farmers would dig as many as twenty wells before they found it. In other places, such as the Moes' farm, they were lucky enough to find water with the first dig and have the well last for over fifty years.

One of the many delightful people I met in North Dakota is a different kind of dowser. Second-generation Norwegian American Juel Smestad (b. 1921) is a *bone* dowser. Instead of locating water with a willow branch, he has the gift of finding bones. In locating people's skeletal remains, he links the living to the dead by enabling them to know precisely where their ancestors lay. In the process of identifying these unmarked graves, Smestad unearths the consequences of judgment, superstition, and prejudice. Some wayward souls were buried outside consecrated ground because the church fathers found their lives unworthy of holy sanction or forgiveness. Others were excluded because they were the "wrong" religion or nationality. Novelist and editor Willa Cather wrote powerfully and insightfully about ethnic tensions and homesteading hardships in the Midwest at this historical moment. In *My Ántonia*, her fictional Bohemian Catholic Mr. Shimerda was refused burial in the Norwegian Lutheran cemetery.[9] Juel Smestad once located the remains of an African-American family buried on the periphery of a church cemetery. "Sure enough I found one outside the fence. See, they wouldn't let 'em in."

Like Juel Smestad, I feel the calling of a dowser—a story dowser. I search for the forgotten or vexing stories of the past, bringing some unrecognized members into the family plot and marking their graves. But I do not always put people at ease by telling them that their ancestors are rightfully placed. My unearthing is often unsettling. I aim to make the reader think deeply and uneasily about these stories, many unhappy, some tragic, others victorious.

Unlike Juel Smestad, I do not leave the bones where they lay. I dig them up, reassemble them based on my best guess of how they fit together, and hope that doing so will bring us closer to understanding the meanings and consequences of actions long ago.

This book took me more than a decade to write after I first visited North Dakota. I now understand that stretch of time not as a series of delays but as a necessary condition for the completion of this project. By doggedly returning year after year, as small discoveries led to new insights, the puzzle pieces eventually started falling into place. People on the reservation came to understand that I was a serious researcher interested in giving back, not a passerby or an expropriator. In various ways people let me know that they not only felt fine about my project, but they wanted to be interviewed, they wanted to show me their treasures, they wanted me to write this book. When I first formally interviewed Dakota tribal member Phillip John Young (b. 1944), he found my questions challenging in a way he had not expected. He told me he was "asking for strength, to know this meaning, so I can help *you*." It is not the historical sources that changed over this decade, but my relation to the living that brings meaning to the departed.

In 2005 I arrived on the reservation in late July, just in time to catch the Fort Totten Summer Theater's production of *Fiddler on the Roof*. Coming from Brandeis University, an ecumenical, secular but Jewish-sponsored institution where such a production would be commonplace, I found the idea jarring, even comical. Until the moment that I saw the blue-eyed Tevye on stage, I did not understand how the play could work on the Great Plains, even as exotic entertainment. The drama is set in a Russian village in 1905. The threat of pogroms hovers as the ominous backdrop to Tevye's efforts to eke out a living by selling milk to the villagers and to marry off his daughters to good Jewish men. Astonishingly, the cast became peasants before my eyes, their stirring performances resonating with the universal truths of the story. The embattled and soon-to-be-landless Tevye and his family could have been impoverished Norwegians forced to migrate or Dakotas ousted from their ancestral lands. The profound pain of dispossession infused the production, making it a deeply North Dakotan story. I realized that my absorption with the encounter at Spirit Lake, a seemingly remote place at an idiosyncratic time, reflected a deeper need to comprehend recurring patterns in world history.

That same summer, I had a change of heart as my responsibility in the reciprocal exchange of doing fieldwork became clearer to me. My calling was to retell and interpret the stories I was being told. As Agnes Greene had pointed out several years before, the interview was mine, not hers. At the end when I asked her, "Is there anything [else] I should know?" she responded, "Ask me. You're the one who wants to know. Ask me. If I know it I'll tell you."

Her clarity helped set me straight. Ultimately, however carefully I listened, however much I let storytellers shape their own narratives, the interviews I conducted were mine. I directed the conversation; I asked the questions; I was motivated to publish. My challenge was to ask the *right* question. But I should never make the mistake of thinking the story I was telling was hers. In the retelling, these accounts became mine, reframed through the prism of my interests. For Agnes Greene, I was not filching her stories, I was constructing my own.

By the time I left the reservation that year, I felt a new sense of validation and respect from others. I had met with the local history group that included both Cherry Monson and Louis Garcia, the honorary tribal historian for the Spirit Lake Dakota. Although Cherry had always been welcoming and eager to share her remarkable archives and personal knowledge, perhaps this time she too recognized that I could do more than poke around. As we were driving across the reservation, Phillip John Young took the initiative to stop and introduce me to Ambrose Littleghost (b. 1932), the pipe carrier of the tribe, and his gracious wife, Anna Littleghost. The manager of the Fort Totten bed and breakfast, Joyce Gross, willingly turned the inn into my base camp by cheerfully taking messages for me and cooking an elaborate breakfast for Ambrose and Anna so that I could host them. After returning home from that trip, I received a card that closed with: "Thanks for making our lives more interesting. Love, Cherry Monson."[10]

Listening to people involves more than hearing their words. It requires respecting and honoring their secrets, joys and sorrows, triumphs and tragedies, and sense of humor. And it requires recognizing their common humanity despite divisions and differences. I understood more profoundly that my scholarly quest reassembled my own disrupted ethnic identity and brought my forgotten and erased family history into view. I could legitimately search for the family I had fantasized about, although my discoveries would not necessarily fill me with pride and admiration.

Dakota and Scandinavian people of Spirit Lake have given me so much of themselves and shared their historical memories. The question remains: What responsibility do I, the historical sociologist—a stranger of particular kind—have to reciprocate?

Social scientists debate what researchers should give their subjects in return for their engagement. Some think that listening is sufficient because the act validates the life of the storyteller. They worry that giving money can be a thinly veiled form of expropriation, trading dollars for answers. What if the accounts were tailored to their monetary value, corrupted by the profits to be made from the opportunity? Others argue that the researcher should give something back. After all, researchers typically hold powerful social positions and use other people's testimonies to advance their careers. Anthropologists have long understood the gift exchange as fundamental to doing fieldwork. Some go further and say the researcher should help mobilize resources for political ends, teach skills, or provide services. Some feminist scholars suggest that you should give something of yourself—friendship, empathy, a relationship—to equalize the interaction and diminish the lopsidedness of the exchange.

Compensation seems like the least Native people could expect from those out to study or profit from them. For centuries, Indians have been ripped off, their secrets exploited, photographs taken, and mythologies revealed, all for the sake of non-Indians' benefit. We have to ask, if the exchange is consensual, does that alter the outcome? If payment is robust, does that make it sufficient? How does paying for stories differ from, say, buying a novel? I gave small tokens of appreciation to my subjects—a flashlight, a calculator, a pen knife, a pie. But Native people also expected to be paid. Money was not an additional nicety or a vulgarity; it established an understanding, a foundation of exchange for the conversation.

My ability to give back in other ways has been hobbled by my outsider status and by my acute awareness of the fine line I walk as someone interested in Native American history as well as Scandinavian immigrant sagas. This book is my effort to reciprocate. I now realize that I came to this project in order to repair my fractured sense of ethnic identity and remedy my placelessness, as a daughter of an immigrant mother and a restless father who thought that frequent moving was a way to repair mistakes and start over. I hope readers will join me in grappling with a history of this space where Native Americans and Scandinavian immigrants lived side by side, each enmeshed in their own people's worldview, but where, 100 years later, they are able to reflect on the stories that both divide and link them.

Acknowledgments

Like every creative project, a book is the product of many people, who share their minds and hearts to make it happen. Those generous subjects who agreed to be interviewed—by me and other oral history collectors—have provided an invaluable service by sharing their stories and insights. The documentary sources from the early twentieth century came alive because of these folks, and others, who have guided me and taught me the cultural logics of the past. Louis Garcia, the honorary tribal historian of Spirit Lake Dakotas, and the late Marcy Young McKay, Dakota tribal member and former director of the Senior Meals Program on the reservation, connected me with elders who could contribute valuable perspectives. Without Louie's "Garcia Messages," translations, vast archive, and generosity of wisdom, this book would be cripplingly lopsided. Hilda Garcia, a constant partner with Louie, helped recruit people to be interviewed and shared her own insights about growing up on the reservation. Similarly, the late Phillip John Young generously gave his time and perspective on Dakota culture. Cherry Wood Monson first led me to my great-grandmother's homestead site and introduced me to the marvel of plat maps. Sadly, Cherry died before her plans for her own museum panned out, but she was an extraordinary history keeper who has left her mark. Seemingly random, serendipitous encounters led others to contribute to the project through interviews, sharing archives, and entrusting invaluable family photographs to me. Many thanks to Cherrie Lane Anderson, Stanley Eliason, Louis Garcia, Brian Greene, Sonja Kanten Haney, John Knudson, Vern Lambert, James Skurdall, and Marlys Peterson Throlson.

Through thick and thin, Grey Osterud has invested intellectual energy in tutoring me on agricultural history and editing multiple versions of each chapter. She has been the best kind of critic, and her discerning editorial eye has immeasurably enhanced the structure, argument, and prose of the book. My steadfast writing group—Mignon Duffy and Debra Osnowitz—has never failed with good humor, inspiration, and constructive suggestions. They joined several colleagues who read earlier versions of the entire manuscript, and the book has considerably improved from their critical engagement: Stephanie Bryson, Mary Childers, Fredrick Hoxie, and Kay Jenkins. Others have read one or two chapters, asked hard questions, and pushed me to clarify my arguments: Gary Anderson, Joyce Antler, Maxine Baca Zinn, Grete Brochmann, Andrew Bundy, Penny Cherns, Louis Garcia, Anita Ilta Garey, Amanda Gengler, Clare Hammonds, Barbara Handy-Marchello, Benjy Hansen-Bundy, Arlie Hochschild, Tom Isern, Lucia Hsiao, Beth LaDow, Margaret Nelson, Carmen Sirianni, Anne Tofflemire, and Harvard's 2012-13 Charles Warren Center Fellows and facilitators: Luis Alvarez, Robin Bernstein, Jayna Brown, Bruce Dorsey, Martha Hodes, David Jaffe, Ann Pellegrini, Kyla Wazana Tompkins, Sara Warner, and Sandy Zipp. I have received constructive feedback from conference panelists and discussants too numerous to mention. I want especially to recognize Gunlög Fur and the workshop she organized on "Indians and Immigrants" at the University of Minnesota that served as an intellectual turning point for me.

Photographs and maps give visual definition to the people and places in the book. For her delight in the faces and stories and her skill at surfacing the beauty of the images, I thank Sarah Putnam who edited the historical photographs. After years of searching for geographers who might be able to help me translate historical plat maps into a GIS analysis, I met Robert Rose, then staff in the Harvard University Map Room. It was pure joy to find someone who instantly understood what I wanted to do, knew how to do it, and then proceeded to work with Mignon Duffy and me to generate gorgeous maps. The map of Spirit Lake region was expertly drawn by cartographer David Deis. Kate Babbitt skillfully proofread and indexed the book.

Responsive librarians and archivists create accessibility as well as a sense of adventure. I appreciate the patient support and guidance provided by: Liv Bengstrom (Norsk Folkemuseum), Forrest Brown (Norwegian-American Historical Association), John Bye (Institute for Regional Studies, North Dakota State University (NDSU)), Elizabeth Carrington (Kansas City Regional Office, National Archives and Records Administration), Carol Culbertson (Vesterheim Genealogical Center), Eunice Davidson (Lake Region Heritage Museum), Jim Davis (State Historical Society of North Dakota [SHSND]), Laurann Gilbertson (Vesterheim Museum), Rhonda Greene (Fort Totten Historic Site, SHSND), John Hallberg (Institute for Regional Studies, NDSU), Curt Hanson (Special collections, University of North Dakota

[UND]), Jack Mattson (Fort Totten Historic Site, SHSND), Jennifer McElroy (Minnesota Historical Society), Shane A. Molander (SHSND), Jean Olson (Superintendent of Benson County School District), Kari-Anne Pedersen (Norsk Folkemuseum), Judith Pinnolis (Brandeis University), Jim Schiele (Lake Region Heritage Museum), Ellen Sieber (Mathers Museum of World Cultures), Sharon Silengo (SHSND), Sandy Slater (Special collections, UND), Knut Sprauten (Historical Publications, Riksarkivet), and Ralph Szymczak (Brandeis University), and Dina Tolfsby (National Library, Norway). With gratitude I thank kin keepers who make it their business to document family histories and genealogies and in this case helped me map the Kantens and Haugens: Verlyn Anderson, Shirley Kanten, Anne Sladky, and Thorlief Solberg. Of the dozens of archives I have visited, the State Historical Society of North Dakota deserves special recognition for its dedication to making its archives accessible. In particular, I appreciate its foresight in sponsoring the North Dakota Oral History Project in 1975 and 1976 and sending interviewers Larry Sprunk and Robert Carlson across the state to capture and preserve invaluable voices in their distinct cadences. My dear cousins Sylvia Hansen Horning and Penny Gosselin interviewed Eleanor Barrett Hansen for me before she died.

Scholars across the globe have engaged this project. For their receptive welcome and generous help early in the project, I want to thank Elizabeth Hampsten, H. Elaine Lindgren, Mary Jane Schneider, Father William Sherman, and Playford Thorson. Other colleagues lent their expertise, suggested things to read or people to contact, engaged in lively exchanges of ideas, and debated possible titles: Guy Abutbul Selinger, Margaret Andersen, Johnny Bell, Betty A. Berglund, Grete Brochmann, Andrew Bundy, Stephen Bundy, Penny Cherns, Peter Conrad, Alice Friedman, Gunlög Fur, Anita Ilta Garey, Naomi Gerstel, Torben Grøngaard Jeppesen, Øyvind T. Gulliksen, Rosanna Hertz, Adam Hochschild, Lynn Johnson, Jytte Klausen, Deb Kanten Kobza, Lori Ann Lahlum, Laura Miller, Jan Eivind Myhre, Peter Nabokov, Grant O'Brien, Jean M. O'Brien, Patricia Kanten O'Brien, Helle Porsdam, George Ross, Lois Rudnick, Faith Smith, Nicholas Townsend, and Michael Witgen.

Several former students who started out as research assistants later became collaborators, coauthors, and friends—special thanks to Stephanie Bryson, Mignon Duffy, Clare Hammonds, and Ken Sun. An army of research assistants has helped comb through the manuscript census, check quotations, transcribe faintly recorded interview tapes, mine Ancestry.com for misspelled names, and search newspapers on microfilm. My heartfelt appreciation for their careful work: Alison Angell, Jennifer Bourque, Nora Bundy, Rosemary Casler, Amanda Gengler, Evan Hansen-Bundy, Lucia Hsiao, Sonja Jacob, Yoon-Jin Kim, Emily Kolker, Valerie Leiter, Julie Morris, Doris Parfaite-Claude, Anne Pollock, Dawn Robinson, Jenna Rosenbloom, and Ida Rukavina.

From the moment I first talked about Indians and immigrants with James Cook, my editor at Oxford University Press, he enthusiastically engaged me. His enduring belief in the project has made it possible to get up at 5:00 a.m. and face the footnotes. I want to thank several institutions for their generous support, which made it possible to take time off from teaching, conduct research, and write: the Charles Warren Center for the Study of American History at Harvard University; the John Simon Guggenheim Memorial Foundation; the National Endowment for the Humanities; and the Norwegian Royal Ministry of Foreign Affairs, Emigration Fund of 1975. The J. M. Kaplan Foundation has awarded this book a Furthermore Grant to enhance the quality of its publication.

From the beginning, my colleagues at Brandeis University have supported my scholarship in numerous ways. Mazer and Norman grants for faculty and the new Senior Faculty Leave have funded travel and research expenses over the years. The innovative Scholar-Student Partnership program provided undergraduate research assistance. The Center for German and European Studies provided critical funds to travel to a Norwegian-American Historical Association-Norway conference in Hamar. Successive deans of the Faculty of Arts and Sciences—Robin Miller, Jessie Ann Owens, Adam Jaffe, and Susan Birren—have supported my leaves and helped create intellectual space at Brandeis University. Administrative staff, especially the incomparable Judith A. Hanley, have been unfailingly resourceful.

Kind relatives and friends provided quiet houses where I could retreat to write or stay while visiting archives. Many thanks to Alice Friedman, Lena Sorensen, Susan Klaw, Peter Del Tredici, Mary L. Bundy, Paula Bundy, William Bundy, Beth Botti, Jon Erik Dolvik, Grete Brochmann, Helle Porsdam, Matthias Mann, Roberta Miller, and Alan Medville. Joyce Gross turned the Fort Totten Bed and Breakfast into a welcoming home. My extended Kanten and Hansen families have answered sometimes nettling queries; for their indulgence and love I am deeply grateful.

My own home has been a vibrant and restorative space. My life partner, Andrew Bundy, has been willing to anchor family while I traveled to North Dakota; he has read and edited endless chapters, accompanied me on long walks, debated fine points of U.S. history and sociological theory, and believed in me. My deeply loving and thoughtful children, Benjy Hansen-Bundy and Evan Hansen-Bundy, cannot remember life before this project. They have joined me on this journey and given me the satisfaction of becoming interested in their ancestors—as role models and metaphors for their own lives.

Introduction: Illuminating the Encounter

AS I BEHELD my great-grandmother's long-vacant dilapidated homestead shack on a hill overlooking the Sheyenne River (see figure 3), I became increasingly perplexed. How did Berthe Haugen, a fifty-one-year-old widow, and her children leave Norway and end up homesteading on the Spirit Lake Dakota Indian Reservation? From reading U.S. history, I knew about European Americans' perpetual expropriation of indigenous people's land and natural resources, as well as the devastating diseases and warfare that reduced Native populations and undermined their autonomy. And I knew that women homesteaded in the American West. But Norwegian women on an Indian reservation? Thus began my own encounter with my ancestral past and my face-to-face meeting with Dakota people whose land the reservation had once been.

A historical sociologist by training, I began a journey that led me out of my geographic and temporal areas of expertise. I confronted two cultures utterly foreign to me, those of turn-of-the-century Norwegian immigrants and of indigenous Dakota people. How did so many newly arrived Scandinavians come to homestead on the reservation? What was the impact of their presence? How did Dakotas, who had been promised territorial integrity, respond to this incursion? In the end, what did the two groups' uneasy coexistence yield, given the paradoxical actions of the U.S. government; the divergence between subsistence farming and industrialized, market-oriented agriculture; and the differing cultural logics of two peoples who were complete strangers to each other? What can we learn about encounters that accelerated a process of dispossession?

Taking these questions as a point of departure, this book explores the underlying historical encounter between immigrants and Indians in the early twentieth century. In the United States we think of cross-cultural encounters as beginning between indigenous peoples and European traders in the sixteenth century and culminating in warfare between the U.S. government and Indian nations in the nineteenth century. But this particular engagement of separate worlds involved Scandinavian immigrants and Dakota Sioux on an Indian reservation in North Dakota *after* 1900. Decades of living side by side created multiple and contradictory layers of conflict, adaptation, resistance, and mutuality within the social relationships on this land.[1]

Encounter on the Great Plains brings into the same frame two dominant processes in American history: the unceasing migration of people to North America, and the protracted dispossession of indigenous peoples who inhabited the continent. The historical encounter at Spirit Lake in a small corner of eastern North Dakota encapsulates the story of conquest and white settlement of North America and the less publicized but equally important story of the dispossession and survival of Native Americans. Further, it demonstrates the consequences of offering land to peasants from abroad in order to recruit laborers for the expanding nation's mission of development. The material wealth and the nationalist mythology of the United States are built upon this history.[2]

The Sisseton and Wahpeton bands of Dakotas whom immigrant Scandinavians encountered were not this place's primordial residents but had themselves settled here in the wake of the U.S.–Dakota War of 1862. They joined another band, Ihanktonwannas (labeled "Cutheads" and Yanktonais in historical documents), who claimed Spirit Lake as their place of origin and the region as their territory, who had not lived in Minnesota and were not part of the war but were nonetheless displaced by it. Reeling from the loss of their historic way of life but still recognized as a sovereign nation, they collectively negotiated a treaty with the United States in 1867 that established the 240,000-acre reservation. At the turn of the twentieth century, when homesteading began, tribal enrollment numbered slightly over 1,000. Dispossession meant relocation and population decline. Native people worked to find a home for their families and make a new life under unfamiliar and unstable legal, environmental, and economic circumstances.

Impoverished immigrants who had set off from their ancestral homeland, too, sought land and a place to remake home.[3] While they did not venture forth as mercenaries or as conscious participants in a colonial scheme, they nonetheless advanced the U.S. imperial project of seizing and transforming North America. White settlers were recruited as instruments of the twin federal policies of westward expansion and the economic and cultural assimilation—or, as many Dakotas saw it, the cultural annihilation—of native peoples.[4] In northern Europe, the governments of Dakota Territory and later North Dakota found a seemingly inexhaustible source of destitute and eager immigrants to populate the region. Those making the journey did not see themselves as serving Manifest Destiny, furthering western civilization, or spreading Christianity among a pagan people, but they nonetheless acted as instruments of colonialism.

Here we confront the human face of expropriation: the land takers and the dispossessed. Spirit Lake attracted Dakotas and Scandinavians from Minnesota who had engaged in armed conflict with one another. Scandinavians anticipated struggles with Native Americans—although for the most part they had not fought in the 1862 war, they had read about it in Norwegian newspapers and in the Scandinavian American foreign-language press.[5] Indians were described as the "Red race," and Scandinavians' attitudes and actions reflected the racism of reigning ideologies.[6] At the same time, they saw themselves as worthy land takers and proficient farmers.

By 1900, as Scandinavian immigration to the United States swelled, few opportunities for homesteading remained. The exceptions were in arid, relatively inhospitable parts of North Dakota and Montana and on Indian reservations. In North Dakota, most settlers were first- and second-generation Scandinavians who were exceedingly poor, had little formal education, and spoke broken, accented English, if they spoke English at all. But they knew that land, provided they could obtain it cheaply, could serve as a foothold and be made to yield a livelihood. Whether they came directly from Norway or Sweden or elsewhere in the Midwest after spending years as landless laborers, they sought to improve their lives through landownership. By 1929, Scandinavians came to dominate as residents and farmers, owning fully one-third of reservation land—indeed, more acreage than Dakotas themselves owned. What does it mean when one group's acquisition of land is predicated on the dispossession of the other?

Four decades following the U.S.–Dakota War, this stigmatized space was the site where dispossession and immigration faced off. The startling 1904 map of the reservation advertised Indian land available for homesteading, where, in effect, the Dawes Act converged with a version of the Homestead Act (see map 2). Published as a broadside, the black (red in the original) checkers mark the unallotted Indian land that homesteaders could newly settle. Like a blotchy plague, the invasive squares appear to creep north from the Sheyenne River. Homesteaders at Spirit Lake lived close to the indigenous people they had just dispossessed; after all, this geographic space was still legally designated as an Indian reservation. Living on the reservation marked its residents—white or Indian—as distinct from the surrounding community. My grandmother, Helene Haugen Kanten, attended a public school just south of the reservation in Eddy Township. She recalled the stinging taunts of the other students who called her a "squaw" because she lived on the reservation. As Dakota women well knew, white people used this racial epithet to mark and degrade Native women.[7]

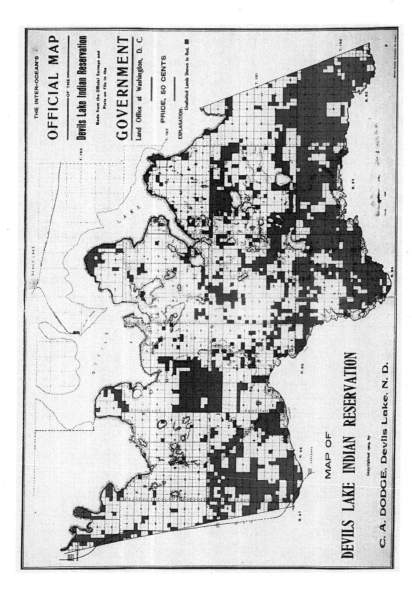

MAP 2 Map of unallotted lands at Spirit Lake, 1904.

This broadside, made from "official survey and plats," advertised unallotted lands available for homesteading on the Spirit Lake Dakota Indian Reservation (then called the Devils Lake Sioux Indian Reservation). Potential homestead sites are marked in red on the original. Published by the *Devils Lake Inter-Ocean,* copyrighted by C. A. Dodge, 1904. (Courtesy Lake Region Heritage Museum.)

MY QUEST

As I pondered the implications of this peculiar situation, I wondered: Why had no one studied this sort of encounter before? Although the two groups converged here, as they did at other times and places, the histories of immigrants and Indians have generally been treated as separate fields of study. Until recently, stories of homesteaders have been told as if they had nothing to do with the fate of Native peoples whose lands they took.[8] Historical chronicles of "pioneer settlers" have privileged white Yankees[9] and European immigrants and cast Indians as a colorful backdrop, an exotic remnant of an earlier era when Native peoples constituted a formidable threat and obstacle to settlement. The history of dispossession has understandably centered on Indian peoples, the horrors of the reservation system, and the continuing loss of land. From Dakotas' perspective, the federal government and its representatives figured as aggressive invaders, white traders appeared as shysters who swindled Indians, and white settlers actively displaced and replaced Native people. Non-Indian farmers who lived on reservations are entirely absent from these histories.

The convergence of federal policy and economic opportunity positioned Scandinavian immigrants and their children to gain from the expropriation of Indian land on the Spirit Lake Reservation. Here they were settler colonialists.[10] Embedded in transnational migration streams, they relocated to find a place to stay indefinitely, not to extend the power of the nation-state but to make farms and families. Like seventeenth-century European colonists, Scandinavians saw the land as "vacant" and "unused." Second-generation Norwegian Palmer Overby (b. 1894), who lived just east of the reservation, articulated his perspective: "There was nobody living up here till 1905, because the Indians had that, you see." In this view, "nobody" inhabited the Dakotas' vast expanses of land. Dakotas' historic strategies for extensive land use were superseded by the logic of private property, homesteading, and agricultural development. Like the U.S. government, Scandinavian settlers privileged agriculture and therefore saw uncultivated land as unused. Most Dakota families cultivated a portion of their land, raising vegetables in one- to two-acre gardens and planting crops, but few raised livestock and grain. Scandinavian settlers knew they could cultivate the soil and use the land well according to their agrarian sensibilities, which dovetailed perfectly with the U.S. government's design. They imagined reshaping the landscape to suit their needs, leaving an indelible stamp on it and making it their own. Despite their poverty and foreignness, they participated actively in a process of dispossession that continued incrementally into the twentieth century, with cumulative devastation to Native ways of life.

The clash of logics about land use in effect, from the point of view of white settlers, erased Dakotas' successes in making homes and adapting to this arid environment. This perspective allowed them to rationalize appropriating the land and exploiting it more intensively. As historian Jean M. O'Brien astutely observes, denying the Native presence made land taking seem justifiable.[11]

Homesteading on the reservation was also a grand, although ill-conceived, experiment in social integration. Plat maps show Scandinavian and Dakota owners' names arrayed on adjoining quarter sections, vividly illustrating the interspersed pattern of settlement (see map 3). Government policies aimed not only to take Native people's

MAP OF

TOWNSHIP 150 N., RANGE 63 W.

of the 5th P. M.

Scale 1¼ inches to 1 mile

EDDY TOWNSHIP

MAP 3 Plat map of Eddy Township, 1910.
Eddy Township (150N, R63W) in Eddy County was platted in thirty-six-square-mile sections. The Sheyenne River divided it, marking the reservation boundary; nonreservation land lay to the south. (Courtesy State Historical Society of North Dakota, Bismarck.)

land and import foreigners who would develop the land with little expectation of short-term profits, but also to promote assimilation through coexistence within a demarcated geographic space. In a period when scientists and governments sorted, categorized, and stratified people on the basis of their perceived race, ancestry, and immigration status and when Southern state legislatures were passing laws that segregated and subordinated black people in defiance of the Reconstruction-era amendments to the U.S. Constitution, the federal government recruited whites to take land on reservations and live amongst Indians.

CONSTRUCTING RACIAL CATEGORIES AND AFFIRMING GENDER HIERARCHIES

The state constructed systems of racial classification to facilitate governance and entry into the country. Indians were subjected to "blood quantum regulation" that in theory parsed the fraction of a person's ancestors who were Native.[12] According to O'Brien, governments imposed classification schemes that served as "tools of colonialism" against Indian peoples.[13] Federal laws specifying blood quantum determined tribal enrollments: to be recognized as Dakota, a person had to have a minimum of one-fourth Dakota ancestry. The regulations required a person to prove their lineage and present evidence of being descended from a tribal grandfather or grandmother. The categories of "mixed blood" and "full blood" contradicted Native practices of deciding group membership based on cultural affinity as well as genealogy. The federal government used the malleable and contested fraction of "blood" as a basis for determining tribal standing in different, sometimes contradictory ways. As it simultaneously promoted integration and "amalgamation," by which it meant intermarriage and the absorption of people with some white parentage into the dominant society, the government strategically aimed to reduce the number of Native people by denying recognition to those whose blood was "diluted" according to its calculus. Over time, by imposing these criteria in conjunction with other serious assaults on Indian people, including war, destruction of natural resources, and efforts to undermine language and culture, the government succeeded in causing a numerical contraction of tribal populations.[14]

This approach to Indians as a racialized minority was profoundly different from the treatment of blacks in the post–Civil War era. Under Jim Crow, African Americans were subject to the "one-drop rule" that identified everyone with any visible African ancestry as black, regardless of whatever Native American and/or European ancestry they might also have, and in effect expanded the nation's black population. Laws, customs, and violence worked to separate and subordinate African Americans, disfranchise them politically, exploit them economically, and segregate them spatially and culturally. As the Australian historian Patrick Wolfe observes,

"Indians and Black people in the U.S. have been racialized in opposing ways that reflect their antithetical roles in the formation of U.S. society." In regard to African Americans, integration and interracial marriage were held up as a specter to fear, not a "solution" to seek. This racialization process consolidated inequality through the law and was applied differently across regions. In the South it segregated growing numbers of blacks from whites, while for Native people on reservations across the continent it applied what Wolfe terms "the logic of elimination."[15]

Assuming that all things indigenous—tribal governance, land held in common, time-honored religious observance, language use—were antithetical to modern American society, the U.S. government sought the assimilation of Native people. Militarily defeated and repeatedly dispossessed, Dakotas were deprived of their customary forms of livelihood and were rendered dependent on the goods, services, and annuities that the federal government had promised to provide in exchange for land taken. Native people worked to make a home for their families and to create a new life under adverse legal, environmental, and economic circumstances. Although they cultivated large gardens, they were not accustomed to or equipped for commercial farming, which by the turn of the twentieth century meant raising large crops of grain, particularly wheat, for sale on the national market. Subsistence on the reservation was a challenge, particularly when Congress retaliated against Dakotas after the 1862 war by abrogating annuities agreed upon in earlier treaties. Thereafter, rations were dispensed only to those *in extremis*, on recommendation of the Indian agent and subject to congressional appropriations. It was not until 1906 that Congress reinstated annuities for Sisseton and Wahpeton Dakotas, who had long claimed they were not enemy combatants in the war but rather had led efforts to protect white settlers and prisoners and served as scouts for the U.S. Army. Even then, these annuities were insufficient for basic nutrition and sound housing.

The process of land taking was gendered as well as racially structured. Not only were women as well as men active participants in the land taking as both individuals and family members, but notions of masculinity and femininity defined the project of continental settlement by white Europeans. The West was infamous as a proving ground for white men and boys keen to earn their manhood as miners, cowboys, Indian fighters, or soldiers. The turn of the twentieth century saw the founding of the Boy Scouts and the presidency of Teddy Roosevelt, the former "Rough Rider" who signed the proclamation opening Spirit Lake Reservation land to homesteaders. Idealized womanhood was portrayed as fragile and refined, the opposite of masculine ruggedness; its most popular constructions expressed white, middle-class, and urban sensibilities. In practice, notions of "true womanhood" were used as a cudgel to judge and stigmatize indigenous, foreign-born, and African American women.[16]

Many immigrant women ignored or defied the gendered strictures of the dominant society. It was my widowed great-grandmother, not her husband, father, or son, who established a farm on the gentle hill near the Sheyenne River. As she ventured to leave Norway and arrived in time to participate in the land lottery, she demonstrated that the dominant gender hierarchy could be subverted to enable her to provide for her family. How did women's landownership shape these communities and offer new options to individuals over time?

Differing histories and competing interests pitted Dakotas and Scandinavians against each other. Scandinavians held crucial advantages, as experienced farmers, as resident aliens with a legal status superior to that of Indians, and as white immigrants eligible for full U.S. citizenship. Yet in the early decades of the twentieth century, when these poor and dislocated people took homesteads on the reservation, these two groups faced common challenges with more comparability of circumstance than a casual backward glance might suggest. Different as they were from each other, Dakotas and Scandinavians shared an outsider status.

Today, after enduring hostility from the dominant culture and struggling to survive in the harsh environment of the Great Plains, Dakotas and Scandinavians continue to live as neighbors on the reservation. Although this book begins with the social conditions and political machinations that allotment entailed, it centers on the influx of whites onto the reservation and the first three decades of their homesteading and farm making. It concludes in 1929 with a platting of the reservation that documented Dakota dispossession and Scandinavian land acquisition, before the Indian Reorganization Act of 1934 ended the allotment policy. I explore the everyday practices of Dakotas and Scandinavians during this cross-cultural encounter. Like other sociologists who have sought to understand how people adapt to new environmental, economic, and social conditions, I want to know: How do groups that start out as "strangers" in an encounter come to coexist in a spatially bounded community?

THE TRANSFER OF INDIAN LAND TO IMMIGRANT HOMESTEADERS

During the second half of the nineteenth century, two major pieces of national legislation encouraged immigration and westward expansion. Passed twenty-five years apart, they were both predicated on the conception that the territorial claims and rights of indigenous peoples posed a barrier to the acquisition of land by white settlers and established a plan for their dispossession. The Homestead Act of 1862 entitled a homesteader to settle 160 acres of land, commonly called a quarter section. Signed into law by President Abraham Lincoln, the legislation stipulated that a homesteader had to stake a claim, "improve" the land by cultivating it and living on it, and file for title, called the "patent," to public land owned privately for the first time. Single women were included in the homesteading legislation, which codified a vision of family settlement. The foreign-born could take land as long as they declared their intention to become naturalized citizens. The land was not free: homesteaders had to pay a filing fee and live on the land for five years and improve it; alternatively they could live on it six months and pay $1.25 per acre, still far below the market price.[17] These lands in the public domain of the United States had recently been ceded by Indian peoples negotiating as sovereign powers.[18] From the perspective of American Indians, therefore, the Homestead Act amounted to a wholesale scheme for further encroachment, violating the terms of the treaties they had recently signed protecting their land. In reaction to the continuing advance by white settlers, Dakota Chief Waanatan, attending a peace commission in July 1868, said, "I see them swarming all over my country.... Take all the whites and your soldiers away and all will be well."[19]

The second piece of legislation was the General Allotment Act of 1887, commonly known as the Severalty Act or the Dawes Act, after Henry Dawes, the Republican senator from Massachusetts who spearheaded the bill. Under this act, reservation land, which belonged to tribes as nations, would be subdivided into individual lots. Adult heads of families were allotted private property in 160-acre parcels; single persons over the age of eighteen years were allotted 80 acres, as were orphans under the age of eighteen; and children, 40 acres.[20] As historian Tonia Compton points out, gender was not explicitly discussed in the legislative debates, but as with the Homestead Act and in an affirmation of women's property rights in many tribes, single women were included.[21] At the urging of Native people, including vocal Sissetons, an amendment to the Dawes Act in 1891 increased allotments to eighty acres for all Indians. Implicitly, this change extended allotment to married women, in effect profoundly differentiating it from the Homestead Act, which purposely excluded married women.[22]

By design, once tribal members had been assigned their own plots, "surplus" land on reservations was opened to white homesteading. Policymakers transferring reservation land to white farmers thought that the subsequent integration would promote the incorporation of Indians into the American way of life. This legislation laid the groundwork for a shift in U.S. policy from conquest to assimilation of Indian peoples.

This particular case at Spirit Lake is a consequence of social structures and local processes—government policies and legislation combined with people's everyday practices—that facilitated systemic land acquisition and dispossession. The reservation system, devised by President Thomas Jefferson, had reflected a strategy of removal of Native people to Indian Territory, by force or negotiation. The result was a shrinking land base, rendering them economically dependent on trade with whites and, later, on the government. Best known are the federal government's seizures of land in violation of treaties to extract valuable resources, such as uranium in the

Southwest and gold in the Black Hills of South Dakota. Less well known are the federal government moves to make reservation land available to white settlement, which brought settler colonists to live on reservations where Indians remained.

Strikingly, the late nineteenth-century reformers organized as "Friends of the Indian" embraced allotment and integration as components of their assimilation agenda, which they saw as the best chance of helping Native people survive into the future. This well-organized and vocal pro-Indian group opposed those who vociferously called for wiping out the Red race.[23] As Frederick Hoxie has pointed out, reformers such as Alice C. Fletcher, probably the most famous agent to allot reservation land, believed that "individual homesteads would protect the Indians from removal and dispossession while it spurred them on to 'civilization.' "[24] As the Friends of the Indian reasoned, the Indian "must be taught industry and acquisitiveness to fit him for his 'ultimate absorption in the great body of American citizenship.' "[25] In response to government efforts to negotiate the implementation of the severalty act, Dakotas argued that the reservation was already theirs because the Treaty of 1867 "provides for a permanent reservation."[26]

Central to the Dawes Act was the primacy of private property. It was not only an economic and political building block of the United States, where yeoman farmers and landholders were regarded as rightful voting citizens, but also antithetical to the indigenous approach to land. As Patrick Wolfe puts it, "Tribal land was tribally owned—tribes and private property did not mix."[27] The logic of reformers had two intersecting premises that suited competing constituencies in the concerned public and the U.S. Congress. The first was that owning land individually in a legal system built on private property would guarantee a base for Indian people in perpetuity, correcting the shortcomings of negotiated territorial rights that had been repeatedly transgressed and proven ineffective in holding the U.S. government and white settlers at bay.

The second aim of allotment was that Indians would come to think of themselves primarily as individuals, not as members of collectivities. In so doing, their allegiance would shift from tribes, nations, and indigenous leaders to themselves and their own "Christian family." These two suppositions converged in the allotment of land and fit subtly but precisely within the "elimination of the native" logic.

At Spirit Lake, Scandinavians were incongruously cast into the role of agents of assimilation, although they hardly represented American culture. Immigrant homesteaders spoke their ancestral languages and came with few resources other than their labor power; even their American-born children spoke English haltingly. These desperately poor new arrivals were themselves targets of Americanization projects and English-only campaigns. The immigrants came to take land but had difficulty accumulating the capital that commercial farming required. They built houses and their own family and community networks with the intention of staying. Although many of the Scandinavians were foreign-born, they had more legal protections and could claim white racial privileges denied to Native people.

The Dawes Act included the promise of citizenship for Indians; indeed, citizenship was showcased as the lure for economic adaptation. Subsequently, tribes and legislatures debated the meanings and merits of that provision, since Indians had intentionally been excluded from the Constitution. Would Dakotas and other Native peoples benefit from "membership in [the] political and geographic community"[28] that constituted the United States? In democratic nation-states, citizenship is desirable primarily because it promises substantive equality and enables people to act on their interests and express their views politically. The Friends of the Indian saw it as central, indeed essential, to the success of reform. They thought that shedding tribal affiliations would enable Indians to succeed as individuals. But Dakotas and members of other tribes had good reason to doubt that the promise of civil and political rights would ever be fulfilled and no desire to abandon their identity, culture, and history, as those promoting citizenship demanded. Shifting federal policies, contradictory court decisions, and state-level discretion over the franchise regularly confused the terms, conditions, and effects of citizenship for Indians, deferring and distorting the entitlements it was supposed to confer.

In the late nineteenth and early twentieth centuries, the United States was segregated and unequal; full citizenship remained largely a white male privilege.[29] As Indian tribes pressed the federal government to recognize their national sovereignty and citizenship on their own terms, the United States was also engaged in contentious debates about the rights of women and African Americans. When multitudes of immigrants and low-skilled workers mobilized to participate in the political process, controversy over who was entitled to vote intensified. So did agitation to exclude immigrants whom some Anglo-Saxon Americans regarded as "unfit" for citizenship by reason of their race-ethnicity, religion, national origin, or culture.

As far as Indians were concerned, heated discussions about autonomy intertwined with disagreements about the possibility or, indeed, desirability of assimilation and citizenship. Scandinavian immigrants could in theory claim the privileges of whiteness, although in North Dakota they were cast as foreign and viewed with suspicion by the surrounding English-speaking society. Nonetheless, the process of naturalization offered "free white persons" an open invitation to become first-class citizens. Indian tribes' status as "domestic dependent nations" gave them some negotiating power with the federal government but also made tribal members, in effect, wards of the state.[30]

Fundamental questions remain: How did individuals and groups exercise influence in households, communities, and politics broadly defined? In what ways did landownership open paths to citizenship and assertions of autonomy? How did dis-possession as a consequence of land taking impede mobilization for political goals that might be shared by Indians and immigrants and their children?

A HISTORY OF CONFLICT

From 1825 on, increasing numbers of Scandinavians came to the United States with the intention of staying. My maternal ancestors, the family of Iver and Anne Halvorson Kanten, left Hadeland, Norway, in 1864 for Fillmore County, Minnesota, a Norwegian portal to the Midwest. They searched for land and a better life, eventu-ally settling in Montevideo in Chippewa County, close to the mission at Lac Qui Parle and the site of Camp Release, where six years earlier Dakotas had held some 256 prisoners of war before they surrendered and were themselves taken prisoner.[31]

A decade later, as immigrants streamed from Norway and Sweden and the mid-western states filled with white settlers, Scandinavians who could not find cheap land in more developed places flooded into Dakota Territory. The peak of Norwegian immigration, from 1876 to 1890,[32] coincided precisely with the moment that the federal government surveyed this territory and made vast tracts of public land avail-able to homesteaders. Although the numbers leaving Norway declined during the 1890s, they surged again from 1900 until the onset of world war in 1914.[33] During this last wave, another branch of my maternal kin, led by Berthe Haugen, landed in North America. When Spirit Lake Dakotas agreed to open "surplus lands" on their reservation to homesteading, Scandinavians—my relatives included—were poised to benefit disproportionately from their dispossession.

White settlers moving onto the Spirit Lake Dakota Indian Reservation were entering a postwar zone. The 1862 U.S.–Dakota War did not unfold here, but its powerful legacy shaped this locality and lives on in memory today. To most students of U.S. history, the year 1862 evokes images of the Union Army's defeat at Harper's Ferry and the bloody battles at Antietam and Fredericksburg. To Native people of the Great Plains, the main theater of war was southern Minnesota. A twenty-mile-wide swath of territory along the Minnesota River had been designated as a reserva-tion for several bands of Dakotas: Mdewakantons and Wahpekutes at the Lower Agency, and Sissetons and Wahpetons at the Upper Agency. German settlers began encroaching on Dakota land, particularly on the north side of the river near the Lower Agency, defying the negotiated boundaries that made it off limits to whites.

The volatile issues that precipitated armed conflict included land taking and the desperate want of food, both in violation of treaty agreements. In the Dakota insur-rection, approximately 500 white settlers and soldiers were killed. So were compa-rable numbers of Native people; no one was immune from the devastation. The traumatized survivors of Sisseton and Wahpeton bands were exiled from their ancestral lands, and some ventured to join Ihanktonwannas in Dakota Territory, which was just being settled by whites and had advanced to the status preceding statehood. The early twentieth-century encounter at Spirit Lake was uniquely shaped by the aftermath of the war and the multiple disjunctures of relocation, for both dispossessed Dakota Indians and land-taking first- and second-generation Scandinavians.

After its victory in the war, the U.S. government extended its control over indigenous peoples, particularly those who had taken up arms. Troops scoured the Upper Midwest, rounding up rebellious Dakotas and sweeping up others in their dragnet, and military tribunals summarily convicted 303 prisoners of killing soldiers and of murdering and raping white settlers. Ultimately, 38 Dakotas were executed, hundreds were interned, and thousands were sent into exile. Congress rapidly abrogated previous federal treaties with Dakotas, and eventually the government imposed new treaties establishing additional reservations further west, including that at Spirit Lake.

Scandinavians entered into this contact zone with preconceptions about the ferocity of Indians' resistance to white farmers as well as their racial inferiority. The notion of a contact zone conjures a unique space where "peoples geographically and historically separated come into contact with each other and establish ongoing relations, usually involving conditions of coercion, radical inequality, and intractable conflict,"[34] as Mary Louise Pratt puts it. Dakotas were profoundly aware of the hypocrisy and betrayal to which the U.S. government could descend. They knew from direct experience that the United States would change the terms of a treaty without previously asking for their approval or even informing them afterwards, and that one branch of government would break a contractual agreement made by another. As Dakota doctor, traveling lecturer, and advocate Charles Eastman wrote, "I learned that scarcely one of our treaties with the United States had been carried out in good faith in all of its provisions."[35] A group of northern Sissetons put it more harshly when considering surrendering to General Sibley, "You know how deceitful and [what] liars the Americans are."[36] The Homestead Act, in essence inviting white settlers to the Midwest, was the perfect example of how outrageously the United States could undermine treaties it had signed just over a decade before. As a defeated people whose territory had once again been confiscated and its means of livelihood further diminished, Dakotas saw few alternatives.[37]

The government constructed reservations to confine and restrict indigenous people. It applied laws of its own making in an effort to further control and eventually eliminate Indians. We can understand reservations as a "racial project," which Michael Omi and Howard Winant define as *an effort to reorganize and redistribute resources along particular racial lines.*"[38] Spatial containment diminished Indians' power, limited their geographic mobility, deprived them of significant natural resources, sealed their political disfranchisement and military defeat, and laid the foundations for ongoing expropriation of their land. The project entrenched racial hierarchies through law, while dividing Dakotas and sequestering them on reservations scattered across a vast territory.

THE CULTURAL LOGICS OF "STRANGERS"

This book begins in the wake of this racializing process. It explores everyday practices during this cross-cultural encounter that unfolded in the midst of protracted legal wrangling that followed military conflict. As these groups viewed each other through a racial lens, up close and with frequent contact, their mutual encounter involved a process of seeing, interpreting, readjusting, and reframing.

Social theorist Alfred Schuetz insightfully cast immigrants as "strangers" who confront a new society, seeking acceptance or at least tolerance, and find their world-view fundamentally incompatible with dominant ways of thinking and acting. In making their approach, strangers attempt to discern and interpret the cultural patterns of the new social group to which they must orient themselves.[39] In effect, they have to comprehend the "cultural logics" of the society they have entered. Cultural logics shape the way a person explicates the social world to him- or herself; they frame expectations about how things should work and how people should behave.[40] Indeed, while not always conscious, cultural logics serve as guides to action. If we define culture as "the shared meanings, practices, and symbols that constitute the human world,"[41] then a series of logics can be understood to explain the world from a particular perspective. Logics are not economic facts, prescriptive directives, or legal constraints, although they can be economic or legal in orientation.[42] Rather, they provide the groundwork for common-sense understanding of the world, or what sociologist Harold Garfinkel calls "practical reasoning."[43] A racial logic is also embedded in the everyday. As Omi and Winant put it, "Race becomes 'common sense'—a way of comprehending, explaining, and acting in the world."[44]

In an encounter, expectations are interrupted and undermined, prompting people to try to elucidate "each other's motivations and intentions." Dislocated people move from being cultural insiders in their homeland to being outsiders in a strange place. As a result, Schuetz argues, newcomers experience a personal crisis of marginality, where they must understand that "from the point of view of the approached group" they are people "without a history."[45] The newcomer recognizes that the approached group's history will "never become an integral part of his biography, as did the history of his home group."[46]

To the reigning, better-established Yankees, Scandinavian newcomers did not have a history, except insofar as they were land-hungry peasants. From the perspective of

Dakotas, Scandinavians were yet another group of white people trying to seize their land. Yankees and Scandinavians did not recognize that Native people had a long record of adaptation, innovation, and change. Instead, they cast Dakotas as fierce warriors, men who were remnants of the past, not people who belonged to modern society.[47] None of the white settlers paid much attention to Native women, even though they were the farmers in Dakota culture and were respected by Dakota men for the many contributions they made. Power enables dominant groups to assert the invisibility of a subordinate group, erase its history, and disrespect its distinctiveness.

At Spirit Lake, identifying the strangers involved designating the insiders. Were Dakotas the principal group? Much depends on where and when you begin. While Dakotas' history, legal status, and relationship to the federal government limited the authority they could exercise, even over themselves, their presence still defined the territory. Spirit Lake was an Indian reservation; without Dakotas it would not, and could not, be a reservation. Dakotas first named the land, used it in particular ways, and observed its sacred qualities. One band of Dakotas, Ihanktonwannas, root their human origins at Mniwakan Cante Paha, which literally means "Heart Hill of the Sacred Water," also called Heart Butte (or "Devil's Heart" by some locals), a striking geologic formation just south of the lake. Mary Louise Defender Wilson (b. 1930, Dakota and Hidatsa) is a descendent of Greater Bear's Lodge, "the Dakota people who claim that as their emergence place." She says that Ihanktonwannas "never came from the east, like many of the history books say." They spoke their own language and practiced their culture as best they could, subject to constraints and conditions. Yet most Dakotas at Spirit Lake arrived there as dislocated people, subordinated by the federal government, deprived of their economic resources, and sometimes actually starving. Were they not equally strangers?

When Scandinavians moved onto the reservation in 1904, Dakotas were demographically dominant, but by 1910 non-Indians outnumbered enrolled tribal members. As indigenous people, Dakotas were marginalized by a culture that sought to diminish, eliminate, absorb, and exoticize them. A racial lens made them perpetual strangers, exiles in their own land. The dominant culture explained Dakotas' behavior, attitudes, values, customs, and political activity as a consequence of their racial identity.

If Dakotas were consigned to the past, then were modern Yankees recognized as insiders? They fiercely defended the governing culture in the diverse society of the West. They spoke English, received a public education, held elective office, and considered themselves rightful Americans. But on the reservation they were few and far between. Representatives of the federal Indian Office, most of whom were Yankees, were government employees with legal authority to make decisions about Dakotas on the reservation. Yet most federal officials, including the Indian agent and, later, the superintendent, were stationed at Spirit Lake only temporarily. Unlike home-steaders, those non-Indians who served the government as administrators, boss farmers, doctors, teachers, nurses, and field matrons would sooner or later be sent elsewhere. Their jobs empowered them to provide services and implement national policy in this place. Legally they held preeminence, but were they not strangers in their own way? As an elite minority, they were regarded with hostility by Dakotas. And, like Dakotas, many white settlers in the Midwest also became skeptical about government officials, whom they viewed as inept, incompetent, insufficiently accountable, or busy enriching themselves by taking advantage of their positions and others' naïvete.

The question remains: Who, here, had a recognized history? If, as Schuetz suggests, strangers become invisible and lose the legitimacy of their past, then who retains vis-ibility? Whose history is told as the story of this place over time? Who can demand that others recognize their history and the claims, honor, and shame that accom-pany it? Scholars such as Jean O'Brien, Fredrick Hoxie, and Alan Trachtenburg have documented nineteenth-century efforts to erase Indians, their history, and entitle-ments from the North American tableau. By writing Native people out of local his-tories, photographing "the vanishing Indian" in order to insist upon Native peoples' imminent demise, staging events to memorialize Indians and thereby imply they had no future, and establishing policies to obliterate indigenous languages, government officials, artists, historians, and writers collaborated in diminishing the power and presence of indigenous peoples on the continent.[48]

Yet Dakotas refused to be erased. They insisted on the veracity of their history and the importance of speaking their language. Dakotas asserted that they were a living people, not a remnant of the past. They took allotments, claimed a place in this refashioned space, planted crops, and participated in Indian dancing and traditional forms of worship as well as attending Christian churches. Living on land marked as an Indian reservation made total erasure impossible. Dakota people challenged government intransigence through federal courts, demanding that the United States honor its agreements and fulfill its obligations to them. They boldly embraced the entitlements of citizenship, exercising the franchise and protesting when county officials denied them their political rights. By enacting valued rituals, demanding that government abide by its treaties, cultivating vast gardens, telling stories, and practicing their culture on the reservation, they survived, adapted, and endured.

In parallel, Scandinavians—Norwegians especially—resisted the prevailing culture and tried to change the economic system of the state. As immigrants with a diasporic mind-set, they came to take land and reconstruct a small-scale version of the culture they left behind. They belonged to farmers' cooperatives and mobilized an agrarian anti-capitalist movement that challenged the unfettered market. While they became naturalized at extraordinarily high rates, they did not use their citizenship to blend into the U.S. context, indeed they established Norwegian schools to ensure their children's fluency in their mother tongue. Unwilling to reject or abandon their own "foreignness," they focused their considerable political energy on their economic grievances, helping the newly founded Nonpartisan League win control of state government in 1916 and make the policy changes that organized farmers demanded.

The remoteness of Spirit Lake and the insistent actions of Dakotas facilitated Scandinavians' parallel efforts to preserve their history and affirm their separate culture.[49] White settlers and Indians understood their uniqueness more deeply through their encounter with each other.[50] In part they cast the differences they observed— such as the use of land, naming practices, religious observances, and how they spent their leisure time—as attributes of race and ancestry. In U.S. society those distinctions revealed hierarchies that were created through law and the everyday exercise of power and privilege. Sociologists Stephen Cornell and Douglas Hartmann argue that racial and ethnic categories are constructed in social interactions, which are shaped by historical circumstances and human volition.[51] Using a racial lens, Scandinavians and Dakotas would have insisted that they could identify someone's race by their outward appearance; features such as skin tone, hair color, cadence of speech, physique, posture, and style of dress were commonly used at the time to distinguish one race from another.

And yet, just as there were dark-haired, short Norwegians, there were fair-skinned, tall Indians, challenging easy categorization. Over the years of living adjacent to each other, they began to view each other with greater subtlety, noticing the use of language and expression, recognizing kinship networks and historical rivalries—Swedes versus Norwegians, and Chippewas versus Sioux—and beginning to understand those differences as traces of ancestral background.[52] Their repeated encounters generated a certain familiarity with each other and their respective cultural practices as they enacted and interpreted boundaries. Being neighbors did not necessarily translate into acting neighborly. They lived on adjoining land, but their social worlds were closed and inward turning. Each group saw its own singular qualities in light of those of the culturally distant other group. As these changed over time, commonalities were discovered, created, modified, affirmed, ameliorated, and rejected. Because of the fluidity, interdependency, and historical contingency of the categories, I prefer to combine race and ethnicity into a single concept.[53] On the ground, the racial-ethnic lens helps us frame the shifting meanings of stranger status and see the clout as well as the stigma it conferred.

Legally codified distinctions that racialized and subordinated Native people kept them separate, but, ironically, the reservation held them in close proximity to Scandinavians. Both groups made determined, collective efforts to secure land, maintain their integrity, and assert political power. Land provided a home base for practicing culture and extending kinship into the future. In their efforts to shun, ignore, or adapt rather than adopt the dominant Yankee culture, Dakotas and Scandinavians led parallel lives that intersected through land, labor, and trade.

Neither adversaries nor allies, they began as strangers in a contact zone; over time they transformed into wary neighbors living in an entangled enclave. The two groups have coexisted in a legally bounded space for over a century. The strong arm of the federal government intervened in, monitored, and undermined Dakotas' lives, while it permitted Scandinavians to navigate their own adaptations as long as they sent their children to school, paid taxes, and learned to speak English. In the process of adjusting to the unfamiliar terrain, Scandinavians faced many of the same challenges as Dakotas. Yet homesteaders gained their foothold as landowners and citizens through Dakotas' dispossession, placing the two groups in antagonistic positions even as both were struggling to make new lives in a demanding political and economic environment. Both groups sought avenues to pursue their political agendas in order to assert cultural autonomy and resist imperatives of the market that privileged large merchants over small producers. Nearly a century later, historical memory keeps wars and land taking and their consequences alive in family and community stories. Indeed, the oral accounts that illuminate these memories, and upon which this book is based, connect our present with this past.

SEARCHING FOR SOURCES: PLAT MAPS AND INTERVIEWS

This book takes an ethnographic approach to history, a particular twist on historical sociology. It is not just about the past, but about the mediated accounts of what people have come to understand as the past. In part, however, the ethnographic character of this book arises from the nature of oral histories themselves. All oral history narratives are necessarily retrospective and shaped by the meaning they give to peoples' lives.[54] I have mostly studied the world of a century ago through the eyes of the living.

My attempts to understand my own family's history are parallel to those of my subjects, who tell stories to themselves and their descendants about where they come from and what brought them here. These reflect not only multiple and sometimes contradictory viewpoints but also the subject's interpretation of others' accounts, which are shaped by the immediate listener and the historical moment (such as the emergence of the American Indian rights movement in the 1960s). To be sure, oral histories reconstruct life as people remember or want to remember it, often devoid of the overt prejudice, desperation, and long-buried feelings that surely existed at the time. But the narratives say much about the memory of the encounter, the cultural logics set in motion, and how those reverberate today.

Because I have sought to understand how two groups with profoundly different citizenship status, language, and culture managed to live parallel but intersecting lives, I have searched tenaciously for sources that articulate each group's point of view but found only checkered sets of documents and gaping holes in the recorded past. Unlike the prominent, whose lives are well documented, most of these poor and marginalized people left little written evidence of what they thought and felt— who they loved, what grudges they harbored, and what triumphs they cherished. Accustomed to working with diaries and letters as historical sources, I found none written at the turn of the twentieth century by Spirit Lake Dakotas and only a handful of letters and memoirs by Scandinavian immigrants. I have searched archives in the United States and Norway, read family and local histories, and scanned newspapers on microfilm and online.

Early in the project, I recognized that land was the primary resource for both groups, so I devoted years to decoding plat maps of reservation land, like the ones first shown to me by reservation resident Cherry Monson on my initial visit to Spirit Lake. The maps from 1910 and 1929 provide time-sequenced snapshots of landownership in the wake of allotment. By searching the U.S. manuscript census, combing through town histories, employing resourceful research assistants, and quizzing reservation residents, I compiled a database that identifies the race-ethnicity of all but 7 percent of the 1,693 landowners on the reservation in 1910.[55] Equally important, I have been able to determine the sex of all but 4 percent of the landowners and to document gendered patterns of landownership. Some land was owned by banks and private companies, and a small proportion was designated for churches and schools. In 1929, none was reserved for the Spirit Lake Dakota nation as a whole.

Dakota life on the reservation was extensively documented by federal employees, who recorded their observations in order to monitor, judge, and control Native people. Since I sought accounts of daily practices and cross-cultural encounters, these rich and detailed sources proved to be surprisingly illuminating. The annual reports of Indian agents and superintendents, as well as field matrons, were the closest to ethnography, slanted as they were by a particular worldview and bureaucratic imperative. Testimonies taken for congressional hearings and in the U.S. Court of Claims have provided invaluable first-person accounts; although they focus on the issues of the day, they rarely speak to the issue of land and coexistence.

The dearth of sources from Dakotas' and Scandinavians' perspective sent me on a seemingly never-ending quest that landed me at the golden door of oral history. To compensate for the absence of primary documents, I set out to interview as many people as possible. I was initiated into the ways of listening and asking questions that Dakotas regard as appropriate. Interviewing relies on give and take between a storyteller and a listener who brings her own questions to the encounter. Listening is as fundamental to historical memory as recounting tales about the past. Honorary tribal historian Louis Garcia (b. 1940) informed me that old Dakota medicine men would not pass on knowledge to just any younger person. The person had to be worthy; the person had to *want* to know, and they had to offer a gift in exchange for learning. Without asking, the person could not hope to learn.

Some members of the tribe understood the importance of listening and profoundly embraced the practice. For example, Ambrose Littleghost (b. 1932), pipe carrier for the tribe, told me how he would stay up late listening to stories being told by his grandparents when relatives visited from Canada. In the 1960s when Garcia first came to the reservation, after listening to older men talking about their grandfathers stealing horses from Hidatsas, "It just hit me like a ton of bricks—these guys are losing their history because this guy's telling stories that [no one remembers].... So I started writing them down." For almost fifty years he has made it his job to listen, learn, and record interviews in notebooks and preserve them in the archives of the University of North Dakota. In a world now organized by written language, the preservation of information requires documentation.

Sustaining an oral tradition requires a conversation. Perfectly illustrating this process of dialog, ninety-year-old Dakota narrator Grace Lambert (b. 1909) told me, "I was a great listener when I was a kid." She relayed an example: "My grandma used to tell me stories. One time she was telling me that they crossed the [river]. I said, 'How did they take the kids across?' I said, 'Did they swim with them on their back? Or what?' She said, 'No no, that's not the way,' she said." Then her grandmother proceeded to explain that horses would pull a floating travois with children across the Missouri River. Grace Lambert listened actively. She would hear a story and then clarify it, constructing theories about how things worked, trying on the cultural logic for herself. Once a story made sense to her, once she understood its internal logic, she could retell it—always referring to her sources. She did not make independent claims to truth, only to what she had heard. "That is what they told me," she said. She would recount where, when, and from whom she heard the story. A good source was someone you knew and could trust. For example, Dakota women first fed their children salt pork (issued by the government) when they were held as prisoners of war. Grace was told the story by a descendent. "She told me herself, but she said that her mother told her that. I knew her mother; her mother was a real old lady by then, when I was born. But she used to ride horseback and used to always come to our house...to visit."[56] Like a footnote, Grace's reference to the origin of her story served as authentication. This was not gossip or hearsay, much less the creation of a nostalgic imagination. Grace consistently affirmed that a particular person said this or that. She did not claim that she herself knew or that what she said was certifiably true, but rather that it accurately reiterated what someone told her.

In keeping with the practices of oral exchange, my interview with Grace Lambert involved the storyteller testing the listener. Throughout our conversation she asked me questions about what I knew. When she first mentioned the U.S.–Dakota War of 1862, she said the white settlers started the armed conflict. "By that man shooting this kid. And what does it say in the history?" In asking me this question, she affirmed that the history recounted in books written by non-Indians can be at odds with the stories she and other Dakota people have passed down and come to accept.[57] Presumably her interest was genuine; she wanted to know which sources I used and what they said. But, as a wise woman, she also wanted to see where I stood in the conversation.

Oral history is central to the cultural traditions of Norwegians and other immigrants as well as to those of Native Americans. In writing about Norwegians who worked at Indian forts in the Midwest, linguist Einar Haugen characterized one immigrant, Halvor Aune, as a "saga-teller par excellence." He respectfully recognized Aune as a man who remembered details and had an unusual capacity for narrative. "He has *fortællerglæde*, the story-teller's joy in his story."[58] For millennia, Scandinavians have also preserved a written record of at least some of their beliefs, legends, and histories.

Taken together, these recollections of the past began to fill the gaps in the written record and retrieve the lost history of the dispossessed and the dislocated land takers. In total, I conducted thirty oral history interviews with those who grew up on and near the reservation, seven of whom were Dakota elders. I also interviewed five members of my extended kin network, searching for common themes and clues to the past. In the late 1960s and 1970s, a surge of attention to the history of ordinary people rather than elites prompted an unprecedented flowering of grassroots-oriented oral history projects. Fortunately, the State Historical Society of North Dakota (SHSND) and the American Indian Research Project (AIRP) in South Dakota had the wisdom to collect stories of elders at that time. Interviews with 128 people comprise the first-person accounts for this book. Of those, 53 percent are from SHSND and 15 percent from AIRP, and they are supplemented by seven oral histories collected in 1993 with those who attended the Fort Totten Indian School on the reservation.[59] All oral history narrators, identified by name, are listed in appendix B, "Oral History Interview Subjects," with key personal information, including year and place of birth, ethnic and tribal affiliation, and the source and date of the interview.

The development of this project has not been a straightforward process. It has involved give and take and multiple trips to North Dakota. Early on, an anthropologist recommended that I visit the reservation and get to know people, as that would help me understand the historical sources. After my first trip, I realized how profound this advice was. Not only did North Dakota scholars point me to key sources, I met generous people—Louis Garcia, the honorary tribal historian of Spirit Lake Dakotas, and tribal member Marcy Young McKay, former director of the Senior Meals Program on the reservation—who introduced me to others who could provide valuable perspectives on the past. Many times, smack in the middle of fieldwork, I would think, "What am I doing?!! I don't belong here. Why did I ever think that I, a total outsider several generations removed from my Norwegian great-grandmother and separated by an even larger gap from Dakotas who remain on the reservation that my family left, could write a book about coexistence a century ago?" Nonetheless, something kept drawing me back—the kindnesses of a few; the fascination of the patchy, incomplete puzzle I was putting together; my own determination to reckon with the silent, yet ever-present legacy of the past. Stories give shape to history, hold together both losses and achievements, and help us make sense of the chaos and conflicts of life and the injustices as well as blessings of the past. How did Dakotas and Norwegians, so profoundly different in their origins and cultures, manage to coexist?

WHOSE HISTORY?

In my search for this history, the ancestry I want to claim troubles me because of my family's role in the dispossession of Dakotas. As tribal elder Agnes Greene emphasized, the story I relate here—however deeply it resonates with those who lived at Spirit Lake—is my own.

The materials on which this book is based are not equally balanced: despite my good intentions and best efforts, the Scandinavian interviews and documents outweigh the Dakota ones. Because of the lopsidedness of the sources and the limits on comparability of evidence, my account leads with Scandinavians' experiences, those of Norwegians in particular.[60] Nonetheless, I work to convey the ways in which political and economic forces created a multilayered reality on the reservation. And I invite others to join me in finding sources, reconstructing narratives, and interpreting this episodically documented history.

Most often, American Indians are relegated to a dead-and-gone past that has been superseded by white settlement, which represents "progress." Their history was rewritten by others and erased whenever possible.[61] Obviously those who lived on the reservation knew otherwise. So what did they know about Dakotas' history and the evolution of coexistence with Scandinavians? Descendants of white settlers have remained frustratingly silent on the matter, taking Dakotas' presence for granted but rarely acknowledging their family's participation in the historical processes that brought them here.

In order to be reflexive, or "rigorously self-aware," I situate myself in the text.[62] I try to understand the ways in which my "partial perspective" is shaped by my disciplinary training; my community of orientation; who was willing to talk to me and be interviewed; what they remembered and what they forgot; my ancestry—Norwegian and Danish—and its cultural mythology; and my kinship ties to a Norwegian homesteader on the reservation who proved up, lived on the land, and then passed her homestead along to her grandsons.

Because my peasant ancestors and most Dakotas left virtually no documents recording their worldview or their deeds, I found insight into their struggles and satisfactions in fiction by some of the great writers of the early twentieth century. Zitkala-Ša (also known as Gertrude Bonin), a Dakota essayist and short-story writer, considered the meanings of the invasion of the United States and its incessant double-talk. Ole Rølvaag, a Norwegian American novelist, wrestled with the dilemmas of ancestral integrity. Two Norwegian Nobel laureates, Sigrid Undset and Knut Hamsun, grappled with the power of land. Willa Cather, U.S. novelist and editor, incisively grasped the immigrant sources of American vitality. And Tillie Olsen, daughter of Russian Jewish immigrants to the Midwest, revealed the ravages of poverty on the soul.

Dakota elder Phillip John Young (b. 1944), member of the Board of Regents for Cankdeska Cikana Community College, was surprised by how much energy it took to be interviewed by a relative stranger. But he clearly saw my path for giving back. "You don't understand. You're white. You come with a nice heart. But give me the strength and the patience to teach *you*, to help you to understand, so you can go and be like [an] apostle—teach the other people what they don't know." He had no compunction about my recording the interviews and donating tapes to the University of North Dakota archive where Louis Garcia had placed his collection in order to make local history more widely available. Beyond that, I was uniquely poised to tell the stories: as an outsider to whom rationales were not self-evident, whose initial ignorance of Native history and culture was similar to that of many white people, and yet had a penchant for writing and a grandmother who used to live on the reservation.

OVERVIEW OF THE BOOK

Encounter on the Great Plains explores Dakotas' responses to encroaching settlers and chronicles the intertwined stories of Indians and immigrants—women and men, farmers, live-in servants, and day laborers—and their shared and conflicted struggles to maintain a language, sustain a culture, and honor loyalties to more than one nation. Together Dakotas and Scandinavians forged an uneasy tolerance and mutual acceptance that grew out of living together through drought, economic depression, and the ebb and flow of family life.

Part I, "An Unlikely Encounter," navigates through the many structural processes that set these two groups on a collision course. Chapter 1, "Indians Never Knocked: Fear Frames the Encounter," begins with the clash between Native and Euro-American visiting rituals and scrutinizes two celebrations held on a single day in 2006: a commemoration of the beginning of white settlement on the reservation 100 years before, and a powwow celebrating contemporary Indian life and culture. The juxtaposition of the two events held in opposite corners of the reservation perfectly illustrates the separation of two peoples living parallel lives for the past century. Chapter 2, "The Scandinavian Flood: Land Hunger, Dislocation, and Settlement," outlines what drove Norwegians and Swedes to leave their ancestral lands and drew them to North Dakota. The next chapter, "The Reservation Land Rush: Allotment and Land Taking," surveys the conditions under which Dakotas lived between allotment, starting in 1890, and the arrival of white homesteaders in 1904 as U.S. policy toward Indians shifted from conquest through warfare to assimilation through private property and education. It investigates the tensions of the allotment process at Spirit Lake as federal Indian agents monitored everyday life while Dakotas strove to cultivate gardens and small acreages, maintain their health and dignity, and press the government to uphold its legal commitments.

Part II, "The Entangled Lives of Strangers," examines the many ways daily life on the reservation both brought Dakotas and Scandinavians together and kept them apart. Chapter 4, "Spirit Lake Transformed: The Nexus of Schooling, Language, and Trade," takes stock of the reservation as white homesteaders began making farms and building commercial establishments in villages and the two groups came face to face with each other. In plowing the earth; constructing villages, churches, and public schools; and planting trees, Scandinavian farmers transformed the reservation landscape. Motivated by commerce and exchange, Dakotas, merchants, and immigrants sought a common language. In chapter 5, "Marking Nations, Reservation Boundaries, and Racial-Ethnic Hierarchies," readers see how the racialization process constructed inequality between groups. Through cognizance of ancestry, language, and growing inequalities in resources, newcomers and Dakotas become more acutely aware of their uniqueness within a stratified racial-ethnic environment, distinct from the national context but powerfully operational on the ground. Over generations, integrated schooling and intermarriage have intertwined Dakota and Scandinavian kinship networks. Chapter 6, "Fighting the Sky and Working the Land," analyzes the ways men and women forged cooperative subsistence strategies and attempted to mitigate their increasing disadvantage in the industrializing agricultural economy. Scandinavians relied on interdependence among kin, community, and cooperatives, laying a foundation for political mobilization around agrarian reform. A small group of Dakota farmers demanded more adequate help from the Indian Office, their legally designated guardians, and weighed the merits of leasing their land versus cultivating it themselves. Most did not farm for a commercial market, but rather grew huge gardens with the goal of feeding their families.

The last part of the book, "The Divisions of Citizenship and the Grip of Poverty," maps differing trajectories of the 1910s and 1920s. Examining how Dakotas interpreted and acted upon their rights as new U.S. citizens and their simultaneous standing as a separate nation, chapter 7, "Divergent Paths to Racialized Citizenship," follows Dakotas to the courts and Scandinavians to the ballot box. With deep criticisms of industrial agriculture but a more optimistic view of the role of government, Norwegians joined the Nonpartisan League, to support farmers and temper the market. Chapter 8, "A Fragile Hold on the Land," explores the consequences for those who endured—Dakotas and a subset of original Scandinavian homesteaders. By 1929, Dakotas owned only one-quarter of the reservation land. Through the sale of land and the fragmentation of ownership as it was passed on to successive generations with multiple heirs, their land base diminished. Scandinavian men consolidated their holdings, Scandinavian women owned more land, and both were slightly better off than before but were still dirt poor by standards of the region.

The conclusion, "Strangers No More," reflects on the outcomes of this history and what to make of the echoing silences that coexisted with enduring attachment to land. The multiethnic community forged in the early twentieth century continues one hundred years later with more intermarriage, intertwined kinship networks, and an expanded base of tribally owned land that goes hand in hand with the contraction of individual Dakota landownership. Throughout, I interweave accounts of these two groups, with the conviction that the crossroads of their histories is where we must begin.

PART ONE

An Unlikely Encounter

1

Indians Never Knocked: Fear Frames the Encounter

DAKOTAS' VISITS TO white settlers' homes often had an element of surprise. Not only were they unscheduled, but Indians did not knock. Dakota elder Grace Lambert explained the cultural practices behind many a misunderstanding. Dakotas had "never lived in houses," so they had no custom of knocking on doors:

> I remember when we were kids when we'd go anywhere; we never knocked on the doors. We just open the door and walk in. Because a tipi had no door. And so you couldn't be standing there knocking on a tipi. [Chuckle.]…They just opened the flap and walked in. So, we did the same. We opened the door and walked in. When I think of it now I always think, "My, we were rude." [Laughs.][1]

Grace Lambert made an effort to understand the logic of white people on the reservation, just as she strove to comprehend her own people's history and practices (see figure 4). Early white settlers told many stories of being startled by the unannounced presence of an Indian in their house. They would hear nothing, feel their skin prickle, and then notice someone standing behind them or in the next room.

The etiquette for entering another's home, based on an unspoken but agreed-upon social courtesy, reveals a clash of cultural logics. Accustomed to tipis, Dakotas did not knock; with wooden dwellings, Scandinavians did. A celebrated Dakota writer, lecturer, and physician, Charles Eastman, wrote: "in an Indian community…there were neither locks nor doors, and everything was open and easy of access to all comers."[2] In contrast, Scandinavians understood their homes as private property and places of familial sanctuary. Honorary tribal historian Louis Garcia recalls that

Solomon Redfox "was a great joker. He'd come into the white farmer's house, come in the door, shut the door behind him, and then he'd knock on the door." By this historical moment, Dakotas understood whites' customs, but they did not always see fit to change their practice, except perhaps in jest. In story after story, encounters with settlers begin with apprehension, involve an exchange, and end with friendly gestures that dissipate hostility even when misunderstandings remain.

The encounter between Dakotas and Scandinavians and other Euro-American settlers was imbued with a mutual fearfulness born of violent conflict. Although Dakotas lost the war of 1862, they killed a large number of white settlers and government soldiers. Fourteen years later, at a place in Montana the Indians called Greasy Grass Creek and whites called Little Bighorn, the Sioux and Cheyenne scored a major victory over the U.S. Army under the leadership of General Custer. Accounts of victory and defeat were fresh in the minds of white homesteaders on the reservation. "The Battle at Little Bighorn was front-page news and often the topic of conversation for years afterward," wrote Cherrie Lane Wood, an early Yankee settler, and her daughter, Cherry Monson: "Ma Lane's first Dakota Territory–born child was delivered less than six years after Custer's death." She continually worried that Native Americans would again take up arms. "She was always planning how she would protect her children if a war party arrived unexpectedly. The outbreak never came, but the fears remained with her during the years she lived in Dakota Territory."[3]

All across the Great Plains, whites were frightened by Indians' military prowess. That alarm was fueled by trepidation about possible retaliation and repressed guilt over their collective misdeeds that surfaced in the knocking exchange. With attitudes shaped by newspaper accounts, family stories, and their own imagination, Scandinavians came to the encounter anxiously expecting conflict. Similarly, whites inspired dread as well as unease in Indians. Native Americans had good reason to fear the U.S. Army. It had a reputation for fighting unfairly, massacring women and children, and vengefully destroying homes and stockpiles of food. The settler invasion following military conflict seemed designed to turn defeat into dispossession. Despite their trepidation, Scandinavians came to Spirit Lake intending to stay.

This chapter narrates the contradictory memories of war that live on today at Spirit Lake and examines the ways that Dakotas and Scandinavians opened doors to each other, or not, in the late nineteenth century. Beginning in 2006 with the coincidence of a Dakota powwow and a centennial celebration of white settlement on the reservation, I weave the present with the past. Dakotas' and Scandinavians' family stories attempt to make sense of their antagonistic history and their edgy coexistence.

THE PARADE AND THE POWWOW

One dusty midsummer day in 2006, the shimmering heat prompted me to roll up the windows and turn on the air conditioning as I drove across the Spirit Lake Dakota Indian Reservation. The odometer clocked only twenty miles between Fort Totten and the Scandinavian village of Warwick, North Dakota, but that short space of time and distance could have been light years transporting me to a parallel universe. Scandinavians have lived on the reservation with Dakotas for a century, but their coexistence has been riddled with apprehension and ambivalence.

This ritual marked Warwick's centennial, celebrating the arrival of white settlers and the establishment of the village soon after the reservation was opened to homesteading. The parade was long, an impressive measure of its importance. It attracted as many participants as observers. Unaccustomed throngs lined the streets as people arrived from Pekin, McVille, Fargo, and Minneapolis to rub shoulders with extended kin and former neighbors. A sizable contingent of flag-carrying Shriners led off, decked out with white shirts and black bow ties, white gloves, and red fezes. Old Glory must have been heavy, as the men's faces were flushed from exertion in the heat. The Shriners carted the big flags on tall poles that spun in the air like those of a drill team as the squad began to disassemble. The men rolled them up, endeavoring to keep them from touching the ground.

The Shriners were followed closely by a 1950s black-and-white sheriff's car. After that came a hodgepodge of antique cars, tractors old and new, beat-up trucks, and elaborate floats sponsored by local institutions such as the Nelson County Arts Council, Farmers Union Oil, and the Sigdal Lutheran Church, "Under same management for 2000 years." Children captured hearts with their horses and various bicycle-pulled entries: a fish-shaped sign for Parker & Emma's Bait mounted on a red wagon; a barrel train proclaiming, "Have a super nice day." The numerous blonde descendants of Norwegian immigrant Ingemund Peterson were shoe-horned into a horse-drawn wooden wagon that, according to the sign, Ingemund had purchased in 1919. Small businesses sponsored carefully labeled cars (e.g., Willys Knight–Vern's Repair, Pekin); many carried smiling people throwing handfuls of candy. A locally renowned Clydesdale team, grand and powerful, pranced out pulling a huge wagon for Darrel's Bar of Warwick. A squat yellow school bus carried the cheering reunion class of 1976. No musical band marched. Presumably, in the early days of the village, some kind of music would have been incorporated—an accordion, a fiddle, a Norwegian folk ensemble, or the Fort Totten marching band. In other predominantly white villages on and around reservations, Indians frequently participated in parades.[4] But not here, at least not today.

The tavern was open for business on the centennial weekend. The small building bulged with people laughing and hanging out the doors, their fair faces flushed from the heat and drink. It is one of the few remaining commercial establishments, along with the school, the Lutheran church, and the post office. With just seventy-five permanent residents, Warwick, like most of rural North Dakota, has been losing population since 1930. The parade embodied the ironies of the day: the endurance of a village that seems almost deserted and has numerous absentee landowners, and the powerful legacy of ancestors whose land taking is celebrated while its consequences for Native peoples are entirely ignored. The visible absence of Dakotas from this event was striking to me, but what reason would they have to celebrate the arrival of those who had built a separate society on the reservation, particularly when their success came at Dakotas' expense?

After the parade, people gathered under the hundred-year-old trees in the town square. Small groups of high school friends and distant relatives reminisced, ate, and caught up. One large multigenerational group wore matching T-shirts that marked their family reunion. A group of revelers invited me to join them. But even as an interested observer with historical ties, I had no real place at the picnic. My grandmother left the reservation in 1910 and my great-grandmother departed in 1935, so none of my kin remained.

Finding myself alone, I hopped in the car and headed to the other side of the reservation to attend the annual powwow, the Fort Totten Wacipi, and arrived in time to see the evening's grand entry. A stranger to each group, I may have been the only person who went to both events.

Just south of old Fort Totten, now a historic site, I pulled into a crowded parking area—a field between the powwow grounds and the rodeo arena. People meandered between stands selling food and exhibiting handicrafts, caught up with friends, and ate popcorn and fry bread. Phillip John Young greeted me. I first met Phillip John through his sister, Marcy Young McKay, when she facilitated my interviewing elders of the tribe in 1999. The two of them invited me to sit with them at the Elder's Day luncheon the following day. Afterward, Phillip John volunteered to drive with me to the site of my great-grandmother's homestead. Chuckling, he said I needed an Indian scout to find my way. The fact that I had been there before did not matter to me; I wanted to see it through his eyes. When I showed him the homestead on a map of Eddy Township and pointed to section 13 next to the Sheyenne River, Phillip John explained that he often hunted there. From that day, he became a willing teacher of Dakota life as he saw it.

We found Louis Garcia, the honorary tribal historian of Spirit Lake Dakotas, dressed in a dance outfit that was strikingly humble in its quest for historical authenticity, a dramatic contrast to other dancers' fancy regalia. Underneath his beaded loincloth and knee bands, he wore a faded pale blue set of long underwear.[5] Across his chest lay a strap decorated with the tips of deer hooves, symbolizing his status as a good provider. His bright red bandana secured a porcupine guard hair and deer tail headdress with a single eagle feather. An anklet of bells on fetlocks fringed out over the beaded vamp of his moccasins. His brightly striped multicolored sash helped frame his body for festivity, but it lacked glamour. Louis's outfit brought to mind Agnes Greene's comment that in the early twentieth century people were too poor to make very fancy costumes. They lacked the wild fluorescent fabrics of today, the spangles of gold, glittery jingle dresses, and shimmering shawls.

In fact, Louis speculated that had Chief Waanatan, who died in 1897, shown up at today's powwow, he would be perplexed. He might ask, "Who are these people? Are they Aborigines from the South Pacific? I don't recognize anything they are wearing or doing." Pan-Indian dance contests and powwows mix tribal cultures as people influence one another and improvise with contemporary materials to create a new Indian style.

A historian by calling, Louis Garcia, who is of Spanish rather than Dakota origin, began listening to stories when he first came to the reservation in the late 1960s. As a devoted Boy Scout growing up in New York City, he spent a lot of time in a feather shop on the Lower East Side. There he met some Dakota tribal members who had been relocated to New York in the 1950s. They taught him to dance and insisted he visit their home at Fort Totten. When he finally did so in 1966, he fell in love not only with the culture but with one of the daughters of a prominent Sisseton-Wahpeton family. Louis stayed, married Hilda Redfox, and continued listening, becoming an important history keeper of the tribe and teacher of carpentry and Dakota culture at Cankdeska Cikana Community College and Lake Region State College.

As the dancers were called to assemble, Phillip John steered me to stand near the drummers. The drumming groups compete for prize money, as do the singers and dancers. A casual group of guys in baseball caps, jeans, and variously labeled T-shirts morphed into a transcendent drumming ensemble. As the singing began, the drums' vibrations seemed to rise from beneath the earth, enveloping the event and its participants.

The circular powwow arena had small covered bleachers to shade people from hot sun or shelter them from pouring rain. The honor guard, wearing white shirts, black slacks, and gloves and carrying flags, led the grand entry onto the *wacipi*. First in the procession was the U.S. flag, reminiscent of the Shriners in the Warwick parade earlier that afternoon. A man bearing a staff adorned with eagle feathers and a medicine wheel followed. As the guard slowly processed into the circle, their feet following the rhythm of the drum beats, they mesmerized the crowd and transformed time and space. Veterans of former and current wars immediately followed. The retinue of princesses and honorary *wacipi* officials came next. And then the dancers. Swirls of color began as specks and filled the powwow grounds with grace and movement, encircling each other as the drums grew louder. The men entered, then the women, and finally the children.

Like powwows of the nineteenth century, white spectators were visible in the crowd (see figure 5). I quickly understood why Indian dancing attracted Scandinavian onlookers a century ago. While the parade formed a line meandering through the streets of Warwick, the grand entry to the powwow embraced the circle, a central symbol of Indian life, as dancers spiraled in. Then, as now, performers re-created their culture, asserting its importance while adapting it to their needs, circumstances, and inspiration. As Louis Garcia cautions, we cannot assume that the rituals of a culture authentically reflect those of one hundred years ago. Nor can we assume that emotional responses to cultural differences were the same as today. Nonetheless, the powwow dancing was more vivid than the sepia-toned historical photographs suggest. We should not misinterpret the solemn faces and frozen poses shown in nineteenth-century photos as evidence of a joyless existence. A richer reality smolders beneath the stylized positions in which the subjects held still for minute-long exposures. The early twentieth-century Independence Day celebrations, complete with picnics and Indian dancing, drew participants and spectators into their fold, lifting them out of daily lives mired in routine and poverty. The celebration of one group's culture satisfied others' fascination with the exotic. The Fourth of July festivities held a century ago at Spirit Lake were more inclusive than the Warwick centennial today. Although in the eyes of Norwegian immigrants Indian dancing may have been a spectacle, it at least signaled their acknowledgment of the Dakotas' presence on this land.

In intertwining lives, Dakotas and Scandinavians fashioned an existence undergirded by land and kinship and punctuated by mesmerizing rituals. A century after this encounter began to unfold, each group celebrated its continuity at Spirit Lake in its own way. Scandinavians commemorated their homesteading ancestors; Dakotas engaged in a contemporary cultural practice. To understand the unlikely encounter between Dakotas and Scandinavians, we must first comprehend the historical forces that brought them to the same place at the end of the nineteenth century.

NATIVE DISPOSSESSION, THE U.S.–DAKOTA WAR OF 1862, AND THEIR REVERBERATIONS

The Dakotas' epic journey is as dramatic as the landscape. Native people at Spirit Lake trace their origins to the Seven Council Fires, Oceti Sakowin, an alliance of Dakota bands that lived in distinct but overlapping ecological and economic systems and communicated through dialects of a common language. The Sisseton and Wahpeton bands of eastern Dakotas that fled southern Minnesota in the wake of the U.S.–Dakota War of 1862 joined Ihanktonwannas, a band of northern Dakotas, to negotiate a treaty and settle at Spirit Lake in 1867 as the herds of buffalo became depleted and they found it more difficult to follow their historic way of life.

For millennia, the ecosystem of the Great Plains supported multiple peoples and cultures through its abundance of wild game and edible plants. Beginning in the eighteenth century, Europeans came to the region and tapped into systems of trade among indigenous peoples, extracting natural resources primarily in the form of animal pelts. "As the foundation that led to the area's discovery by Euro-Americans, the fur trade stimulated exploration, was a prime factor in the destruction of Indian culture, and brought the first white people to settle the area."[6] The early French traders did not intend to destroy Indian culture or even to take their land. They ventured forth to do business, and their efforts, supported by colonial governments, eventually rendered Native peoples economically dependent.[7] Offering tools, beads, cloth, and weapons, the traders sought to create new needs that would link Indians to Europeans and motivate them to continue harvesting animals for exchange. Importantly, these men established kinship ties, which facilitated exchange, by marrying Native women.[8]

European contact, trade, and settlement transmitted infectious diseases to indigenous peoples, devastating their populations and disrupting their cultures. Demographers conservatively estimate that in 1492 approximately 7,000,000 people inhabited North America. By the last decade of the nineteenth century, the indigenous population of that area was closer to 375,000, or at most half a million.[9] In the Great Plains region, epidemics of smallpox, measles, and cholera decimated entire tribes during the nineteenth century.[10] The fur trade in this region ended around 1867, primarily from overharvesting of animals.[11]

Between the combined effects of European diseases, excessive hunting of bison, invasion of white settlers, and U.S.—Indian wars, Native peoples' power declined along with their numbers. The loss of their resource base destroyed their ability to hunt as they had for as long back as oral accounts reached. As Mary Louise Defender Wilson (b. 1930) said, Dakotas depended on the buffalo "for everything practically." Louis Garcia explained the consequence, "Land and buffalo went together. No buffalo meant less value to the land."[12]

Sissetons and Wahpetons had spent the better part of the two previous centuries in the territory that whites later claimed as central and southern Minnesota. These hunters and horticulturalists had moved seasonally, setting up camps and establishing villages where they cultivated gardens along the Minnesota River during the summer. Along with Ihanktonwannas, whose territory ranged north of the James

River and east of the Missouri River, and other tribes, they hunted buffalo on the prairie. Dakotas fought territorial disputes with their longtime enemies, Ojibwes, over the north-south divide in Minnesota and northern Dakota Territory.

Setting the stage for U.S. continental expansion at midcentury were two treaties that the federal government negotiated with Dakotas: the 1851 Treaty of Traverse des Sioux and its subsequent modification, the Land Cessions Treaty of 1858. The Treaty of Traverse des Sioux ceded most of Dakotas' territory in central Minnesota down to the Iowa border in exchange for a cash payment, a twenty-mile-wide reservation along the Minnesota River from the Mississippi to Lake Traverse, and annuities for fifty years. In 1858, a delegation to Washington further negotiated the Land Cessions Treaty, which ceded the ten-mile swath of reservation land on the northern side of the Minnesota River. Because of misunderstandings of terms, lack of tribal representation in the delegation, and a Senate confirmation process that made changes without consulting Dakotas, these treaties generated enmity and distrust, setting Dakotas and whites on a collision course that ended in war.

The Outbreak of War

Because the 1862 U.S.–Dakota War is almost as hotly contested today as it was 150 years ago, I hesitate to say more than what historians of all persuasions now agree on. Outraged at the U.S. government's betrayals and violations of its treaties, Dakotas took up arms and began killing white traders and settlers in southern Minnesota on August 18, 1862.[13] The land cessions that had recently been negotiated stimulated an expansion of white settlement that crowded Dakotas and displaced wildlife, diminishing their hunting territory. The failure of the 1861 harvest meant that Dakotas suffered from extreme hunger through the summer of 1862, while white traders refused to extend credit as they normally did. In an act reminiscent of food riots in early modern Europe, in early August Dakota warriors broke into a warehouse at the Upper Agency to get food.[14] Compounding the problem, the U.S. government was late in delivering contractually agreed upon annuity payments in the form of food and money, sending available supplies to the Union Army instead. Although Dakotas' most immediate grievances were against white traders and the federal government, they resented white farmers who aggressively took land and refused overtures to engage in reciprocal exchange, a longstanding practice between earlier white settlers and Dakotas.[15]

Dakotas' sense of place entitled them to their territory, and they expected others, including white settlers, to respect their rights. Historian Gary Anderson illustrates the complexities of this stance for Dakotas who in earlier times spent the summers cultivating gardens near the Minnesota River and the winters in the woods. Among the converging disputes that led Dakotas to take up arms in 1862, he points to the encroachment of German settlers who moved onto the northern side of the river while it was still formally part of the Dakota reserve and reduced access to "their established hunting grounds."[16] Misunderstandings of major proportions unfolded.

> After cold weather set in, the boomers moved into the abandoned summer lodges of some remnants of Red Iron's and Sleepy Eyes's Sisseton bands. When spring arrived and the Indians returned, the first serious confrontation took place. The Dakota women "became enraged and struck the ground with their fists to indicate that land belonged to them." The Germans refused to be intimidated even after the young Dakota warriors threw down the survey flags and began killing cattle. Only the arrival of the army prevented violence.[17]

Imagine witnessing that confrontation and watching women furiously pounding the earth. Their ferocity conveys their wrath and deep sense of prerogative. Those cultivated plots were theirs. They had cleared, planted, weeded, and reaped the land's bounty every year as they returned to the same spot. As they saw it, their temporary absence during the winter did not negate their right to it. Cultivating the same patch of land along the river year in and year out established, and, in their eyes, consecrated their claim.

Internally, Dakota opinion was divided about how to deal with the acute food shortage and how best to confront the U.S. government for its refusal to honor treaty agreements.[18] Sissetons and Wahpetons, who lived toward the northwestern end of the large Dakota reserve along the Minnesota River, were generally opposed to taking up arms against the United States. Historically they had been more hospitable to whites; more of them had converted to Christianity and shifted from a mix of hunting and agriculture to primary reliance on farming. Several bands of Sissetons and Wahpetons were hunting buffalo in Dakota Territory north of the Sheyenne River when the initial attack occurred. According to Anderson, even among those Mdewakantons and Wahpekutes who lived farther southeast along the Minnesota River, where warriors had set up a lodge, there was longstanding polarization about the best way forward for Indian people.[19] Chief Little Fish reported on the actions of noted chief Waanatan: "After we got the news a council was called by Wa-a-na-tan and Standing Buffalo, and they told their people that this was not their affair what had been done; it had been done by the [Mdewakantons], and that none of the young men should go and join in this, but all keep together and quietly go back to their village."[20] Nonetheless, once violence ignited, some of those who had opposed an attack were pulled into the conflict. Many noncombatants, at the time and since referred to as "friendlies" as distinct from "hostiles," helped settlers escape harm and liberated some from captivity once the war was underway. Some acted as scouts for the U.S. Army in exchange for the promise of payment and land.[21]

After the battles and bloodshed of the six-week war, Dakotas were either imprisoned or exiled from Minnesota. In 1863, when it punished Dakotas by terminating their treaty entitlements, Congress indiscriminately included Mdewakantons, Wahpekutes, Sissetons, and Wahpetons, presuming that they had all participated equally in the conflict. Dakotas in Minnesota were effectively dispossessed of the rest of their land. In the wake of the hostilities, many fled the area, afraid of vengeful troops who sought to punish all Indians. Dakota elder Agnes Greene (b. 1915) said, "They were chased out of Minnesota."[22] According to historian J. Michael McCormack, although only a small number of Dakotas took up arms, "fearful Minnesotans found it easy to accuse all Indians," including the noncombatant Winnebagos and Ojibwes. In the diaspora that unfolded, some bands sought safety across the border in Canada; others found refuge with extended kin in the area that would become South Dakota and formed the Lake Traverse Indian Reservation. "After Congress had its revenge by abrogating all existing treaties early in 1863, many Sioux bands," including bystanders and pacifists, "migrated to areas of refuge and security and so the forest and waters of the Devils Lake region became a haven."[23]

Entangled Family Stories of the Conflict

When I asked respected tribal elder Grace Lambert about her family, she began with the events of the summer of 1862 to explain her family's journey and its relationship to land at Spirit Lake. She shared with me a long and complex account of her understanding of what sparked the conflict: "They were supposed to have massacred a town, or something. My ancestors weren't educated or anything but they used to talk about that. They always said that it was started by an egg." Intrigued, I queried, "An egg? How so?" She continued:

> These Indians were already on kind of like a reservation. They were already close to a fort, Fort Snelling…. They said that the government wasn't sending in the rations for them to eat because they couldn't hunt or anything; they were just kind of captives like, and remained on the reservation there, and the only thing that they could eat was what was given to them from the government…. They said that the government hadn't sent it in. This was what the Indians were talking about, see, I didn't read it in no book or anything, this was just what I heard the elders talking about.
>
> They were saying that these two kids were going towards where the warehouse was, but eventually, I suppose, maybe that was a little town, or a village. They were

all white people who lived there. This man lived at the end of the village; he was kind of like a farmer, and he had chickens and everything. These two Indian boys were going and one was a chief's son, and when they got close to that chicken coop, they went in. And that man was watching them through this window in his house. And he came out and he was standing there and…I guess he took his gun with him too, outside. Because these two kids, they were teenagers, they were about fifteen or fourteen years old, and they came out and they had an egg in their hands that they must have taken from…the nest. One of the boys said, "I dare you to break that egg." And he said, "That's easy," and he dropped it and of course it just broke on the ground. And I guess the man aimed and shot the boy. So the other boy ran home. But see, he killed the chief's son. And when that boy ran home back to…the reservation where they were…he told them. So that was how the war started. The warriors…went back and that's how come that thing was destroyed, that place, what they call the massacre.

Grace understood that the historical record contained competing renditions. Some published accounts of the war also contain stories about an egg, although the significance of this incident is debated.[24]

Of the approximately 500 white settlers and soldiers killed in the war, only a small proportion was Norwegian.[25] Nonetheless, like everyone in the region in the aftermath of the bloodshed, Norwegian immigrants were traumatized and decided to relocate. The war prompted them to move north and west in hopes of greater security in a place that was less crowded and less racked by conflict. Formally established in 1861, Dakota Territory beckoned as it opened land to willing settlers. Some ventured directly to Nelson, Eddy, and Benson counties, where they lived in the vicinity of many of the Dakota people who had also fled Minnesota.

Norwegian farmers have family stories that, like Grace Lambert's, begin in 1862. The Fordes left Norway and settled among other Norwegians in Belmont Township, approximately fifty or sixty miles south of the Minnesota River where the war centered. As warnings about the eruption of violence reached the community, settlers began making plans to defend themselves. A week into the conflict, on Sunday, August 24, 1862, as Louis Garcia recounts, "fifty warriors under Chief White Lodge traveled down the Des Moines River" to that part of Jackson County near the Minnesota-Iowa border. For reasons not entirely clear, they targeted a Norwegian settlement just north of the Lake Okoboji area where Inkpaduta and his warriors had taken revenge against forty-two white settlers in 1857.[26] When, armed with tomahawks and guns, White Lodge and his men reached Belmont Township, they began killing local families and destroying property. In total, thirteen Norwegian men, women, and children were killed and three were seriously injured.[27]

Like the accounts of the Dakota Conflict writ large, the story of this incident is told in multiple, sometimes contradictory versions. In an oral history with the State Historical Society in 1975, Oscar T. Forde (b. 1895) repeated the story passed down to him from his father, known as Big Ole, who was a boy when the warriors entered his home:

My grandfather and grandmother and the family came to Minnesota in the early [eighteen-]sixties, thereabouts. At that time there were very few settlers there, and there were a lot of Indians too, around that time. Some of them were very peaceful, and others, of course, could be riled up if they got hold of some liquor or something like that. And, it seems that it had been rumored around for some time that the Indians were on the powwow.... They were making trouble, see. Some of the folks, the neighbors there, had gone to church and they'd taken their guns with 'em. And, my grandfather and grandmother stayed home, kind of looked after the farm and so on. He was out feeding the hogs early in the morning, just about daylight, and the Indians were lying on their tummies, up above on a little hill.... You know how they go down, they'd pour the swill in the trough?... And as he raised up, the arrows, they were all shot at one time, the arrows hit him. I think there was four to five arrows that hit him in the back, and of course killed him instantly. Just slumped back over the pig pen again, and was there. And then of course, they started to holler and scream and came running towards the house. And by that time the [people in the house] rushed down in the basement somehow. And there was a young couple there, had been married and had one young child.... They said they knew that... if they took the child down there it might cry. And of course, they'd all be killed. So, instead of going down in this hideout, they stayed up and the Indians came in. In the meantime, my father who had been standing back to the door, he was eleven years old, he was a big boy, he was going to hold the door closed, so the Indians couldn't come in. Well, that was just a joke. They just broke the door open and came in. And Dad got away and he started to run down this slope, it was kind of a ravine. And someone had dug for a well there, and didn't get any water, so the grass had just grown over it.... They'd shot him once, with an arrow, and they hit him in the elbow here. But he fell into this hole, and just stayed there. And some of the Indians, some stayed in the house, some started to look for him, and they couldn't find him so they just got disgruntled and they went back up to the house again.[28]

The 1910 history of the incident written by Arthur P. Rose corroborates the main facts.[29] Although distant from the central battles of the war, the Belmont massacre profoundly shaped the mind-set of Norwegian settlers who came to North Dakota. Not only were Norwegians the only victims, but approximately half of all the Norwegian lives claimed in the war were lost at Belmont. Curiously, this story is told without its historical context. If one did not know that a war raged between Dakotas and white settlers and the U.S. government, Oscar Forde's account would make the attack sound random, an act perpetrated by vindictive Indians who were "riled up" and "on the powwow."

I had occasion to interview another descendent of the Fordes of Jackson County, Norman Forde (b. 1914), the grandson of Little Ole Forde, who was Big Ole's younger brother. The version told to him detailed what occurred after Big Ole's escape. The Indians killed the young mother who stayed upstairs in the house and left her body lying on the floor with the nursling at her breast. The horror in the telling stems from the iconic image of a baby suckling a dead woman. From the perspective of the Norwegian settlers, killing the parents and orphaning the infant was an inhumanly cruel act and a terrifying message to the survivors. Considered from an Indian perspective, it was an act of mercy; the Indians preserved the life of the innocent child. Oscar T. Forde ruminates, "It's funny, they didn't want to kill that little baby, isn't it? They left that little baby right there, sucking this blood from the breast." Despite the chaos in the heat of passions, it is not surprising that the infant was spared. While many infants and children were killed during the war, Dakota men may have exercised compassion in this instance, seeing the baby as innocent of any offenses committed by its parents. However, Rose's account specifies that the "infant" was two years old and was found in the blood. The child may have been still nursing, but this story may be apocryphal. Oscar Forde seemed to still be wrestling with how to explain the act of fearsome warriors sparing a baby, when they appeared so hardened to tenderness or compassion.

At the end of his recollection of family history, Norman Forde concluded, "From there on, I don't know really what happened.... that's about as much as I remember." Oscar T. Forde, a generation closer to the event, had more to say:

> Pretty soon my dad got out of this little hole, and he started to run towards this church, where he knew there were a lot of neighbors. When he got there, he told 'em what had happened. And he was so exhausted, that he just dropped over, in sort of a faint, I guess. And they all got excited there in the church. They picked up their guns and they all started to run to their homes. And pretty soon, someone said, "Well, how 'bout [Big Ole] Forde, he's not here with us," see. And there was one fella that said, "Well, I better go back and see what's happened to him." They went back and they found him. And they helped him and they took him along, got some of the neighbors there, and went for two

or three days. And the worms had started to accumulate in his elbow here. You know how the gangrene I suppose had set in and the worms were there. And one fella says, "Well, we got to do something about that." He took a gunshot shell, twelve gauge or something like that. He broke it in two, took the black powder and poured it in his arm, here. And touched a match to it. Shwt! Just burned it out, see. Course it got rid of the worms all right, but it left his arm so that all his life, he would have his arm just come down like.... I could tell Dad blocks and miles away, far as I could see, whether it's him or not, the way he walked.

Oscar's account revels in his father's grit as a wounded messenger of imminent danger. Whatever obtuseness may have accompanied his ancestors' land taking near the Iowa border, where five years before white settlers had been killed by Inkpaduta, he forgave them. He could interpret their and his father's tenacity as evidence of masculine bravery, and hence his inheritance.

Eventually Big Ole Forde, who had been shot in the elbow, and his younger brother, Little Ole, ventured to Nelson County, North Dakota, where they were the first homesteaders in what came to be called Forde Township. After meeting Big Ole many years later and learning his story, Archie Redfox, Sr. (Sisseton-Wahpeton) commented, "I wonder why he came to live by the reservation near us."[30] Norman Forde assured me that proximity to Dakotas was not an issue for his great-uncle or for his grandfather, Nils Forde. "I think the danger was kind of over. They farmed up here in Nelson County quite a while" before they moved to Hamar, on the reservation. "No, they never had any Indian problems up here." Like other amazed Scandinavian settlers, Norman implicitly compared 1862 to the present day. Despite their initial trepidation, once they were living here in the company of Dakotas, Scandinavians discovered that the period of violent conflict was behind them. Their foreboding tapped into their unspoken awareness that they were again agents of dispossession of those same Dakota Indians. Their own victimization allowed them to relinquish responsibility for Indian displacement. Oscar saw himself as an innocent descendent of a boy who was shot at random. Scandinavians' apprehension reveals not just lingering fear but also flickering recognition that Dakotas' wrath was warranted. Their worry was diluted by generation and distance from the site of trauma, although not from the people involved in the suffering.

As the hostilities drew to a close in September 1862, many Dakota warriors surrendered to General Alfred Sully and handed over their prisoners of war. Of those Dakotas captured, tried by military tribunal, and jailed for the winter, 303 were sentenced to death. President Abraham Lincoln commuted the sentences of all but 38. Their group hanging on December 26, 1862, stands as the largest mass execution in

U.S. history, and to this day the fairness of the trials and the sentences continue to be challenged.[31]

The Tragedy at Whitestone Hill

The following year General Sully and Brigadier General Henry H. Sibley were ordered to find those who had not been captured immediately after hostilities ceased and compel them to surrender. As many Sissetons and Wahpetons sought refuge in northern Dakota Territory, they continued hunting and raiding white settlements. Ihanktonwannas, their fellow Dakotas who had not participated in the hostilities in Minnesota, also continued to hunt buffalo, but with less success. The generals' quest brought them to a place in Dakota Territory south of Jamestown, between the James and Missouri rivers, called Whitestone Hill, where they planned unsuccessfully to rendezvous.

Controversy about the facts and the framing of the incident at Whitestone Hill hangs as a shadow over relationships on the reservation today, as it does about the larger war. In his search for marauders, General Sully and his troops descended upon a Dakota encampment of approximately 300–400 lodges.[32] Early in September, a circle of Tetons and another of Ihanktonwannas were camped around a lake next to Whitestone Hill, preparing for the oncoming winter. Mary Louise Defender Wilson explained, "The general didn't understand that they were *not* a group of people who had anything to do with what happened in Minnesota." Repeating what her great-grandmother told her, Mary Louise described the situation—Ihanktonwanna children and women were curing buffalo meat while the men were away hunting.

> The people were not hostile. They simply told him who they were, but evidently, they didn't want to believe that. And they made them give up whatever they had, like, that could be used as a weapon. Knives. There weren't any younger people in there who had other types of weapons. And they were all given up, and then they fired on them. And the children. My great-grandmother always said, "Well, they ran as well as they could."

Given the evident aggressive intent of Sully's mission, once Dakotas became aware of the larger number of soldiers, they made efforts to negotiate a truce while women and children were taking whatever they could and evacuating the site.[33] Nonetheless, the soldiers charged, without good communication or coordination. The assault resulted in approximately 150 Dakota deaths, according to Sully, but he added that "Indian reports make it over 200."[34] Army losses amounted to 20 killed and 38 wounded.[35] North Dakota historian Elwyn Robinson called "the battle" the "bloodiest ever fought on North Dakota soil."[36]

Many at Spirit Lake today speak of Whitestone Hill as a massacre of Dakota women and children. Jack Reeves (b. 1918), son of early Yankee homesteader Clyde Reeves, could only shake his head and look down at the floor when Whitestone Hill was mentioned. An avid member of a local history group, he regarded General Sully's actions as rash and shameful. Mary Louise Defender Wilson said the people resented "what the general did to them there at Whitestone Hill." In a letter written to his father two months after the tragedy, Samuel J. Brown, a nineteen-year-old interpreter at Santee Sioux Agency who had previously scouted for Sibley, wrote:

> I hope you will not believe all that is said of 'Sullys' successfull expedition,' against the Sioux I don't think he ought to brag of it at all, because it was, what no decent man would have done, he pitched into their camp and just slaughtered them, worse a great deal than what the Indians did in 1862, he killed *very few* men and took *no* hostile ones prisoners, he *took* some but they were friendly Yanktons, and he let them go again....It is lamentable to hear how those women and children were slaughtered it was a perfect massacre."[37]

Adding to the devastation, the following day Sully's troops burned 400,000 to 500,000 pounds of dried buffalo meat that had been stockpiled in the camp, as well as tipis and household goods left behind, destroying Dakotas' winter food and remaining supplies.[38]

In the aftermath, 156 people were taken prisoner and kept at a military camp—32 men and 124 women and children.[39] Along with others, Mary Louise's great-grandmother was taken on a forced trek to a prisoner-of-war camp, which she found "a horrible frightening experience" because men marched with their weapons on display all the day long. Dakotas viewed that open exhibition of arms as a threat of further violence and aggression. They also feared being poisoned, so initially they refused to eat the food they were given. After they were released, they returned to their people.

Ihanktonwannas were compelled to go to Standing Rock, which became a reservation in 1873, in the heart of Dakota Territory. Relocation made subsistence difficult. Previously, according to Mary Louise, "many of them wouldn't come over to this side of the river, because, well...they see the land was different, and they were accustomed to that fertile land and raising their crops. They always did corn, beans, squash, and melon." Ihanktonwannas were punished and relocated in the aftermath of the war, despite their lack of participation in or proximity to the fighting.

The ensuing diaspora made Sissetons and Wahpetons settlers in a territory where they had hunted but was not their home. From the perspective of the government, rebellion continued to lurk as a possibility, with mail routes and white settlers as potential targets. Those Dakota bands that surrendered at Fort Totten, "a mix of Dakota people," negotiated a treaty with the U.S. government establishing the Devils Lake Sioux Indian Reservation. Tribal member Eunice Davidson recalled the way her grandmother would wistfully talk about southern Minnesota: "That's where their land was. That's where she was *from*. That's where her mother and her grandmother and her great-grandmother [were born]." In other words, Minnesota was home.

Destitution and disease were rampant on the Spirit Lake reservation, similar to what we might find today in a wartime refugee camp.[40] Recognizing the extreme deprivation of Dakotas, General Sibley wrote to the Secretary of the Interior on December 28, 1867, with an urgent plea to help them: "They are almost naked and starving, barely subsisting on what fish they can obtain, and as there are no buffalo or other game at this season, they must receive speedy succor, or many of them will perish."[41] He pointed out that the government's postwar objective had been to gather Dakota bands together on a reservation, which (it went without saying) he had been instrumental in accomplishing. His own role in the enterprise would be compromised if the government reneged on its agreement:

> The bands at Devil's lake, having abandoned their hostile attitude, expect the promises of the government to be fulfilled, and as they have received neither provisions nor clothing up to this time, I respectfully urge that, unless they receive speedy succor, they will be driven by sheer necessity to resume their habits of pillage of the whites, and thus renew hostilities which it has cost a large expenditure of blood and treasure to bring to a close.[42]

Sibley understood this catastrophic situation as an invitation to rebellion. He called upon the government not to recreate the very same conditions that had provoked the eruption in Minnesota. The harsh neglect appeared to be a form of retribution against Dakotas by a government that defaulted on the agreement he had negotiated. This treatment undermined the honor of Sibley's promise to meet Dakotas' basic needs, which had been instrumental in persuading them to surrender. Temporary funds only partially met the needs of people, who, in effect, were being collectively punished for the war.

DISPOSSESSION AND APPREHENSION FRAME THE ENCOUNTER

Because the federal government's Indian containment program depended directly on white settlement of the continent, immigrants were central to westward expansion, as the government of Dakota Territory clearly understood. Its Office of Immigration actively recruited foreigners from northwestern Europe, sending agents as far afield as Norway and Sweden.[43] Recruitment propaganda played to stereotypes of these national groups. Sociologist Kendric Charles Babcock found that Norwegians were not known to be as gregarious as people from southern and western Europe, who migrated elsewhere in the West to work in mining or industries concentrated in urban centers. They were, however, seen as "strong-limbed, sound-hearted, land-hungry."[44] North Dakota historian Elwyn B. Robinson took stock: "Perhaps even more than the other Scandinavians and the Germans, the Norwegians were individualists. They had a strict, puritan moral code, and were a pious, serious-minded, and introspective people; yet they were often excessive in fighting, drinking, and love-making."[45] Despite the questionable veracity of these ethnic characterizations, they held a firm place in the popular imagination. The railroads, financially invested in having more people and products to transport, underwrote and encouraged development.[46] Native Americans faced the insatiable appetite for land and natural resources that impelled European immigrants and American settlers.

Dakota writer Zitkala-Ša emphasized the foreignness of whites, especially their odd and repulsive appearance. In one short story, her protagonist observed: "Large men, with heavy bundles in their hands, halted near by, and riveted their glassy blue eyes upon us."[47] In another story Zitkala-Ša's central character conveyed her mother's warning "about the poverty-stricken white settlers, who lived in caves dug in the long ravines of the high hills across the river."[48] Indian resentment, which the settlers feared, was a central theme of the story. "A whole tribe of broad-footed white beggars had rushed hither to make claims on those wild lands."[49] Her mother held white men, who preached Christianity but sold liquor, responsible for the deaths of her brother and daughter. "He is the hypocrite who reads with one eye, 'Thou shalt not kill,' and with the other gloats upon the sufferings of the Indian race."[50] Antipathy over the violation of treaties and expropriation of Indian land may not have been evident at every turn, but it was a backdrop to interactions between white and Native people. White settlers, who surrounded Spirit Lake Reservation in border towns such as Minnewaukan and Oberon in Benson County and Sheyenne in Eddy County, brought with them stories of war with Native people in South Dakota and Minnesota. Thomas Pearson (b. 1894) recounted a story of his grandfather's confrontation with a "great big Indian" (most Indians grew in the telling). "Grandpa had said, 'Let's move away from here. It's dangerous to live here.'" After they left South Dakota for Iowa, the family that bought their property was killed by Indians. "So Grandpa moved out in time. So I tell you, it wasn't good." In 1890 they left Iowa, walking all the way to Eddy County, North Dakota, to find land. They then walked back to Iowa to get their belongings and moved to a section several miles from Fort Totten. On the eastern edge of the reservation in Tolna, Nelson County,

Palmer Overby reported that his family "traded with the Indians" and insisted that they had "no problems." That expectation of problems—that amorphously lingering possibility of violence—took the Dakota Conflict as its referent. His mother came from near Montevideo, Minnesota. "That was with that Minnesota massacre they had down in there, in the early days." As if frozen in time, that threat lurked in the shadows, a sharp contrast to their current reality. With little understanding of treaty violations or land encroachments, Scandinavians remembered only that Dakotas killed white settlers. Treating Indians as a hostile people of the past, they found their living, breathing neighbors startlingly benign.

One notorious warrior, White Dog, or Sunka Ska, seemed to take pleasure in frightening white people (see figure 6). In his travels around the region, White Dog would wear a tomahawk in his belt and boast about his participation in the Minnesota War and his collection of white scalps—eleven by some counts, by others ninety-nine. He expressed his disdain for whites to those who showed up at his home near Horseshoe Lake. According to Lloyd Olson, a Norwegian interviewed by Louis Garcia, "White Dog would scare children" who followed him all around Warwick. "He would turn quickly and stomp his foot," and the children, including Lloyd, would run. White Dog "got a big charge out of doing this."[51] He may have resented being treated as an oddity, a subject of ridicule as well as myth. But the stories suggest that White Dog understood that inspiring fear signals power and used it to his advantage as well as for his amusement.

Along with apprehension of Indians in particular, white settlers expressed alarm about difference in general, the unaccustomed ways of life they encountered in this new and intimidating environment. Many recalled being unnerved by howling winds, which they mistook for coyotes or perhaps wolves. Most immigrants came from places that were culturally homogeneous and relatively isolated. In Minnesota, Shirley Kanten's (b. 1914) grandmother, Anne Halvorson Kanten, a Norwegian immigrant, lived across the river from the Christian mission at Lac Qui Parle, where the opportunity for land taking undeniably resulted from the exodus of Dakotas. Surely stories of the war were fresh, complete with numerous accounts of kindness as Dakotas saved neighbors and friends from certain death or ushered them surreptitiously from the boundaries of Camp Release. Dakotas would come to the Kanten farm to buy dairy products, and in turn the Kantens would buy lumber from them. Anne exhibited some fear in these exchanges. She "used to be kind of scared, but…all they came for was to get milk….[Laughs.]" Shirley Kanten explained that the foreignness of the visitors made her grandmother apprehensive. "It was just the idea they were different. It was a completely Scandinavian area, in the Watson area, for a time—there were a few outsiders, but…Italians came in, to work the railroads, so even that was scary, she'd say." In this report, Shirley empathizes with her grandmother, but also interprets her fear as misplaced. The comparision of Italians to Indians reveals that she considered her grandmother's fear of difference groundless and both groups harmless. Born as she was in 1914, a profoundly different moment in Indian-white relations, she saw the Dakota Conflict as safely in the past and her family's farm as securely located in an immigrant enclave.

In this multiethnic polyglot region, there were many opportunities to be fearful. Households tended to be isolated, and strangers were plentiful. In the absence of inns, passing travelers would seek food and shelter at ordinary houses. Norwegian American memoirist Barbara Levorsen reported, "Mama had little to fear from the Indians, but she was terrified of the wandering peddlers,"[52] who were rumored to be Syrian and Arab (decidedly not European). Gypsies surface in people's stories as a kind of traveling spectacle. Swedish immigrant Emma Beckstrand Casper (b. 1886) spoke frankly of her prejudice: "That was one time a load of gypsies [was] coming. I was sure scared of them though. Cause there are so many... and I don't know, I don't like them."

The Totten Trail that connected reservations and forts across North Dakota continued to be used by Indians even after the forts were demilitarized. Discussing early nineteenth-century New England, historian Daniel Mandell astutely remarks that in a postconflict economy, dislocated people are likely to search for seasonal work.[53] To white settlers, even those who had relocated repeatedly, Indians' itinerancy resembled their supposedly nomadic former life as hunters. As bearers of weapons, Indian hunters could be mistaken for warriors, and settlers feared the implicit threat. Many oral history accounts tell of Indian travelers on their way to visit relatives or attend a powwow at another reservation. Barbara Levorsen recalls her Norwegian mother's rising fear: "Perhaps it was after she came to America that she heard how merciless, cruel, and bloodthirsty the Indians were to the white settlers. This fear remained with her for many years. Still she went out to Dakota to be an early settler herself. Here she did not have long to wait to see Indians, as they passed nearby on their treks to pow wows at Fort Totten or somewhere on Strawberry Lake."[54]

Curiosity generated ambivalence, balancing fear with the desire to witness a spectacle. Scandinavians, like white Americans, exoticized Indians. By the turn of the twentieth century, with Indian wars at an end and Indian people vanquished and living on reservations, Native Americans were cast as a "vanishing race" by the dominant culture and government officials.[55] They assumed, indeed willed, that in an economic contest of the survival of the fittest, Indians were doomed to fail. Despite a few victories, they had lost militarily, and the proliferating white settlement across the continent proved that domesticated fenced farming beat out free-range hunting and ranching. A growing romanticism about the Native American past fed an art market of Indian goods and photographs of the "lost race."[56] White settlers anxiously anticipated possible acts of revenge, but marveled at clothing and religious practices that they perceived as so different from their own. Barbara Levorsen tells a story on herself as a young girl. When a wagon pulled up at their gate with an Indian man and two women in it, "I, having heard so many hair-raising stories about Indians, forgot caution and rushed down to the gate to get a good look at them. I stared at them with open curiosity and they stared impassively back at me."[57] No doubt the Indians found her behavior rude, but had encountered it before.

Contact with indigenous people was minimal unless white folks lived on or near reservations or watched Indian dancing on the Fourth of July. Historian Barbara Handy-Marchello observes that in North Dakota "most settlers had little contact with Native Americans."[58] Encounters were regionally specific, although stories were ubiquitous. A person living in Grand Forks in 1910 could imagine Indians as people of the past and never meet someone of Native ancestry to challenge that view. Even in 2013, it is possible for a North Dakota resident not to know about Native American history or simply associate Dakota people exclusively with the Spirit Lake casino.

In assembling seven volumes of letters that immigrants sent back to Norway, literary scholar Orm Øverland observed their profound silence about Indians. Only one mention of Native Americans surfaced in the collected letters from 1895 to 1904. Even the volume covering the period of the U.S.–Dakota War had few accounts or references. Øverland's probing discussion of this absence concludes, "The most important point to be made…is that they were rarely paid any attention at all."[59] In Ramsey County, to the north of the reservation, contact occurred primarily when whites went into the town of Devils Lake. The German Polst family reported, "No there weren't any Indians up there." No Indians worked on farms; none lived in the area; no Indian children went to these country schools; and none even passed by. Through segregation and confinement, Native Americans became an oddity, a spectacle, seen only on "Indian Day" at the Chautauqua or on a trip to Fort Totten. In dramatic contrast, whites living on the reservation could not ignore the presence of Dakota people; indeed, they were neighbors.

Time and again stories of the Great Plains tell of children from white and Native communities being incorporated into a tribe without distinction. This practice fed the fear that Indians might possibly take children—not to harm them, but to raise them as their own. Barbara Levorsen's Norwegian neighbors, Ole and Mrs. Rodne, who came to join her extended family, struggled with these fears. Their homestead shack was not far from the Totten Trail, and one day some Indians camped nearby. "When darkness came and the child had gone to sleep they stole out of the shack and into the planting of young trees where they spent the nights as they were afraid of being attacked in the shack. (No doubt the Indians knew where they were.)"[60]

Mamie Larson (b. 1884) relayed a parallel family history and the fear her parents felt, however ill-founded, at the idea of their children being kidnapped:

> Maybe we were afraid of the Indians....There was an Indian scare once, when we were small kids, I can remember. They said there was a war dance in Sheyenne. But I don't know, it didn't amount to much....They told us kids that they had a well out there that wasn't very deep. They were going to hide us down there, because *they stole white children.* Yeah. They did, too. And so we were kind of scared, us kids.

The Ghost Dance, which spread enthusiastically among many tribes in 1890, struck fear in the hearts of settlers. They perceived gatherings of Indians as threatening. Indian agent John Waugh wrote that at Spirit Lake no one "joined the hostiles," that is, those in the Ghost Dance. But he chided the "timidity of some of the settlers near by" for overreacting and creating alarm when none was warranted.[61]

Most likely the war dance rumors recalled by Mamie Larson were tied to regional unease. Concerns about kidnapping may have stemmed from the disputed origins of a white child Wasicupazi ("Yellow Haired White Man"), nicknamed Irish Mike, who was adopted into the Spirit Lake tribe. Louis Garcia explains the logic from Dakotas' perspective: "They would, during periods of warfare or whatever, take in a lot of women. And then their children would be incorporated into the tribe, the same way the Eastern Indians took in a lot of white people. They would capture the white—especially a boy—to replace a fallen warrior. And so, that person whether they were black, yellow, or white was taken into the tribe." Mamie grew up in Sheyenne, herself virtually adopted by the Mattson family, not far from where Irish Mike and his family lived. Seeing him speak Dakota, identify as a tribal member, and even receive an allotment must have given some credence to this anxiety.

Indians had reason to fear white settlers. They knew that with one family came others, and Indian land was vulnerable. In 1901, Dakotas held councils to discuss the U.S. government's request that they release unallotted land to white homesteaders. Responding to a proposal to build a bridge across the Devils Lake narrows, which would link white settlers in Ramsey County directly with the reservation, Little Fish, one of the Sisseton hereditary chiefs, expressed apprehension. "For my part, I do not want a white neighbor. He may get on a drunk and knock me senseless."[62] For sound historical reasons, Chief Little Fish was skeptical about the government's willingness to follow through on its promises: during the war and after, he had witnessed mistreatment of Dakota people and more than one tussle between whites and Dakotas, particularly when alcohol was involved.

HOSPITALITY MITIGATES THE FEAR

The practice of reciprocity held the potential to link these apprehensive people and assuage their misunderstandings. Hospitality was a cultural logic that Dakotas and Scandinavians both embraced. In Dakota culture generosity was valued as highly as bravery, and honorable men were generous.[63] Societies of high-status men served to promote, ensure, and regulate care for the elderly and sick. In her short story, "A Warrior's Daughter," Zitkala-Ša wrote about the protagonist's father, a chieftain known for his valiant deeds in war. "He was also one of the most generous gift givers to the toothless old people."[64]

Sissetons and Wahpetons on the reservation, who had rejected other Dakotas' pleas to take up arms in Minnesota, had many stories to tell about saving the lives of white settlers. On the reservation, hospitality was extended to newcomers. Louis Garcia tells the story of a German immigrant, Fredrick, who stayed with the Solomon Redfox family during his first winter in North Dakota. The entire family was fascinated by his wooden shoes. While Fredrick looked for land and work, Solomon Redfox taught him to speak English.

Norwegians claimed a heritage that also privileged hospitality, but instead of focusing on honor, it valued providing for the unfortunate. Harkening back to mythic progenitors, in her memoir Agnes Reiten Hared interpreted this principle: Norwegians were "always ready to share food and shelter among their own. In fact, this was a tradition laid down by the Norse god Odin, and it was long the custom of the Viking housewife to prepare a basket of food, lay a white cloth over it, and hang it from the eaves of the house for the wayfarer."[65] With this cultural gem that her family brought from Norway, Agnes clearly demarcated the boundary of her obligation—to help among *her own*. But what about others?

On the Great Plains, as in Norway, being a generous host was a sign of a good housewife and by association that her husband was a good provider. With villages and farms scattered over a vast area, traveling to do business, share labor, or visit kin required staying at another's house and being fed. Dakota elder and storyteller Mary Louise Defender Wilson said, "Of course, whenever you went anywhere, people would always share their food with you." Second-generation Norwegian American Mamie Larson de-romanticizes the hospitality of early settlers by explaining the absolute need for mutual aid on isolated homesteads: "People never come to your house but what you had a meal for them. You don't think about that now. Well, you don't have to, you can get a meal wherever you want.... Course you know they'd come a long ways and they were always appreciative because they knew they needed it."

The issue of hospitality between Indians and white settlers was more complex, mediated by inequality and mutual wariness. Dakotas had local knowledge, but sometimes the newcomers brought more resources. Yet the widespread poverty and absence of amenities meant that Indians and migrants had material needs in common. Food was the most frequent medium of exchange, even if the specific kinds of food were different. As wild game became less plentiful and Dakotas living on the reservation found it harder to feed their families, they sometimes turned to white settlers who appeared to have more. They expected to be treated in the same way that they would welcome a visitor to their home. Ellen Mattson Roach wrote, "It was not an uncommon thing in those days to have an Indian walk into your house and ask for something to eat, which he always got, of course."[66] But this raises the question: If they did not ask, would the food be offered?

Dakotas expected food as an acknowledgment of reciprocal obligations. Their sense of entitlement came from certainty that white society owed them a great deal. They had previously held dominion over the land and now faced dire hardship, generated not just circumstantially by white land taking. Their requests were based on their own cultural logic that hospitality would assuredly be forthcoming.[67] From this rather different stance, whites often interpreted this expectation as "begging." Second-generation Swedish American Edd Johnson (b. 1886) said Indians would visit his off-reservation community: "Some of the neighbors was a little scared when they come around. But...they was pretty peaceful. Sometimes they'd beg a little bit to eat, and get a loaf of bread or something like that." The unease lying beneath this assessment of peacefulness hints at their perception of a lurking threat if they did not comply. Certainly some accounts of killings by Ínkpaduta's warriors in Iowa in 1857 and the war in Minnesota suggest that whites' refusal to honor reciprocal obligations provoked the conflict.[68] Other whites simply saw their visitors as hungry people in need and acted accordingly.

Despite their general trepidation of Indians in the context of lives lost in the U.S.–Dakota War, Nordic newcomers were repeatedly surprised when they had "no trouble" with Indian visitors. Extending hospitality normalized relationships and established good will. Ella Dolbak (b. 1880) reported that her Norwegian mother was not afraid of Indians, although she and her siblings were. "We were just ascared of them. We had it in us that we were going to be careful." She recalled the children's misinterpretation when her family was visited by an Indian she did not name:

> Mother said, "I looked at his feet," and oh it was kind of late in the fall, and she thought that he was cold on his feet. She didn't have any bread that day.... She pointed to his feet, "Are you cold?" she says.... She used to spin; she had a spinning wheel.... She spun the yarn, and balled it up, and made mittens and

stockings and that. And she gave the Indian a pair of stockings. [Laughs.] She thought that he was cold on his feet. [Laughs.] And he smiled and he seemed to be so glad. And took those stockings, my mother said, and walked off. But we laughed at it afterwards that we didn't think he was cold on his feet, but she thought so.

The Indian visitor understood Ella's mother's generosity and the reciprocity it implied. It pleased them both. The children failed to comprehend what their mother knew well: people appreciated the gesture of a gift.

When asked about experiences with Indians, Ida M. Hendrickson (b. 1893) said, "They'd come. They were friendly.... They'd come around and sell plums. And then once when they come around Mama took the dish pan out. She was making donuts.... And the squaw was sitting in the back seat, in the back of the buggy. And then she took her skirt. She wanted Mama to put donuts into her skirt. And they were so happy when Mama did that.... Never had any problem with them" (see figure 7). Again, the expectation was of trouble—conflict, hostility, or at least misbehavior— so that "no trouble" deserved notice and comment. Dakotas valued the gift giving. Still, Ida's mother did not invite the visitors inside the house, which presumably she would have done with another Norwegian family. If white settlers failed to respond with generosity, divisions would ossify. As Handy-Marchello puts it, "Sharing food is such an important element in building community that the refusal to offer food to visitors or those in need must be seen as a means of delineating community boundaries."[69] Not everyone treated Indians the same way they would treat those whose ancestry they shared. Some "responded in ways that would have been considered extremely rude among their European American neighbors."[70]

Dakotas' hospitality went beyond reciprocal exchanges, however, and deeply inverted what Scandinavians embraced. They practiced a culture of redistribution, not accumulation. The generous "give-away" was a gesture that both marked the high status of the person making the gift and honored the recipients. In fact, Charles Eastman wrote, "Public giving is a part of every important ceremony."[71] Judge William L. Gipp, a member of Standing Rock Tribal Council and a Tribal Court judge, explained in 1976: "Our Indian way of life is just the opposite of the White! See, the white man is out to accumulate just as much as he can and the more he can accumulate the higher his status becomes. The Indian was the other way. The more he could *give* was a status!"[72] Johnson Williams, a Sisseton-Wahpeton living in South Dakota, articulated a common Dakota critique of white culture:

A white guy it seems like he lives mostly for money. And he'll go to any length to get money. [Chuckles.] And that's what we can't understand.... He's pretty tight with his money, too. Then some they are very generous. And among Indians...it's not like that. What you have is meant to be shared....To them [whites] it's money, money, money. Hurry, hurry get all the money you can. And they'll probably steal their own...mother's or their own father's eyeballs if they got a chance to make any profit out of it. That's what them Indians can't understand.[73]

Accumulation of money or land implied greedy selfishness. In Zitkala-Ša's short story, her protagonist, Blue Star Woman, reflects: "The generosity of her friend had often saved her from starvation. Generosity is said to be a fault of Indian people, but neither the Pilgrim Fathers nor Blue-Star Woman ever held it seriously against them."[74] The importance of providing for others was inculcated in children. According to Charles Eastman, "It was our belief that the love of possessions is a weakness to be overcome.... The child must early learn the beauty of generosity. He is taught to give what he prizes most."[75] In a searing critique of modern society, Eastman lamented the effects of adaptation, "As a child, I understood how to give; I have forgotten that grace since I became civilized."[76] Using "civilization" ironically, both Zitkala-Ša and Eastman reveal the contradictions of a culture that claimed superiority for itself.

Louis Garcia explained the logic. "Indian people were very generous—give away things. But then you have to look at the society that they were in; how could you carry all of this stuff with you? In modern terms, I mean, if I said, 'Well here, you can have this widescreen TV, here, take it!' You know, 'Oh, gee, I got a widescreen TV!' then all of the sudden it dawns on you, 'I gotta cart this twenty miles to the next camp!'...And so you know to give away these things." Dakotas placed a premium on being able to pack up camp and move along quickly. That meant material goods were more cumbersome than beneficial. As Dakotas moved seasonally, there was a limit to what a person could carry in the way of food, tools, cookware, and sacred objects. Equally important, giving blankets, horses, and food to others not only signified status but triggered an obligation to reciprocate, if not in kind, then in loyalty.

Proximity increased opportunities for sustained contact, for visiting, for generosity, for familiarity—and for setting limits on all forms of interaction. Carl Goranson (b. 1911), a second-generation Swede who lived in Oberon, gave his perspective on relations with Dakotas, revealing the sensitive issues stemming from coexistence:

The Indians were getting somewhat tamer. Livable. There were times when there were a few scary moments I guess. In fact the government wouldn't allow them to camp, over three days at a time, to break 'em up, for fear of them...recovering some of what they thought they'd lost. The government would break them up....I don't say that in a derogatory manner. For the simple reason there's 1400 Indians on the Sioux reservation, and among them I have oceans of *good* friends. Good clean people.

By referring to Indians as "tame," Carl framed them as previously wild and therefore markedly different from himself. His emphasis on their cleanliness cast them as previously dirty, relegating them to a primitive stereotype. Boasting, Carl saw himself as the friend of numerous Indians, none individually named, like indistinguishable drops of water merged into the sea. We must view this claim skeptically because we do not know how the Dakotas Goranson identified as friends viewed him—we do not have their accounts. Historically, claims of friendship could be self-serving, like the race liberal who claims "some of my best friends are___" (fill in the blank).

Being thrust into close proximity meant Dakotas had to endure intrusion and occasionally offensive comments and behavior. Dakota elder Agnes Greene acknowledged that becoming familiar with people made for more hopeful relationships. But she pointed to gaps in understanding—people who lived ten miles from her knew little of her way of life. In her late adulthood Grace Lambert became a teacher of the Dakota language and grew interested in establishing détente with her white neighbors, who she conceded were here to stay. "I was always wishing for better relationship with the white man, 'cause after all, we've just got to abide with them. We kind of live together no matter what. And we may as well as face the music and say we better buckle down and become friends, and act like we like each other."[77] Unlike Carl Goranson, she did not pretend to have white friends, but she realized the wisdom of a more engaged coexistence.

Second-generation Norwegian American Einar Severson (b. 1892) recalled a visit by an Indian family to his childhood homestead in Nelson County on the Totten Trail (see figure 8). "Indians that moved from Wisconsin and up here, and they used to come right through our yard. That was the Fort Totten Road, to down here where Fort Totten is now" (see figure 9). His account, full of pathos, reveals the boundary his father enforced:

I remember one time there was an Indian family come in a covered wagon. And they stopped at our place. And they had a baby born. And he died, he died on the homestead there, when they stopped overnight....They asked him if they could bury him on, anywhere out here on this land. "Well no," Dad said, "you can, we'd rather have you go off of my property and bury it right on that road that comes," right on, the [Route] 32 comes into town here. So they buried him right, right by the road. I think we're driving right over the grave....I imagine it went up in bones when they built the road the second time.

It is painful to imagine how the Indian parents must have felt. They lost their baby while in transit, and then their request to bury him where he died was denied. Einar's father's proprietary sense about his land converged with his aversion to Indians and his possible concern about their repeated returns to pay tribute to their departed child. Would he have done the same to a Norwegian family passing through? Without embalming, a dead body would quickly decay. For health reasons and presumably emotional ones as well, immediate interment was required. So the family had to bury their infant near the road. In England, burial by the roadside was an ignominy reserved for criminals and heretics. The fictional community in Nebraska depicted in Willa Cather's *My Ántonia* refused to allow the corpse of Mr. Shimerda, a Bohemian who took his own life, to be buried in the Norwegian cemetery. The newborn Indian baby and the suicidal man could find a resting place only by the side of the road. In retrospect, Einar Severson struggled with the cruelty of his father's act. To this day, the Severson family guards the grave. When road improvements are made, they oversee the process to make sure the grave is not disturbed.[78]

* * * * *

The clashing etiquettes of how to enter a neighbor's home reveal the jarring chasm between these distinct yet fundamentally interconnected histories. On that celebratory day in 2006, contemporary Scandinavian Americans commemorated their past by eliding the conflict-ridden history that gave them a place on the reservation. Unlike their homesteading ancestors who did not and could not ignore the fact that they took Indian land, the centennial disregarded that crucial information. Nor did the Fort Totten Wacipi turn its attention to the history that allowed Scandinavians onto the reservation. Eschewing nostalgia, Dakotas celebrated the present, creating a new Native American culture, while honoring service to the military and national pride.

This book attempts to fill a silence, putting conflict and mutuality back on the historical map at Spirit Lake. Notably, early reservation residents coexisted without violence. My own journey into this contested time engages me in prickly entanglements as I attempt to understand how Dakotas received Scandinavians, went about their lives, and managed to survive. I seek to grasp how Scandinavians reconciled their vision of themselves as fair and ethical people with their role in land taking. Let this account serve as an invitation for others to join me in reconsidering what this past means for our present and future.

2

The Scandinavian Flood: Land Hunger, Dislocation, and Settlement

WHAT COULD POSSIBLY draw a person accustomed to the green mountainous beauty of Norway to the rolling brown plains and golden wheat fields of North Dakota? Land. A deeply rooted desire for land motivated Norwegians to cross the Atlantic and journey halfway across the continent. In North Dakota was not just land they could own, but large, flat plots of rich, dark soil. J. Olson Anders described his father's reaction to the James River valley in 1881. "To his eyes the endless undulating prairie, flat as a floor, was an inspiring sight. No back-breaking root-grubbing drudgery here!"[1] Stanley Eliason (b. 1939), grandson of immigrants Knudt and Bridt Fredrikson, spoke about its appealing qualities: "The delight that they saw with this land, how easy it was to plow compared to what they had to deal with in Norway." He emphasized the stark contrasts between the two countries:

> Norway is a very rocky place. What isn't in rocks is in different kinds of heather and what not and it takes an awful lot of work; and everything was done by hand. Now my father came himself in 1911 when he was eighteen years old, and he went back to Norway in 1919 and was offered... the farm back there because he was the oldest son. But he'd already been working out here with this big machinery, big tractors and all, and back in Norway it was still all by hand. He just didn't want to have any part of it.

Highly fertile flat land had no match for a farmer, particularly with machinery to ease the labor.

The oral accounts of immigrants speak to their practical aspirations; the romantic notions that Americans often held about themselves were conspicuously lacking. Rasmus Yri matter-of-factly explained: "My reason for emigrating to America was to better my economic conditions. There was no political reason for moving. Norway is a democratic country of a longer history than America. In fact, the idea for political freedom, freedom of speech, and freedom of worship are bits of thought taken from the Norse people."[2] Unlike those immigrants who sought religious or political freedom, he viewed his native country as setting a standard for democracy. But his economic prospects there were limited.

The land, however appealing, was not benign. Subject to the whims of "the Nature," as Norwegians called it, land was also cruel. It demanded sacrifice. Historian Barbara Handy-Marchello articulates the paradox: "The bond between family and farm was both beneficial and tyrannical: land was a powerful benefactor that supported large families over generations, and land was an enemy that drained families of money, health, hope, and sometimes even life."[3] And it harbored dangers of conflict with Native inhabitants. These leave-taking stories weave contradictory threads—isolation and loneliness with community and camaraderie, frequent mobility with long-term rootedness, the thrill of possibility with wrenching dislocation. All hold grains of important truths.

A NORWEGIAN AMERICAN DREAM

In 1911 Waldemar Ager pointed to the promise Scandinavian immigrants sought. Writer and editor of *Kvartalskrift*, a Norwegian-language journal published in Wisconsin, he set out to take stock of the Norwegian settlements in North Dakota. Had the land lived up to its promise? Ager's journey brought him to villages on and around the Spirit Lake Reservation: Hamar, Tokio, and Pekin. Impressed by the potential he saw, he remarked, "Everything is, so to speak, in its genesis."[4] A few miles southeast of the reservation, the Fredrikson family farm stood as an exemplar of the American dream, Norwegian-style. Today, looking at the farm in Pekin and hearing stories of its early twentieth-century prosperity, it is easy to imagine the hopeful enthusiasm it inspired. Fertile fields stretch out to the horizon in all directions. A three-story clapboard house stands proudly next to a smart, red, gargantuan barn, with docile cows, strong horses, and dogs alert and ready (see figure 10). As he toured the farm of Knudt Fredrikson, Ager observed that "the big house is new and could have been taken out of a large city's best residential area."[5] Then, to whet the appetites of his readers, he inspected the family's conveniences:

He took me down to the cellar and showed me the big central furnace. The whole house is heated with warm water and there are radiators in all the rooms. He shows me the bathroom, modernly equipped as in the big cities. A big windmill pumps water up to a large tank on the third floor and that is how water pressure is obtained.

We walk over to look at the barn. It is, here as elsewhere in the older settlements, colossal,—a real giant building. And well he needs it; for it holds 20 horses in addition to cattle. Also everything here is modern. Everything is calculated to make work less toilsome, to save effort where possible.[6]

Knudt, younger brother of immigrant Ole Fredrikson, first homesteaded in 1891 (see figures 11 and 12). He worked the land, married Bridt Krosbakken, and had five children (see figure 13). Their house, built in 1905, was paid for with the profits from only two or three years. Surely the labor-saving amenities were especially important to Bridt, as women were responsible for hauling water and heating homes.

However exceptional, the Fredriksons' achievement in the remote heartland stood as a testament to an attainable dream. How must the Fredrikson farm have looked to the landless in Norway? How could Knudt and Bridt have accumulated so much wealth in so few years? Such swift success and upward mobility was unthinkable in Norway. A person could not count on luck, but someone had to get it, people reasoned. Why not them? Even the "wheat miners," as Wallace Stegner called them, who came to extract and exploit natural resources, knew the work would not be easy.[7] The Fredriksons were willing to rise early, work to exhaustion for twelve- to fourteen-hour days, and utilize the labor of their children—the more the better. Here, in America, was possibility. While most farmers would never get rich, they could own their own land and feed their families into their old age. For that they could sacrifice; for that they would strive. Household improvements and landownership could not protect them from all hardship. A year after building their grand home, Bridt died in childbirth. The land she owned jointly with Knudt stayed within the family, as did the forty-acre pasture she had inherited. Knudt remarried a few years later, and his second wife, Nellie, threw herself into raising the children. After Knudt's death in 1919, she managed the farm enterprise. Her stepchildren later inherited the land and kept the farm in the family.

In the United States men and women could start new lives. As Waldemar Ager understood, that possibility must have felt like an exhilarating freedom, despite the hardships and twinges of guilt at deserting their native land. Immigrants could leave behind their shame, whatever the stigma. As historian Ingrid Semmingsen explained,

"People fled to America to escape debt, child support, and paternity suits; unwed mothers emigrated, especially those who were expecting a child."[8] Stanley Eliason reports that three of his Fredrikson great-uncles left sons and daughters in Norway in the 1880s. The question of those children's legitimacy lingered, and whether they received support from their absent fathers remains unclear. Stanley also notes that there appear to have been problems with alcohol in his family back in Norway. His successful grandfather, Knudt Fredrikson, had been active in the temperance movement in North Dakota. Stanley speculates that in so doing he was trying to solve family problems, much like many others.[9]

THE EXODUS

In the nineteenth through the early twentieth centuries, the Norwegian economy did not expand enough to absorb young people. Norwegians depended as much on their country's coastline as on its forested mountains for their livelihoods, which centered on fishing, shipping, and harvesting wood as well as farming. One-quarter of the land was covered by forests, while only 3 percent was considered arable, and even that was rocky and unsuitable for large-scale farming in most areas. Yet 90 percent of the Norwegian population lived in rural areas.[10] Trade was essential to Norway's well-being.

The swelling numbers of her population and the lack of opportunity at home meant that Norway became a major source of the flood that hit North Dakota. It left an aching gap in its wake: the ratio of emigrants to those who stayed behind was second only to that of Ireland, famous for its mass exodus.[11] Innumerable households and families suffered dislocation. In the fifty years between 1865 and 1915, three-quarters of a million people left Norway, a country of barely over two million in 1900. By 1910, as historian Odd Lovoll calculated, "every third Norwegian, counting only the immigrants and their American-born children, resided in the United States."[12] Sweden and Denmark also sent emigrants to North Dakota, although fewer in number. Of the one million Swedes who immigrated to the United States between 1850 and 1930, a significant proportion lived in urban areas (61 percent in 1910).[13] Danes came later to North Dakota than the other Scandinavians, and like Swedes were more likely to scatter across the state rather than live in concentrated, visible communities as they had in Iowa.

A cultural restlessness took hold similar to that which they imagined had motivated their Viking ancestors—*vanderingers*, or "wanderers," who made countless moves. The livelihood of many Norwegians required travel; people who lived along the coast and fjords and worked in fishing or shipping were especially mobile, but so were those in the uplands. Semmingsen observed, "Mountain men were traveling folk, and communications were good across the mountains along century-old paths. It has been said that the mountain folk traveled farthest, that they were the cosmopolitans in this age. The lowland people were more settled, their world more constricted."[14]

Gripped by "Amerika fever," more and more Norwegians left.[15] Tom "Buck" Snortland (b. 1917) elaborated on the contagious enthusiasm that seized his family: "I could never figure out how a Norwegian fisherman could come out to the prairies. But there is a similarity to the ocean and the prairies." As a second-generation Norwegian American, he queried a relative back in Norway about the mass migration. His kinsman reported,

"You could never believe it," he said. "It was like a fever." Of course we were propagandized by the railroads that wanted pioneers to go west. But he said… "The people, they *had* to leave. They *had* to come to the promised land. A hundred and sixty acres of black soil," which would be something in Norway. My dad was eight when he came, I don't know how old his dad was, but his dad too, who was in his sixties, the later sixties, actually had a stroke and dragged one leg, he said, "No way am I staying here," he said. "If everyone else is going, I'm going too." (Snortland's emphasis)

The Snortland family story speaks to the social momentum and kinship ties that compelled people to leave, despite their deep attachment to place.

In America, as in Norway, some of those internal migrants kept moving, looking for a better opportunity in another place.[16] Those who tell their stories here are those who eventually stayed put. Orris G. Nordhaugen (b. 1901), a third-generation Norwegian from Leeds, North Dakota, characterized his grandfather as a "roamer" who thrived on mobility. His wanderlust appeared to be a character trait. For others it was foolhardiness or courage. As Semmingsen acknowledged, "Even migration can become a habit, and these stepwise emigrants may have moved several times before they settled."[17] In analyzing the framing of Native peoples by New Englanders, historian Jean O'Brien points to the ironies of "English notions about fixity and place" that "figured centrally in dispossessing Indian peoples."[18] Colonists had uprooted themselves to move to another continent. Yet local historians referred to New Englanders as settled and Indians as nomadic. Euro-Americans continued their colonial expansion westward and Native people returned home after seasonal rounds. These numerous accounts of Norwegian *vanderingers* reveal them to be willfully wandering, much like New Englanders who kept migrating until they found economic opportunity.

The Scarcity of Land and Pinch of Poverty

In Norway, only a fraction of the rural population owned land. Many more people toiled for landlords on farm units called *gaards*, small-scale estates that consisted of noncontiguous lands supporting many people with multiple occupations. Most of the laborers on the farm were called cotters, or *husmenn*, who paid rent by working or in cash.[19] Looking back at her parents' place of origin, Barbara Levorsen describes conditions for *husmenn*, which her mother characterized as "virtual slavery."[20] "They could live in a little house and have a small plot of land on which to grow potatoes and such, but to pay for these privileges they were at the landowner's beck and call the year around. The wife worked at the big 'gaard' also, and the children started at the age of nine, by herding sheep or cattle."[21] In addition to the farm laborers, "tailors, shoemakers, baking women, seamstresses and women who took care of meat after butchering, came to the 'gaard' and some remained for weeks."[22] With little machinery available, cultivation was labor intensive (see figure 14).

The land did not guarantee sufficient food for adequate, year-round nutrition. Einar Severson reported that in the 1880s his parents "were starved right out of Norway." He recalled that in an effort to stave off hunger pangs, "they mixed ground birch bark with their corn meal and stuff to make it bulkier so that it would last longer." In good years, farmers only fed such rough fodder to their animals, but in bad ones they had to resort to eating indigestible things themselves. While not all emigrants were equally impoverished, the fear of destitution propelled many to depart.

In Norway, as in some parts of Denmark and Sweden, the system of inheritance ensured that farms were not broken up but instead passed from father to the eldest son, so younger sons and all daughters had to find alternative means of support.[23] Land and kinship were deeply intertwined in Norwegian law and culture. Freehold land tenure was ownership not burdened by obligations to a feudal lord or noble landlord. "Traditionally, farms were thought not to belong to individuals only, but to all related kindred if the farm had been in the possession of a family for a certain period of time."[24] The aim of the centuries-old practice "is to secure that agricultural property over a certain size remains within families who own land. The system prevents land from going to the free market. Land is subject to certain rights held within a family."[25] Eldest sons had an entitlement to the land, an *asetesrett*, an allodial right, that acted not precisely the same as primogeniture but gave them "the right to inherit the farm intact in payment to the other heirs."[26] By the nineteenth century, most farms were too small to divide. The premium placed on keeping the farm undivided led many younger children of landowners to migrate or become cotters if they remained.[27]

Most landless youth entered farm labor and domestic service, at home and abroad. There was virtually no arable land even to purchase, especially in fertile areas. Linking the land to the number of male children, Shirley Kanten explained the Halvorson Kantens' motivation for emigrating in the 1870s: "They had really no choice but to leave Norway, because they couldn't get any more land if they had bigger families. There was no land available. You think of them starting out with six little boys." With homestead land in the United States and such an ample supply of labor, the Kantens could look forward to a viable economic future.

In his autobiography, Tosten Mikkelsen Lillehaugen reflected on his early life in Norway. As a young man he worked out, saved money, and in 1878 concentrated on securing his own farm and all the necessary components to make it successful. "If I was to be a full-fledged farmer, I had to have a wife. So now I had to try a little along that line, too. But seeing I was going to be busy, it was not wise to make the distance too great. I tried my luck in the immediate vicinity and the final answer was 'Yes, she supposed so,' seeing I had a place where she could live and call home."[28] We can imagine Tosten's sigh of relief, as he then referred to their marriage as something that "was taken care of." His bride, Sigrid Gjeldaker, while perhaps not bowled over by Tosten's decidedly unromantic approach to courtship, was at least assured of the security of a house and land.

Tosten reflected on the economic challenges of farming in Norway during the 1870s. "Many farmers went bankrupt during this time."[29] According to his own calculations, he was suffering a net loss of about $100 every year. "I went to my father-in-law and told him our situation. But he belittled my worries and said it was not any worse for us than for other people."[30] Even so, his father-in-law offered to sign for a loan at the bank. Still, Tosten pondered the possibility of going to the United States. His father-in-law "said he thought with my family backing it was not necessary to think of things like that. I replied that it looked as though every one had all he could do to take care of himself. Besides, I did not like to sponge on my relatives for a living, but I wanted to support my own family. And I was sure, barring ill health, I would be able to do that. He told me he would have to think it over."[31] His father-in-law left the decision up to him. Tosten and Sigrid moved first to Wisconsin, then to Minnesota, and finally to Walsh County, Dakota Territory, in 1887.

Not all farm laborers and farmers had the kind of family resources available to Tosten Lillehaugen. After 1880, the character of Norwegian emigrants shifted. Ingrid Semmingsen writes that "in the 1860s it was primarily a family emigration."[32] Later, young and unmarried individuals predominated. They were more likely to be landless, poor, young, and single. "In the wave of the 1860s about a fourth of the men were between fifteen and twenty-five; in the 1900s nearly two-thirds of them were."[33]

By the end of the century emigrants were more likely to be from the rural lower classes and the urban laboring classes. Gladys Jorgenson Peilor (b. 1916) told of her father, who left Norway in 1893 when he was eighteen years old because "there was nothing to do." His family was poor, and there were no jobs. Similarly, her mother left Norway and sought work as a domestic in the United States. Domestic service was an expansive job category that involved a great deal of physical labor and relied mostly on foreign-born women. In 1900, among employed Scandinavian-born women, 62 percent worked as servants or laundresses.[34] Women workers were in demand in households and on farmsteads, and the flow of immigrants from Europe and Scandinavia generated a supply.

Poor and hungry people who stayed in Norway had to rely on religious charity. In contrast to the United States, in Norway church and state were not constitutionally separate. The Norwegian Lutheran church exercised enormous power by teaching an all-encompassing worldview and keeping records of births, baptisms, marriages, and deaths. Significantly, the clergy oversaw internal migration. In order to leave a parish, a person had to get an "attestation" from their local pastor. To travel internationally, a person had to see the sheriff or police to obtain a passport.[35] The church collected alms for the poor from all those who were able, and the funds were put into "the box." The local minister, who distributed those funds, was a person of great authority.

My great-grandmother, Berthe Haugen, received funds from "the box." She and her husband, by whom she had five children, eked out a living on the Lynghaugen farm, where they were cotters. Her husband died of tuberculosis in 1890, leaving her with few resources and reduced labor power. Two years later, she gave birth to a daughter. The father of this child was a farm laborer much younger than Berthe who went on to marry and have a legal family of his own. The courtship practice of bundling—spending the evening in bed together—did not appear to hold the same leverage for widows that it did for women who had never married; this man was not expected to marry the widow who bore his child. Norwegians customarily tolerated premarital sexual relations, in part as a way of testing the woman's fertility.[36] Prenuptial births were often linked to a forthcoming marriage, and while the church frowned upon the practice, it was nonetheless common.

Berthe continued to live in abject poverty and sent her older daughters out to work. She had younger children to support and now a sullied reputation to bear. When Berthe broke her leg she had to send her nine-year-old out to work as well. Emigration to America seemed like a way to live with more dignity and, hopefully, garner more resources. In 1900, Berthe's eldest daughter, Inger Randine Haugen, then twenty-three, ventured alone to explore the possibilities in North Dakota. Two years later Berthe followed with two children and a grandchild in tow.

Despite the hardship and limited opportunities, most people stayed in Norway. The simple lack of a job does not explain who left and who stayed behind. What prompted some people to relocate and others, who occupied a comparable position, to remain? Research across countries shows that historically, it was not total desperation that prompted most people to emigrate. In fact, the most destitute could seldom afford the cost of passage. Emigrants possessed some education, enough resources to move, and gumption or an adventurous spirit.

Transnational Labor Markets and Kin Connections

Incentives to direct their dreams toward the United States, rather than to Sweden or England, included higher wages, an abundance of jobs, and most importantly, vast amounts of land available at low prices. Wages for agricultural laborers were about three times higher in the United States than those in Northern Europe at the time: the premium for skilled labor was even greater.[37] In the United States, as in Europe, the industrial revolution created a huge demand for unskilled labor that immigrants helped meet. Scandinavians concentrated in industries such as shipping in New York, lumber camps and farming in the Midwest, and domestic service everywhere.

Johanna Tvedt was seventeen when opportunity arrived in the mail. Her eldest sister had migrated to Nebraska, and she and her new husband sent a ticket for another sister to come. In Norway, her mother, a widow with nine children, did not have an easy time of it. However, the invited sister did not want to leave, so Johanna stepped into her shoes. In 1905, she went straight to Kerney, Nebraska.

America had appealed to Johanna because she thought that in a few short years she would become wealthy. Life in Norway had been constant work, but she found that it had been nothing compared to what was expected of her in America. Obligated to her sister and brother-in-law for the price of the passage, they put her to work. The hired man was released so that Johanna would not suffer from idleness and beside[s] her house work she cultivated corn and did other farm work generally required of a hired man. In only a matter of days Johanna found that America was not going to be such a paradise. In fact the lack of money made it impossible for her to even pay the postage for letters home, let alone return herself.[38]

Once she worked off her passage, she found a job as maid, and eventually made her way to North Dakota. Although she left her kin in Norway and then her sister and brother-in-law in Nebraska, her move drew her closer to other relatives and offered her greater economic opportunity.

Helping hands reached across the ocean, connecting rural Norway to the heartland of the United States. The labor shortage in North America meant that farmers scrambled to hire people whom they knew to be reliable workers. Virtual open doors to entry facilitated the transnational movement of Scandinavian workers, as did steam-powered ocean liners. As Semmingsen put it, "the individual Norwegian-American farmer received his younger siblings or nephews and nieces gladly, at any rate in good times. They could perform valuable services on the farm as long as they had the patience to stay."[39] As the case of Johanna Tvedt shows, this arrangement often took the form of an agreement whereby a ticket for passage to the United States was exchanged for a year's work.[40] With little but labor power to offer, health was a pivotal resource; without it, immigrants knew they were doomed.

Often the employer who loaned the passage money was a relative. In other cases, a worker might help recruit his or her brother, sister, or cousin to come from Norway—as long as they were young persons capable of hard work. Hans C. Hanson of Warwick, North Dakota, was someone Ingemund Peterson (b. 1894) called a "big man": he owned land and had a perpetual labor shortage. He needed more men, even outside of harvest season, and he needed domestic help. International transportation and active kin networks meant that he could draw from the pool of surplus labor in the Norwegian countryside rather than going ten miles north to Devils Lake.

Evin Peterson, Ingemund's older brother, arrived in 1914 and began working for Hanson. He recruited his sixteen-year-old sister, Anna, back in Lillehammer and lent her money for passage. As Anna prepared to leave in the spring of 1915, a question lingered as to whether her older brother, Ingemund, could join her, for a job awaited him as well. When I interviewed him at age 105, he still lamented the missed opportunity of traveling with his sister. He worked as a carpenter on a farm a fair distance from his home. Then "I got a call from Ma that my papers was [ready]. I just went home and started to get ready for the next boat.... [Anna] just got to Warwick a little bit before I started out in Norway.... I had my birthday on the boat. I think that was Sunday the sixth of June. I wrote to her, because she didn't know if I wanted to go or not.... And then I got to Warwick at the same time as my letter." Ingemund's job was to "haul school kids" in an era before buses when country schools could be several miles away. He worked at the Hansons' through the summer, and then went to Montana with his brother, Evin, to work in the lumber camps for the winter. The following spring, in 1916, his father came and began working for a nearby farmer. His mother and six other children came later that year. Too late to homestead and too poor to buy land, Ingemund's parents lived as tenant farmers and day laborers.

The sense of prerogative born of this type of recruitment is reflected in the prideful response of Nels Knudson (b. 1888) to an interviewer's queries about his motivation for immigrating. As a sixteen-year-old in Norway in 1904, Nels considered his limited options. He recounted his deliberations with his mother. When the interviewer asked, "Why did you come?" Nels, in his typically argumentative style, shot back, "Why I came?!! Good night! Why did *you* come?" The interviewer replied, "I was born here." Nels snorted: "They didn't ask you. I was asked if I could come." From Nels's perspective, he was invited to the United States. He explained the crucial conversation with his mother: "Now, I'll tell you. I wanted to be a sailor. But she says 'No!' my mama did. 'I'm not going to sit up every night and wonder where my boy is. But you can go to North Dakota. You got two uncles over there.'" His mother, who apparently had veto power, was willing to send him abroad to someone she knew. So Nels left Norway for North Dakota.

The stories connect siblings, aunts, and uncles in the job-seeking process. Emma Beckstrand Casper's story begins in Sweden. Her family sent her eldest brother to Litchfield, Minnesota. He returned home and took Emma and her sister back to Minnesota. In 1904, Emma worked a year for her uncle, who had paid the $80 for her ticket. Two more brothers came later. Emma continued to live and work there until 1908, when she moved to Crary, North Dakota, where her sister was working and had secured her a job. "She come first, and then I come. And they had a job for me already, so I come to Nicholson's, Harry Nicholson's in Crary. And I worked there one year." She then met and married Otto Casper, a man she knew from Litchfield, who homesteaded north of Warwick on the reservation. Later, her brother lent the young couple some money. "He helped us, so we could get started farming there, see."[41] She lived there the rest of her life.

THE INFLUX INTO DAKOTA TERRITORY

Describing the influx of immigrants as an overwhelming act of nature, Cherrie Lane Wood (b. 1886), born to a Yankee family in Dakota Territory, commented, "There's an awful lot of Scandinavians in through here. But when we first was here, when I was little, there wasn't any. They came in just like a flood."

While the constant inflow of immigrants turned the Yankees into a minority, it overwhelmed the state's Native American residents. From 1890 to 1910, when North Dakota's population tripled, the Indian population continued to decline, reaching its nadir in 1910. The reasons for the decline are complicated, but chief among them were the destruction of the Indians' economy and way of life and the poverty and diseased that followed.[42] By 1910, Native American Indians constituted just 1 percent of the state's population; most lived on reservations. Indian numbers decreased as the white population exploded.[43] As a result, the ratio of Indians to whites in the state dropped dramatically, from 428 Indians per 10,000 whites in 1890 to 112 Indians per 10,000 whites in 1910.

By 1910, approximately 70 percent of the state's population consisted of first- and second-generation immigrants, people whose language and culture originated outside the United States. Native-born whites with at least one foreign-born parent comprised 43.5 percent of the population, and another 27.1 percent were foreign-born whites, while "native-born whites of native parentage" comprised 28.2 percent. Negroes, as African Americans were then called, comprised only one-tenth of 1 percent.

Of those born outside the United States, approximately 40 percent were Scandinavian: 29.4 percent came from Norway, another 7.8 percent from Sweden, and 3.4 percent from Denmark. Of the non-Scandinavians, Russians were the largest group (20.4 percent); most were "Germans from Russia," ethnic German Protestants who had lived in the region near the Black Sea for generations.[44] Germans from Germany constituted another 10.6 percent of foreign-born whites. When Cherry Lane Wood decried the Scandinavian deluge, it was more than her prejudice speaking.

In a land of immigrants and displaced people, the question "Where are you from?" probed for details about journeys as well as origins. Behind the query lay a person's relationship to the land. Place does not simply imply a set of boundaries defining farms, towns, and counties; it connotes a social geography of moves, relationships, and kin connections. "If you don't know where you are, says Wendell Berry, you don't know *who* you are."[45] The link between land and history situates a people in time as well as space.

Norwegians recognized themselves as shaped by place, which located them in relation to their heritage. When Ingemund Peterson relayed stories of his past, he embedded them in the history of those around him—where they lived, where they came from, and to whom they were related. In telling me about his first job in North Dakota, stories kept surfacing about the big farmer, Hans C. Hanson, who employed him: "H. C. Hanson was born in Norway and come over here when he was a year and a half or two years old. Ya, he come from... Buxton down by Hillsboro.... The Mrs. was from Hillsboro." Ingemund mapped people geographically, ethnically, and genealogically. He situated people in space as well as in relationship. He employed the Norwegian tradition of introducing yourself by saying where you are from and identifying others in the same way.

Renaming the Scandinavians

Norwegian naming practices symbolize the linkage between the people and the land. Norwegians had two last names—one derived from the father and one from the farm. The patronymic naming system in this Lutheran country assigned children a Christian name, often that of a close relative in the older generation. A last name specified paternity and sex. Hence a child was designated the son or daughter of the biological father. For example, my maternal great-grandmother's name was Berthe Halvorsdatter Lynghaugen. Berthe was the *datter* of Halvor Evensen, who was the son of Even. In effect, Berthe's genealogy, as recorded in the church records, was encoded in her name. Upon marriage, her name did not change; she continued to be described as her father's daughter, although she would also be addressed as her husband's wife. Her children would take her husband's name, each with a gendered twist.

Berthe's identity was also linked to the name of the farm where she was born and lived—Lynghaugen. Literally, her name means heather (*lyng*) on the hill (*haugen*). This part of her name was, in effect, an address. Many farm names were descriptive as well. My maternal grandfather's family was from the Kanten farm, from the Norwegian word meaning "the edge." The farm name placed Berthe on the land in a particular location. If she moved, her farm name would change. For example, Lester Skjerven (b. 1895) explained, "My dad's name was originally Espegaard. But then he bought the Skjerven place in Norway, and then he had to take the name of the *gaard*, see. And they stayed by it." The Lynghaugen farm owed Berthe a place to live and a small garden plot. Even though she did not own the land, she belonged with it. The norms that governed farming in Norway were profoundly different from those in the United States. The land had an obligation to the workers. In law and in custom, the cotters who worked the land were entitled to a plot for a garden and a minimum share of the harvest. When land was sold, the new owner had to assume the obligation to the cotters. As a result, the workers were assured of a place to live, although it yielded a meager, inadequate subsistence. They had some claim on the land and its produce, regardless of who formally owned it. Consequently, the farm name was more powerful than an address, because it linked the individual to a system of social rights.

That connection to land and the security it pledged were severed in the move to North America. That moment of transition often coincided with a change in name. Berthe shortened her name to "Haugen," contracting the long farm description and dropping her connection to her father. Scandinavian names proved challenging to monolingual English speakers, discouraging the less tenacious from even attempting. Their pronunciation flummoxed outsiders, and like Dakotas' names, the meanings, stories, innuendo, and history that were implicit in names were incomprehensible. Immigrant narratives recounting passage through Ellis Island offer an abundance of instances in which names were misheard, mispronounced, misspelled, disregarded, and disparaged. At this gateway for millions, unschooled and arrogant officials used the power of their position to stamp those who were arriving with a new, often unwelcome, name.

Land taking created a similar filter. Third-generation Norwegian American farmer Helmer Dahlen (b. 1899) told the story of his father's brother, Ingebret Ellingsen Dahlen. "When they filed on land, either the paper was too short, or something. The Dahlen didn't get on his name. Then they didn't pay no attention. Later I found that his name wasn't on there, and they said, 'Oh you can easily change that by going and paying twenty bucks.' And he says, 'Heck no.' He's going to keep Ellingsen. [Laughs.] So one of my uncles' name is Ellingsen." In effect, that uncle used the patronymic, Ellingsen, while others used the farm name, Dahlen. The lack of standardized spelling meant that members of the same family could bear names that sounded the same but looked different, such as Skurdall, Skurdell, and Skurdahl.[46]

My mother's father's family name went through some of the same permutations as the Dahlens', although their multiplicity seems more purposeful. Once the sons and daughters of Iver Halvorson Kanten left Branbu, Norway, and arrived in Minnesota, some chose the farm name, Kanten, and others used the patronymic name, Iverson. The family story maintains that because the family was so big and their patronymic was so common, they used their farm name to distinguish themselves. Interestingly, my great-grandfather, Andrew Iverson Halvorson Kanten, can be found in the U.S. census using different names in different decades. In 1875 he is Andrew Halvorson; by 1900, when he owned land just south of the reservation in Eddy County, he is Andrew Kanten. I suspect he was Andrew Iverson for a while in between. Each name coincides with a move, with buying and selling land. Perhaps when homesteading was a one-time right, having different names served a useful purpose. New names must have been convenient for starting a new life, avoiding the law, marrying again, or any number of imaginable reasons.

Some people yearned for that American snap, a name that would not mark them as foreign even when their accents did. Erick Erickson Subsjoen shortened his last name to Stubson to make it easier to pronounce.[47] My great-aunt Kjester Haugen became Esther. Still others wanted to distinguish themselves from those around them. Lars R. Larson (b. 1895) recounted his father's journey from Norway in the 1880s. Originally, his father was called Lewis Larson, but upon his arrival in North Dakota he found many other men named Lewis, so he chose to become Lars Larson. Curiously, that would have marked him more clearly as Nordic, but perhaps that entered into his deliberations.

Kinship, Ethnic Concentration, and Leapfrog Migration

Newcomers followed established migration flows, moving west, seeking the sound of their native tongue. J. Olson Anders wrote, "Like all immigrants, father had at first a strong emotional preference for his own nationality."[48] His father took land in southeastern North Dakota on the edge of a settlement with some Norwegians, although the presence of other ethnic groups nearby rankled him.

In recounting their journeys to North Dakota, virtually all Scandinavians speak of either a kin connection or a community contact that brought them to a particular place. They often moved several times, in what Semmingsen describes as leap-frog stages, before they finally settled permanently. Immigrants already knew someone here from "back home"—in Europe or in another state—when they came to North Dakota. Carl E. Goranson, a Swede, explained his theory of migration: "It just depends on who settled first and then who wrote back and said 'come.'" Bjorne Knudson (b. 1911) explained the logic of his newly married parents' process of emigrating from Norway. "They figured they had to go somewheres where someone would know 'em, or they'd probably starve to death. [Chuckle.]" They landed in Chippewa Falls, Wisconsin, where Mrs. Knudson had a brother, and from there gradually made their way to North Dakota. This process created the ethnic concentrations that Father William Sherman has called a "prairie mosaic." Much as today we mark distance by travel time, not just miles, so geography was measured by the sequence of ethnic communities. This approach to taking land was not exclusively Scandinavian, but they seemed to embrace it with great fervor.

The search for enough land to support a large extended family kept driving people west. In a moving biography, Carrie Young casts her mother, Carrine Gafkjen, as a rugged individual who set out to homestead on her own. In fact, a close reading reveals that a cousin lived nearby and a friend was just catty-corner across the road. Carrine's brother, Ole, came later. "Ole was not a trailblazer. He had followed my mother out to North Dakota only after she was well settled on her homestead with husband and children, and he had been lucky enough to acquire the 160-acre farm across from hers, where there was already a small house and barn."[49] Palmer Overby described the clustering of kin and friends. "They settled in a group, see. Like the Lundabys.... That's the way they come in, see." Oscar T. Forde told the story of his father's first winter in North Dakota, when he dug a hole in the bank of the Sheyenne River and trapped weasels, muskrats, and beavers. He sold the hides in the spring, loading them in his wheelbarrow and walking approximately 125 miles to Fargo. He then went back to Hayfield, Minnesota, where his girlfriend lived. When he returned, "He brought about five or six families with him. They all wanted to come up there. And he told 'em about this place where they could homestead. So they came with him.... They brought a yoke of oxen and a wagon, so they could haul quite a lot of stuff with 'em." In 1902, Lester J. Rendahl's (b. 1912) mother and her brother homesteaded on adjacent plots. They built a shack on the line bordering the two quarters. Another brother, Madius, came later. After his dad's brother married his mother's sister, there came to be a "bunch of double cousins." Migration from other parts of the Midwest replicated the process of emigrating from Scandinavia. Shirley Kanten explained the move from Fillmore County, Minnesota, where her family initially landed, to Chippewa County: "They couldn't get land anymore." By that time, homestead land was no longer available; no land was for sale either. So, she reports, "They started to move up this way...along the Minnesota River, mostly, and kept going until they found land." Not coincidentally, much of the Dakota reservation and the sites of battles were sparsely settled in those postwar years. As the next generation came of age, many moved north and west to North Dakota. Shirley explained, "Great-grandpa owned a lot of land, but...he had a large number of boys too." The Norwegian principle of providing land for sons still applied in the United States. Shirley's great-grandfather was concerned about all of his sons, not just his eldest.

Norwegian settlements followed the waterways of the Midwest. Carlton Qualey documented this pattern in his extensive demographic study of Minnesota and North Dakota.[50] Norwegians settled along the Minnesota River and the Red River and, in North Dakota, along the Sheyenne River and the James River. The Sheyenne, which is not a wide river, flows east, entering into the north-flowing Red River near the city of Fargo. From its origin in Sheridan County, the Sheyenne meanders south through Benson, Eddy, and Nelson counties, all solidly Norwegian.

Logically we could argue that river valleys provided an ideal combination of resources: water for drinking and washing, wood for fuel and building, fish for food. But not all ethnic groups attempted to settle along rivers; this pattern is quite distinct to Norwegians. In his oral history, Palmer Overby explained: "They settled the river first." Palmer's father was advised by the Norwegian locals to take his land along the river, rather than south of it, because even though it was flat, it was "hard to get water. And when you do get a well, it wasn't fit to drink." Palmer reported, "We drank river water for years.... You never got sick out of river water. You could swim any time of the year.... You never got any itch or anything because it's fed by springs." Eventually, in the 1880s, outbreaks of cholera from the James River prompted people to use it sparingly and abandon it as a source of drinking water.

When asked to explain the logic of settling along river valleys, Shirley Kanten talked about her own family's path from Minnesota: "They were very much dairy people, because they lived along the rivers." When I asked, "Why did that mean, dairy?" Shirley replied, "Because there was so much they couldn't farm." Being a naïve interviewer, I said, "I see," which I really did not. So I sought further clarification, "Because the land was too wet, is that it?" Shirley put me straight: "Too hilly." She explained. "See, I grew up on a farm that was right along the Chippewa River, and there's...several acres that are not tillable, but they make good pasture land." Dairy cows require pasture and water. Shirley Kanten's theory explains the need to be near a river, although it is not clear which comes first, the river or the cows. Later in life Helmer Dahlen's uncle criticized his grandfather for settling in Nelson County on hilly land near water and with trees rather than flat land in the valley that would be ideal for wheat cultivation. Helmer reasoned, in defense of his grandfather, "You had quite a few cattle. Wood and grass, water, see. That's what they looked for." Perhaps their interest in dairying explains why women are more likely to own land near lakes and rivers. Women were primarily responsible for milking and caring for cattle in North Dakota, as they had been in Norway, and for hauling water and chopping wood, so they would want to be clustered near water and trees.

Within Scandinavian communities ownership meant proprietary control of land that was subject to governmental laws and taxation. Importantly, land was alienable; it could be kept or sold in perpetuity. As the foundation of individual and family wealth, land should be accumulated, cultivated, relished, honored, and then passed along to the next generation. Cultivating the land meant owning it. Many Scandinavians held fast to the notion that land rightfully passed through male heirs who worked the land. An argument that unfolded in Willa Cather's *O Pioneers!* between Alexandra Bergson, daughter of Swedish settlers, and her brothers, Lou and Oscar, forcefully lays out the issues of the power of cultivation and the status accorded women in farm management and inheritance. Lou and Oscar asserted that because they had toiled in the fields, they owned the land, even if the title was in Alexandra's name. "We worked in the fields to pay for the first land you bought, and whatever's come out of it has got to be kept in the family."[51] Lou and Oscar were outraged that Alexandra was contemplating giving land to her suitor and longtime friend. They further insisted that even though Alexandra had successfully run the family farming enterprise since their father died, vastly expanding their land holdings and experimenting with new crops, they owned the land and held the power. "'The property of a family belongs to the men of the family, because they are held responsible, and because they do the work.'"[52] The dispute over gendered labor and precisely what rights accompanied which kind of investment was subject to ongoing negotiation. Scandinavians, like the fictional Bergsons and the Dakota women reclaiming their fertile plots along the Minnesota River, felt that cultivating the land entitled them to it. They aimed to build a successful farming enterprise and establish a foundation for a family legacy.

DISLOCATION, INSANITY, AND GENDER

Many hypothesize that dislocation leads to insanity. Immigrants' lives were full of hardships, some of them crushing to the human spirit. Second-generation

Norwegian Lillian Jensen (b. 1902) said, "I remember my father saying those folks that homesteaded with him...were either in an insane asylum or dead." The long winters, the isolation, the physically exhausting toil, the longing for home—all contributed to some settlers' disorientation.

In the popular imagination, it is the women, not the men, who proved unable to handle pioneer hardships; they were supposedly too fragile to manage the isolation of homesteading. One enduring source of the image of the beleaguered woman unable to cope is *Giants in the Earth*, Ole Rølvaag's novel about Norwegian immigrants to Dakota Territory.[53] So powerful is this portrait that even those unfamiliar with the book have absorbed its message.

The oral narratives of this project raise and deliberate about the theme of the excessive toll homesteading took uniquely on women. Weighing the evidence, Lillian's husband Clarence L. Jensen (b. 1899) recalled, "I visited the Jamestown Asylum one time, years ago. And they said there were a lot of women in the hospital there, at the time, who had been...all alone, on these lonely prairies in the early days, and had gone insane because of it. Whether that's true or not, I don't know."

Historian Barbara Handy-Marchello argues that the trauma of homesteading on the prairie did not affect Norwegians or women with special force; no one immigrant group or gender was hit harder than others. She notes that historians have not been immune from gendered misconceptions: "The fictional homesteading woman can barely be distinguished from some historical treatments—a sad victim of isolation, wind, dust, fear, and overwork."[54] While rates of hospitalization for mental illness were not significantly different in North Dakota than in the East, immigrants were institutionalized at higher rates than the U.S.–born residents of the state. Handy-Marchello elaborates: "Immigration encompasses a complex of stressors related to mental disorders, including the distress of cultural isolation and separation from family, and, for some North Dakota settlers, disappointment in the promise of 'free land.' Another possibility is that some individuals inclined toward mental instability may have been more likely to emigrate in the first place."[55]

The pervasive gender assumptions about mental frailty have been disproven empirically. In fact, women were less likely to be institutionalized than men. In his 1932 meta-analysis of the mental illness of Norwegians in Minnesota, Örnulv Ödegaard found that men had a much higher rate of insanity than women (controlling for age and proportion of the population). The only exception was during the 1890s, when women were disproportionately institutionalized.[56] Those afflicted were in their childbearing years, isolated, separated from other women, and at risk of giving birth without the help of a female community.

When queried, many women adamantly rejected the point of view that rendered them and their mothers victims. Asked if she thought pioneering was tough on women, Ida M. Hendrickson said, "Oh no. I don't think so." Her neighbor, Ralph E. Seastrand (b. 1901), skeptically interjected, "Well, I don't know." Ida Hendrickson immediately retorted: "Well, I know when mother used to sit and talk…and they said, 'Are you going to Dakota to freeze to death?' And she said, 'I've never frozen and I've never starved.' And she'd been here all these years." That indignant response, asserting that women were tougher than the culture gave them credit for, came through repeatedly in the oral narratives. Norwegian American Helmer Dahlen remarked on his grandmother's stoicism, "She never complained." His wife, Ruth Dahlen (b. 1904), a former school teacher, referred directly to *Giants in the Earth*. "Judging from the books I've read, there were women who went crazy." After asking whether the interviewer had read the book, Helmer countered that "it was harder on the men. He froze to death." Ruth acceded that Per Hansa, the hero of the book, had sacrificed his life, but then she brought up childbirth without anesthetic as an indicator of hardship. Helmer brooked no argument with that, although in Rølvaag's novel childbirth was not Beret's complaint. In reflecting on his own history, Helmer pointed out that his family was not isolated. "They were all working together." Then Ruth recounted an accident that her father suffered his first summer on the farm. "He thought this was a God forsaken country. I think my mother adjusted more quickly than he did." Yet contrary experiences did not necessarily upend the mythology.

Immigrants longed for the relatives they left behind and for their native land. The difficulty of traveling along dirt roads, which were barely more than prairie trails and were frequently ravaged by the weather, contributed to immigrants' sense of isolation. To Norwegian immigrant Martha Lima the North Dakota landscape meant unfamiliar and uncomfortable openness: "We have a very wide—to my taste a much too wide—view from our house. Greatly do I miss water, river, mountain, and woods."[57] As she lamented, North Dakota appeared barren and expansive—more like the open ocean. Some women emphatically expressed their dislike of the landscape, which they linked to their isolation on remote homesteads. Swedish immigrant Emma Beckstrand Casper put it vividly: "On the farm out there, I sure didn't like it. I was so lonesome, so that was terrible. You know in those days there was nothing, no trees, or no roads…just a lot of snow in the wintertime." In reflecting on whether his parents liked the country, Lester J. Rendahl fastened on the fact that they made a decision and stuck to it. Liking it was irrelevant. Changing their minds would have meant admitting defeat. "They just decided this is what they were going to do. It was tough. I know it was tough for them. I don't think I ever heard them say they were going to give up."

Unfortunately, Rølvaag's long shadow conceals women who homesteaded land in their own names and thrived because of it. How did this novel so effectively commandeer the framing of these issues? According to literary scholar Øyvind T. Gulliksen, "Despite the fact that Rølvaag strove for authenticity in *Giants in the Earth*, he also cleverly developed the character of Per Hansa into an American frontier '*ur*–farmer', in exactly the idealistic version Americans dreamt of during the 1920s."[58] In fact, he knew from gathering historical evidence that many immigrant stories contradicted this mythic portrait. Gulliksen describes a remarkable exchange in which Rolvaag's colleague, Clarence Clausen, recommended that he alter the novel's storyline so as not to be deceptive. Based on archival letters, Gulliksen writes, "Clausen had seen strong husky women settle on the prairies, stark contrasts to the often-paralyzed women in Rølvaag's manuscript. In Clausen's experience, it was more often the male immigrant, his father for instance, who had sat in the prairie cowshed singing Norwegian songs, full of tears and feeling homesick for Norway."[59] Yet stories of women suffering "from depression and despair" were told and retold until they became a kind of folklore. Handy-Marchello observes that "they also served to deny women credit for their constructive role in the homesteading process and to assign blame for some families' failures."[60]

As I researched my family's journeys, I uncovered many ways that migration can disguise family ruptures. My grandmother's sister, Aagodt Haugen Beck, constructed a family myth by insisting that her husband had died in Norway. Aagodt had married Johan Olsen Bekken, a *kemigraph*, or lithographer, with dark hair and grey eyes. They sent their three-year-old son, Christian, to North Dakota with his grandmother, Berthe Haugen, two aunts, and an uncle in 1902. However, I discovered that Aagodt and John Beck, as he came to be called, and their one-month-old infant, Olaf, crossed the Atlantic *together* in 1903, made their way to the heart of the continent, and reunited with their extended family. Three years later, John stopped living with Aagodt and their two sons. Perhaps inventing his death proved easier than explaining his emotional unraveling in the migration process. He showed signs of despondency that may have surfaced earlier but became more pronounced once they settled in North Dakota. His parents had immigrated to Roseau County, in northern Minnesota, where records show John was arrested for erratic behavior. He subsequently spent brief periods in newly built asylums for the mentally ill in Illinois, Washington, and Minnesota.[61] A skimpy paper trail reveals that the "Examiners in Lunacy" at the State Hospital for the Insane in Fergus Falls, Minnesota, declared him insane and admitted him on February 9, 1907. One doctor noted that John "refuses to answer questions," so few clues shed light on his condition. When the intake form asked, "Has the patient shown any disposition to injure others?" the doctor wrote, "No." When it asked, "Does the disease appear to be increasing, decreasing or stationary?" the doctor wrote, "Increasing." John was deeply depressed and disoriented.[62] This story flips the narrative we have come to expect.

John Beck was released from the state hospital later that year and recommitted in October 1910, where records describe his ailment as "imbecility." They indicate that he was "unable to grasp ideas intelligently" or carry a conversation, and his memory was "very bad." Seeking to avoid assuming financial responsibility, Minnesota officials remanded him to North Dakota. After a court hearing in Devils Lake, John was described as "depressed and somewhat demented." He was admitted to Jamestown Insane Asylum, about twenty miles south of Sheyenne, with a diagnosis of "manic depressive psychosis," a freshly minted mental health term indicating dramatic mood swings. Most entries in his hospital record describe him as almost catatonic, unwilling to engage in conversation and eating little. When admitted he weighed only 132 pounds, had an abnormally rapid pulse, and showed evidence of tubercular lungs.

Two years into his hospitalization, John appeared agitated and managed to escape for several hours. The attendants found him sleeping by the James River and brought him back to the asylum. In the following years he made two additional escape attempts, but never made it out of the building. The entries in his file were few and far between, describing him as spending most of his time in bed and uncommunicative. When John Beck died of tuberculosis in 1928, the asylum notified his "sister" (actually, his sister-in-law), Inga Rustom.

Equally startling as the madness that seized John Beck was the completeness with which Aagodt distanced herself from him. Unlike her ability to escape her past by leaving Norway, her visible estrangement needed explanation in her residential and kinship networks. She had to invent his death in order to avoid justifying the way she effectively discarded him. Migration proved an opportunity for her while it destroyed him.

Some women went beyond asserting their endurance and rewriting their life stories to articulate their love of North Dakota and of farming as a way of life. Yankee Cherrie Lane Wood returned to North Dakota in 1907 at age twenty. Her mother cautioned her against marrying a farmer, so, of course, she went right ahead and did. She loved North Dakota with a passion. "Ma Lane said, 'Dakota is a harsh land for the pioneer woman. It's a man's country.' "[63] She worried about the drudgery and loneliness of homesteading. Cherrie Lane Wood found none of that: "Loved this country ever since. My folks thought it was awful. Anyone that lived in a beautiful state like Seattle, they should come out here and like it. I liked everything about it.... I was never on a farm before in my life, except when I was two years old.... But I loved it. Of course, I had the man I wanted, too." She elaborated: "I was just cut out to be a farmer's wife and.... I liked the cold weather. I liked everything about it."

* * * * *

Perhaps more aptly than Rølvaag's *Giants in the Earth*, Willa Cather's *My Ántonia* accurately captures the spirit with which many immigrants and self-selected Yankees infused the homesteading and settlement experience. In this story of the Nebraska plains, Ántonia's father reluctantly left Bohemia at his wife's urging and was devastated by the homesteading experience. It was he, the gentle musician, who committed suicide. Perhaps having a sense of personal agency was key to thriving. Energetic and lively young immigrant women—Scandinavian, Bohemian, and German—made the town of Red Cloud a vibrant, hopeful place. Working as domestic servants, they rose to almost any challenge, raced to weekend dances, laughed, felt joyful, and resisted being worn down by the burden of work—at least before marrying and bearing children. Their native-born counterparts in town sought middle-class respectability and remained colorless, inactive, provincial, and entrapped in narrow conceptions of proper womanhood. Embedded in families and communities and immune to the dictates of bourgeois culture, the immigrant girls and young women did not worry about the stigma of working in the fields. Some creatively used their ingenuity, skills, and sexual appeal to fashion a different kind of life for themselves. For example, Lena Lingard in Cather's novel, determined not to repeat the life of her mother, who was depleted by pregnancy after pregnancy, developed a dressmaking business that enabled her to become financially independent, eschew marriage, and support her mother. Cather understood that a homesteading life offered real possibility as well as tragic loss. She saw the zest with which immigrants made new lives in America.

While Willa Cather suggested that immigrants saved American culture from its stifling preoccupation with bourgeois respectability, she neglected to examine the ways they simultaneously wreaked havoc on the land they came to possess. Their settlement and commitment to a multigenerational family legacy displaced a recently conquered Native people, who became their new neighbors.

3

The Reservation Land Rush: Allotment and Land Taking

IN THE RETELLING, my taciturn Norwegian grandmother, Helene Haugen Kanten (b. 1891), dramatized her narrative about the land rush at Spirit Lake: "[My mother] took land; she took homestead on the Indian Reservation. And that's where they chased the Indians off, you see, and took the land away from them." After I turned the tape recorder off, she crisply conveyed how she viewed the situation: "We stole the land from the Indians." The drama comes from the self-judgment implied by her phrasing. The concept of *taking* land as opposed to buying or settling it found widespread usage in the early twentieth century, but it sounds illicit. And the phrase, *took homestead*, reflects the Norwegian American way of framing the process. Helene clearly felt the tug of culpability, at least in retrospect. It is impossible to know whether she had felt that way as a young, observant Lutheran. How did she justify her mother's actions if she determined that her mother, with her assistance, had stolen land?

In point of fact, Dakotas had to agree to sell unallotted land before it was homesteaded, so it was not stolen, but rather taken legally. Further, her reckoning that Native people had been "chased off" expressed her feeling memory but ignored how these events unfolded as Dakotas continued to live on the reservation along with newcomers.

Helene's moral stance undoubtedly would have found many sympathetic Dakotas and is consonant with a judgment about the whole of U.S. history that is rife with deception and betrayal of Indian people. Undoubtedly she knew that Dakota people had been ousted from Minnesota by military force. Living among them on the reservation as part of the homesteaders' land rush must have made her acutely aware of the ravages of dislocation, inadequate nutrition, and poor health. In registering her own agency, Helene nominally accepted her responsibility as a settler colonist. Her acknowledgment made Dakotas' invisibility impossible. At the very least, proximity created conditions for recognition and visibility.

Fundamental to the changing conditions for American Indians is what Frederick Hoxie calls "the assimilation campaign," which, following military conquest, rested on three pillars: landownership, citizenship, and education.[1] This chapter explores how the project unfolded at Spirit Lake as Dakotas were wards of the government, their land held in trust, and their daily lives monitored by the Indian Office. Twelve years after Dakotas took allotments, other dislocated and economically marginalized people, Scandinavian "strangers" in particular, moved onto the reservation. This chapter probes the sometimes enormous gap between the Indian Office's stated policy and its on-the-ground execution, examines the post-allotment living conditions of impoverished Dakotas, and outlines the processes that led to Scandinavian ownership of the majority of land on the reservation.

ALLOTMENT AS AN ASSIMILATION STRATEGY

Fort Totten was the administrative hub of federal authority for Devils Lake and Turtle Mountain and stood as a symbolic center of the reservation. Dakota elder Grace Lambert observed that this proximity was not coincidental: "If you have ever noticed that all the reservations were at a fort because they wanted the soldiers to look after us. They were afraid we might rebel and have a war or something." The fort system was indeed a testament to the U.S. government's fear of further rebellion on the part of Indian people and a strategy for controlling and patrolling the Great Plains. Military troops saw indigenous people as subordinates—their charges and former enemies. Spirit Lake Dakotas had been calling for the military fort on the reservation to be dismantled at least since 1886. According to the Indian agent, "The Indians are very anxious to have the troops removed, and it is very desirable that their wishes in this respect should be complied with, as their presence here is no longer necessary, and everything in connection with the post is demoralizing and a source of trouble and great annoyance, as there are but few men in connection with the Army who are willing to admit that an Indian has any rights which a soldier is bound to respect."[2] He and members of the tribe agreed that the fort buildings would make an ideal site for the industrial school for boys.

In the wake of the massacre at Wounded Knee in December 1890, a tragic low point in the federal treatment of Native peoples, a shift in U.S. Indian policy facilitated this transformation. Federal troops killed more than 200 mostly unarmed Lakota men, women, and children on the Pine Ridge Reservation in South Dakota. In effect, the massacre ended military conflict between Indians and the

U.S. government, communicating what Thomas Biolsi calls the "threat of mass terror."[3] The government demonstrated that it would ruthlessly crush Native peoples even if they did not try to defend themselves. Within a week of the massacre, Fort Totten was decommissioned. On January 5, 1891, stewardship of the fort shifted from the U.S. Army to the Bureau of Indian Affairs. Two weeks later it opened officially as the Fort Totten Indian School.

As another centerpiece of the assimilation project, the Dawes Act of 1887 was designed to subvert the way Dakotas historically understood and negotiated use of land.[4] Tribal member Phillip John Young articulated the fundamental principle that underlay the Dakotas' alternative understanding: Indians felt "you *couldn't* own land because it's not yours" (Young's emphasis). Louis Garcia emphasized the alien logic and the coercion involved: "The European concept of land ownership [was] thrust upon the Indian people." Control of a territory had entitled people to use the land and its bounty.[5] According to Garcia, "it was a matter of survival if another group came in and was using their resources, which happened all the time. So they guide by a hill or a river or something, it was the boundary." The right to *use* the land for travel or hunting might be claimed and negotiated between groups, but no one exercised exclusive ownership equivalent to the concept in U.S. law, which implied proprietary control in perpetuity.

It was not resistance to land in severalty, separately owned land, that most impeded Dakotas' quest for self-determination, but rather the actions of the federal government. In recognition of Indians' lack of familiarity with private property ownership, the Dawes Act stipulated that allotted land be held in trust by the U.S. government for twenty-five years, reasoning that this would give Indians time to adjust to land-owning logic and family farming.

The price of this protection was that tribal members were wards of the government, denying them autonomy. In practice, the federal government's constriction of Indians' rights as wards of the state meant that many important decisions were taken out of the hands of Dakotas—how they used their land or whether they could mortgage the property. Nor could they sell the land; first they had to petition for the patent to the land and prove their fitness, or "competence," to act independently. If the government wanted to rebuild independence among Dakotas, which it had systematically attempted to destroy during the previous century, then it had to provide the means for achieving self-sufficiency. As Charles A. Eastman wrote, "How are we Indians to learn if you take from us the wisdom that is born of mistakes, and leave us to suffer the stings of robbery and deception, with no opportunity to guard against its recurrence?"[6] Specifically, the United States should honor its legal commitments to Native people and provide the proper tools for running a farm, as it had promised. The government's contradictory policy, founded on a notion of yeoman masculinity (as opposed to Native American manhood, or universal personhood regardless of gender), conceived of all Indians as male and simultaneously undermined what it purported to do.

The Indian agent oversaw the daily affairs of the government bureaucracy, mediated relations with the Indian Office in Washington, D.C., and listened to the needs of the Indian people—or failed to do so—as they brought their issues to him. Notoriously, agents in charge of reservations were profiteers who misappropriated funds and enriched themselves by selling government provisions intended for Indians, making sure Indian people were undersupplied and their own pockets full. Not all were dishonest, but they were political appointees hired without regard for qualification, and those who tried to do their job well were overshadowed by those whose greed undermined their integrity as well as their credibility with Indian people. In his autobiography, James McLaughlin, the third Indian agent at Fort Totten, wrote of the agent's expansive powers: "Justice was necessarily administered by the Agent, and sharp correction was sometimes given those who could not be restrained by the tribal rules."[7] Agents held the authority to rule on competency and influenced how tribal members used their land and monies in trust.

Agents sometimes married into the tribes they served. Like the fur traders of earlier generations, they gained a kinship advantage from their integration into the community. At Spirit Lake, James McLaughlin, a self-described "major" and "friend of the Indian,"[8] married Marie Louise Buisson, of distinguished Dakota heritage—granddaughter of a prominent fur trader and Mdewakanton woman and daughter of a Civil War veteran. Precisely how McLaughlin's formal kinship with Dakotas altered his affinity for Native culture and sympathy to Indian political issues remains an open question.[9] Opinion about him was divided, but the loyalties that did exist were strong. When he transferred from Spirit Lake to the Standing Rock Sioux Reservation in 1881, many of the Ihanktonwanna (Pabaksa) band of Dakotas accompanied him "because they admired Agent McLaughlin."[10] Later in his fifty-two-year career with the Indian Office, McLaughlin returned to the reservation multiple times to negotiate key agreements and preside at government ceremonies (see figure 15).

The successor to McLaughlin, John W. Cramsie, had served at Fort Totten since its inception. He married Mary Jane Buisson, younger sister of Mrs. Marie Louise Buisson McLaughlin. Cramsie spoke some of the Indian language, although he relied on his wife to translate on the reservation.[11] He saw himself as an advocate for Dakota people, and his reports were peppered with references to the rightful debts owed Dakotas.[12] As an enforcer and mediator, he vacillated between wanting to honor the commitments his employer made, embracing the ideology of potential Indian self-sufficiency, and criticizing the egregious ways the government undermined its stated goals by reneging on legally binding agreements and under-resourcing Indians' farming endeavors. Yet, revealing his paternalistic orientation, Cramsie would refer to "my Indians" when explaining his affinity for the Dakotas' position and its logic.[13] The unusual empathy Cramsie expressed for Dakotas' political and economic situation receded with successive agents and superintendents.

Choosing and Assigning Allotments

Well before the Dawes Act was passed, most Dakotas at Fort Totten Agency were "located upon individual claims" scattered around the reservation where they had vegetable gardens and farmed "wheat, oats, barley, corn, and potatoes."[14] When the different bands of Dakotas first arrived after the U.S.–Dakota war, they settled in clusters across three districts—Wood Lake, St. Michael's Mission, and Crow Hill— that reflected a traditional approach to setting up camp. In Minnesota, Dakotas lived in villages organized by *tiyospaye*, a "larger family of related household units" that was more significant than individual households.[15] These kin clusters remained, indicating a strong Dakota preference for proximity to kin and continuity of camp circles.[16]

After passage of the severalty legislation in February 1887, Cramsie seized the initiative and hired a surveyor to commence surveying and allotting land. The Indian Office immediately ordered him to cease and desist as the legislation specified that a special agent be commissioned to oversee this complex process. By the time Cramsie received the orders he had assigned seventy-one allotments, which, he acknowledged, "will have to be all gone over again."[17] The following year he urgently pressed his superiors to move forward, "as the Indians are desirous of having a paper to secure them in their possession." Fast work would save him "trouble and annoyance"[18] as Dakotas impatiently pushed to straighten out the mess his foolhardiness had created. But Dakotas were skeptical about allotment and its promised outcomes.

When the first allotting agent, Malachi Krebs, arrived at the reservation in 1889 and met with the tribal council, he had to confront Dakotas' many objections, particularly in light of their previous agreements with the government. First, they insisted that the Treaty of 1867 reserved permanent land for them, which as a tribe they collectively owned.[19] Second, they challenged the way that reservation boundaries had been drawn. In a misreading of the original treaty and its designated landmarks, 64,000 acres had been lopped off the reservation. By 1889, white settlers already lived on that land in Benson County. But Dakotas demanded that "the western boundary line [be] re-established, as provided for and agreed upon by the treaty, and the white man removed in order that they may select their lands as provided for in the allotment act, viz, in the choicest portion of the reservation, through which a railroad runs and affords convenient and proper facilities for shipping their surplus grain."[20]

A third grievance aligned with objections voiced by Sissetons in South Dakota, that men over the age of eighteen should receive 160 acres, not just those twenty-one years and older, as had been specified in the Devils Lake treaty. Dakotas argued that a nineteen-year-old man was capable of cultivating a full farm, perhaps even more than a seventy-year-old man who by virtue of his age and the legislation would receive a full quarter section. Sissetons pressed hard on the equalization of allotments, not just on the discrepancy between young and old men. " 'This reservation,' they said, 'is our common property; we, our wives and our children, have a right to an equal share in it. Among white men, when land is left to a family, the law divides it equally. You say we are now citizens under the same law as white men. We wish to be treated as citizens.' "[21] Sissetons convinced the Board of Indian Commissioners, who recommended an amendment to the severalty act; that was done in 1891.

Fourth, they asserted that, by treaty, they were not subject to taxation on lands held in severalty. They strongly objected to the suggestion of taxation as a component of citizenship. Fifth, they saw no benefit to imposing white society's laws on the reservation, "which would render them liable to arrest and punishment by the white man for any infringement of the white men's laws, which they know nothing about." They elaborated that "white men are anxious to get possession of their lands, and that the law would be enforced for every trivial offense for the purpose of driving them out of the country with this end in view."[22]

Sixth, they opposed proceeding in the absence of Cuthead Sioux (Pabaksas, or Ihanktonwannas), who had joined them as original signatories of the 1867 treaty establishing the reservation and were rightfully entitled to allotments.[23] Finally, Dakotas also pressed a long-festering grievance that later gave rise to a suit in the U.S. Court of Claims. They demanded "money also due them, under old treaties in Minnesota, that was confiscated in consequence of the outbreak in 1862 by other bands of Indians; that they did not think it just treatment that they should be punished for the offenses of others."[24] Dakotas challenged the United States to make amends by honoring its obligations.

In the end, Dakotas' objections to allotment were not to owning land per se, but to letting the U.S. government set the terms when it had proved so untrustworthy in the past. They foresaw citizenship manipulated as a means to apply unfair standards to their circumstances, leaving them at a grave disadvantage, with the ultimate goal as dispossessing them of their land. This interpretation proved prescient given what would unfold in following years.

The process of allotting resumed with the arrival of special agent Joseph R. Gray in 1890 and the congressional appropriation of funds to pay for the 64,000 additional acres in 1891.[25] A government report acknowledged divided opinion on allotment: "The men who have heretofore been known and recognized as chiefs or leaders are as a rule opposed to the allotment of lands in severalty."[26] Ultimately, however, a sufficient number of adult men signed the agreement to participate in the process. By September 1890, land had been allotted to 653 tribal members, 397 males and 256 females,[27] out of a population that had risen to 1,038 Indian people (485 males, 553 females), indicating that Dakota people living elsewhere had come to the reservation to be allotted.[28] In 1892, the new Indian agent, John H. Waugh, reported, "The Indians are all well satisfied at the results of taking their land in severalty."[29] By 1894, 1,032 allotments had been made, amounting to approximately 100,000 acres, or about 97 acres per person on average.[30] Importantly, the government did not set aside surplus land for future generations. As Agnes Greene put it, "They had lots of land, but we didn't get it"[31] (see figure 16).

While no extant historical documents inform us of the particularities of selecting and assigning land, kinship clearly shaped Dakotas' preferences.[32] Many but not all Dakotas got land they already occupied. A story told by tribal elder Agnes Greene dispels the notion of voluntary choice in the allotment of land: "My grandparents *had* settled already in Stump Lake. And they had log cabins." She emphasized that "They *lived* there. That was their home; they had a garden" (Greene's emphasis). Stump Lake lies a few miles east of the reservation's official boundaries. She continued, "They pushed them off and they gave them land by Hamar. It's between Warwick and Hamar, in that area. They gave them each, I think it was forty or eighty acres. I think it's eighty. Then…they gave them each a paper. There was about two or three families." When I probed about how much say they had in their selection of allotments on the reservation, Agnes Greene asserted that it was none: "No, they just give it to them."[33]

Many people's allotments were divided in two separate acreages: eighty acres of hilly wooded lands and eighty acres that were flat and arable. While none of the descendants of allottees whom I interviewed knew how their families or the government made decisions about location, the principles of Dakotas' historic land use unfolded in a discernible pattern.[34] That involved moving their tipis "from one part of the reservation to another every season"[35] to maximize their resources. Grace Lambert described Dakotas as "always roamers looking for food and a place to stay during the winter months." In 1893, about 300 farm families on the reservation cultivated an average of eleven acres. Of those, Indian agent Ralph Hall wrote, "there are twenty or thirty families who can and do take care of themselves without any assistance whatever; but the most of them live from hand to mouth."[36] Access to timber was important for building material and fuel and as a product to sell—although Indian agent F. O. Getchell reported in 1902 that "resources of timber were greatly reduced by the military occupancy, and is now after years of wood-chopping and hauling by the Indians well nigh exhausted."[37]

The consequence of that pattern was that the southern, flatter part of the reservation—with land more conducive to farming—was not allotted and thereafter made available for homesteading. According to the assessment done at that time, only a fraction of the reservation land—about 41,600 of the 240,000 acres—was recognizably "tillable," that is, able to support cultivation. "The reservation as a whole is much better adapted to stock raising or mixed farming than for exclusive grain growing, being rough, broken, rolling, and stony."[38] The soil was "light sandy and gravelly loam" and subject to "lack of moisture" because of low annual rainfall. In effect, Dakotas were trying their hand at agriculture with the deck stacked against them.

This pattern of allotments disadvantaged Dakotas in the market-oriented single-crop economy. Ignatius Court, among those in the tribe who kept a shrewd eye on agriculture, recognized this problem and lobbied the agent for a change (see figure 17). Court had already worked in various capacities on the reservation, including as postmaster, and later served as a judge in the Court of Indian Offenses. Because of his role as an interpreter, he had been one of the legal witnesses to the signing of the certificates of allotment selection. His uncle, Left-Handed Bear, Matocatka, one of the Wahpeton chiefs, appointed him to a Spirit Lake delegation to Washington in 1898.[39] Perhaps in response, agent F. O. Getchell wrote to the Commissioner of Indian Affairs explaining that having an allotment split into two separate places hindered farming, since Dakotas or the whites to whom they leased the land had to transport their equipment from place to place. If they decided to sell, Dakotas' land was worth less than it would have been as a consolidated quarter section, which was easier to cultivate.[40] Although consistent with their practice of mixed land use, division of allotted land in this way made it difficult for Indians to succeed as farmers.

Tracing Genealogy and Verifying Heirship

Private property required owners to be able to trace legal kinship over time and across generations, if for no other reason than to determine what should happen to land when someone died.[41] Under U.S. law, if no will had been filed, land would be inherited by next of kin; first in line were a spouse and children. But if the deceased was not married, or if no written record of a marriage or children could be found, then determining rightful heirs was difficult, since the system was based on written documents rather than oral testimony.

In 1902, recognizing that deciding inheritance posed serious problems, Congress passed the "Dead Indian Act" to establish a procedure whereby heirs could be identified.[42] If no heir was identified or the heirs wanted to sell, allotted land could then be sold with the approval of the Indian Office.[43] Because Dakota naming practices, like those of many American Indian tribes, did not include family names or make descent obvious, tracing genealogy required knowing tribal history and kin relations over time. Births and marriages were seldom recorded, except episodically by a church or the Indian court.

This set of issues assumed huge proportions a decade after allotment because keeping land within a family over time was critical for Indian people. In his 1903 annual report, agent F. O. Getchell pointed out that "more than 33 1/3 percent of these original allottees were dead."[44] Simultaneously, the Dead Indian Land Act offered an avenue for land-seekers and speculators to acquire land, even before the reservation was opened to homesteading. As a result, land was transferred out of the hands of Dakota tribal members and into those of white landowners, Scandinavian and non-Scandinavian alike.

Significantly, the task of determining descent became the responsibility of the agent, who was insufficiently knowledgeable about Dakotas' complex kinship system to ensure that all potential heirs were identified. Getchell complained of the enormous amount of time he spent trying to resolve inheritance issues; tracking relatives across generations required making sense of what he saw as the "extremely tangled condition of the family relation among the Indians, under their tribal mode of marriage."[45] Dakota kinship practices included a tradition of polygamy, although, as one Indian agent noted, almost all Dakotas were "monogamists."[46] They recognized divorce, and both women and men could remarry without stigma. Moreover, Dakota kinship terms were not identical to those used in Euro-American culture. For example, Dakotas used the term "mother" to refer not only to a person's biological mother but also to her sisters, reflecting the important role of aunties in socializing children.

With each subsequent cohort, the number of owners multiplied as most land continued to be held in trust. Soon a single plot of land might have a hundred or more co-owners. Phillip John Young talked about his grandparents' allotment: "Now it's chopped up into about a zillion ways because each member had ten kids.... cutting it up and cutting it up. So, it's down to nothing now, pretty much. Less than one percent you own, a decimal point." Even when "dead Indian land" was not sold off and inherited land was kept in trust, the benefits of owning the land diminished with each generation.

RENAMING THE INDIANS

In the United States, tracing kinship demanded anglicized family names that linked generations and marital partners, identified paternity, and, when used consistently, had legal standing. Lineage was important to Dakotas, but it was commonly known and did not have to be embodied in a surname. Ella C. Deloria (Yankton Dakota), linguist, ethnographer, and member of the Standing Rock Sioux tribe, said in a public talk in 1969, "There was no need for a family name among the Dakota because there was no property to inherit."[47]

In nineteenth-century assimilation efforts, schoolteachers and ministers arbitrarily assigned anglicized names to Indian people at every juncture. Children were given "Christian" names when they started school, many anointed with monikers of presidents and other distinguished white men or common names such as Henry and William.[48] Grace Lambert explained that when her grandfather went to receive his allotment, "they gave 'em names. They couldn't spell it, I suppose, or something, and they just gave him a white name. He was given the superintendent's name, I heard. I don't know if that's true or not. The superintendent at that time's name was Sam Young. A lot of them were baptized by the priest and given names by him too."[49]

The matter of names became a hotly debated national policy issue—should indigenous names be translated, family names tacked on to protect property, or left alone?[50] Representing the compromise in the Department of the Interior, Hamlin Garland, novelist and reformer, proposed and then launched a project dubbed "Renaming the Indians." Worried about land fraud perpetrated against Native Americans because of their complex system of naming, he supervised the process of translating Indian names into English and assigning family names systematically. He appointed Charles Eastman to undertake the task of chronicling and translating names of all those on Sioux reservations. To do so, Eastman came to Fort Totten in September 1905 for about two months. As a bilingual native speaker, his translations were supposed to be sensitive to Dakota culture and tasteful in English, and still meet the needs of law dealing with private property and inheritance.[51]

The clashing cultural logic of naming becomes starkly clear in Zitkala-Ša's fictional story of Blue-Star Woman. An elderly woman comes to the tribe and claims to be a descendent of a tribal member. The fact that she is old and landless and claims membership prompts the tribe to take some responsibility for her. She must provide genealogical proof of her ancestry in order to be enrolled in the tribe, yet she insists on observing the taboo against saying the name of the dead frivolously. "The unwritten law of heart prompted her naturally to say, 'I am a being. I am Blue-Star Woman. A piece of earth is my birthright.'"[52] She faces a dilemma because of the gulf between her values and the legal system: "Blue-Star Woman was her individual name. For untold ages the Indian race had not used family names. A new-born child was given a brand-new name. Blue-Star Woman was proud to write her name for which she would not be required to substitute another's upon her marriage as is the custom of civilized peoples. 'The times are changed now,' she muttered under her breath.

'My individual name seems to mean nothing.' "[53] When confronted with the need to prove her relationship to the tribe, Blue-Star Woman says, "I do not understand the white man's law. It's like walking in the dark. In this darkness, I am growing fearful of everything."[54] Zitkala-Ša adroitly points to the irony of a culture that described itself as "civilized" and claimed to honor individualism yet required that a woman abandon her birth name and take that of her husband upon marriage.

In Dakota culture, naming a child—especially a first-born—was a special occasion marked by a give-away and often a feast. A baby's name would mark gender (girls' names often ended with "win") and could indicate kinship status or birth order, such as Caske (eldest son) or Tokaza (grandchild). A child was often given another name later.[55] A give-away marked a moment of honor for Grace Lambert when she was named Waunsidawin, "Merciful Woman."

I always just appreciate that old man for giving me that name. They usually give names to children that are well thought of. And my dad died before I was born and so when I was born, why, my mother thought that since I didn't have no father I should have an Indian name, to be recognized that I was born legally.... She made a big kind of celebration for the elders. They put up a tipi and several elders came, and one of them, his name was "Good Road" in Indian.... She got him to name me and he was a very quiet man, but I am just noisy. I wonder why. They always say that you take after whoever names you,...their character and all. But his character was pretty good and I, of course, I made all kinds of mistakes too, but most of the time I kind of behaved myself. And I think I would be pleasing to that old man, as far as I went anyway. But that's how I got my name. And they usually gave things away when they did that. My mother said she gave a mare with a colt and that tipi and a lot of things, other small things like blankets and stuff. Then, she said, she gave a feed; they all ate.[56]

With each name comes a story. Charlie Cree (b. 1895), who was from the Turtle Mountain Band of Chippewas and attended boarding school at Fort Totten, ruminated about some of the names he had been given. When he was two or three years old and very ill, a healer, Mrs. Ryingson, named him "Flying with the Wind." She said, " 'That little boy is going to die on you. Bring him over, I'll doctor him.' So I still got scars where she punched me. Old [Zemackwa], they're religious people. So she gave me a name."[57] Later he was called "Charlie Eagle Eye" after his grandfather's father.

At the same time that the U.S. government was trying to neutralize and depoliticize Indian culture and Americanize immigrants, the stories behind Indian names captivated a larger public. Names carried exotic distinction, an association with the western frontier, the era of a more physically vigorous and honorable life, and a romantic interpretation of vision quests, which were practiced as a coming of age ritual in some tribes.[58] Numerous travelers and settlers in the West would boast of their Indian name, conferred in friendship and honor. For example, Solomon Redfox dubbed his American neighbor, Jack Reeves, "Dirty Face." Louis Garcia reports that the Cavanaughs would regularly give their white employers Dakota names, but not inform them of the real translation. The employers would be so pleased to know they had an Indian name that they would go to town and brag to whomever would listen. Dakotas had the last laugh.

CONDITIONS ON THE RESERVATION

The administrative matters of the reservation, largely conducted by the Indian agent and, later, the superintendent, were run out of the main office at Fort Totten (see figure 18). Other government employees, some of whom were Dakota, included the boss farmer, an additional farmer, an interpreter, a blacksmith, cooks, a doctor, a nurse, a field matron, and school staff, including teachers.[59] Powwows were prohibited and off-reservation travel restricted. Grace Lambert explained the demise of customary observances: "Everything was called pagan, and they were scared of them."[60] The spread of the Ghost Dance among Indians across the country in the early 1890s inspired fear of an uprising. Tribal member Eunice Davidson (b. 1951) recalled her grandmother articulating the antagonism toward constraints imposed by the Indian Office: " 'They had to change our ways, and we couldn't speak our language, couldn't dance,' she said, 'and that was very hurtful.' " Agnes Greene put it bluntly, "The government was trying to control the Indians, so you didn't dare have a powwow in the earlier days." Many forms of recreation, such as card playing, were banned. "*You were a prisoner of war*,"[61] she concluded (Greene's emphasis). In effect, the agency office exercised far-reaching control over Dakotas' everyday lives.

In accordance with Indian governance, Dakotas held councils with leading men of the tribe who conferred among themselves, acted on behalf of the tribe, and sent delegations to speak and negotiate with representatives of government. Dakotas' nation-to-nation relationship with the United States meant that any grievances regarding their treatment or condition needed to be taken up with federal officials. Sometimes they traveled north to Devils Lake or testified at a hearing in Minnewaukan, the Benson County seat on the western border of the reservation; at other times they marshaled the resources to send a group to Washington, D.C., to meet with congressmen or the president. Tiyowaste, or Little Fish (1825–1919), Waanatan (1828–1897), and Matocatka (1828–1905) were the last hereditary chiefs to exercise leadership on the reservation.[62] Unlike other tribes, Spirit Lake Dakotas did not have a business committee or councils organized around specific topics. Like other reservations, Spirit Lake had a Court of Indian Offenses, staffed by three Dakota judges, and a system of Indian police. The court's effectiveness depended on the high regard accorded the particular Dakota leaders as they mediated local disputes. Particularly because of the confusion over legal jurisdiction, county and state judicial systems were reluctant to adjudicate conflicts among Indians.[63]

In the years between allotment and the reservation land rush, conditions for Dakota people at Spirit Lake improved little, if at all. Although the government claimed to promote farming, food insecurity continued to be a major problem. Dakotas lacked work animals and proper farm equipment. They had to rely on cattle instead of horses, for example, "which makes the work much more laborious and tedious."[64] Agent Cramsie used a meaningful yardstick to communicate the human cost: "For lack of horse teams to do our harvesting we will lose more than double the amount of grain necessary to feed the Turtle Mountain Indians."[65] The frustration at the undercapitalization of farmers and the resulting inefficiency and waste redoubled Dakotas' anger over the government's saying one thing and doing another. A decade later, agent F. O. Getchell encapsulated the operating formula: "Poor teams and poor plows resulted in poor plowing."[66] Agent Ralph Hall reported how a Dakota man responded to the vagaries of wheat farming. "One old Indian told me that in future he would only plant potatoes and corn, as that always furnished him something to live upon, while his wheat crop was either a failure, or when he raised one, it took all of it to pay his debts."[67] Scanty harvests translated into inadequate food and exacerbated endemic health problems.

The damage wrought by disease and poverty threatened Dakota people as a collectivity. High mortality, and what demographers call "diminishing replacement" rate, meant fewer children, decreasing tribal enrollments, and increasing "dead Indian land" on the market. Although precise mortality rates are hard to come by, the annual reports enumerated deaths: for more years than not, they exceeded the number of births. Disease and malnutrition hit young children and elders especially hard. In 1901 after an outbreak of smallpox at Turtle Mountain and two cases at Spirit Lake, agent F. O. Getchell assured the Indian Office that "every man, woman, and child on the reservation was vaccinated, whether willing or unwilling."[68] Dakota population at Spirit Lake declined from its peak of 1,098 in 1894 to 986 in 1910 and 980 in 1931. In the Indian communities on the reservation, the devastation was more a chronic condition than a sudden catastrophe.

Undernourished, impoverished people living in crowded conditions were more vulnerable to tuberculosis, which was spread by person-to-person contact through sneezing, coughing, talking, and singing via "microscopic droplets released into the air."[69] According to historian David S. Jones, "tuberculosis caused far more morbidity and mortality among the Sioux than among even the urban poor of eastern cities."[70] One key preventative measure was improved nutrition; another was the ventilation of houses, an especially vexing problem in log huts that were sealed tight through the long winter. When Dakotas lived in tipis with smoke holes at the top, ventilation was not an issue, and seasonal relocation allowed them to refresh their campsites. However, making their new log dwellings warm and comfortable while allowing for fresh air was not easy. As late as 1913, only 225 out of 250 Dakota homes had wooden floors; the others still had dirt floors.[71] Some Dakota families still lived year round in tipis or tents on their property, which they viewed as more hygienic, warmer, and less smoky than log houses (see figure 19). Without electricity, running water, or a sewage system, everyday tasks in the household and barn required prodigious effort and heavy labor. Women had to haul water, wash clothes in big tin tubs, and heat the house and cook food using campfires or stoves that burned wood or cow chips. During harvest, some Dakota families used their houses to store their wheat while they lived there themselves or moved in with relatives.[72]

Prevention of the spread of disease could be the most effective kind of healthcare intervention authorities could make. As a gendered complement to the "boss farmer initiative" to teach Indian men about agriculture, the Indian Office developed a program aimed at teaching women skills in housekeeping and childrearing, the domestic linchpins of the assimilation process.[73] As historian Rebecca J. Herring points out, reformers thought that once "Indian families began to inhabit permanent houses on their allotments," the need for instruction was more acute.[74] The field matron program, which first received funds in 1891, sought to "promote the civilization of the Indians, particularly with respect to their home life and surroundings."[75] The charge of the field matron included instructing women in a broad range of domestic labors: house cleaning, food preparation, laundry, sewing, care of the sick, childrearing, care for domestic animals, adorning the home, and observance of the Sabbath.[76]

At Fort Totten, the public health approach taken by Carrie Pohl, the field matron employed from 1913 to 1916, sought to reduce contagious diseases by bringing her professional skills to bear in her work, and it served as a bridge to the explicit public-health efforts undertaken by the Indian Office in the 1920s.[77] Unlike those who preceded her, Carrie Pohl left an extensive paper trail—almost three years of daily field notes that she submitted to the superintendent—that enables us to follow her visits to Dakota households on the reservation. Armed with her twin missions of teaching domesticity and preventing the spread of disease, Carrie Pohl mixed her cultural biases and harsh judgments with her considerable skill as a nurse to offer advice and assess the condition of Dakota homes. These detailed descriptions, like the agency reports, are laced with Eurocentric judgments. Nonetheless, their great specificity allows us to picture households and to understand Dakotas' reactions to Pohl, as refracted through the lens of her notes. So, for example, she registers her disapproval of Mrs. Jackson's housekeeping, which prompted the superintendent to call in and reprimand the Dakota woman. Another tribal member, Mrs. David Hopkins, expressed resentment at Carrie Pohl's actions. Defensively, Pohl accused Mrs. Hopkins of keeping a "very dirty" house and dismissed her reprisal as an excuse to resist instruction. Although, in keeping with Dakota hospitality, most welcomed her, some avoided her intrusive presence. She claimed that she never found Mrs. Smiley Smith at home: "If she sees my teams in the neighborhood she leaves for fear I will call."[78] Nonetheless Pohl would peer through the windows in Mrs. Smith's absence and record her appraisals, which she continued to pass along to the superintendent.

Many Dakota women lacked the most basic resources necessary for rudimentary housekeeping. For some, simplicity stemmed from their attachment to their own culture. Pohl noted, "Pretty Bird and wife have no furniture just the old Indian way."[79] Tribal member Eunice Davidson recalled an elder who lived next door in a canvas tent but eventually built a house of wood. "They had gotten her a fridge one time and she wouldn't use it. She didn't like it," so she put it out in her yard. Some Dakota families suffered leaky roofs on log cabins or holes in summer tents. Carrie Pohl observed, "Mrs. Louisa Black Cloud home is a little hut ready to tumble down, found what little furniture she had soaked with rain: one dresser, one dish cupboard, one table, and one stove." Despite this situation, she admitted that Mrs. Black Cloud "would be a fair housekeeper if she had anything to do with"[80]—that is, resources or money. As she witnessed the daily conditions of rural poverty, Carrie Pohl gradually developed greater empathy and became less harsh in her judgments. The longer she worked, the more often she conceded the potential for improvement if Dakota people had "anything to do with."

Pohl taught Dakota women about the causes and prevention of prevalent contagious diseases, particularly tuberculosis and trachoma, a common eye disease that begins as conjunctivitis or "pinkeye" but, when left untreated, causes scarring and eventually blindness. She made home visits and delivered lectures to gatherings of the Indian Temperance Society, the church at Wood Lake, a Catholic convention, and the Indian Women's Sewing Circle.[81] When she initially made her home visits, she observed: "Little care is taken in familys where trachoma or tuberculosis exists to keep from infecting other members of the family."[82] Many acted on her advice as best they could: "Called on two Indian familys, Iron Cloud and Albert found three tubercular children in familys, had Indian woman put beds out of door; also gave instructions for cleaning. Called again in the P.M. found the floor scrubbed and all bedding out of doors also sick children out of doors; found tent near the cabin gave instructions to have sick children sleep in tent which they promised to do. The Iron Cloud cabin had only a dirt floor."[83] Pohl made a concerted effort to bring families what they needed to install screens on their windows and doors, enhancing ventilation in log houses and keeping out flies. Over time, just as Carrie Pohl became more understanding of the obstacles facing Dakota women, so they became more receptive to her. Some would ask her advice in childrearing; others would request that she procure medicine from the agency doctor for them.

These intermittent efforts to interrupt the devastations of reservation living and improve agricultural production were paired, starting in 1904, with integration.

"OPENING" THE RESERVATION TO WHITE HOMESTEADERS

A key element of the Dawes Act cast thousands of acres as "surplus," in effect creating an opportunity for white homesteading and another round of dispossession. After allotment, as North Dakota historian Elwyn Robinson disingenuously put it, "As the Indians began to live by farming and on government rations, it became obvious that some of *the reservations were much larger than they needed to be.*"[84] Bjorne Knudson, whose Norwegian father homesteaded hilly reservation land, explained his understanding: "They decided to give the Indian people so many acres of land to each individual Indian. Well, after they have done this, there was a lot of land left over. So then the federal government says, 'Now what are we going to do with this land?'" The innocence of this perspective removes culpability from those who designed the legislation to dispossess Native people of more land.

The severalty act stipulated that whites could homestead on reservations only after tribes agreed to relinquish the unallotted land in return for payment. In 1901, James McLaughlin returned to Fort Totten Agency as U.S. Indian Inspector to discuss this matter with Spirit Lake Dakotas. By November 7, 216 adult male members of the tribe (out of 296) had signed the document agreeing that unallotted reservation land could be made available for homesteading.[85] In his annual report, agent F. O. Getchell ruefully observed that Congress failed to approve the agreement in a timely way, thereby effectively nullifying it.[86]

Nonetheless, two-and-a-half years later, on April 27, 1904, after some debate about the terms of the agreement (such as, the fee per acre), Congress finally passed legislation specific to Fort Totten.[87] According to the *Sheyenne Star*, the Land Allotment Act of 1904 was greeted with a "hail of joy" in the surrounding Scandinavian and Yankee communities.[88] Just over a month later, President Theodore Roosevelt signed a proclamation announcing the plan, its terms, and timetable and declaring that the "Sisseton, Wahpeton, and Cut-Head bands of the Sioux tribe" of Spirit Lake Reservation "had ceded, conveyed, transferred, relinquished, and surrendered, forever and absolutely...all their claim, title, and interest of every kind and character in and to the unallotted lands."[89] The wheels were set in rapid motion as the Land Offices in Devils Lake and Grand Forks prepared for the onslaught.

Organizing the Land Taking

Given the high demand for land and recognizing the "wild scramble" that had occurred elsewhere,[90] the federal government assigned Judge Richards, the official responsible for overseeing the Oklahoma land taking a few years earlier, the job of designing a lottery to select homesteaders. The first 600 randomly chosen people won the right to claim a quarter section of land for $4.50 an acre and a pledge to improve it. As with the Homestead Act, married women could *not* enter the lottery; women had to be over twenty-one and single, widowed, divorced, or head of household. The rules favored adult men, who could enter whether they were single, married, or widowed as long as they were at least twenty-one.

Undaunted, on August 9, 1904, Miss Carrie Fisher of Grafton, North Dakota, stood first in line at the Grand Forks Land Office when it opened to register people for the lottery. She was followed by a "long line of women"[91] who wanted a chance to homestead. Over the course of two weeks, 15,076 people entered the lottery, and many of the names drawn were those of women.[92]

What made women want to own land? In the face of dispossession as a people, Dakota women could preserve land by accepting allotments. Historically Dakota women owned everything associated with the household—the structure itself, furniture, cookware, and the like. Therefore it was a small shift to conceive of them owning the ground upon which a home was anchored.

For non-Indian women, homesteading provided a one-time opportunity to establish a place to live, provide a means of income and self-sufficiency, make an investment, gain leverage in the marriage market, and offer insurance in old age. Single immigrant women, whose primary occupation in the United States was domestic service, found this potential appealing. Young, unmarried, and enterprising women sought economic and social opportunity by homesteading (see figure 20). While few went into farming independently, some used their homesteads to leverage resources to do other things, such as finance an education. Lois Olson Jones's (b. 1918) aunt had been to millinery school, "so she had a trade": the land was an investment to help support her. Widowed women, regardless of age, shared many of the same obstacles to self-sufficiency faced by married and single women. They had few employment options, particularly while raising children, and homesteading enabled them to support themselves and their families.

Land was a necessary means for both groups to cultivate gardens, provide a home for themselves and their families, have a space of their own, and sometimes yield an annual income. It provided an economic as well as cultural foothold. Having security in land could also facilitate leaving a bad marriage. Dakota women could do this more easily than Scandinavian women, because they had the power to divorce men without stigma, and in the process they retained possession of the household goods. Those who owned their homes could rent out rooms and become boardinghouse keepers. Anna Mathilda Berg, known as "Tillie," came to North Dakota from Sweden, and in 1905, at the age of thirty-four, took a homestead on the Spirit Lake Reservation across the road from Berthe Haugen in Eddy Township. When Warwick resident Clara Haugland died, her sister, Mina, came to live with the new widower, Iver C. Haugland, to take care of the baby. Haugland, a Norwegian immigrant and banker at the Farmers and Merchants Bank, ended up marrying his sister-in-law. Mina felt reluctant to live permanently in her sister's house with all of her belongings, however. As a result, Iver Haugland traded his land and house in Warwick with Tillie Berg—the whole kit and caboodle, including dishes—for her homestead.[93] Sociologist Elaine Lindgren wrote, "This home, with its four bedrooms and fine furnishings, provided her with a livelihood; she ran it as a boardinghouse, usually renting to teachers,"[94] for forty years.

Owning land gave women the power to say no. When Norwegian immigrant Bertine Sem proved up her claim in Bottineau County in 1904, she had three neighbors witness that she had lived on the land and cultivated eighty acres. "Satisfied that she was in fact a *bona fide* farmer, the government granted her a deed to the land."[95] She married almost immediately thereafter and started a family with Erick Sannes. The couple then decided that they needed to cultivate more land. "Most farmers used their land as collateral to buy more land, but Bertine, who had worked so hard to retain the title to her land in her own name, refused to risk mortgaging her farm. She insisted they find another way."[96] Her independent ownership of that land allowed her to veto a financial maneuver that would risk her long-term financial security. She could do so because her name was on the title. Her authoritative voice, vested in land, shaped the direction of the household enterprise.

The *Sheyenne Star* reported that less than a year after the land lottery three-quarters of the 100,000 acres had been claimed.[97] Gust A. Berg (b. 1889) explained how it worked for his father, Gust S. Berg, an immigrant from Sweden: "He drew a number and he [had] to come back and...pick out the land.... They drove out with horses from Devils Lake to...show 'em the land, see. And they give him three places, he could [pick] which one he wanted." John Henry Kennedy was number thirteen in the lottery. His low number gave him an advantage: "We had good soil out there." Clyde Reeves drew a high number in the lottery, so "he had to wait a year and got what was left of the choices,"[98] according to his son. Reeves had worked on a dairy farm near Doyon in Nelson County, saved up his money, married, and entered the lottery. Clyde and Eva Reeves ended up northwest of Warwick on what has come to be called Reeves Lake.

Indian superintendent Charles Davis observed Dakotas' response to the white homesteaders' arrival: "The opening was conducted in a very orderly manner, the Indians manifesting a very keen interest, and many members taking an active part in securing settlers and finding suitable locations for them."[99] Presumably Dakotas' knowledge of the lay of the land, the quality of drainage, and good places to hunt benefited the homesteaders. And no doubt they were curious, but while they agreed to this arrangement, there is less evidence that they embraced it. When I asked Eunice Davidson how her grandmother felt about white homesteaders on the reservation, she reported that she remained silent on the matter. "A lot of them didn't want to talk about the past 'cause it was really hard for them." Their land losses were great, and mistrust of white people dated back to the Minnesota war and the relocation to Fort Totten. Her grandmother did say, "We were mad at the white people for what they did to our land."

Proving Up, Making Farms, and Failing

The homesteading process on the reservation followed the same protocol as that used for non-Indian land. Although homestead land on the reservation was not free, it was a boon. As Gust A. Berg put it, "They had to pay four and half dollars an acre. And that is a lot of money them days." Homesteaders paid $720 for a quarter section, in contrast to cleared land in Nelson County, for example, which sold for $20 an acre, totaling $3,200.[100] In light of the fact that an average day laborer earned one dollar a day and worked seasonally, the difference amounted to years of paid work.

In the long term, the cost to homesteaders was high: relocation, backbreaking labor, and participation in the usurpation of Indian land, which incurred resentment. Through working the land, transforming it, and living on it, they could take title. Like allottees, homesteaders had to have the land plowed. In contrast to earlier generations, by 1905 homesteaders were not using oxen to break sod but were hiring a steam-powered rig instead. Gust A. Berg explained, "Fella by the name of Crommett broke up a lot of this land.... I think it was ten plows he had behind a steam rig." Edgar Crommett, who came from Illinois, lived near Warwick and became one of the larger landowners on the reservation, amassing almost one thousand acres by 1929. Through sod busting he was able to accumulate cash and purchase more land, which was virtually impossible for a farmer who relied primarily on his or her crops to raise capital. After the sod was broken, homesteaders still had to clear the land,

and both men and women were on call for the hard physical labor that farm making required. They also had to buy equipment and seed and erect buildings, which could cost up to one thousand dollars.[101]

The costs to Dakotas, by contrast, were immeasurable: further erosion of the tribal land base was accompanied by the social and economic intrusion of immigrants and Yankees. Land loss and resentment created what Eunice Davidson's grandmother, Alvina Alberts (b. 1912), called a "black heart," weighed down with pain and sorrow, which was passed down from generation to generation. The tribe was supposed to benefit financially from the payments for the land and, from the perspective of reformers, the Americanizing influence of the white settlers.[102] In the eyes of the broader public, land sales amounted to a gigantic windfall. In May 1905 the *Sheyenne Star* ran the headline: "Fort Totten Indians Paid: $60,000 Disbursed at Devils Lake to New Citizens." The story detailed: "Each adult received $84 and each child will receive his share when he becomes of age."[103] Local newspapers across the country, like the *Sheyenne Star*, regularly reported on lump sums paid to Indian nations, which contributed to the perception that Indians became rich from land sales. The implication was that if they were poor, it was because they misused their money. Yet, that $84 would have been insufficient to ward off starvation for a year.

When homesteaders were poised to take title, they had to present their case to the Land Office registrar, Ole Serumgard, a second-generation Norwegian. He assessed the veracity of each claim and took formal testimony from two witnesses. Subsequently homesteaders had to publish an announcement in the local paper, giving naysayers an opportunity to rebut. For example, Warwick's *Weekly Sentinel* announced: "Notice is hereby given that Ida M. Olson of Tokio, ND has filed notice of her intention to make final commutation proof in support of her claim."[104]

My great-grandmother, Berthe Haugen, built a place on her homestead in Eddy Township in April 1905 and proved up seven years after moving onto the land. She initially broke about twenty-five acres and planted flax. Later, she diversified her crops, growing wheat, oats, and barley, and also cut about twenty to twenty-five tons of hay. On her claim form, she said, "I have twenty-one acres fenced. Have rented my pasture to a neighbor who grazes about ten head of cattle there." Two witnesses, Norwegians John Borgerson and Osmond Thorson, who were her neighbors on the reservation, gave testimony on her behalf[105] (see document 1).

Claim shacks provided just enough space for living and establishing residency, a key requirement for taking homestead land. Wood was scarce, but settlers wanted more than the sod huts inhabited by homesteaders a generation before. Berthe Haugen's dwelling was twelve by fourteen feet, with a small second story, while her barn was fourteen by sixteen feet. Log houses such as those occupied by Dakotas

4—196.

Department of the Interior

United States Land Office ___Devils Lake, N. Dak.___

Serial No. ___01215___

Receipt No. ___110679 - 112434___
___652713 - 935760___

Certificate.

Homestead.

DEVILS LAKE
Indian Lands,
Act of April 27th, 1904.

June 18 _____, 19 12.
(Date.)

It is hereby certified that, pursuant to the provisions of Section 2291, Revised Statutes of the United States,
___Berthe Haugen___

has made payment in full for ___SW¼___

_____ Section ___13___
Township ___150 N.___, Range ___63 W.___, ___5th Prin.___ Meridian,
_____, containing ___160___ _____ acres.

Now, therefore, be it known that, on presentation of this
Certificate to the COMMISSIONER OF THE GENERAL LAND OFFICE, the
said ___Berthe Haugen___

shall be entitled to receive a Patent for the lot above described.

Res.H.E.No.320. _____, Register.

NOTE.—A duplicate of this Certificate is issued to the claimant as notice of the acceptance of the proof and payment, and of the allowance of the entry by the Register and
Receiver.
The original is forwarded to the General Land Office, with the entry papers, for
approval by the Commissioner of the General Land Office and issuance of patent.
The duplicate copy forwarded to the claimant should be held until notice of issuance
of patent is received.
In all correspondence concerning the entry in connection with which this Certificate
issued, refer to the NAME OF THE LAND OFFICE and the SERIAL NUMBER noted hereon.

APPROVED _____ SEP 1 4 1912

By _____, Division ___C___

JUL 15 1912

Pat No. 293210 Sept. 23 1912

DOCUMENT 1 Berthe Haugen's Homestead Entry, final proof, 1912.
Berthe Haugen was issued this homestead certificate by the U.S. Department of Interior for Indian land at Spirit
Lake. After living on the land for seven years and offering proof that she had improved it by cultivating the land,
planting trees, and building structures, she was granted title.

were not unusual. Even after proving up, homestead shacks continued to be used as
living spaces or as shelters for animals.

Homesteaders who had family members with them had an advantage. Proving
continuous residency was difficult for people who had jobs or responsibilities

elsewhere, or who just plain got lonely. In partnership or with a family, a person could accomplish a great deal. For example, James Skurdall (b. 1942) tells of his Norwegian grandfather, Anton Skurdall, staking a claim in McHenry County, west of Devils Lake, which he never finished proving up. Because he worked for the Great Northern Railroad, he could not live on the land continuously. Skurdall reports: "While they had the land, my grandmother and my father's three oldest siblings spent the week on the claim and were joined by my grandfather on the weekends. If my grandmother, Rena Skurdall, was as hardworking on the land as she was in town, it was probably she mostly who made the improvements to the claim."[106] Discontinuous residence was grounds for denying or challenging a claim.

Building a viable farm required not just an investment in land and equipment, but also skills and social capital. As agricultural historian John Hicks observed, "Farm labor, as those who really knew patiently explained, was skilled labor. A boy who had grown up on a farm knew many things that only years of experience could teach."[107] Many people who entered the land lottery had little knowledge of agriculture, while others had farmed in different climates. Bjorne Knudson's father had been trained in carpentry in Norway. According to Bjorne, "Then he decided to really do it big and he was gonna go farming. So…[Chuckle.]" Those who had farmed were unlikely to be so foolishly optimistic. Lottery winner T. O. Berg had been a shoemaker in Fergus Falls, Minnesota. Men and women worked at various jobs in order to accumulate enough capital to launch their homesteading venture. The women in Amy Mosbaek's (b. 1923) family toiled as domestic servants in boardinghouses in Devils Lake, "cooking and cleaning, and laundering and that sort of stuff.…In those days there wasn't much else for women to do."

Yet many homesteaders failed. Nationally, 60 percent of the two million homesteaders who filed an initial claim failed to prove up.[108] For immigrant newcomers, the transformation from homesteader to landowner or, for the less fortunate, to renter or sharecropper could be short and swift. Staying and making a life on the reservation was harder than most homesteaders had imagined. Some did not like the farming life and left. Even in the best of times, not all those who were skilled and committed succeeded, as a bumper crop that lowered world grain prices could undo a year's work and leave a family destitute just as easily as a failed crop.

Opportunity elsewhere lured settlers away just as it had attracted them to North Dakota. The drought of 1910 coincided with the Canadian Pacific Railroad's decision to make thousands of acres available for homesteading up north in Alberta and Saskatchewan. Some saw the opportunity as a chance to start over. In Benson County, Joseph Olson (b. 1894) reported, "The big movement was about '10.…They hiked for Canada. Scandinavians were mostly here then; they all skinned out." My own family, a cluster of Kantens, Borgersons, and Bensons, left Eddy County that year to homestead in southern Saskatchewan (see figure 21). Curiously, the family account did not present the move as precipitated by disaster, but rather by the promise of more land for a growing family. Approximately fifty miles from the newly founded Kantenville stood Wood Mountain Reserve, a place where Dakotas harbored Sitting Bull and other warriors in the aftermath of their battle with General Custer in 1876. Yet again, the Kanten migrations entangled with Dakota history. Barely eighteen and with an infant in tow, Helene began the process of homesteading a second time.

Like many who came unprepared, Jewish immigrants struggled with farming. Alfred Thal (b. 1899), a second-generation German Jew who grew up in Lakota, a small town twenty-five miles east of Devils Lake, discussed the two Jewish settlements in North Dakota—Painted Woods and Devils Lake—that ultimately disintegrated: "Free land was something that they had never heard of a Jew holding in Europe. So they didn't know what they were getting into. They came out here, and no place to live, and nothing was modern. They didn't know one end of the horse from another. Just weren't built or understood anything about agriculture. They suffered a miserable time out here," and their settlements "collapsed." Linking the history of Jewish people to the legal discrimination against them, he concluded: "They were not suited to farming.... Never in their past history had they been able to have land." The small Jewish population north of Devils Lake near Garske had no place to worship and had to rely on an itinerant rabbi to teach their children.[109] Based on his research and interviews with Jews around the state, Thal explained: "Ninety percent of the settlers would sell their land as soon as they could get title to it, which gave them enough capital to move into some small surrounding town and establish a store. I would say that 40 to 50 percent of the settlers became merchants in this area. The rest moved either west or east."[110]

Those who stayed might profit from those who left. Norwegian American Oscar T. Forde spoke of the benefits that accrued to his father, who sought to accumulate more land. "Some of them would come and they'd go. Homesteaders. I think he bought some of their land that way." Farmers on the reservation could buy land from homesteaders who failed, those who relinquished their claims, those who had had enough and wanted to take what profits they could, or those who just gave up.

Land Sales and Accumulation

Within U.S. agriculture, Yankees had a competitive edge because of their facility with language and their familiarity with the dominant economic and legal systems. Oscar B. Wood brought an enterprising outlook and a valuable set of skills. "Oscar saw the vision of what this land could be and not what it was."[111] He was a farmer who understood economies of scale and the value of accumulating land: "He took up as much as he could right around here. And then, every time he could get a piece of land, he took up another piece of land. I just loved it and so did he." His wife, Cherrie Lane Wood, also a Yankee, felt no qualms about this strategy (see figure 22). "We had to just take up the places we could. Or buy a little hunk here and a little hunk here. And he stood up on that hill over there, one day he and I was looking at, he says, 'You know Cherrie, I'm going to own all this land in here.' Well, he did."[112] By 1929 Oscar Wood owned 1,560 acres on the reservation. He was equally canny in his choice of marriage partner. In her memoir, Cherrie Lane Wood attributes her love of North Dakota to her relationship with her husband and her engagement in the enterprise. But only a few homesteaders succeeded in building a large-scale farming operation. By 1929 Berthe Haugen had just her original 160 acres—no more, no less. Her ambitions were more modest: to support herself and her family into her old age.

Typical of development across the West, the reservation attracted a handful of outside speculators. Frederick H. Stoltze, who worked for the Great Northern Railroad, became the largest landowner on the reservation in 1910, owning an astonishing 2,766 acres. He first came to the area to plat towns and buy them up at the behest of his employer.[113] Always an absentee landlord, Stoltze lived in St. Paul with his wife, children, and a slew of servants, where he also ran a lumber and coal business. The magnitude of his purchases required large amounts of capital, which most settlers could hardly imagine.

Other people approached homesteading as an investment, to generate some capital for the long run or to begin their family farming operation. Barbara Handy-Marchello makes clear that most immigrants were not speculators: "They came for 'free' land, for land at a price, for adventure, for opportunity, to practice their religion openly, or simply because their family and friends were already in Dakota."[114] Lois Olson Jones had two uncles and two aunts who took land on the reservation: she conjectured that "maybe it was just a way to get started." Patrick Langstaff (b. 1915) explained the dominant approach to taking land: "Farming was a way of life.... Most people... didn't come there to get rich. They came to have land, and something of their *own*. But then it seemed like they wanted to escalate farming work, where you could get rich at it. I don't think that worked out too much."

Although homesteading served as white settlers' main avenue to the reservation, because of the Dead Indian Land Act, more land became available for sale as allottees died. Dakotas could make bids on the land—and some did—but most lacked the resources to do so. Tribal member Eunice Davidson recalled her grandmother's resentment of whites who made purchases. "She didn't like 'em buying up the Indian land. She wasn't angry with the Indians who sold it, but she didn't think that was right. She said... 'Don't ever sell the land.' Both my grandmas did." Perhaps this clear mandate responded to the loss of land a generation before. Eunice's great-grandmother, Ehnaiyotankewin, who had received an allotment, sold her entire 80 acres to Norwegian farmer Albert K. Johnson in 1912. Because she was deemed "incompetent" and her land was held in trust, she had to get the government first to provide the deed to the land and then approve the sale. Curiously, the Indian Office agreed on condition that her husband assign half of his allotment to her. In effect, the series of transactions meant she purchased 78.6 acres from her husband for $1, and then sold her allotment to Albert K. Johnson for $1,048.[115] By the time she died in 1927, she still had land in her name, as did her husband, although he had less.

One tag-team that took advantage of what it saw as an opportunity came in the partnership of three Norwegian cousins: T. A. Luros, Edgar Anderson, and Morton Anderson, all of whom worked at the Crary Bank at some point (see figure 23). In December 1903, four months prior to passage of the Land Allotment Act, they purchased land on the reservation. Robert Kiciwakankan, heir of deceased allottee John Tawiyukcanwastena, sold eighty acres in section 19 of Minco Township to T. A. Luros and Edgar Anderson.[116] In the late teens, Morton Anderson quit his job at the bank in order to pursue his goal of buying and managing large tracts of land. As he amassed holdings, he tirelessly purchased land from Dakota allottees and their heirs: 160 acres from Oyeckinyewin (or Josephine Kiciwakankan) in 1916; 40 acres from Louie Langer in 1920; 80 acres from Tawacinwastewin in 1923; and so on.[117] This successful banker–cum–land manager came to own the equivalent of two entire sections in Minco Township by purchasing land from Dakota heirs and allottees, and also from Scandinavian immigrants. His acquisitions, in effect, transferred land from Dakota to Scandinavian ownership.

One result of the concerns raised by the rapid sale of allotments out of the hands of Indians on many reservations and a response to the challenges posed by indigenous customs of kinship and naming was the passage of the Burke Act in 1906. Making the situation even more confusing, Congress revoked the citizenship that had been granted to allotted Indians and extended indefinitely the period when allotment land could be held in trust. By delaying full citizenship beyond the twenty-five-year period specified in the Dawes Act, it gave discretionary power to the Commissioner of Indian Affairs to determine competency and citizenship. As the Board of Indian Commissioners pointed out, "It creates a presumption that the allotted Indian is not to be a citizen of the United States,"[118] instead of the opposite, and put the burden of proof on the individual.[119] In effect, the Burke Act extended wardship for those Native Americans presumed not to be competent—which meant all Indians until proven otherwise. Tribal member Eunice Davidson reacted with offense when she read probate records that declared her ancestors and others "incompetent."

She saw the label as a ploy to pry land from Indian people. The law set up a double bind: either be declared competent and risk losing your land, or do not seek to be declared competent and continue to have no control over your land.

The consequences of homesteading, buying, and selling meant that by 1910, while Dakotas still owned close to their original allotment amounts, 99,038 acres collectively, Scandinavians had amassed 49,489 acres, more than any other Euro-American group and almost half of the land available for homesteading.[120] Scandinavians comprised about half of the Euro-American landowners on the reservation, or 19.6 percent of the total. In comparison, Yankees were 7.4 percent of landowners. Dakotas constituted almost 60 percent of the landowners, but owned less than half of the land, just twenty years after allotment.

* * * * *

In the decade leading up to allotment, Dakotas were suffering hardships but were also eking out a subsistence by cultivating gardens and planting crops on land near their homes. The Dawes Act and its sequel, the Land Allotment Act of 1904, created the conditions that enabled homesteaders to settle on Indian land at Spirit Lake at the price of Dakota dispossession. To citizens and foreign-born immigrants who could become naturalized citizens, the legislation offered an exchange of land for labor, money, and displacement of Native people. Scandinavian settlers moved onto the reservation, quickly became dominant demographically, and lived as neighbors with Dakotas.

As American Indians, Spirit Lake Dakotas could not freely use their land in ways consistent with U.S. conceptions of proprietary control. Because of the trust status of their land, allottees did not exercise autonomy or decision-making power over land, financial expenditures, or everyday activities. Living on a reservation created a sometimes tense, always dependent relationship with the U.S. government that was structured by law and mediated by the Indian agent and federal employees, which until 1890 included soldiers.

In contrast, Scandinavian settlers were freeholders. Divergent histories and differential legal status meant that Dakotas and Scandinavians both revered land but exercised profoundly different degrees of control over it. Indeed, the law empowered Scandinavians to act consistently with their belief in private property, which was the foundation of the legal system and the agricultural economy. Scandinavians and Yankees sought to own land for themselves and embraced the logic of land accumulation, which gave them a considerable economic advantage. Even though Scandinavians came as poor people, they devoted their collective energies to taking land and making farms. Those who failed or decided the effort was not worth it moved on.

Scandinavian migrants' and immigrants' lack of self-consciousness about being settler colonists—in effect, the beneficiaries of a giant land grab—resulted from their sense that they made farms solelythrough their labor and investment. With few exceptions, most homesteaders did not grapple with the ethical consequences of their actions. Unlike earlier settlers across the Great Plains, however, they could not avoid directly and immediately confronting the fact that they were settling on Indian land.

PART TWO

The Entangled Lives of Strangers

4

Spirit Lake Transformed: The Nexus of Schooling, Language, and Trade

BORN AND RAISED on the reservation, Bjorne Knudson told a story of his family's entangled world: "We had an Indian family...[that] lived right in the middle of our pasture. And he was very poor. He owned his own land, but he had a big family, several children, some very beautiful girls, and one or two boys. I went to school with the boys, so I knew them pretty well. Anyway, they got to the point where they didn't have any money to buy food, so he would come to our place every day at noon.... They did this for one solid winter, this family. Come every day, just like he just belonged to the place. My mother, she would set a place for [them]." No questions were asked, no overt invitations extended, but Mrs. Knudson came to expect to feed the family and made them feel welcome. Most likely lunch with the Knudsons was the only meal the family ate. As Bjorne put it, "times were tough" (see figure 24).

Central to Bjorne's account is the curious phrase, "like he just belonged to the place." In fact, the family *did* belong to the place; they owned the land on which the Knudsons lived. As tenant farmers, the Knudsons worked the land, cultivated it, paid for their use of it, and considered it theirs. Their logic of renting property meant they could treat it as their own, complete with boundaries and privacy. Yet their Indian landlord felt entitled because it was his land and his family lived there. At haying time, without planning with the Knudsons, he simply appeared and began working. In exchange, he expected sufficient hay for his own horses, which was fair in the Knudsons' reckoning.

Even if he hadn't owned this particular plot, the reservation was his. Norwegians took up residence, even ownership, but in a larger sense the reservation still belonged to Dakotas, who had rights to hunt and fish across the reservation regardless of who "owned" it. After a lifetime of living there, Bjorne still seemed startled by the action and could not let go of his logic of bounded property. From Dakotas' perspective, the Knudsons did not have exclusive rights. At the same time, they shared the imperative to feed those who were hungry and practiced reciprocity. So the situation worked. Despite their parallel lives, with the clash of some logics and the convergence of others, routinized contact on the reservation through schooling, labor, and trade meant that Dakotas and Scandinavians had to confront their preconceptions and prejudices about the other group on a daily basis. Historian Mary Neth found that everyday interaction could "undermine ethnic stereotypes and build personal ties among members of different ethnic communities."[1] Their strangeness to each other fostered misunderstanding, yet coexistence brought greater familiarity.

Through the nexus of commerce and common work, the two racial-ethnic groups came together and became accustomed to one another's habits and the sounds of their language. Through leasing land, they found a shared understanding. The stories of Scandinavian newcomers speak to the confusions of the encounter in this space that happened to be an Indian reservation. Both Dakotas and Scandinavians were targets of Americanization campaigns and resisted through their insistence on their cultural distinctiveness and use of their mother tongue.

OPEN LAND, BROKEN LAND

Norman Blue (b. 1905), a Sisseton-Wahpeton from South Dakota, called a reservation where white people lived "a broken reservation."[2] Indeed, the dynamic influx of homesteaders fundamentally altered land use. Parceled sections marked the platted boundaries within which homesteaders plowed narrow, upturned furrows, built fences to contain their livestock, and mowed wild grasses for hay. Benson County built roads, and the Great Northern Railroad laid track to transport people, building materials, and crops. By 1910 the open landscape of the prairie was buried beneath layers of trees, roads, fences, and farms, like an ancient village under volcanic ash. Louis Garcia pointed out that some landscapes became unrecognizable, in large part because trees disguised the subtle contours of the topography. "You look at the old pictures and you can see for miles and there's not a tree in the way."

As part of the Great Plains ecosystem that had sustained people for millennia, the area around Devils Lake had supported bison and waterfowl in abundance. Baw Jensen (b. 1894), a second-generation Norwegian who lived west of the reservation, recalled hunting as a child and seeing one hundred acres of geese in flight overhead, darkening the sky. The cultivation of the land and deliberate poisoning of rodents, such as gophers and field mice, affected the entire food chain. The decreased rainfall starting in the 1900s translated into a gradual receding of Devils Lake, which meant that fish had a harder time surviving in the increasingly alkaline water. Local papers proposed stocking fish and commented on the waning number of badgers.

The presidential proclamation of 1904 that opened the reservation to homestead-ing also designated 1,674 acres around the highest geographic point on the reserva-tion, which Dakotas called White Horse Hill, as a national game preserve. Dakotas protested that they had not sold the acreage to the U.S. government, and in 1909 they sent a delegation to Washington to contest and negotiate.[3] The following year Congress awarded the tribe $3,120 for the land, considerably less per acre than the homesteaders paid or the sale price of land set aside for churches and schools. In 1917 and 1918 the preserve was stocked with bison, elk, and other game that had roamed the Great Plains for eons. Second-generation Swede Mauritz Carlson (b. 1948) found it odd that the U.S. Fish and Wildlife Service decided "to preserve the buffalo. Kinda like a national emblem of how we conquered the Indians: We killed the buffalo." In addition to confiscating the land, the government named the preserve, "Sully's Hill." Like Mount Rushmore in South Dakota's Black Hills, the retitled hill asserts the supremacy of the victor in the midst of the vanquished, hon-oring General Alfred Sully who, as Dakotas saw it, dishonorably massacred Dakota women, children, and retreating warriors in 1863.[4]

Contests over place names erupted as newly arriving homesteaders embraced the popular philosophy that the West invited not only claiming and reshaping but also renaming. Writer Wallace Stegner articulated the sentiment: "It had no places in it until people had named them."[5] He meant, of course, Euro-American people. But Dakotas had names for places all over the Great Plains that marked geographic for-mations and the history of indigenous events—wars, tragedies, and miracles. Some places on the reservation retained their names and thus Dakota history. According to Louis Garcia, Shin Bone Lake northeast of Warwick derived its name from an event critical to the survival of a band of Dakotas in the spring of 1866: "Someone remembered seeing some buffalo fall through the thin ice and drown a year or two past. The Dakota rushed to the northeastern corner of the lake, where they retrieved the leg bones of the drown[ed] buffalo, cracked them, and boiled them in water to make a broth which saved the people. The shin bone, or tibia was one of the leg bones used to make the soup."[6]

Unlike Dakotas, Scandinavian settlers did not view the reservation as broken, but they would have acknowledged that the land became "pretty well broke up," as Gust A. Berg put it. They witnessed what they interpreted as indigenous cultural continu-ity all around them. In the initial years of white settlement on the reservation, coex-istence was riddled with uncertainty on both sides. Anxieties about this encounter were evident among the new homesteaders, who had intentionally decided to take land among Dakotas. Gust A. Berg recalled, "I was scared to death of them Indians because they said, 'they'd scalp people.' See, they made me believe that. And I was scared to death. Then the Indians come over there one day…by the name of Fox." Visiting with Solomon Redfox dissipated Gust Berg's fear.

Everyday contact created the conditions for familiarity and exchange. Cherrie Lane Wood reflected, "I'd never seen an Indian before.…And I had heard about the Indians and I knew they grew around there too." Then one day she was sitting in the barn while her husband was milking the cows. The roar of driving rain masked small noises. A Dakota man entered the barn and did not notice her. Initially frightened, Cherrie soon realized that "Indians weren't something to be scared of. I wasn't scared of another Indian in my life."[7] She lived on the reservation from 1907 until she died in 1979. Her daughter, Cherry Wood Monson, wrote, "The family had no fear of the Indian neighbors that they knew and did business with since they were friends."[8] Familiarity dispelled fear as the contact zone was transformed into a neighborhood.

Cherrie told a more edgy story about an open confrontation between her husband, Oscar B. Wood, and his new neighbor after he moved onto the reservation. "Oscar was finishing this second well when an old Indian [Wambdikuwa] came storming over and threatened him with a gun." Apparently Oscar's horse had been roaming around, perhaps on Wambdikuwa's property. The nature of the violation was not clear, but it incited Wambdikuwa to take up arms and show this newly arrived white whipper-snapper who was boss. Oscar greeted and talked with him. His daughter reports that Wambdikuwa "became a lifelong friend, and they laughed about this incident many times. Oscar's early training as a neighbor helped him thereafter in his relations with the Indians. Once his word was given, it was kept. The Indians learned to trust him. Eventually he formed many close friendships with his new neighbors."[9]

FROM SEGREGATED BOARDING SCHOOLS TO
INTEGRATED DAY SCHOOLS

The federal government used education as a major instrument for assimilating Indians as the Office of Indian Affairs mandated that Natives be "Americanized." Upon arriving at government schools, teachers cut students' long hair and forbid them to speak their own language. The boarding school system was designed to break the link between children and their parents and dissociate them from their culture and language. Attendance was compulsory, and those who resisted might be forcibly taken from their families.[10]

The local precedent was the Grey Nuns School, established in 1874 adjacent to St. Michael's Catholic Church. In 1891, the Fort Totten Indian School, also for boarders, expanded Dakotas' options. Because of overcrowding, some students were sent from Spirit Lake to board at national schools such as Haskell in Kansas and the Hampton

Institute in Virginia, which had been established for freed blacks and began accepting Indian students in 1878. Many parents "resisted sending young children any farther than the reservation boarding school," and some refused school altogether.[11] Dakotas objected not to learning English and literacy per se, but rather to the gendered twist that inverted notions of Dakota masculinity. Agent John H. Waugh expressed his belief that parents were prejudiced against the schools because they taught boys to do girl's work—such as milking cows, sawing wood, and, I suspect, agriculture in general, which was designated as female labor in the pre-reservation era.[12] Clearly schooling humiliated boys who no longer had the option of growing up and earning honor as men, as had their grandfathers before them.

The Grey Nuns, informally called the "Sisters' School," enrolled primarily Dakota children until they reached the age of twelve. In contrast, the Fort Totten Indian School mixed children from the Turtle Mountain Band of Chippewa with Dakotas, much to the unhappiness of parents and children alike. Indian agent F. O. Getchell reported in 1902 that "runaways were frequent and persistent. The principal excuse among the parents was that their children were abused by their old enemies the Chippewas." A skeptical Getchell refused to accept the charge: "I am satisfied that the greater part of this complaint was concocted by the children themselves, and was without foundation."[13] Parents were outraged over the treatment of Dakota children in the tribally integrated school. After children reached age twelve, they could no longer attend the Sisters' School, so the older boys would return home, in effect ending their education and losing the English skills they had acquired.

Members of the tribe advocated for a day school on the reservation, similar to those that existed on other reservations. Getchell reported that the parents "promise good things, if a day school were given them."[14] Through persistent lobbying, Dakota parents and tribal leaders persuaded a doubtful Getchell of the soundness of their plan. The Waanatan School, named in honor of the Dakota chief who had recently died, opened in the 1902–1903 academic year to serve older Dakota boys. Getchell reported that attendance was high until it came time for spring farmwork, when it dropped off.[15] A few years later, Charles Davis, Getchell's successor as superintendent of the reservation and former head of the boarding school, closed the Waanatan School, noting that its average attendance was only sixteen, which did not warrant an entire school. Thereafter older boys were either transferred to off-reservation boarding schools or stopped attending.[16]

Going to boarding school meant being wrenched away from family and being forced to speak a different language.[17] School officials would drive up, load children and their belongings in the car, and whisk them away. Hilda Redfox Garcia recalled the bravery of her father, Archibald "Archie" Redfox, just a "little guy," as his own father prepared him for the authorities to take him to school. Archie recounted his father's message: " 'They're gonna come, you're gonna have to go to school.' And to know this, and not be afraid, trust your parents, that it's supposed to be something good." Hilda marveled that "he wasn't afraid."

Dakota people I interviewed and those who participated in the Indian Boarding Schools Oral History Project expressed conflicting and ambivalent opinions about schooling. The Fort Totten and Grey Nuns schools were harsh and alienating, and physical conditions at these institutions facilitated the spread of dangerous diseases such as tuberculosis. At the same time, some former students said that they had learned a great deal (see figure 25). Bertha Demarce (b. 1911) claimed, "I learned everything from the sisters," including crocheting, rug making, cooking, and how to raise chickens.[18] There appears to be a significant gender divide in how boys and girls experienced and responded to boarding school. More women than men reported being obedient and liking school; the boys seemed to suffer more from the loneliness, harsh discipline, and humiliation of the system's rewards and punishments.[19]

Had they the choice, most would not have traded the physical hardship they suffered at home for the emotional deprivation of boarding school life. Demus McDonald (b. 1945) posed the conundrum that he found so confusing as a child: that "someone who was supposed to be so holy could yet…be so mean."[20] Phillip John Young, who insisted that he had not wanted to attend school, spent a year at Fort Totten Indian School, and after the death of the grandparents who had been raising him, he was sent to Wahpeton Indian School for the third and fourth grades. In spite of his reluctance, Phillip John said, "I liked it though. They were mean; they were no good; they were hateful. But I learned more underneath that strict environment than any of all the environments I've ever had." He recounts the teachers' punishments for speaking in Dakota: "They washed your mouth out with soap, and spanking…. They didn't want you to talk your own language."[21] In retrospect, Phillip John appreciated acquiring the tools required for economic survival (see figure 26). Similarly, Peter Belgarde (b. 1944), who had been tied to a chair so school officials could cut his hair when he first arrived, ran away many times as a young student, but also valued "the discipline I was taught."[22]

Alvina Alberts (b. 1912) attended the Sisters' School and insisted that she preferred going hungry at her grandmother's over the loneliness and harsh discipline doled out by the nuns. Their practice of striking a child's hand with the sharp side of a ruler broke several bones in her hands that went untreated. Alvina reports, "I was afraid of the sisters [at] first. But after a while I had a shell around me all the time, something protecting me."[23] While her parents missed her, her father insisted that she receive an education. He told her and her brothers, "I want you to go to school, all of you, and learn to talk real good English so they can't put anything over on you. You'll know everything they're saying and everything they're doing."[24] While she stayed, her brothers ran away multiple times and would be returned to the school by her father. Alvina enjoyed learning, but felt that boarding school was "so cold, so lonely, so like, 'What am I doing here? I don't belong here.' "[25] She recalled seeing nuns push children's faces into their plates of food if they did not eat. "That could very well have happened to me, but I was feisty. I just took that plate and shoved it, got up from my chair, and I stood back. That sister just looked at me up and down and turned away and never did anything. That was one thing we learned; you can fight back. Maybe that's why, like I said, they weren't so bad to us. Maybe because we were fighting back."[26]

Grace Lambert's account of her mother's experience at the Grey Nuns School emphasizes how schooling attenuated her mother's cultural ties with her people at the same time that it provided her with much-needed care: "My mother was always in the Sister School, because she became an orphan when she was eight years old. And she stayed in the Sister School until she was eighteen and she got married, and went home. So Ma said she never knew nothing about the Indian ways of doing things. But her grandmother, I guess, used to teach her lots of things after she was married, because she *had* to cook and sew and do the things the Indian women did."[27] Although the transmission of Dakota practices was profoundly interrupted, the rupture was not irremediable. When Grace herself attended the Grey Nuns School, she struggled with English: "The people did go to school at a late age in them days because it was hard for us to get started. We only spoke our Dakota language. I didn't even know a word of *yes* or *no*. . . . I had to learn from the beginning and that was pretty hard." Grace viewed her schooling ambivalently. People said the nuns "were mean, but I didn't think so. . . . I learned an awful lot from them." Looking back, she concluded that the benefits of her education outweighed the negative parts of her experience.

Crowded and hazardous conditions in the boarding schools proved fatal for many children; they acted as caldrons of disease and magnified Indians' health problems. In 1916, Indian superintendent Charles Ziebach reported, "The Sioux children have a much higher rate of tubercular glands, than the Chippewas. About 50% show some enlargement of the cervical glands. Twenty per cent show pulmonary lesions."[28] He pointed directly to the conditions at the boarding schools, where children were packed together and ventilation was inadequate: "As the children are crowded twelve to eighteen in a room, with just enough room between the beds for a small child to walk between them, the condition of the air when they arise in the morning is easier imagined than described. With so many in one room sleeping so close together, any infection travels over the whole room in one night."[29] The healthcare provided the children was utterly inadequate. The school hospital was full and the school nurse impossibly overworked. Staff turnover was unacceptably high in reaction to the severe working conditions: "There have been five changes in this position in the last year, and the present nurse is about to resign."[30]

Upon leaving boarding school, young people faced the disorientation of returning to a culture to which they no longer entirely belonged. Agnes Greene began attending the Fort Totten Indian School around the age of five because there were no day schools near her home. Her parents were "taking my brothers to school, and I wanted to stay and for punishment my mother let me stay in here. I liked it, till I got sick, then I came home." She struggled with learning a new language and culture. During summer breaks, "you talked nothing but Indian."[31] As Peter Belgarde put it, "It was almost a relief from a burden when you got back home and could be Indian again."[32] In her short story, "Four Strange Summers," Zitkala-Ša, who had attended boarding school herself, illustrates the limbo in which young people returning to the reservation found themselves. Her female protagonist says, "My mother had never gone inside of a schoolhouse, and so she was not capable of comforting her daughter who could read and write. Even nature seemed to have no place for me. I was neither a wee girl nor a tall one; neither a wild Indian nor a tame one."[33] Once back on the reservation, she dispensed with shoes and wore moccasins. She felt excluded from white society and wanted to sustain her kinship ties and racial-ethnic identification. Similarly, historian Wilbert Ahern summarizes a key contradiction of the Americanization project: "The reformers' expectation that schooling should result in individuals who had more in common with white contemporaries than with their home communities and relatives were naïve about both the strength of culture and the racism of whites."[34] Some Dakotas celebrated their children's education with give-aways, and others kept them out of the system as long as possible. Segregation from immigrant children was absolute until public day schools opened on the reservation.

Once Euro-American families owned land on the reservation and paid taxes, public schools run by the county and financed by property taxes were built in areas reserved precisely for that purpose—sections 13 and 36 of each township. Long before the battles of the 1950s and 1960s, the racial-ethnic integration of public schools unfolded quietly on the Northern Plains, with remarkably little national notice. Public day schools presented an opportunity for Indian children to live at home and learn with white students rather than be sent off to boarding schools. In October 1905 the Benson County School Board established the two public school districts on the reservation: Free People's (in Warwick) and Fort Totten (see figure 27). The 1907 teacher's report for the Free People's School lists ten students in attendance. The major complaint was, "We need a schoolhouse." Thankfully, the condition of the outhouses was "good."[35]

Tensions quickly developed around who was to pay for Indian children's education in public day schools. Since the federal government was perceived as obligated and richly capable of funding the endeavor, white residents of Benson County felt it was not their responsibility, particularly when Dakota allottees paid no property taxes. Downplaying the problem, in 1910 superintendent Charles Ziebach wrote: "The number of Indian children in attendance at public schools is very limited. Those children who do attend the public schools are mainly the children of parents who are practically white, and are not affiliated generally with the Indians."[36] Ziebach's disparaging reference to "inauthentic" Indian children regardless of their tribal status, and his language of bloodedness reflected the government's obsession with blood quantum and its constructions of purity. Unless the Indian Office paid Benson County for public school attendance, or Indian parents were full landowners and taxpayers, whites complained that Indian children unfairly attended school without the equitable financial contributions of Indian people. Political controversy over financing the education of Indian children intensified over time.

Some white people who grew up on the reservation fondly recounted their experiences at integrated elementary schools. Alvin Kennedy (b. 1897) remembered playing with Dakota children: "One Indian family, that lived about two miles from the schoolhouse, was a boy and a girl that went to school there. Louie and Selina Demarce." Patrick Langstaff recalled that in the 1920s "I think we all kind of got along together. When we went to school there…like Tokio, there was few Irish families, too,…and heck, in that school, Indian children went to school there, too, and there was Norwegian, Germans, and some of even French-Canadians went to school there. We all seemed to get along. We didn't shoot each other like they do now. [Laughs.]" His perspective is that of a second-generation German who married and raised a family with a Native woman. Integration and peaceful coexistence were values he held dear.

Dakotas who attended integrated schools did not characterize interactions on the playground as harmonious. Grace Lambert recalled painful comments made by white children with whom she attended the Grey Nuns School. "We were kind of ashamed of ourselves after a while because we didn't know as much as the white kids that went to school with us.… They would just make fun of us; pronounce how we were talking English. We didn't know the English well, so we'd say words real different. So we would quit talking English too and talked Indian.… They said 'Oh, you dirty Indians' and 'lousy Indians' and everything." As Grace recounted this experience of mockery and harassment to a Homemakers Club decades later, a Polish woman attending the meeting said: "Mrs. Lambert, I faced same situation myself. I am a Polack and we eat a lot of garlic and it smells.… When I'd go into the school room, 'There comes that stinking Polack.' [Laughter.]"[37] In retrospect, these women could see their shared humiliation in being targeted by schoolchildren because their ancestry marked them as "other."

The U.S. school system, whether run by the Indian Office or by the county school board, mandated that all children speak English. Agnes Greene recalled, "That was hard. You talk Sioux and then you went to school. You talk English, you come home, you talk Sioux. So when you went back to school, you had to learn again. [Laughs.]" Grace Lambert recognized the brutality of the system, but in retrospect thought it might have been the only way to learn. "I am very grateful that they were very strict with us.... They used to pound us on the head and everything, and pull our ears if we were talking Indian. That was the only language we knew! And so we had to learn the other language.... It was the same as a lot of white people, the immigrants that came over. They had to learn a different language too."[38]

As if to prove that point, second-generation Norwegian Gurine Moe (b. 1890), who grew up in Nelson County where few children went beyond the fourth grade, said about her schooling: "We didn't get very far. Three months in the fall and three in the spring. And we couldn't read an English word. When we come home our folks didn't speak English. We spoke Norske. So by the time it started [again], we'd forgotten everything." Immigrants' children were not sent away to boarding schools to disrupt cultural transmission, but they did face ridicule for speaking a foreign language and eating unfamiliar food, and were bombarded with Americanizing messages.

Not all day schools that immigrants attended enforced the English-only policy. The mischievous schoolboy bubbled forth from ninety-two-year-old Julius Fjeld (b. 1884) as he described learning English in elementary school. Laughingly he explained that only a few of his schoolmates in Nelson County could speak English when they began school. "We wasn't supposed to talk Norwegian, but we used to cross the road and we'd talk all the Norwegian we wanted to." Although they, like Dakota children, were forbidden to speak their native tongue, some Scandinavians had teachers who were less strict, or who were Norwegian themselves and tolerated a bilingual environment. Second-generation Norwegian Einar Severson, who was born in Nelson County, said, "I couldn't hardly talk a word. No. My mother, she never learned English at all.... I talked Norwegian right in school. [Laughs.]" Thor Peterson (b. 1913) started school at Minco: "I was lucky we had a Norwegian teacher, too. I couldn't speak a word of English when I started. She taught me, talked to me in Norwegian. Didn't take long to learn English." Norwegian was so pervasive in some areas that when Mamie Larson's children, who grew up speaking Swedish, began school, they faced a language challenge: "The children *all* talked Norwegian. And our kids, I guess they couldn't understand the Norwegian either. So, they stuck to their English, then. We had started English in Sunday school out home, so. They got a little English there" (Larson's emphasis). As children are wont to do, they ridiculed those they perceived as different from themselves or who in some way exposed their own vulnerability. E. R. Manning (b. 1900), whose father was a Yankee newspaper publisher, recalled making fun of children who spoke broken English, even though his Norwegian mother spoke her own language at home.

Like Dakotas, immigrant parents found reasons to resist the U.S. school system and used language as a vehicle to inculcate and reinforce their children's ethnic identity. Historian Ingrid Semmingsen found that Norwegians were skeptical about female teachers, the apparent lack of discipline at school, the unevenness of teachers' training, and the secular character of instruction.[39] Unlike the Swedes in this area, the Norwegians made a concerted effort to teach their children to read and write in their ancestral tongue, primarily through Sunday schools. E. R. Manning, who attended Norwegian school on weekends, most vividly remembered learning a few cuss words. Ada Engen, born to Norwegian homesteaders near Aneta, explained, "Mother subscribed for a Norwegian children's magazine that we read. They were anxious that we learned to read Norwegian so we could understand the church. Religion and Norwegian were synonymous."[40]

In their attachment to language and its link to ancestral religion, Dakotas and Norwegians shared a cultural logic. However, their skepticism about American education and value of learning English did not become an occasion to forge common cause.

THE LANGUAGE MOSAIC AND LINGUA DAKOTA

With popular anti-immigration campaigns in the United States, public opinion and government policy converged to pressure Native Americans and foreign-born adults to speak English and to espouse an exclusive national identity. During the 1910s, as war raged in Europe, English-only campaigns across the country heightened animosity toward the many non-English speakers. The federal government was well aware of the staying power of a language community, which was a major impetus for policies that attempted to destroy transmission of tribal languages. In 1913, 55 percent of Dakotas spoke some English; 40 percent could read and write English. At that point, Dakota was still the dominant language, and agency employees, including the farmers, doctors, and field matrons, had to have interpreters working with them. In 1914, Indian superintendent Charles Ziebach wrote, "The Indian does not understand and the farmer cannot explain it to him, which results in misunderstanding and disgust on both sides."[41] As an ethnic enclave, the reservation served a useful purpose for Dakotas in maintaining language, much to the dismay of government officials.

Language was an important cultural medium that Norwegian immigrants utilized to differentiate "us" from "them" in the process of displacement and relocation. Linguist Einar Haugen found that in 1814, when the country separated from Denmark, which had exercised linguistic authority, Norwegians made language one of their most important symbols of "national individuality and independence."[42] According to the 1910 census, 18 percent of North Dakotans who had been born in Norway reported that they did not speak English, compared to approximately 9 percent of Swedish-born and Danish-born residents of the state.[43] These figures only roughly indicate language use; just because people could speak English does not mean that they did.

In this multilingual environment, people sought out language communities that practiced their distinctive culture. Immigrants and Indians alike listened for familiar sounds and clustered in kin-based settlements that are visible on the plat maps. According to Mary Louise Defender Wilson, for Dakota people language groups divided along multiple lines, reflecting history as well as culture. Barbara Handy-Marchello writes, "Fear of losing one's culture to English-language and American customs or to other European immigrants motivated settlers to build communities with cultural boundaries."[44] In her memoir, Barbara Levorsen told of the joy some immigrants found in meeting someone from the same village or valley in Norway who spoke the same dialect and might have news of the folks back home.[45] As Lori Lahlum puts it, shared language and culture helped mitigate the extreme "strangeness" of the new land.[46] The language community solidified an identity and served as a means of transplanting ancestral traditions onto American soil.

But it also stigmatized foreigners. Ingemund Peterson felt the sting of not being able to speak in the dominant language (see figure 28). In the fall of 1915, he and his older brother headed to Montana in search of employment. "I couldn't understand anything, but Anton, he been at it for many years, so he was quite a English. He could talk. But the boss, one day [they] come and took Anton someplace, gonna do something else, and the boss come over to me and started to [talk]. I was just standing there. I had nothing to say....I was just like a dead horse, standing there." Ninety years later, the humiliation of not understanding remained etched in Ingemund's mind.

Some families embraced the message of acculturation. Lois Olson Jones recalled, "Grandpa was of the opinion that if you're in America, you learned English, so Swedish wasn't spoken in Mother's home." Evelyn Jahr Greene's (b. 1935) father, who was American born but grew up speaking Norwegian, would not teach his native language to her. "I would say, 'Daddy, teach me how to speak Norwegian.' And he'd say, 'No, you're an American. You speak American.'" He would speak Norwegian to his neighbors, but not to his daughters or his wife (who was not Norwegian).

In the 1940s, when Hilda Redfox Garcia was little, a generational divide separated her from her grandparents. Dakota, the language of elders, was spoken at home. Hilda explained that her maternal grandmother "would only talk Sioux," although she knew a few words in English. In her recollection, the elders intentionally did not teach their children. "All the older people, they speak to each other in Dakota, and we spoke English." In interpreting their behavior for herself, and for me, she explained, "They didn't want that for us, they didn't want what they had to go through." She told me a story about her mother's experience in boarding school, where a student had been speaking in Dakota and refused to stop when the teachers admonished her. As punishment, they "put her downstairs in the basement. And my mom said, 'I'll always remember her crying, "Please let me out, please...."'" She said, 'I'll always remember that.' That must have been awful." Hilda reasoned that her parents wanted to "protect" the children, so they strove for English fluency at home.

Amidst these pressures to acculturate, I was intrigued to find evidence of active opposition to learning English. Unquestionably, maintaining a foreign language in the United States sustained a separate national identity. Norwegian Americans debated the value of maintaining their distinctiveness, and some demonstrated their stance through action. Efforts to retain and transmit the mother tongue abounded in Nelson, Eddy, and Benson counties. Children attended church-sponsored "Norwegian Schools" even while enrolled in "English Schools." Lutheran church services were conducted in Norwegian well into the 1930s as people expressed a preference for what Semmingsen called the "language of the heart."[47] Many Norwegians rejected the prevailing American ethos of abandoning their culture of origin and disappearing into the English-dominated mainstream.[48] As Gurine Moe put it, "Those old timers from Norway, they didn't care for this English stuff. 'This Jankee stuff,' they said. [Laughs.]" They argued that the multiplicity of people who brought the best of their cultures with them enriched U.S. civic life.

Geographic concentration made it easier to reject the use of English, as well as to sustain cultural practices and ethnic identities. Ellen Sanvik Rue (b. 1897) explained that in 1915, when she arrived from Norway at the age of eighteen to work in Eddy County, she did not need English: "I couldn't speak English. I had to learn it. But then, most people talked Norwegian around here, so it wasn't too hard." In her memoir, Carrie Young, a second-generation Norwegian, wrote: "To me English seemed like an anemic and ineffectual language compared to the robust Norwegian. Stories told in Norwegian were funnier or sadder or grimmer."[49] Remarkably, protected as she was from mainstream communities, Barbara Levorsen's interior life and mental frame of reference was anchored in the Norwegian American community. "Though my parents were born in this country, and even my great-grandparents are buried here, I had become in thought and speech an immigrant."[50] Still, Levorsen recognized the shift that occurred after the Great War and the cessation of immigration in 1924 as ethnic groups succumbed to pressures and altered their identities and practices.

In exploring the transatlantic linkages between Norway and Norwegians on U.S. soil, historian Jon Gjerde found that immigrants and their children "maintain allegiances to the United States and to their former identities outside its borders."[51] Øyvind T. Gulliksen refers to this dual affiliation as "twoness." With a "twofold identity," immigrants could embrace their new country while believing that "the old world was not to be discarded but would remain an inspiration and source of pride in the new."[52] Norwegian immigrants' deep ties to history, land, and kinship in their homeland profoundly shaped their outlooks, frames of reference, attachments to their ancestry, and cultural practices in the United States.

In spite of the emphasis on conversing in Norwegian, many stories reverberate with intergenerational tensions in the shift to English. Some accounts emphasize children's adaptability and parents' encouragement, even if English was not spoken at home. Bjorne Knudson's father, Morris, found employment as a carpentry teacher at the Fort Totten Indian School and had to communicate with his students. According to Bjorne, he did not speak Dakota, but he did speak English. "He gradually learned from us kids, I believe, and neighbors. As soon as we started going to school.... My mother too, they picked up the English language." Immigrant parents feared being ridiculed by their children. Second-generation Norwegian American Mamie Larson recalled growing up in an adoptive Swedish home: "The old folks...they understood English, but they couldn't talk it. So we kids, we talked English to them, and they answered us in Swedish. They understood it...but they just didn't want to swing to talk in English, because they felt they couldn't pronounce it right. And they didn't want to be criticized by kids."

Rather than learning English as the standard-bearers of Americanization would have preferred, some people instead learned the language of their neighbors. This process was most often prompted by commerce and trade and by shared labor, although sometimes the impetus came from romance and kinship. Lois Olson Jones's Swiss-Irish father learned Swedish so he could talk to his mother-in-law. Second-generation Irish-Scotch-German Alvin Kennedy also learned to speak Swedish: "I got so I could understand quite a bit. The Mrs. was Swedish." Lois Olson Jones's grandfather, so urgent in his push to teach his children English, also encouraged the use of Dakota at the family dinner table. "I learned how to speak a little Sioux from him....He made friends with the Indians and we always had Indian people that...came for a handout, sometimes they came to give us something.... We had to learn to speak to them, as well as they were trying to speak our language." Mauritz Carlson reported that Andrew Zetter, a neighbor of Swedish heritage, "talked Sioux."

Grace Lambert reported that her parents could communicate with white neighbors because "they understood sign language and they used little sign languages too, to tell us what they wanted." When I asked, "Did any of them learn Dakota?" she replied: "Well sure, some of them did. The men especially because they did a lot of working *with* the men.... So they had to communicate all the time and help each other and everything. I think that was how they kind of learned to understand each other. But the women didn't get together as much, or often as the men did."[53] Their shared work drew men into the swirl of immigrant peoples using multiple languages. When I asked Ingemund Peterson how he communicated with fellow workers on a harvest crew, he explained: "Make motions," his effort at emulating an age-old Native system of communicating across language groups. But rural white women living on scattered homesteads were more isolated from non-kin, as were Dakota women. Even immigrant women engaged in paid employment were more likely to be in domestic service or farm labor. If they worked for someone who shared their ancestry, which was common, then the work environment was not conducive to learning English.

NODES OF COMMERCE AND EXCHANGE

While children from different cultures met each other in the local schools, residents on the reservation primarily engaged with one another through trade and labor. Businesses multiplied as the population grew, attracting and mixing people from various walks of life, and providing jobs[54] (see figure 29). The promise of development in the region inspired the building of the grand Benson County Courthouse in Minnewaukan and the stately post office in Devils Lake. Commercial centers sprang up to complement Fort Totten, the administrative heart of the reservation, and St. Michael's, the site of the Catholic mission and the Grey Nuns School, benefiting from the constant flow of federal funds and jobs. The two planned villages, Warwick and Tokio, joined Sheyenne to the south and Oberon to the west of reservation borders, flourishing as markets and transportation hubs and drawing both visitors and residents[55] (see figure 30). Superintendent Ziebach managed astonishing amounts of money on deposit at local banks: in 1910, First National Bank branches in Sheyenne held $24,973.13; Minnewaukan, $19,829.28; and Devils Lake, $48,451.80.[56]

By 1915, when Ingemund Peterson arrived, Warwick boasted a post office, a lumber yard, a general store, and numerous saloons. When I interviewed him at the age of 105, Ingemund vividly recalled "that day I come to Warwick" and the warm embrace of a greeting in his mother tongue. He conjured himself on the train with no English language skills and the conductor alerting him as they powered through Tolna that his stop was next. "I seen that old conductor, he was jumping around; he was like me is now." After getting out at the station, "I had to take my brown heavy suitcase down on the wooden platform.... I started down two steps, down to the sand pile there. That was all sand in Warwick, just like them buffalo holes.... I took my suitcase and walked down.... I walked and walked." He came to an old building, which must have seemed strange in such a recently built place, a "big awful building, with not very big windows. Then that was the restaurant. But I kept on walking by them stores, the grocery store and the barber shops, and the pool hall was on that one block there.... I couldn't see no one inside behind there. It didn't look like a store in Norway a tall. It looked more like an Indian [store]. [Chuckle.] All at once somebody hollered to me: 'Come back, come back.' He called me. I turned around and went up on the planks again." It was H. C. Hanson, the farmer who had sent for Ingemund. As things transpire in small villages, the train conductor had spoken to the livery man, who told Hanson, whom he knew to be in town, that Ingemund had arrived. "Hanson he come out in the door and hollered, 'Come back again.' Ya.... He was standing in the door, and I come up there and I took off my cap, because in Norway we always did that. Ya.... and Hanson said, '*Ta pa dej lua.*' Oh ya, he talked Norway and he was born in Norway. And he liked to talk Norway.... He talked English at home all the time, but oh, '*Ta pa dej lua.*'... He took me along to the restaurant.... We had something to eat."

Ta pa dej lua—"Put on your cap." To Ingemund Peterson, those few Norwegian words were as welcoming and delightful in the telling as they had been when he had heard them eighty-five years before. They communicated to him that he had arrived in a new land that rejected the formal hierarchies of the inland Norwegian communities where taking off one's cap was a necessary sign of respect paid to one's superiors. H. C. Hanson was telling Ingemund in no uncertain terms that in America such deference was obsolete. Even though he had hired Ingemund to work on his farm, they were on equal ground. That he could convey his message in Norwegian made it all the more meaningful. In effect, Ingemund was stepping into the uniquely Norwegian American world of the kind that Ole Rølvaag promoted—a multicultural environment that accepted the use of Norwegian language but was American in its egalitarian values.[57] With, of course, the immediate and striking exception of Native Americans and their legal subordination.

Central to cross-cultural brokering were traders and storekeepers on and off the reservation who had regular contact with Indians and Scandinavian settlers, military officers, and government officials. The *Warwick Weekly Sentinel* observed: "A large number of Indians were in town recently and while here did considerable trading. A good town to trade in."[58] Merchants knew when annuities and land fees would be paid to tribal members. To prevent unscrupulous behavior on their part, in 1905, Indian agent Davis used written orders to authorize purchases. In compliance with

Indian Office policy, he reported: "The undignified effort of merchants and others to sell to the Indians things they did not need, and at largely augmented prices, was reduced to a minimum. The Indians took their cash and went to the several nearby towns and made their purchases in their deliberate manner, almost universally paying their debts."[59]

Part of what distinguished traders on and off the reservation is that, like the early white settlers, they "engaged in substantial communication with the same Indians over an extended period of time."[60] As the Indian trader from 1877 to about 1912, Frank Palmer, who spoke Dakota and married a tribal member, functioned as a kind of cultural mediator. A Civil War veteran born in Ohio, Frank moved to Dakota Territory in 1884 and then worked at Fort Totten. Legendary as a mail carrier who had survived a deadly Indian attack,[61] he was in a prime position to seize opportunities as the regional economy expanded. In an oral history interview with the State Historical Society, his daughter Marie Palmer Tharalson (b. 1895) said, "Dad would accept grain or produce as pay for what the Indians purchased." He also accepted herbs, medicinal products (such as snakeroot and ginseng), and furs (such as skunk, coyote, badger, and fox) that he shipped to St. Paul for sale. "I guess there was an awful lot of crookedness that went on too," she remarked. The Indian trader was supposed to be supervised by the Indian agent. "But I guess if you're a friend of his, why, you get by with murder if you wanted to." By 1910, Palmer was one of the biggest landowners on the reservation, which lends credence to Agnes Greene's assertion that some reservation employees were profiting from their position at the expense of Dakotas.

In order to coexist with their neighbors, store owners and traders needed to learn some Indian language. The Jensen siblings' father owned a general store, the Wigwam, in Oberon, which sits on the western border of the reservation. According to the Jensen brothers, he had pretty good relations with Dakotas who traded with him and spoke some Dakota. As evidence, they told of an Indian woman the family employed to help with the labor-intensive chore of laundry. Elward "Baw" Jensen (b. 1894) reported that their mother hired her to "come there and rub on the board for her, name was Susie. And she was a good old lady. They liked her real well. But she would never eat with the rest of us. She'd always want to eat alone." Taking them into her confidence, Susie warned the family against Dakota women she thought they should not trust.

Socially, trade normalized relationships as people came in contact with one another and became familiar across their differences. An informal trader and beadwork collector, Lillian Wineman (b. 1888), of Norwegian and German Jewish descent, told about her congenial relations with Dakota people: "We'd say, 'hau koda.' They were glad when you said, 'hau koda,'" which means "hello, friend." Wineman, who lived in Devils Lake, made numerous trips to the reservation to trade and visit during her long life (see figure 31). Like other white people's self-descriptions as friends to the Indians, Lillian's claims must be recognized as one-sided. When I asked Louis Garcia how Dakota people might have responded to her, he said, "At least Lillian Wineman tried to learn a few words of Dakota. This must have endeared her, even if her gender protocol was not correct."[62]

F. W. Mann was one of the more successful merchants off the reservation. Grace Lambert attributed the store's success to its founder's character: "The old old Fred Mann that really started the store, I guess, he treated the Indians very good. And then he talked a little of their language, too."[63] He first established a general store in 1884 in Devils Lake, and his sons joined him in the business. His store was "where everybody went and traded. Clothes. Groceries."[64] His son, E. Earl Mann (b. 1887), described the business's trading relationship with Dakotas: "They never had much money.... For just the ordinary load of wood, as a rule, we tried to have the Indians buy a certain amount of provisions, the common things that they would want, and then to have some cash on the deal." The Manns were clearly in business to make money, and they were also invested in maintaining good relations with Indian people, who were important customers. When interviewed by the State Historical Society, E. Earl Mann cast the relationship between his father and Dakotas as one of mutual trust. "It seems to me in my recollection that most all of the Indians who came over there, they became friends. They were very friendly. We knew them all." At the age of eighty-nine, he could reconstruct some of the conversations he would have with Dakota customers. "We'd say, 'ta'ku.' Ta'ku, that meant, 'what do you want?' or 'what can I do for you?' And the man would say, 'wahpe'—it's tea. And you'd say 'to kais sa'pa'—was it green or black?" He recalled that his Dakota customers preferred black tea.[65]

E. Earl Mann provided some insight into merchants' accumulation of property. They could expand their land holdings by granting credit. While he defended the Mann Store's practice of extending credit to farmers as prudent, he acknowledged that farmers with large land holdings could run accounts up to $1,000. He asserted that some storekeepers used credit as a strategy for obtaining land from debtors who were unable to pay. "Eventually, the merchant went into the farming business."[66] John Weninger, a second-generation German and lifelong bachelor, is a case in point; by 1910, he owned 1,190 acres on the reservation. He came to the area in 1884 with the clear agenda of accumulating land. His store in Oberon helped generate the necessary financial resources.[67] According to Carl Goranson, people called him "Dutch" for his miserly ways. He owned "oceans and acres of land. He'd loan people money to buy it, and had to foreclose. Never hardly washed, that you knew of. Still he could cook the best pork chops and cook the best apple sauce of anybody in the country." Clearly a man of contradictions, he was nonetheless wily in his business dealings.

Even though the federal government prohibited the sale of alcohol on the reservation, taverns abounded in the towns, and makeshift gathering places emerged when locals trafficked in moonshine after passage of the Nineteenth Amendment in 1919. As third-generation Norwegian Barbara Levorsen put it, "Alcohol was the scourge of the settlements. Perhaps it was a blessing that towns were few and far away and were infrequently visited, as the saloons or 'blind pigs' were many and inviting."[68] Alcohol could often be purchased at the drug stores as well, as it was marketed legally for its purported medicinal uses. Drinking and fighting went together, stirring up an explosive mix in interracial interactions, particularly given the scandalous history of whites using alcohol to swindle and manipulate Indians.

Churches grew hand in hand with the saloons, although houses of worship tended to be more segregated than commercial establishments. Bjorne Knudson observed that at his church "you never see Indian people. No. If you do, that is very rare." Bjorne, like most Norwegians, was a practicing Lutheran. The U.S. government turned to religious institutions in the 1870s to administer Indian policy through educating and Christianizing Native peoples.[69] At Spirit Lake, this initiative translated into missions by Episcopalians and Catholics. Language played a key role in dividing religious congregations and reinforcing cultural divides between Scandinavian Lutherans and Dakota Presbyterians and Catholics.[70] Early Presbyterian missionaries had translated the Bible into Dakota and sought indigenous people to become ministers of their faith. A small Episcopal ministry survived, complete with its own cemetery on the reservation. In 1913, the more dominant Catholic and Presbyterian churches counted 300 and 250 communicants, respectively.[71]

At times religious affiliation seemed less important than the practice of Christianity. In the summer of 1929, while in transit between Fort Totten and Lake Traverse Sisseton Reservation, the Redfox family was visiting kin and picking berries. They camped at the dump grounds near Binford, North Dakota, where they would sometimes rummage for salvageable items. After setting up camp, Mrs. Louise Redfox Two Bear gave birth. As Christians, the family valued the spiritual importance of baptizing the newborn child. Given the high incidence of infant mortality among Dakotas, they urgently sought assistance. The following morning they successfully conscripted Reverend Mathias Borresen Ordahl, a Lutheran minister, to come out to their camp and baptize the baby (see figure 32). Although the Redfox family was not Lutheran, they warmly received Reverend Ordahl, who arrived with his daughter in tow.

Second-generation Norwegian Bjorne Knudson had contemplated the philosophical roots of these distinct religious preferences and peppered his explanation with his own interpretations of Dakota practices: "The Indian people are very superstitious. Yeah, they are. I don't know, they're different than the white people."

Through claiming whiteness and asserting difference, he explains his own cultural logic. "Now as far as their religion is concerned, I still maintain that deep down in their heart, they still prefer their own religion instead of coming to the white man's church." Mary Louise Defender Wilson put it differently: "Along with our own way, well then they also went to church."

Of course Christian religions can also be superstitious and mythic, which Bjorne might even concede. Scandinavians were not exempt from contradictory spiritual observance. A group erected a statue of the Nordic god Thor elsewhere in North Dakota, which Mary Louise reported was "on top of our sacred place. Well...at least they had some inkling that it was a powerful place." Even if some today would reject Bjorne's characterization of Dakota people as superstitious, his deep interpretation is basically right: many Indian people prefer their traditional religion to the Christianity that was imposed upon them. In their own narratives, Dakotas express both appreciation of and resentment against their treatment by priests and nuns.

LEASING LAND

Land became to Dakotas what cows were to Scandinavians: a key source of cash. When I asked Dakota Hilda Redfox Garcia how land was used in her family, she said, "It was leased out. To a farmer who farmed it." Hilda's grandfather, Solomon Redfox, received an allotment, inherited others, consolidated them, farmed, and passed the land along to his son, Archie. In Archie's generation, except for the lot he and his family lived on, the land was leased out. When he died, Hilda and her siblings inherited that land. Their ability to earn income from leasing land meant, in effect, that they became landlords to white farmers. Most important, leasing allowed Dakotas to live on a portion of the land but not have to cultivate it themselves.

From the perspective of a Dakota or Norwegian landowner who was not farming his or her land, renting it out was a smart strategy. Tenants paid in cash or crops—from one-third to one-half of the yield.[72] The landowner could either use the crop (e.g., hay to feed cattle and horses) or sell it. Tribal member Eunice Davidson reported that "a lot of white people leased land from my grandpa," typically through a sharecropping agreement. Dakotas' willingness to lease land to white farmers on a case-by-case basis provided much-needed income that may have exceed what they earned as farmers themselves and was consistent with Dakotas' sense of territorial use.[73] In this way the shared logic of letting another use the land in return for a fee enabled Dakotas and Scandinavians to find common ground.

The fervent desire for land that drove the passage of the allotment acts in Congress did not abate in the early twentieth century. Grain rewarded economies of scale, while cattle required more pasturage in an arid region. On the reservation, as available arable land became scarce, farmers who could not buy additional land turned to leasing it. Mary Neth explained: "In contrast to the South, where tenancy was almost universally an indicator of rural poverty, tenancy in the Midwest did not necessarily correspond to a certain income level. Midwestern farm tenants sometimes worked the best land and the largest farms."[74] As Neth pointed out, leasing land offered farmers a means to expand their cultivation capacity without investing money or incurring greater debt. The rate of farm tenancy all over North Dakota grew; by 1920, 31 percent of farms in the north central states were rented.[75]

Over time, U.S. policies shifted from encouraging Indians to achieve agricultural self-sufficiency through farming (the Dawes legislation had prohibited leasing allotments) to promoting leasing and then to selling their land to white farmers.[76] At Fort Totten, some superintendents saw leasing as providing crucial resources to Indian households; others worried that it created disincentives to farm the land. Nationally, Frederick Hoxie finds, "agents encouraged this process, pointing out that rentals provided their charges with capital for equipment and seed and suggesting that industrious neighbors stimulated Indian advancement."[77] Superintendent Charles Ziebach wrote of another advantage of leasing: "As the land must all be broken up, and as much of it bears considerable stone which must be removed, it is impossible to lease it for one year."[78] In effect, white renters could be relied upon to clear land, provided that they were offered sufficient incentives (e.g., a five-year lease), which would later benefit Dakota farmers by requiring less land-clearing labor.

Policy aside, it became a common assumption on the part of both Dakotas and Euro-American farmers that Indian land was available for leasing, for either pasture or cultivation. When Bjorne Knudson's father needed more land to plant, he rented some north of Fort Totten: "This land was Indian land of course." Cherrie Wood summed it up: "Yes, we rented land from the Indians quite a bit…until we did buy it.…Everybody rented." Clearly, she and her husband Oscar had a long-term strategy of land accumulation, and buying land from Indians met their needs.

The land-holding investment strategy of some homesteaders created absentee white landlords as well. The Bergs paid rent to a doctor in Iowa who owned the land they lived on when they were first married. They also rented from Ida Olson, one among several "lady homesteaders" in Lois Olson Jones's family who held on to their land long after they moved away. Lois's Uncle Albert Olson, who moved to the Pacific Northwest, also retained his land until he died.

As landlords, Dakotas had to collect rent, a task that was complicated by whites' superior legal position and Indians' subordination to the superintendent. From all accounts, however, landowners had more leverage in the bargain because they controlled a scarce resource and could find ways to circumvent the Indian Office. They could be choosy about their business associates.[79] These negotiated arrangements led to irritations and disagreements, as well as successful business relationships. Ingemund Peterson recalled his interaction with his lessor: "I rented land, a little land, a little hay land, a little farmland from him. So, he come to my place. I had that rented for many years so he come and got his payment. It wasn't very many dollars we paid for a piece of Indian land them days. But he come…and got his money.… So he'd come in the house and had coffee and a little bit to eat.… He was good enough to take his few dollars right from me; otherwise I had to get to Fort Totten and then he'd get it back there." This convenient arrangement saved travel and meant an annual face-to-face meeting.

This form of commerce necessarily built upon ongoing social relationships. Jack Reeves's father, Clyde Reeves, rented land from a nearby Dakota man, with whom he had a good relationship. Before this man died, he told his wife that Clyde Reeves should be able to rent his land for as long as he wanted. She honored that request. Jack strongly approved of this kind of honor. He felt that was how neighboring and business relationships should proceed. He also interpreted some Indians as "pestering" white farmers for money. As he saw it, Indian landlords would raise the rent and then farmers could not make any profits from the crops. Dakota landlords would come out to the farm to collect their rent, sometimes in advance of the agreed-upon time. This procedure differed from that of mortgages obtained from banks, which would be repaid after the harvest. One of Jack's friends told him that if he had known what a nuisance it would be to live on the reservation he would not have done it. Given the historical patterns of deception and exploitation of Indian people, Dakotas' mistrust of white farmers was reasonable. As the party with leverage and with critical income hanging in the balance, Dakota landowners had to be confident about outcomes.

The immigrant Norwegian Knudson family had multiple tenant-landlord relationships over the years. When Bjorne was twelve, his father sent him to plow a field they were renting from the recently widowed Mary Blackshield. She was one of a handful of Indian women who made efforts to expand their land holdings. When "dead Indian land" was put on the market, she made bids to purchase more. She resourcefully used her land to generate an income to support herself and her elderly mother.[80]

Because the field was far from his own house, Bjorne had to spend the week at the home of Mrs. Blackshield, whom he had never met before:

> Dad rigged up a set of a full line of equipment, horses and plow and a wagon and everything, and he told me just exactly where to go…but when I got north of Fort Totten, there were no roads hardly, just trails, and I kinda got lost. So I stopped along side of the road where an old man was plowing with

horses.... His name was LaRose, he was a French Indian, very nice fellow. He told me where to go.... So I took off with my horses. When I pull into the yard at Mrs. Blackshield's, there was an elderly Indian lady outside... plastering her chicken coop with mud.... She had mud from her face clear down to her toes. [Laughs.] But it was a kind of a yellow clay and that was what the Indian people used, if they could find that kind of a soil to plaster their buildings with, their log buildings. She knew I was coming. She says, "Put your horses in the barn" she said. "I know you're supposed to stay here and I know your dad real well." And she says, "There is feed in the bin." She says, "There's hay in the upstairs. Take care of your horses," she says, "and come in and supper will be ready."

Well, I wasn't too enthused. At that particular time I wasn't really hungry [laughs] because it just made me wonder what kinda household this would be where I had to stay. But when I stepped into that home, I got the biggest surprise of my life. That lady was all washed up; she had a nice clean dress on; everything was spic and span. There was a tablecloth on the table. [Chuckle.] ... She lived in a two-room house, but it had an upstairs. And it had a plain floor, not pine, but a fir floor. That floor had been scrubbed so it was almost white. And it was one of the best, as good a meal as I've ever eaten. I stayed there about a week.

Mrs. Blackshield had been "spotting" her chicken coop. It was common to prepare log buildings for the winter by filling the gaps between the logs with clay.[81] Young Bjorne knew that women working on farms got dirty; his own mother was a prime example. But he did not know Mrs. Blackshield, and he was put off by her initial appearance. In retrospect, he was amused by his fear of the unknown. "Mrs. Blackshield was a well-educated lady. [Laughs.] She had taken many prizes cooking and baking and exhibiting products like that on the fairs in the [county]. Of course, I didn't know this. I thought she was just like some other Indian neighbor that we had, just common people. But she was a well-educated Indian lady." He reckoned that he gathered the nerve to enter the house "because I knew that Dad would *never* send me to a place that wasn't fit to live in."

While Mrs. Blackshield did her best to make Bjorne feel at home that week, he continued to be intimidated by her mother, who lived with her. Education diminished the distance between Dakotas and Scandinavians, but there remained a huge gulf of understanding when facial expressions, customs, and cultural markers could not be interpreted, or could easily be misinterpreted. "I have to say this about her mother. Her mother did not like me. She could not speak English but she would sit and stare at me so I was almost afraid of her. Because I could understand why the Indian people didn't care much about the white people in those days. I imagine that was the reason for it."

The young Bjorne, who did not speak Dakota, and Mrs. Blackshield's mother, who did not speak English or Norwegian, experienced a cultural standoff. From Bjorne's perspective, an elderly lady sitting quietly in the corner who made no gesture of friendship must be angry. His cultural estrangement was mediated through a lens tinged by guilt. He inferred her motives for not liking him: "They still say it today, that the white man came into this country and took their land away from 'em. And they weren't reimbursed properly for it." Bjorne Knudson knew that Dakotas got a raw deal. Yet his family lived right there on the reservation. His father was employed by the Fort Totten School teaching carpentry to Indian children. His mother ran the farm that they homesteaded. In effect, their livelihoods were dependent on the dispossession of Dakotas and government efforts to assimilate them via schooling. Bjorne was aware of all that. So he interpreted the ancient mother's steady gaze as disapproval and dislike. "That lady was at least a hundred years old. She'd sit in a chair and she'd mumble to herself all the time. Now, whether she was talking Indian, I don't know. She was really an old lady.... She just sat in that one particular place. But I could tell by looking at her that she didn't like me. Uh uh. No."

What might the situation have looked like from the perspective of Mrs. Blackshield's mother? In her culture, young people were expected to defer to elders. She may or may not have liked him personally. Certainly she knew the horrors white people had perpetrated on Indians, although we do not know her specific history. The intimate encounter would have compelled her to exercise careful discernment about this young Norwegian boy entering her daughter's house and plowing her land.

Leasing could ease complicated inheritance issues, because if inheritors leased, they could share a divisible form of income. The fact of multiple heirs complicated the agreement for white renters as well as Dakotas, however. Patrick Langstaff explained that, if one piece of land was owned by multiple people, one inheritor might try to lease it to someone and pocket the money him or herself. "You had to be careful [laughs] you didn't get hooked into something like that. [Laughs.]" You could have dozens of unhappy owners asking for money. Leasing from a single owner "saved a lot of headache."

Meeting the terms of the agreement in a context of mutual respect was key to the success of this symbiotic exchange. Bjorne explained his philosophy of coexistence. "I went to school with Indian people. I worked with Indian people. I had Indian people work for me when I farmed on the reservation. I never had any problem with them.... I treated the Indian people like I treat anybody else, because they are human beings and they've got problems and the whites have problems."

In complete accordance with such a philosophy of bridge-building human relations, Ambrose Littleghost, a pipe carrier for the tribe, told me that the best way to

get respect is to show respect. He asserted that the gift one gives will return to someone in kind. He tried not categorize people on the basis of their ethnicity, but rather
tried to respond to them on the basis of their displayed humanity. He claimed that
he did not pre-judge others; instead, he gave them a chance to reveal their decency
through their actions.

* * * * *

After white homesteaders moved onto the reservation, the land was not all that was
utterly transformed. Human relationships were laden with baggage, carrying guilt
and resentment as they were viewed from personal vantage points shaped by distinct
histories and orientations. Scandinavian and Yankee settlers brought biases and
cultural preferences with them, as did Dakotas. Although these groups sometimes
offended one another, they managed to live together as they established farms and
raised their children. The reservation context required tolerance, as clashes of logics
had to be negotiated. Local institutions of trade—formal and informal, economic
and social—acted as crossroads, creating points of contact and exchange. In turn,
that interaction enhanced familiarity and reduced encounter anxieties. Lives intertwined through shared schooling, often uncomfortably. Some cultural mediators—
especially merchants and some individuals and families—made efforts to cross
language barriers and to reach beyond racial-ethnic divides. However much homesteaders made claims to the land, Dakotas continued to act "just like they owned the
place," because in a larger sense they did.

5

Marking Nations, Reservation Boundaries, and Racial-Ethnic Hierarchies

CURIOUSLY, ONE COMMUNITY event drew the dispersed enclaves together: Independence Day. Notwithstanding its ironies, this celebration of the moment when the thirteen colonies rejected British rule became the centerpiece of ceremonial life on an Indian reservation filled with non–English-speaking Dakotas and Scandinavian immigrants.[1] That the country's founding was based on the dispossession of Native peoples went without comment. The Fourth of July featured pageantry, American flags, and firecrackers. It was an occasion to race horses, play baseball, and stage competitive games. Everyone picnicked, a welcome break from the heavy farmwork of midsummer. Second-generation Hungarian Annie Hilbert (b. 1896), who lived west of the reservation, discussed the importance of the event for a region with so many foreign-born people: "That was the nation's holiday and they were proud enough to be living here and making it their nation. So they were very particular about keeping up the Fourth of July." In effect, folks participated in symbolic citizenship, which Nancy Cott defines as "an attachment to a political community."[2] Independence Day festivities brought multiple communities together across the ethnic checkerboard, honoring the creation of a new nation while ignoring the contradictions that lay before them.

Synonymous with this salute to U.S. history was Indian dancing. Numerous non-Native narrators recalled going with their families to Fourth of July picnics at Wood Lake or Fort Totten where Dakotas performed. Collie and Charles Stedman, among many others, cited the Fourth of July as the most memorable holiday of their childhood. Harriet Watts Birkeland wrote, "We never saw Indians in Illinois. It was exciting to go to Ft. Totten while the Indians camped there in the summer and watch their dances. They wore costumes of skins and bells and feathered head-dress when they danced and sang their war songs. They scared me but I found they were friendly."[3] Scholar Lucy Maddox writes, "For many white Americans, their only contact with Indian people was through the medium of performance, and for many American Indians, their only way of representing themselves to white Americans was through performance."[4] Indian dancing served as an entertaining spectacle for white settlers. Ironically, on the reservation, the Fourth of July meant participating in or watching Indian dancing.

Why did Dakotas engage in a pageant that they might well reject on fundamental historical and political grounds? Why celebrate the formation of a nation that had expropriated their land, subordinated them, and still threatened to render them extinct? Significantly, Independence Day provided an occasion to practice their culture in a context where it was otherwise heavily regulated and sometimes prohibited. The assimilation project deemed dancing a remnant of a "primitive" way of life that was to be eradicated. Louis Garcia points out that in the face of government policies to destroy Indian culture for all time, Indians seized with a vengeance on any occasion for sanctioned cultural observance.[5] According to historian Clyde Ellis, "Indian people use dancing to negotiate new social and cultural realities and protect tribal and community values."[6] Importantly, according to scholar Tisa Wenger, dancing was a form of religious observance that, depending on the tolerance of the Indian agent and how much he tried to regulate the practice, tribes could celebrate on their own terms.[7] Many tribes, Dakotas among them, argued that based on the constitutional right to freedom of religion, they should be allowed to dance. As dancing affirmed Dakotas' ancestral pride and honored their historical distinctiveness, the Fourth of July became the perfect forum to meet a variety of needs.

Because her strongly Christian family did not partake of Indian dancing, Dakota elder Grace Lambert had a unique perspective on the Fourth of July: "No, my parents weren't into Indian dancing and like that. They were more religious people. I suppose that's why I am like that too. But, since I was a kid that's all I knew.... So they never went to Indian dances *unless it was Fourth of July*. Then we'd come one day, just for the Fourth of July, and we would participate in their games and everything for the day. But we always went home. We never camped, but this place used to be full of camps." Because it was part of a patriotic spectacle, watching did not compromise her parents' religious philosophy and practice. When I asked her to explain why the Fourth of July was so special, Grace replied: "I liked the Indian dancing because I wasn't used to it. I didn't see too many of them when I was a kid. So when I got to be teenager like, I enjoyed it. That regular Kahomni, where two people dance together, was more like dancing the white man way. And I used to like to watch that because some of them were real fancy dancers. [Laughs.] It's fun."[8] These social events brought Norwegians and other ethnic groups into the audience as well. Meeting multiple purposes, they provided exotic entertainment for non-Indians, and provided an opportunity to practice and affirm culture for Dakotas.

On the reservation, daily contact regularized the encounter and exchange and hence the ground rules for interaction across cultural divides. As they became neighbors, they confronted and marked their differences in everyday life. Alfred Schuetz articulated the process of moving from strangers to ambivalent neighbors in a common place: "A face-to-face relationship presupposes that those who participate in it have space and time in common as long as the relation lasts.... For each partner the other's body, his facial expressions, his gestures, etc., are immediately observable as symptoms of his thought."[9] Amidst the ups and downs of agricultural work, mixed landownership, and community rituals, contact familiarized people with the practices of others on the reservation in what Schuetz called a "community of time." Allotment and land-taking patterns created racial-ethnic concentrations in the context of integration. Here, unlike segregation in the region, the co-residence of Dakotas and Scandinavians reduced their social distance.

While they could not remain invisible to each other, *neighboring* did not often accompany being neighbors. A social mosaic—made of oddly shaped pieces with ragged, sharp edges and definite borders—overlay the geometric uniformity of the invisible platted grid. Dakotas and Scandinavians socialized in limited ways, on special occasions, and attended separate houses of worship. As historian Mary Neth found in much of the Midwest, the "face-to-face character of neighboring practices reinforced these ethnic, racial, religious, and geographic boundaries."[10] The illogic of prejudice and its attendant insistence on racial-ethnic hierarchies, endemic to the United States, permeated the reservation, but not without a local twist. Historian Daniel Mandell observes that in colonial New England, "Anglo-American prejudice remained an unavoidable aspect of Indian life. This bigotry drew from a rich mixture of old fears and emerging ideologies."[11] Coexistence heightened some prejudices and tensions and softened others. While the superintendent in 1919 could observe that "the white people and Indians get along together very well,"[12] eighty years later Bjorne Knudson could concede "prejudism" on the reservation. Both groups ascribed distinctions of "looks" and "blood" as they used ancestry and history to explain their differences. Adopting a group identity necessarily excluded others. Over time, reservation inhabitants began to intertwine their kinship networks through marriage and adoption.

As residents of a common geographic space—still legally and socially recognized as an Indian reservation—they created a community of sorts within a structured enclave. Through ownership, they invested in the land, rooted themselves, and hunkered down for the long term. Ultimately, they forged a link created by a commonality of circumstance and off-reservation bigotry that lumped them together.

INDIAN DANCING, "INDIAN DAY," AND CHAUTAUQUA

By the early twentieth century, as federal policy increasingly emphasized agriculture, the Indian Office's practical concerns overlay its broadly stated political and reform principles: dancing distracted people from farmwork. Still, in the 1910s, superintendent Ziebach wrote with some tolerance: "I do not regard the old time Indian dances, as indulged in by these Indians, as harmful. They are not permitted to practice the dances which are barbarous in nature or harmful to themselves. These dances are regulated by this Office and they are allowed only at such times as will be of no detriment to their crops or stock."[13] Louis Garcia writes about the profound shift in masculine culture that took place once Dakotas lived at Spirit Lake. Men could no longer earn honor as warriors, at least until World War I when local Dakotas began enlisting in the army.[14] The purpose of the men's Peji Wacipi, or Grass Dance Society, was "to serve the people, set an example to the young men to have steadfast valor in war and generosity in peace."[15] However, given the demise of warrior culture, the Grass Dance Society's "main purpose was to promote generosity."[16] The Grass Dance continued to be performed on the reservation on multiple occasions.[17]

Dancing also occurred on "Indian Day," an oft-remembered highlight of the annual Devils Lake Chautauqua, a month-long gathering similar to a state fair (see figure 33). It featured educational exchanges, political lectures, and exhibitions of new technology. At the height of the Chautauqua movement in the early twentieth century, 12,000 sites around the country hosted events that drew an estimated 30 million people.[18] According to the 1907 program for the Devils Lake Chautauqua, Dakotas "came in full Indian dress, bringing their own tepees, and performed grass and war dances and displayed many of their native crafts and beadwork"[19] (see figure 34). Typically, Chief Little Fish would give a speech to an enthusiastic audience and the Fort Totten Boys Band would perform. Dakota elder Grace Lambert interpreted the events on the north shores of Devils Lake as an opportunity for cultural exchange: "They always invited the Indian people to come and do their Indian dancing and the hand games. . . . so that the white people could know that the Indian had sports too." But Grace never went. She explained that unless a family included performers, the difficulties of travel and the high price of entry prevented Indians from attending.[20]

Agnes Greene, whose mother was a powwow dancer, showed me a postcard of a dance troupe, her mother at the center dressed in her finery. "That's the way they dressed when they went to Chautauqua." She commented that white people in attendance would buy the outfits after Indians performed. Struck by the contrast between this and Grace Lambert's accounts, I asked Agnes Greene to confirm that in fact her grandmother and grandfather had also participated in "Indian Day." She replied: "We all did. We went. They all danced. It was *Chautauqua Day*, so most Indians went. They were camped out for two days or something."[21] For Dakotas who went to dance, it was "Chautauqua Day," not "Indian Day." Dakotas were Indians every day; they went to the Chautauqua once a year to perform or sell their crafts. In this regional extravaganza Dakotas were included, not as curiosity seekers mingling with the crowds, but precisely because they were different.

A meal was promised in exchange for their performance. Agnes Greene said, "They didn't get paid or anything. They went as kind of a friendship deal.... They just got along, then the white people will be there...and they danced around. People come and watched." However, when I asked if she thought, as Grace Lambert did, that the dancing was an opportunity to teach white people about Indian culture, she said, "To me it wasn't. You were there, you're an Indian, you can't change it.... [Laughs.]"[22] She saw her identity and practice as a fact that white people could accept or not. She felt no need to explain herself or to teach whites about her way of life, although she did embrace the performance as a goodwill gesture.

While the Devils Lake Chautauqua did not pay equal tribute to all the ethnic groups on the Great Plains, it did hold a "Scandinavian Day" as well. In 1906, a year after Norway's independence from Sweden, the Chautauqua sponsored a lecture on the history of Scandinavian emigration to the United States.[23] Unlike Indian Day, it attracted wider participation because a substantial number of Scandinavians attended the Chautauqua regularly (see figure 35). Nonetheless, impoverished people living on the reservation seldom went. Scandinavian Day featured North Dakota's demographically dominant group and extended a "friendship deal" to those native-born residents who might have felt some hostility toward the newcomers.

Like Independence Day, regional events such as the Devils Lake Chautauqua brought Dakotas, Scandinavians, and others into shared public space to celebrate the nation and themselves. Even as the reservation became a recognizable montage of nationalities, this structured ceremonial encounter affirmed their shared circumstances and revealed their bold assertions of custom and ritual-accentuated differences. Through this process, each acknowledged the other's existence.

RACIAL-ETHNIC GEOGRAPHY

Because so many in North Dakota were first-generation immigrants or migrants, except for Ihanktonwannas, everyone seemed a newcomer. Sisseton and Wahpeton Dakotas had lived on the reservation for almost four decades and continued to struggle to adapt to this bounded and stigmatized space. With the predominance of people born in foreign countries who spoke languages other than English, the question of ancestry and identity seemed pressing and immediate. The process of sorting and grading—locating people on a racial-ethnic map—created distinctions that necessarily excluded some while privileging others. Being poor and beleaguered—whether indigenous or foreign—stimulated antagonism, misunderstanding, judgment, and prejudice, but occasionally roused compassion for and collaboration with one another. According to Michael Omi and Howard Winant, when race cannot be located or identified it creates a "discomfort and momentarily a crisis of racial meaning."[24] The effort to classify and mark boundaries is a kind of encounter anxiety, linked to being strangers and reacting to difference. Because social categories are initially unknown and uncertain, the moment also creates contingent possibilities.

The reservation demographics made race-ethnicity, while constructed and fluid, a category with urgent social consequences. Anthropologist Dhooleka Raj notes that in conversation, people ask questions with the intention of marking difference or foreignness and then attribute personal distinctiveness to culture. Curiously, because cultural differences are so evident and in need of explanation, people experience a "nostalgia for culture."[25] Indeed, on the reservation, a fondness for an idealized past existed in tension with tragic events—especially war and poverty—that drove them to this place. People fastened their remembrance and interpretation of culture onto race-ethnicity. On the reservation they noticed national origins and assigned racial-ethnic identities at virtually every turn.[26]

What Are You?

Ancestry, or national heritage, acted as a vocabulary of reference, a mooring that located people in history as well as place, and invariably became part of the conversation with oral history subjects, whether prompted or unsolicited. In a typical, if forceful, rendition of this placing, Gust A. Berg, in his booming auctioneer's voice, bluntly asked his interviewer, Larry Sprunk: "What are you?" This probe into heritage assumed the ethnic geography of the state, where visible and audible markers of ancestry carried forward for generations.

Sometimes the query was confrontational. North Dakota Oral History Project interviewer Larry Sprunk pressed U.S.-born Cherrie Lane Wood about her complaint that all of her neighbors were Norwegian (see figure 36). When she began to list them, he remarked: "It doesn't sound like all of them were Norwegian. So you must have retained some of your Yankees when the Norwegians came in." Cherrie Lane Wood replied, "Yes, there's some. The Ruttens over here were Dutch. I guess they were German....But the Scandinavians really did invade this country. They came in. What are you? Scandinavian?" Clearly she saw her own racial-ethnic group as the legitimate inhabitants and Scandinavians and other immigrants as invaders.

In her view, Dakotas did not warrant discussion. Larry quickly assured her he was German, but Cherrie would not have withdrawn the implied insult even if he had been Scandinavian. She later complained that the Scandinavians had "gobbled up" the Methodist church in Warwick, so she no longer attended. Then she confided: "I got a lot of Scandinavian relations, so don't tell anybody that I said that." Interestingly, the hyphenated extension that we use to denote ethnic origins—Scandinavian-American or German-American—is dropped in this North Dakota conversation. Larry could have been a new immigrant or a third-generation German, and it would not have mattered to Cherrie, because the category held a meaning that endured into the present and was not simply a marker of an earlier time.

How did residents who spoke different languages become aware of the subtleties of one another's kinship networks, family histories, and cultural practices? When I asked Dakota elder Grace Lambert whether she had white neighbors near the farm where she grew up, she said, "Yes." I then asked if any of them were Scandinavian. Her answer revealed her inattention to the distinctions that preoccupied the Euro-Americans. "I wouldn't know. Right close to us, the next farm, it was a little farm, it must have been twenty acres or something; the white man's name was Woolsey. Is that a Scandinavian name?" When I said I doubted it had Scandinavian origins, Grace Lambert searched her memory, trying to be helpful. "East from where we lived was another man that lived there, a white farmer, and their name was Valinsky. Is that…?" I suggested that was probably a Polish or Russian name, not a Scandinavian one. This kind of ethnic parsing was not relevant to her social categories. "Oh, is it? Oh well, they were the white men there."[27] The Indian–non-Indian divide overshadowed ethnic nuance. The specific ancestry of Euro-Americans did not seem to obsess the Dakota subjects I interviewed to the same degree that it did Scandinavians and other white settlers. In reverse, while Scandinavians adopted the language of bloodedness, with few exceptions they were not attuned to tribal enrollments or band loyalties. Patrick Langstaff stated that, from his perspective, white people were more culturally distinct from one another than Dakotas were from other Indians. I suspect his position is simply the reverse of Grace Lambert's. Across the divide, it was hard to differentiate.

The interchange made me understand how profoundly parallel lives could maintain their detachment. It is not as though Dakota people did not take note of ancestral backgrounds. They were acutely aware of having to share the reservation and the Fort Totten Indian School with Turtle Mountain Chippewas, their historic enemies. They heard different languages spoken and knew that Scandinavians and other European immigrants talked about the "old country." Many recognized Norwegian farmers as a distinct category, but the racial-ethnic distinction between Indian and non-Indian reigned supreme.

Racial-Ethnic Hierarchies Based on "Looks," "Blood," and Economic Circumstance

The operating assumption at Spirit Lake was that appearance reflected "blood," which was presumed to be a measure of purity and authenticity. Among Indians, tribal membership, band affiliation (Sisseton-Wahpeton, Ihanktonwanna, Mdewakanton), and bloodedness were imposed by the government but were also enacted, as historian Melinda Meyer argued, as a form of ethnicity among Indian people.[28]

The reservation vocabulary of bloodedness filtered into Norwegians' discussions about ethnicity, race, and ancestry on the reservation, not just in relation to Dakotas. For example, Bjorne Knudson proudly announced himself as "full-blooded Norwegian," signaling his ancestral authenticity as someone born to Norwegian immigrants. Like all matters genealogical, the facts got more complicated when I started digging. While I was looking through the 1920 census, which specifies the birthplaces of a person's mother and father, I discovered that Bjorne's parents both had a parent born in Sweden.[29] In effect, that made Bjorne half Swedish. But his presentation of self, his identity, was tied up in being "full-blooded" Norwegian. I found numerous contradictions, decade by decade, as memories blurred and presentations of ethnicity changed, depending on the political and social imperatives of the time.[30]

The national hierarchy of racial-ethnic privilege had local manifestations and contortions. When Agnes Greene's son mentioned that there were Germans from Russia who lived in the area, Mrs. Greene exclaimed, "They were treated just like the Indians." Her son agreed, "They weren't treated very good at all."[31] Her comparison placed Indians at the bottom of the racial-ethnic hierarchy, especially in off-reservation schools and, as others have confirmed, at businesses in Devils Lake. When I asked Agnes Greene what she thought about her Scandinavian neighbors, she conceded that in general there was harmony. "On [the] reservation, they were all right. I mean, *they got along with us.*"[32] She centers the consideration where she thought it belonged: Dakotas' pride of place. She was clear about who should accommodate whom: Dakotas were the center, and white settlers joined them on the periphery. Whites might own land, but the reservation belonged to Dakotas.

If Indian heritage was considered shameful or stigmatizing, someone could use it as a slight, relegating another to the bottom of the social hierarchy. Marie Palmer Tharalson, daughter to Fort Totten Indian trader Frank Palmer (who was Yankee) and Maria Prang (a German immigrant), recalled in an oral history with the state historical society, "My mother was always accused of being an Indian. She was very dark, but she was German right straight through." Note that she says her mother was "accused," as though being Indian were a crime. Implied by the government push to "amalgamate," less was better. Similarly, Evelyn Jahr Greene emphasized the importance of "looks" in relaying the tensions between her father and her mother's mother. She explained that her maternal grandparents met "in a woolen mill in New York. [My grandmother] always said she came down from Canada. And my dad would always say, 'I know you're Indian.' And she would get madder than a wet hen. I mean, she didn't want to be.... At that time, it was not good to be an Indian." Evelyn thought that her grandmother's features suggested indigenous ancestry. As a woman who married a Dakota man and has children and grandchildren who are enrolled tribal members, Evelyn fiercely asserted the worthiness of that identity. She championed her grandmother's remarkable accomplishments as a midwife who worked alongside "Dr. Snyder here in Devils Lake. She delivered 163 babies.... She was somebody, that's who she was."

If Indians were at the bottom, pressed to disguise or discard their heritage as they moved in broader society, at the top of the racial-ethnic hierarchy were native-born whites who spoke English, the Yankees—or "Jankees," as the Norwegians would pronounce it, with a disdainful accent on the "Jank." Most came from the East and the Midwest. Members of this group ran the national government, held most state elected offices, controlled the public schools, and had the greatest influence in local politics. As the dominant group they were, presumably, to be emulated as well as feared. Memoirist Barbara Levorsen described her mother's antipathy to Yankees. "She disliked my speaking American, discouraged it in any way she could, and instilled in me a feeling of inferiority toward 'yankees' that has been a battle to overcome."[33] Clearly, her mother felt a modicum of defensive superiority over the dominant group, and was resolutely invested in maintaining her Norwegian identity. As a third-generation Norwegian American, Levorsen grew up in a household where that hostility and resentment remained strong as Yankees exercised their power to sanction, exploit, or exclude groups. "It seemed that the 'yankees' could take the settlers' good butter, fresh eggs and hard-earned cash, but to take their hand in friendship was another matter."[34]

Among Scandinavians, despite their numerous and obvious similarities, Norwegians and Swedes joked through their historical enmity and local tension.[35] Norwegian demographic dominance reversed the historical relationship between Sweden and Norway. Old World national rivalries, informed by centuries of resentment and colonial tensions, played out in North Dakota. Carrie Young, whose Norwegian family lived in the northwest corner of the state, writes: "We knew only a few Swedes and Danes. There was a much quoted adage, always spoken ironically and accompanied by plenty of laughter: Norwegians run deep, Danes run merry, and Swedes run best."[36] As she explains what she sees as the glimmer of truth in the joke, she concedes that the Swedes excelled: they seemed to be more ambitious and to assimilate more quickly. The irony was laid bare, however, in a joke told by

Norwegians, that the Swedes *think* they are better than everybody else. In a culture wedded to radical egalitarianism, obtuse self-importance was no compliment.

Within bounded physical proximity, social distance separated racial-ethnic groups, especially along the Indian-white divide. Mary Louise Defender Wilson observed that at Standing Rock, "These people…didn't have much to do with the newcomers." When asked about socializing with Dakotas, Gust A. Berg replied, "Oh no, not that. But we'd meet 'em like in Tokio or Warwick." When his wife, Annie Berg (b. 1899), chipped in, "They were friendly," Gust concurred, "Yeah, they were nice people." But they drew a line around social activities that few ignored. When Larry Sprunk asked her whether ethnic groups mixed at dances or social events, May Gunning (b. 1887) gave the same answer as the Bergs, an emphatic, categorical, and automatic "No." Some families on the reservation were known as "Indian haters," identified by Dakotas as people to be avoided because they were untrustworthy and generally hostile.

Other Norwegians on the reservation, such as Evelyn Jahr Greene and Ingemund Peterson, reported that Dakota neighbors would visit them regularly. Evelyn, who grew up on the reservation, characterized her parents as quite socially tolerant, not making racial-ethnic distinctions in who was welcome in their home. Their shared poverty was a powerful equalizer: "We were so poor we didn't even realize we were poor. Everybody else had it just as tough as we did." Evelyn's best friend was an Ojibwe girl who went to school at St. Michael's. "I don't think there was any dividing line. Really. Absolutely.…We had people that would stop by for coffee. And we always had…something to eat.…And coffee was always on the cook stove."

Cherry Wood Monson wrote about her parents' hospitality on the reservation (see figure 37). She recalled their nearest neighbor, Lou Merrick, whom they employed on the farm:

He was a Sioux with dark complexion and long braids. Lou returned to the Reservation after his years at Carlisle. Lou came often and for various reasons. Every Thursday morning Cherrie made doughnuts. On one such morning, Lou walked in without knocking. He felt free to make himself at home since they were great friends. Lou went directly to the table with the fresh hot doughnuts and said, "Have a doughnut, Lou." Cherrie smiled. She enjoyed cooking when someone enjoyed eating. "That was good," said Lou to himself; "Better have another one." Oscar came in and joined him before they started the activity they had planned for the day.[37]

This comfortable relationship evolved in the context of proximity and working together.

Living on the reservation marked its residents—white or Indian—as distinct from the surrounding community. My family told and retold a story about the day my grandmother, Helene Haugen Kanten, as a pre-teen, rebelled against her prejudiced, ill-behaved teacher. Because she did not come to North Dakota until the age of eleven, what little English she spoke was laced with a strong Norwegian accent. She was literate in Norwegian, but had attended school in Norway only to about third grade. Tired of being ridiculed by her teacher for inadequate English and by students who taunted her by calling her a "squaw," one day she exploded with frustration. She wrestled the teacher down on a bench, sat on her, and with a shaking finger scolded, "You be good. You be good." Imagining her as a big, strong farm girl capable of physically overpowering an adult was easy. But we marveled at the idea of our aged grandmother—calm, quiet, sitting with her thumbs twiddling or hands busy with needlework, and long grey braids fastened atop her head—unleashing her fury. According to the story, the teacher ceased to pick on Helene after this incident.

Differences between those who lived on the reservation and those who lived north of the lake continued for decades. Indeed, tribal members today relay accounts of business establishments that scrutinize them with suspicion or refuse to serve them. After living with relative racial-ethnic tolerance on the reservation, Evelyn Jahr Greene received a rude awakening when she boarded in Devils Lake so she could attend high school. "I was always considered one of those 'Tokio girls.' There was a dividing line, not that I was considered a Native…but I didn't have any money. I had one dress." In a school that required girls to wear dresses every day, that proved a painful stigma. "That's when I started realizing that there were different kinds of people—the haves and the have nots." The "haves," from her point of view, imperiously looked down their noses at others. The "have nots" were those who lived on the reservation—Dakota and Scandinavian alike.

Intermarriage, Adoption, and Bounded Kinship

Although kinship was rare in the immediate post-homesteading era, racial-ethnic groups eventually became intertwined through heterosexual marriage and adoption. In the earlier times of fur trading, military occupation of the continent, and an uneven sex ratio among Europeans and Americans, marriage between white men—Scots, French, and Yankee—and Indian women was not unusual (as witnessed among Fort Totten employees in the past) and served the interests of both groups.[38] The reverse relationship, of white women and Native men, was much rarer.[39] Scattered evidence suggests that cohabitation did occur between some of those Norwegian bachelor farmers and Dakota women that did not result in legal marriage. One of my great-aunt Aagodt's sons is rumored to have been among them.

But early in this encounter at Spirit Lake, first- and second-generation residents on the reservation largely avoided romantic involvement with "others." Faced with the choice, would Dakota parents have preferred their daughter marry a man from the Turtle Mountain Band of Chippewa or a Norwegian bachelor farmer? Inferential evidence suggests that marriage preference would go to a Native of another tribe over a white person of any ethnicity.[40]

Sociologists have long documented the power of proximity in marital partner selection. While Scandinavians and Dakotas shared a geographic space, they spoke different languages, worshiped at different churches, and recognized the social and legal chasm between them. Geographer John C. Hudson finds that marrying within the group "produced a kind of clannishness."[41] As Norwegian American David Davidson (b. 1944) pointed out, ethnic communities "stick together" in clusters, and "that's usually where you end up finding your mates." An observant chronicler of boundaries on the reservation, David nonetheless married a Dakota woman.

Norwegians tended to marry other Norwegians. Norwegian historian Ingrid Semmingsen called them "by far the most exclusive group on the marriage market, even of the Scandinavian nationalities. Danes were more cosmopolitan in their choice of mates, and the Swedes were intermediate."[42] The next most common practice was to marry someone from another Scandinavian group. As historian Dag Blanck puts it, "when Norwegians and Swedes started marrying outside their own groups, they became each other's favorite partners."[43] Those most likely to marry within their ethnic group were those with strong ties to their religion and language. Illustrating the power of bounded ethnic communities, Grace Pearson (b. 1903), a second-generation Norwegian, explained how she came to marry someone like her husband: "His cousin married my sister. So they had excuse to come down there. There was two girls down there. [Laughs.] There was four brothers, and my mother always said, 'How do you know which one you want?' she said, 'because they all look alike.' I says, 'They don't look alike at all, to me.' [Laughs.]"

This pattern of mate selection did not necessarily involve conscious prejudice or even overt ethnic preference, although it could. When I asked Bjorne Knudson about the importance of being in a Norwegian community, he replied: "I don't think so. We had English people; we had Swedes; we had Danes; all kinds of denominations. . . . I belong to the Sons of Norway Lodge, but so what? I belong to the Elks; I belong to the Odd Fellows Lodge. [Laughs.] It is all the same to me." But when I asked him about the ethnicity of his wife, he admitted, "She is Norwegian." In ruminating about marital choices, Helmer Dahlen, also a third-generation Norwegian, said, "I don't think they had anything against [others], but they liked their own people best, I suppose." He then generalized, "That's the way with all nationalities." J. Olson Anders tells a story of some Swedish neighbors trying to break up the courtship of his Norwegian father and Swedish mother. Before they married, the neighbors switched and stole her mail and tried to convince her that a nice Swedish bachelor would be better suited for her.

Within European royalty as well as Native American tribes, marriage exchange bonded clans, groups, and nations, establishing alliances and creating kinship ties. Once Dakotas were confined to the reservation with travel constricted, their marriage market changed. Tribes across the country had become concerned about land when white men married into a tribe, gaining the attendant legal and social privileges of kinship. Motivated by concern about dispossession via marriage, in 1888, Congress passed a law that prohibited white men who married Native women from inheriting their land.[44] Euro-American men and Indian women still married—for example, Ed Lohnes, a Ramsey County commissioner, married Chief Waanatan's daughter, Mary, also known as Blue Nest Woman.[45] Intermarriage could act as a hedge against prejudice or at least heighten accountability for negative attitudes. Over time, racial-ethnic boundaries were breached more regularly. In the 1970s, Norwegian American Berdella Overby (b. 1903) cautioned, "You don't dare talk about anybody now because they're intermarried." Living just off the reservation in Nelson County where tensions had long simmered between Irish Catholics and Norwegian Lutherans, she was concerned about the intermixing of religious groups as well as racial-ethnic ones.

Reflecting government policy, Indian agents urged Dakotas to engage in "Christian marriage," regardless of whom they married, which meant partnerships legally sanctified by the church, and to have only one spouse at a time, since polygamy had been a Dakota practice. In 1920 Indian superintendent Samuel Young reported, "It appears to me there is less intermarriage between the Indians and the Whites than formerly, but that the two races are coming to understand each other better."[46] Some Indian Office employees not so subtly said, as William Beyer did in his 1927 annual report, "Intermarriages will be the logical solution of the Indian problem."[47] He lamented that there had not been a great deal of "intermingling of races."[48] Despite social condemnation of intermarriage, government officials envisioned the dilution of Native culture when Indians married non-Indians and assumed that in the long run Euro-American culture would prevail and Indians would blend into white society. Unlike marriage between blacks and whites, the government sanctioned marriage between non-Indians and Indians.[49]

Prior to 1930, Scandinavian-Dakota marriages were rare and intermarriage between Indians and whites remained highly controversial in both groups. Describing his enclave on the northern part of the reservation, Ingemund Peterson referred to several intermarriages, historically more common, between French Canadians and

Metis or Ojibwe. There was "even one Norwayan." In the early 1910s, Norwegian immigrant Peter Fields married Mary Jane Bergie, an Indian woman fifteen years his junior. When field matron Carrie Pohl visited their household, she would distinctly note her full name: Mary Jane Bergie Fields.[50] Clearly the union rankled her. Tribal member Henry Buisson's second wife was Ingeborg Neilson, a Norwegian immigrant, with whom he had two children.[51]

Unions across racial-ethnic boundaries meant a change in identity in subsequent generations. They created a deeper kind of intimacy. But they did not, and could not bridge all the gaps and social divides, even with the link of kinship. In fact, they complicated rather than erased them. David Davidson spoke of the pain his grandson felt when he discovered that David was white. As a young boy, the child had not noticed. Of course he loved his grandfather, who married and had children with Eunice Abraham Davidson, who was a tribal member. The boy burst into tears when David explained his Norwegian ancestry to him. He protested, " 'No, Grandpa isn't white. He isn't white!" He had been brought up in an environment that included the embrace of his interracial grandparents, but whites were enemies to be avoided, not the people you loved.

Adoption, a common practice in the nineteenth and early twentieth centuries, filtered through many of the narrators' stories as another way that racial-ethnic boundaries were crossed or maintained. As sociologist Viviana Zelizer argues, in agricultural societies the labor of minors, especially teenaged boys, made children valuable additions to the household economy.[52] With high rates of maternal mortality, care for orphans was often provided through adoption. Dakotas' practice of incorporating children into the tribe reflected their expectation that children who needed a home would find one. The mysterious presence of Irish Mike, a white baby who was adopted into the tribe, prompted competing explanations. Some posited that he may have been taken in an Indian raid. Second-generation Swede Mauritz Carlson reasoned that occasionally white people heading west in covered wagons contracted smallpox and died, leaving a nursing baby who might survive until rescued by a passerby. One Dakota version of the story, documented by Louis Garcia, suggests that the infant was simply abandoned on the prairie, found by Dakotas, and brought up by the tribe.[53]

Because of high mortality rates, large families, and inadequate resources, adoption was common within Scandinavian families as well, although perhaps without the inclusiveness that Dakotas practiced. There were no stories of Scandinavians adopting Indian children, or vice versa.[54] Second-generation Norwegian Dagny Skurdell Bilden was four years old when her mother became ill with "dropsy," was hospitalized, and was warned that her prognosis was dire. She conveyed the casual way that adoption was anticipated and discussed:

Concerned that she hadn't improved, she visited Dr. Bennett at Aneta, with me clinging to her skirts. I heard her ask the doctor, "And if I die, what will become of my children?" He replied, "Well, I'd like to have a little girl, so I could take this one!" I was frightened and began to cry, for surely I didn't want to be separated from my family. Thank God, Mother started improving, and in several months she was back hard at work. She lived to be seventy-eight years old. She had made new black dresses for all the girls, so that they would have been prepared for her funeral, if she had passed away.[55]

Other stories had less happy endings. Evelyn Jahr Greene tells about the childhood of her father, Nicholas Jahr, born to Norwegian immigrants in Wisconsin. His mother died when he was about seven, so his father, Cristian Jahr, who worked in lumber camps, pulled him and his older brother out of school and sent them to a farm in South Dakota. The boys, then in third and fourth grade, worked for their room and board until they came of age. Nicholas later moved to North Dakota and homesteaded thirty-six acres on the reservation, where his father later joined him.

Mamie Vik Larson, whose parents left Norway for Jamestown, North Dakota, suffered a different kind of family dismemberment. Her mother contracted typhoid fever from drinking river water and died in 1888, when Mamie was four years old. Like Cristian Jahr, Mamie's father could not care for the three children himself and continue working, yet he was deeply reluctant to give them up for adoption. He found homes for them, but not in the same place. Mamie's sister was taken in by a lawyer's family in Jamestown. Mamie and her brother, Bruce, were sent to Sheyenne to live with a successful Swedish family, the Mattsons. Mamie tells the story:

Father had just filed on three quarters of land right outside of Jamestown that we were moving on that spring, when mother died.... So, of course, he had to let go of the children. Well, after we had gone up here, then Mrs. Mattson and the lawyer there, they wanted to adopt all three of us, which he should have done. But he just couldn't just see it that way; he thought he was going to get us children back. And of course we stayed on and on, and he had all kinds of trouble getting started on his farms. And so I grew up here, [with] the Mattson family.

Despite her father's desire to keep his family together, he could not. His temporary solution, fed by his reluctance to release legally his children, turned into a decade of hardship and separation. In retrospect (and perhaps at the time), Mamie could see the advantages of regular adoption and realized that she could have more easily made the transition had her father simply let go and admitted he could not care for them. Instead, she spent her childhood in limbo, never quite belonging to the Mattson family and always yearning for her father.

THE TENSIONS OF MUTUALITY AND PERCEPTIONS OF INEQUALITY

Mutual aid was the bedrock of survival on the plains, both among Native peoples and among Scandinavian immigrants. The notion of a self-sufficient household fails to capture the full picture of economic and social interdependence on the reservation. As anthropologist Seena Kohl cautioned, "Many discussions of frontier settlement have emphasized pioneer characteristics of individualism and self-reliance. However, it is important to remember that cooperation and mutual aid were as common and certainly as important for survival."[56] Mary Neth contended that farm people were embedded in this web of interdependence and "understood their lives through these social relationships, created by social interaction and by the labor that dominated their lives."[57] Dakota elder Mary Louise Defender Wilson discussed the tension within Dakota culture between individualism and collectivity, both of which were important. "You had to learn to be yourself and not be worried about what someone else was going to say to you, or . . . [that] they might make fun of you." She asserted that individuals had to "state [their] views on matters that are important to the people. And try to have discussion about it." The cultural logics of Dakota life demanded both: "We have stories about when you must work together as a group and then when you should be individualistic."

Did becoming neighbors mean being *neighborly* with each other? While ethnic differences abounded and boundaries were enforced, poverty was a great equalizer. As Gust A. Berg put it, "Pret near everybody was alike. There was nobody had anything." The standard of living was low but appeared relatively equal across the Euro-American and Scandinavian groups. Most whites were farmers, even though some families owned more land and some had more resources to utilize it. Hardship was expected, and people judged their own circumstances by the community standard of living. The perception that "everybody was alike" fell apart when Indians were incorporated into the picture. Group solidarity that helped build a Scandinavian community simultaneously excluded Dakotas. Their safety net came from kin, the local community, the church, and, for Indians in desperate need, sometimes the government.

For both Scandinavians and Dakotas, hardship was a state of mind as well as a set of conditions we could try to measure. Retrospective accounts are necessarily refracted through political and economic change. Now that consumer goods have become a marker of status and well-being, it is difficult to imagine life without them. After the Great Depression and World War II, with the increased availability of consumer goods and greater disposable income, what people owned became more of a visible standard they used to assess their own well-being and compare themselves to others. In his novel *Growth of the Soil* (1917), Nobel laureate Knut Hamsun explored the mind-set of settlers in the north of Norway that found parallels in North America. "The settlers didn't make themselves suffer on account of goodies they hadn't got; art, newspapers, luxuries, politics were worth exactly as much as people were willing to pay for them, no more; the growth of the soil, on the other hand, had to be procured at any cost. It was the origin of all things, the only source. The settlers' lives sad and empty? Ho, that least of all! They had their higher powers, their dreams, their loves, their wealth of superstition."[58]

In the early twentieth century, surrounded by poverty, most white people on the reservation did not feel deprived. They carefully observed one another's land use and crop yields, learning from each other as they also judged one another. At the same time, they were reluctant to call attention to themselves for being outstanding or inadequate.

Providing sufficient food for the family was an accomplishment, and as people cast their eyes about, they saw others struggling as they were. Some likened ethnicity to a class category that trumped other distinctions. As Cyrene Bakke Dear wrote, "There was not much class distinction in those days. Most of us were Norwegian."[59] She understood that not helping someone in trouble could mean immeasurable suffering. Farm families produced almost all of the food they consumed, and having enough to eat was a measure of well-being. The Knudson family "always had plenty. We never were out of food." Shirley Kanten told a story about her father exploring land for his family in Saskatchewan. "They lived in just a shack, but... he said, 'We had plenty to eat. For breakfast we had bread and milk, for dinner we had milk and bread, and for supper we had both'! [Laughs.]"

That sense of well-being was not always shared by Dakotas. The appeal of boarding school's three meals a day reflected their greater food insecurity. From Grace Lambert's perspective, the relative equality of circumstance on the reservation was undermined by racial-ethnic differences in class position. Indians had fewer resources than whites, which made all aspects of agricultural labor more difficult. Capital translated into equipment: "They did have wind mills, which we didn't have. We pulled our water up by pulley, with a rope. And we dropped the rope down with the bucket so it would sink in and get full of water and then we would pull it up." For women, whose job it was to haul water to the house, this difference had daily consequences. Buckets filled with water were heavy—a full five gallons weighed forty pounds—and burdened those who had to carry them to the house or the barn. Grace Lambert also observed the differences in the scale of farm operations. Referring to white farmers, she said, "They had great big troughs because they had way more cattle than just one cow." Dakotas did not keep enough chickens to sell eggs: "Whereas a white farmer probably had maybe a hundred chickens.... So they can afford to sell some and eat. But the Indian had only twenty.... If there was nothing else to eat they'd have to eat all the twenty eggs in one day and they wouldn't have nothing left to sell."[60]

At the same time, Lambert was aware of the difficulties whites faced in farm making: "Well, they were struggling too, just the same as we were. They weren't any richer than we were, but we didn't know it at the time. But now when I think about it they were starting too.... And so it was kinda hard for them too."[61] In retrospect she realized that land-holding whites occupied only a marginally better economic status than Dakotas, but it still generated resentment.

With great equality of circumstance and without abundance, kin and neighbors provided the primary safety net in times of shortage or crisis. Domestic goods that were produced and distributed by women were central to community exchange and give-aways.[62] Participation, discretion, and control in that system of redistribution can be understood as a kind of efficacy. Sociologist Rosabeth Moss Kanter finds *efficacy* to be a more appropriate term than *power*, because it conveys "the ability to mobilize resources…rather than domination"[63] She elaborates that efficacy "accumulates" through activities and alliances. If we conceive of mutuality and neighborliness as a gendered type of efficacy, then we can also think of withholding help as a means of asserting division. Both were manifest in everyday interactions.

Like Scandinavians, Dakota households were "embedded in extended-family networks which functioned as important reproductive units,"[64] as anthropologist Patricia Albers puts it. Dakota women were the linchpins of those networks, placing them at the crux of reservation social life. As neighbors, women's gifts and exchange were not fleeting but were part of a sustained mutuality. Receiving help—in the form of goods, labor, advice, and support—obligated recipients to give later on. Their connections with others also gave women leverage in their intimate relations. Other studies have shown that community involvement weakened the ability of male heads of household to exercise arbitrary authority and behave abusively.[65]

In effect, mutuality was a long-term strategy for survival and a key foundation for women's position within families and in the community. The question remains: Did Dakota and Scandinavian women share resources, knowledge, and labor in a reciprocal way? Bjorne Knudson recalled, "There was hardly any welfare that I can think of when I was a youngster. If you didn't have any means to buy food you just went without food. And the Indian people were the same way." He told of multiple instances when his family exchanged food and labor with their Dakota neighbors and landlords. Dakota elder Agnes Greene talked about the safety net that was based on neighbors helping neighbors in need and returning the favor when their positions were reversed: "We had good neighbors. They'd give us some, so we always had it. [Laughs.]... You help each other. You give them some money then or something. Then [later] they help you."[66]

Exchange across racial-ethnic lines was sometimes a gesture of mutuality and at other times a payment for labor. Near the southwestern corner of the reservation, the Swedish Carlsons were neighbors of Joe Irish (son of Irish Mike), who had a spring on his land. Blenda Carlson (b. 1930) recalled how her family, who had no spring, simply helped themselves to Joe's spring water. They admitted that someone else—for example, a white person—might have charged them a use fee. But Joe Irish did not. In turn, the Carlsons did not charge the Irishes for the corn they took from their fields, which they regularly did. It was a mutually agreed-upon exchange that was not formalized or written down, but taken for granted. E. R. Manning, whose mother was Norwegian, recalled weekly contact that involved the exchange of food for moccasins, not tit for tat, but over time: "Indians were very close to us. They'd come in.... a woman by the name Annie Grey Wind, and she'd always come in about noon, not every week, but quite often. I was just a kid. Mother would set the table, and we'd all eat together. She would eat with us, and she had a couple of kids. Then Mother would give her some of our cast off clothing.... And she'd always give us moccasins. So I had moccasins, I'd wear moccasins all the time." Grace Lambert recalled how white folks "would come and bring us all kinds of stuff like [jelly], and sometimes we worked for that, instead of money. Maybe they might give us a couple chickens too or something."[67]

The Woods were large Yankee landowners who lived in a Dakota enclave and employed Dakota laborers on the farm and in their household. According to Cherrie Lane Wood, she and her young Dakota neighbor, Elizabeth, were helpful to each other:

Seldom did Cherrie need to ask Elizabeth to help her. When Elizabeth saw a need, she quickly and efficiently took care of the problem. A pot on the stove needed stirring and Elizabeth would probably finish the meal. The baby needed a bath and she would spend a great deal of time caring for the youngster with no thought of pay other than friendship. No doubt these two learned much from each other since they had such diverse backgrounds. Circumstances had provided them with an opportunity to discover and enjoy their different cultures. Often Elizabeth would explain an Indian custom. Cherrie would listen and learn. She was fascinated with the stories of Indian life. She learned many of the words of the Sioux language, but she never mastered it.[68]

This story, while told from the Woods' perspective, reveals that both parties made an effort to extend themselves, to reach beyond the comfort of their accustomed way of living. Elizabeth was neighborly, kind, and helpful. She must have seen the Wood family as providing some resources for her as well. No comparable stories exist of Cherrie going to visit Elizabeth and helping her with cooking or childcare; we do not know the story from Elizabeth's perspective.

A potential breach in the relationship surfaced many years later when Elizabeth confessed to Cherrie and Oscar that she had been taking sugar from them over the years. "Cherrie was surprised. Stealing was not acceptable in Cherrie's world, but it was a way of life for Elizabeth. The girl continued, 'Every time you left, I came in with my paper sack and filled it.' Cherry eventually found it easy to distinguish between early day Indian thefts and early day white thefts. If you left sixteen dollars on the table, a white man would take it all. An Indian would maybe take four dollars and leave you twelve."[69] The neighbors did have something to offer. Elizabeth acted on her notion of appropriate redistribution of scarce resources—in this case, sugar. Her action revealed that she thought the Woods family had a surplus, which must have been true since Cherrie did not notice the pilfering. Elizabeth may have seen the sugar as payment for the labor she clearly contributed to the household. Interestingly, in a confessional sign of friendship, Elizabeth eventually told Cherrie of her deeds.

Under conditions of dire hardship, caregiving was an important skill that was shared, sometimes across racial-ethnic lines. The Carlsons told about how Dakota artist Peter Black Cloud credited them with saving his child's life. In return for advice for treating the croup and later a ride to the doctor's office, he gave them one of his paintings. The poverty that ravaged so many Indian households was accompanied by endemic diseases that did not affect Scandinavian settlers to the same degree. Dakota tribal member Alvina Alberts fondly recalled her aunt who had become a healer. She learned home remedies from white folks and "Indian ways of healing" from her mother, whom she described as "quite the woman."[70]

With determination and resourcefulness, healers and midwives cared for others. Professional healers such as Dr. Carter in Warwick treated Dakota patients, and they would bestow treasured items in payment and gratitude. His next-door neighbor, Marion Skurdall, remembered Mrs. Carter hanging a full feather headdress on the clothesline to dry in the backyard.[71]

RACE-ETHNICITY AND GENDER IN PATTERNS OF LAND HOLDING

Land, platted and parcelized, gave material heft to the dividing line between haves and have-nots. By rooting kinship deeply in landowning, residence and cultivation brought people together and drove them apart. In 1910, six years after the reservation was opened to white settlement, the two largest landowning groups were Dakotas

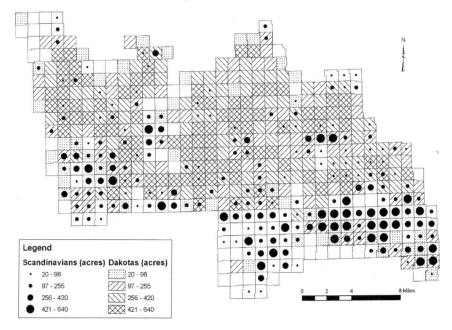

MAP 4 GIS Map of Scandinavian and Dakota landownership, 1910.
Generated using Geographic Information Systems (GIS), with a database developed from plat maps. This map arrays racial-ethnic concentrations of land ownership on the Spirit Lake Dakota Reservation.

and Scandinavians. Map 4 arrays the concentration of the two groups across the reservation. Even with split allotments, Dakotas concentrated in communities across the northern, hilly part of the reservation and in the four historic districts. Similarly, Scandinavians clustered as near each other as homesteads would allow, in areas of unallotted land on the southern half of the reservation and along the Sheyenne River.

The average size of land holdings was critical, as the history of agriculture on the Great Plains demonstrates. That the average acreage varied dramatically across ethnic groups reveals something about their history and legal status as well as land taking. On the reservation, allottees and homesteaders could acquire more land only through purchase or inheritance. Their chances for success as farmers rested in part on the size of their acreage. The smallest average parcels of land belonged to Dakotas: 99 acres. The Scandinavians' average land holding was 149 acres. Although they owned, on average, half again as much as Dakotas, compared to farmers across the state their holdings were modest, reflecting a strategy of owning land to support a family rather than accumulating land to attain wealth.

The largest Scandinavian landowner in 1910, Goodnow Torrison, a naturalized immigrant from Norway, held a total of 535 acres on the reservation, nothing on the scale of the second-generation German merchants and speculators. However,

Torrison was a trader; he ran a hardware and lumber store in Oberon.[72] The next largest acreage, 480 acres, was owned by John Walde, a Norwegian bachelor farmer who was assisted by his brother and sister.[73] Most others did not come close. Among Dakotas, Robert Wakaksan also owned a comparable 480 acres, accumulating considerably more than his original allotment. Next came Felix Dance Eagle, who owned 240 acres. Most others owned only their original acreage, or less.

Significant numbers of women in each racial-ethnic group owned land on the reservation. Because of this unique moment in North Dakota settlement, through homesteading, allotment, and purchase, women had access to land, and they seized the opportunity. In comparison, in most times and places, according to Mary Neth, "women had access to the most critical resource of farming—land—only through their relations with men."[74] In other words, white women came to own land through marriage to a landowning man or through inheritance. Notably, through lobbying and negotiations, Dakota women had a right to an allotment, whether they were married or unmarried.

In 1910, 379 Dakota women held land in their own name. As a group, they constituted 38 percent of Dakota landowners. At the time of allotment in 1890, females constituted 53 percent of enrolled Dakota tribal members. By 1911, the female proportion of the population at Spirit Lake had declined so that their numbers were equal to those of men. Their demographic decline suggests that the two decades post-allotment were harder on women than they were on men. Theoretically, the proportion of landowners should reflect their population at 53 percent. Historian Tonia Compton's research on the Nez Perce documents that allotment precisely reflected the female population (51 percent).[75] Complete allotment documents are not available, making a systematic assessment of the process impossible. Certainly the decline in the proportion of women and girls negatively affected landowning totals—but we have to ask why women lost their land in greater numbers. The growing scholarship on the indigenous ownership of land tends to neglect gender, with a few notable exceptions. This dearth makes this analysis of landowning at Spirit Lake all the more important, but it lacks a comparative base.[76]

The proportion of women among Dakota landowners is astonishingly high in comparison to that among non-Indian women. In her studies of homesteading, which was just one path to landownership, Elaine Lindgren found that women claimed an average of 10 to 12 percent of homesteads in North Dakota.[77] A 1920 study that examined the ownership of farms rented to tenants in the north-central states found that only 8 percent of the owners of North Dakota farms were women, although the regional average was about 16 percent.[78] By that measure, Scandinavian women on the reservation, who constituted almost 14 percent of Scandinavian landowners, fell near the regional average.[79]

The amount of land women controlled is also important in assessing gendered relationships on the reservation. Consistently across the region and across ethnic groups, men owned more land than women.[80] However, Dakota women came close to parity with men; on average, they owned 95 percent of the amount of land that men owned in 1910. This parity may reflect the consequences of inheriting land in equal shares. When allottees died, their land was divided equally among heirs, male and female alike. Over time, the disparity between men and women narrowed, and Dakota women continued to be major land holders in the tribe. In contrast, Scandinavian women owned approximately 81 percent of the average acreage of Scandinavian men on the reservation. Through owning land, the lives and livelihood of Dakota and Scandinavian women and men were interwoven. These women's propensity to own and retain land was a common characteristic produced by their circumstances, which had both distinct and shared features that developed as a shared logic in their otherwise separate lives.

* * * * *

Just as the dispersion of homesteading on the reservation intermixed land uses, so too did it mingle people from diverse cultures. Dakotas' and Scandinavians' generally nonintersecting lives nonetheless intertwined through rituals of nation, mutuality and occasionally, kinship. Through reciprocity and co-residence, a zone of contact was transformed into an integrated enclave of coexistence.

The jagged, distinct edges of mosaic tiles fit together to create a whole. Sharp legal boundaries delineated the geographic borders of the reservation, while prickly social ones marked its interior. Annual community pageants emphasized ancestries in a common context that simultaneously marked their differences. In everyday life grounded in the land, those living on the reservation experienced an equality of circumstance that fostered symbiotic coexistence. Norwegians' and Swedes' primary reference group was other poor Scandinavians rather than Dakotas. Their average land holdings were half that of the state as a whole, and women's average acreage was smaller than men's.

Because bountiful harvests and profitable commodity prices could never be guaranteed, owning land did not ensure adequate nutrition, access to cash resources, or freedom from poverty. This problem fell with special force on Dakotas, whose average land holdings were two-thirds that of Scandinavians. As they cast their eyes about, non-Indians appeared better off, however marginally. In fact, all non-Indian ethnic groups owned larger average holdings land than Dakotas. Everyone was acutely aware of the reservation–non-reservation divide as they shared a stigma imposed by the larger regional community because of their poverty and their association with Indian-ness.

6

Fighting the Sky and Working the Land

UNDER THE WARM summer sun, people on the reservation had little warning of the cataclysm to come. They went about their routine chores, milking cows, weeding gardens, putting up fences. They were optimistic about the crop yield this season. During the two previous years, 1914 and 1915, farmers had produced "the largest crop harvested on this reservation,"[1] and prices had risen as wheat found an eager market in Europe, where the Great War was raging. Late in the day on the sixth of August, a storm developed north of Devils Lake, and the hail began wreaking havoc as it moved across the countryside. Gaining in force, winds swirled into a tornado, skidding southeasterly and skipping like a stone onto the reservation, bouncing across Warwick and Hamar. Livestock disappeared into the funnel. Buildings collapsed. The tornado ripped roofs off houses and barns as it whipped through Pekin, gained momentum, and mowed into McVille.

In its wake, trees lay uprooted and crops flattened. Characteristically, tornadoes could destroy one crop and leave an adjoining field untouched. According to the *Tolna Tribune*, "The Catholic Church in Bergen Township was completely wrecked and the Sigdal Church was also demolished." Tom Rude in Nelson County lost seven head of horses. Many barns were completely ruined, with damages estimated to total $200,000 in Tolna alone. The Knudt Fredrikson barn, so grand and seemingly imperious, stood with its roof torn off. Much of the second-story pile of hay remained, with ragged splinters jutting out like tatters of unraveling cloth (see figure 38). The clapboard house fifty yards away stood undisturbed. Nearby, grain elevators disappeared.[2]

As the labor of decades was destroyed in minutes, the storm's ferocity showed no reason or mercy. Seeking shelter on her farm outside of Hamar, Aagodt Haugen

Beck hunkered down in the barn with her four-year-old son, Erling Bennet, in tow. The howling wind battered the barn, tearing it "to pieces" and knocking down a rafter that fell on the small boy. It broke his neck, and he died instantly.[3] We can only imagine what a loss of this magnitude felt like to Aagodt, as she left behind an outsized silence. The boy does not appear in family records, his life and death absent from the family tree. Aagodt had two older sons, children of her first marriage to the troubled John Olson Beck. But this child was born of her common-law marriage to Ole A. Borgerson. In March 1916, she had finally taken steps to divorce Beck, who remained in the Jamestown Insane Asylum. Two weeks after the divorce was final, Aagodt legally married Ole.[4] Perhaps her pregnancy prompted them to marry before the birth of their second child. Having legalized their relationship, the tragedy of Erling's death must have felt all the more harsh. Aagodt's fortitude helped her to keep going. She went on to have two more children.

Tenacity had to be part of a farmer's character, even irrationally so. Norman Forde's grandfather rebuilt his barn, which had been struck by lightning three different times. Nils and Jette Forde had homesteaded with a resilience that made it possible for them to stay despite the fickleness of Mother Nature.

> There was lightning that hit the barn the last time; burnt it up. People said he should change place; they thought it was something in the ground that drawed lightning. He had a cement floor in that barn and everything, and he built up four barns in the same place.... I seen the last one burn. They had it half built up again, and it blew down. They said he...should change places for the barn. He says, "I'll build them up as fast as they go down," he says, "in the same place." So he done.

Other people tell similar stories of lightning striking—burning barns and homes, killing people and livestock. Jette Forde's seventeen-year-old brother, James Alstad, had been working in a general store in Ottofy, North Dakota, when lightning struck him dead. As Cherry Monson reports, "Everything on the shelves was charred.... Even the matches in the boxes were brown but no fire started."[5] Second-generation Norwegian Lester Rendahl declared, "We were kind of fighting the sky."

Farm families' susceptibility to the weather was matched only by their vulnerability to capitalist markets. The risk-taking farming required meant that it attracted those who could handle uncertainty and retained those who had few alternatives. The gritty and resilient minority who endured had a commitment to the land. Because risk was endemic to the enterprise, people who worked the land had to be willing to advocate for themselves within the political economy, accept the inherent precariousness of any year's harvest, and endure. An upturn in the markets, such as that during World War I, could always be coupled with a random hail storm or a drought of major proportions. In any five-year period, farmers could expect two years to be bad.

Because, as Lucy Russell (b. 1883) put it, "farming is a gamble," farmers had to develop means to mitigate risk—the ravages of the weather and the markets. First and foremost, they understood deeply that farming was a family enterprise. Risk was further allayed by sharing labor in the community and via cooperatives. And finally, in a cash-poor economy, marginal farm families made every effort to provision themselves and to generate income in whatever way possible. This chapter explores how families organized the division of labor and managed community interdependence to provide subsistence needs and strengthen their perch on the land.

CULTIVATING LAND AND INTERDEPENDENCE

Most farmers viewed themselves as poor people who valued living off the land. While they did not expect to be powerful, they did have a sense of incomparable purpose. "We are the people that feed the world," Lois Olson Jones declared with great pride. Patrick Langstaff claimed that the farmer is "the most important person in the nation.... You look at history. No nation ever amount[ed] to anything unless they had that stable food supply." After a pause he gave an example, "Egypt built the pyramids.... It only took a small portion of people to raise food; the others could take up other enterprises." Like builders of other great civilizations, as he saw it, farmers provide a foundation for the North American economy.

Labor was the nexus of social organization in rural communities, according to historian Grey Osterud.[6] Proximity was key to the continuity of relationships and mutual helpfulness with work. That is not only *why* farm families lived near kin, shared labor is *how* they managed. Lois Olson Jones made it clear that her grandfather needed adult sons to farm with him, which meant living near him. When two of her uncles moved to the Pacific Northwest, she mused, "I suppose it was hard for Grandpa to maintain what land he did have without any boys to farm with him.... Albert was the one that farmed most of it, but then he had his own thing over in Benson County." Living near extended kin made close collaboration possible.[7] Scandinavian households may have been nuclear in structure, but they relied on extra-household help in practice. Dakotas were likely to live in multigenerational households, or to have several dwellings on one piece of property that supported the extended family.

The uncertainties of farming meant that diligence and hard work did not consistently lead to success. For Dakota farmers, the Indian Office judged every part of farm activity; in 1910, Indian superintendent Charles Ziebach took stock of Indian farming on the reservation: "Although nearly all of the Indians cultivate a small por-tion of their allotments, about 50 percent of them follow strictly agricultural pur-suits. The area cultivated by each Indian, who carry on farming operations, ranges from a field of 25 or 30 acres to a farm of 300 acres." In the wake of drought that year, Ziebach worried that the "*almost total failure* of crops" would discourage farming amongst Dakotas, "more especially those who are farming on a small scale."[8] The "additional farmer," assistant to the boss farmer, detailed some of the ways Indians pushed back against government policy. "They do not think it worthwhile doing any work on their land, of course I try to encourage them to work their land any-way."[9] He observed how hard it was to convince Dakotas to keep farming in the face of repeated failure. This moment exemplifies anthropologist Thomas Biolsi's argu-ment that the mission of the federal Office of Indian Affairs was to force Indians to "acquire the habit of industry, one of the main components of civilization."[10] He contends that they continued to "compel Indians to labor, even when that labor was irrational and nonproductive."[11]

Gendered Labor and the Power of "We"

In the agricultural economy of the Great Plains, Dakota and Scandinavian women's labor was essential to agricultural endeavors and family well-being. Thoroughly believing that only men could be farmers, historian John Hicks nonetheless argued that the viability of farming in the Midwest depended on the labor of a man, his wife, and their children: "The larger his crop of boys and girls old enough to help with the work the better he was able to handle his labor problem."[12] Historian Barbara Handy-Marchello aptly characterizes adult men and women as "partner farmers."[13] She writes, "Marriage and family stability depended on the economic contributions of both husband and wife."[14] This conception renders the interdependent work that spouses did visible and important in ways that conventional portraits of women as helpmeets or housekeepers ignore. Indeed, she argues, poor families could not afford to let go of women's productive labor.

While the principle of family labor was shared by Dakotas and Scandinavians, the customary gendered division of labor among Dakotas was turned upside down in the transition to agriculture. In this transformation, responsibility for growing crops was shifted uneasily and incompletely from women to men. Historically, it had been women who cultivated crops, while men hunted and fished. However, U.S. govern-ment policies were designed to turn Native men into farmers and make women their helpmeets. Their tool distributions and educational programs privileged men in agriculture and the cash economy and relegated women to domesticity. In practice, however, Dakota women cultivated gardens and also worked in the fields.

The indispensable labor provided by partner farmers placed a premium on het-erosexual marriage. As Carrie Young insightfully observes in her biography of her Norwegian mother, "Homesteading men were desperate for wives."[15] The fact that men outnumbered women gave those women who lived in North Dakota some leverage in their marital and economic choices. Households headed by single men found it necessary to hire domestic labor. Bachelor farmers regularly paid women to cook, bake bread, and do laundry. The recognition of the importance of women's economic partnership can be seen in Marie Olson Frank's (b. 1889) proud report of her husband's good sense in choosing her. A second-generation Norwegian, she reflected on her courtship with her German husband, whom she married in 1906 at the age of seventeen. "He was going with a teacher. But I guess he figured I'd make a better farmer's wife." Marriage to a skilled and hard-working person partially rem-edied a core labor shortage.

Women consistently framed their joint endeavors with a "we" perspective. In her letters home to Norway, Sigrid Lillehaugen speaks in the first-person plural in reporting on crop prices and farm activities. "We have put up well over 100 tons of hay and we have rented out just as much from the other quarter that we have taken as Homestead Land."[16] Sigrid mindfully conveyed the many ways she embraced the farming project. It was part of her worldview and projected her own centrality to the enterprise. Effie Hanson similarly took the authoritative "we" position as she described her work in the garden: "The children and me dug 23 bushels [of potatoes] & put them in the cellar while John was helping the neigh-bors thrash.... We...got 2 of the neighbor men to help finish & we had over 150 bushel to put up in the cellar and besides that we give a neighbor some of the small ones and the pigs got some of them."[17] From Effie's point of view, the farm enter-prise was hers as much as her husband's. She knowledgeably reported on many different parts of the farmwork, including seeding, thrashing, crop yields, and market dynamics.

In effect, women's "we" approach to agriculture called attention to their contribu-tion. As women asserted their joint role in ventures that ranged from planting to harvesting and selling livestock, regardless of whether or not they toiled alongside their husbands in the fields and attended the auctions, they called attention to their partnership (see figure 39).[18] That assertion of legitimacy and visibility fought against a culture that minimized the work women did, even as it depended upon their labor. Some historians argue that these efforts were oriented to the long term, as women claimed their rightful place in running the enterprise, and kept a watchful eye on what would happen to the farmland after their husbands died.[19] Since access to land was critically important in sustaining their livelihood and family legacy, positioning themselves as entitled to inherit had significant consequences.

Although work was gendered—most tasks were labeled as appropriate for one category of person and not for another—and a division of labor prevailed, families had to exercise flexibility, which Osterud calls the hallmark of rural labor.[20] Their hardscrabble existence necessitated imaginative adaptation as well as tenacity in a context of interdependence. Handy-Marchello found a fairly gender-neutral ethic within "an integrated system of productive and reproductive labor."[21] Women regularly performed what was conventionally regarded as "men's work" in the barn and in the fields. And in times of high seasonal demand or family crisis, men did "women's work"—cleaning house, caring for small children, and working in the garden. While the trade-offs may not have been strictly proportional—women helped men more than vice versa—the result was more overlap between men and women than the deeply gendered labels would suggest.

Teamwork was how Grace Pearson, a second-generation Norwegian, cast her approach to farming. "You've got to work together. . . . You gotta get up and take your share." She threw herself into whatever had to be done. She described loading manure in the barn for use as fertilizer: "When he'd go out in the field, he'd push the manure boat into the barn, and then I'd put all the manure on the boat. Then when he come home, he'd put the horses on it and take it out. [Chuckle.] So we sure did a lot of dirty work." Dakota tribal member Mrs. James Lohnes helped "her husband put in the spring crops."[22] When men worked out for wages, which they often did, women were left in charge of the farm and took responsibility for routine chores. Grace Pearson elaborated: "In the fall, he'd run threshing rigs and that, and then I'd stay home and do the chores at home, milk the cows." Dakota elder Grace Lambert recalled her young married life when she was "strong and mighty" and her husband walked miles to work: "I was a healthy woman. . . . I had to haul water. My husband worked [out]. . . . So I stayed home and did the work."[23] Rural women performed hours of backbreaking labor in the fields and the barnyard, as well as in the house. The imperatives of farm making and farming demanded flexibility.

Assignment of chores considered gender-appropriate varied by group. In addition to cultivating crops, historically Dakota women dried meat, tanned hides, snared small animals and birds, and foraged for edible fruits, vegetables, and roots on the prairies (see figure 40).[24] Mrs. Norman Blue, Sisseton-Wahpeton from South Dakota, recalled that when breaking camp "Dakota women they do all the work. They take the tepees down and carry everything."[25] Grace Lambert described the disparities between women's and men's work: "The woman she did *everything*: she carried the water, she did the cooking, she went to get the wood, she took care of the baby, and she *had* the baby and everything" (Lambert's emphasis).[26] Then she reflected on the value associated with gendered work among Dakotas: "But the men were kind of treated like they were kings or something. When they brought back the game, they appreciated it because they were going to have something nice to eat; meat was really special to the Indian people." She went on to point out that men also "made the roads, trails.... I think that's why they always felt a little bit better than the female."[27]

Likewise, consistent with practices in the old country, Norwegians seemed likely to disregard conventional American gendered boundaries or interpret them flexibly.[28] In Norway, although the farm economy was diversified, dairying was central, and women were responsible for the care and feeding of cattle. In summer, young women and children would take cows to graze in the high mountain pastures (the *saeter*), milk them, and make cheese and butter. Rasmus Yri recalls going to stay at the *saeter* when he was eight and his sister was ten; his mother would join them once a week to make cheese.[29] According to Barbara Levorsen, when women worked with livestock in Norway, they felt no disgrace in it. But in the United States, it connoted poverty and foreignness.[30]

While farm making called upon everyone to adapt to rugged conditions, Norwegian and Dakota women continued working outdoors much longer than Yankee women did.[31] Their labors may have earned them respect among their men folk and neighbors, but their willingness to toil at what were conventionally regarded as men's tasks brought them scorn from the outside community. American society constructed racialized dichotomies as a way of defining middle-class white womanhood. The bourgeois feminine ideal of dependency and delicacy differentiated white women from the practices of hard-working black, Indian, and immigrant women.[32] Historian Ingrid Semmingsen wrote that Yankees "took it for granted that immigrants would do the hardest work and get the least pay."[33]

Indian women historically had been viewed by white society as unequal drudges because they worked hard and, from the dominant culture's perspective, Indian men did not work hard enough.[34] Some Native American feminist scholars suggest that in the transition to reservation life, men's primary responsibilities—hunting and being warriors—were almost entirely disrupted, while women's continued in much the same vein.[35] Ironically, the strenuous and skilled labor that made women integral to economic endeavors of their family and community prompted others to cast aspersions on them. Reformers sought to "elevate" Native women by confining them to domesticity, which they saw as appropriate to a higher form of civilization. On the reservation, however, both Dakota and Norwegian women seem relatively oblivious to these messages as they went about their lives, worked on their farms, and raised their children as best they could.

There was a gender label for most tasks in the barn, barnyard, household, and fields, and a preferred hierarchy for who should do them. In regard to fieldwork, men were first, big boys second, hired men third, women next, and smaller children last.[36]

Those gender and age prescriptions were flexible, however, as necessity dictated getting vital tasks done with whatever labor was available. Carrie Young reports, "Even in later years if my brother wasn't home and my father couldn't get a hired man my mother would often go out into the fields and help my father rake hay or operate the binder that tied the wheat into sheaves."[37] Like Johanna Tvedt, whose sister and brother-in-law discharged their hired man when she arrived from Norway so Johanna would not be "idle," Scandinavian and Dakota families used women's labor to replace, not just supplement, the work of hired men. At Mrs. John Waanatan's house, David Hopkins's daughter was working "in the place of a hired man."[38]

Importantly, individual women expressed preferences for different tasks and arranged their work accordingly when they could. As a child, Grace Lambert was partial to indoor work: "I didn't like to work in the garden. So I had to be the housekeeper. I had to take care of the house and put on the water for whatever was supposed to be cooking. Had to keep the fire going until things were done. So I used to work in the house most of the time. Did the ironing and sewing, and patching things for my little sisters and brother."[39] In contrast, Carrie Pohl reported that Mrs. James Bear "enjoys working out of doors best. She had a good garden last summer and is putting in her garden this spring."[40] Hattie Iron Lightning took "care of the home while her father and mother take care of a garden and do the outside work."[41] Evelyn Jahr Greene recalled that her mother "would rather work outside than anything in the house." In fact, according to Evelyn, her mother, who grew up in a nonfarm Yankee household, was so uninterested in housework that she had to be taught domestic skills by her Norwegian father-in-law. "He used to help my mother because she wasn't too good at cooking and all that stuff." Still, she was an energetic person and liked doing fieldwork. "I can remember after we moved to Devils Heart.... She'd work with my dad, right alongside with him." When a neighbor would come by, Evelyn's father would stop to visit, but her mother would keep working.

Children's Work and the Work of Children

In the early twentieth century, as in the nineteenth, children had responsibilities to the family and the kin-based economy.[42] Everybody worked, or everybody starved. Starting at the age of seven or eight, children had chores that included pumping, carrying, and dumping water; weeding the garden; feeding the chickens; shooing birds from the fields; and stacking firewood. As they got older, they started milking cows, picking stones, pitching hay, shocking wheat, and driving tractors. Farmwork gave people freedom from the industrial logic that threw the work-family balance off kilter, although that flexibility did not make it easy.

Younger children helped their mothers. Second-generation German Patrick Langstaff recalled that he started to milk cows when he was about ten. "Everybody had to help. 'Course there was a lot of work on the farm.... Like you had a big garden, you helped your mother take care of that too." He also assisted with picking all kinds of wild fruit. "There used to be a lot of wild strawberries—my mother was great for that—June berries, wild grapes, strawberries, choke cherries, Bing cherries, and wild raspberries....When berry time came, I was ready to go. [Laughs.]" Norwegian Bjorne Knudson and his siblings helped their mother do the farmwork: "Dad was always out working, a lot of time he'd never come home for a whole week. So as soon as we was able to do anything, we were out there, helping her....Done all the chores." Evelyn Jahr Greene gathered eggs and dug potatoes. At age seven or eight, Thor Peterson started helping his older siblings pitch hay and pick rocks. In Ella Dolbak's family, children would sit on the shocks of drying grain and chase away wild geese. When Tom Pearson was seven or eight years old his parents would not let him use the hayfork because they feared he would be in danger of losing his hand. So he was responsible for walking with a light team of horses. "My hands would get sore.... I was so sore that a lot of the times, I kinda *cried*."[43]

However well integrated children were into the family labor force, they first required care and attention. Rural living conditions and agricultural endeavors gave men and women the ability to combine childrearing with full-time work and to share it flexibly to meet the needs of the household economy.[44] As in other agricultural communities, when rural women felt the tension of competing demands, they could manage the workload by distributing tasks and getting help from others.[45] Women found ways to do their chores while caring for young children; the cows had to be tended and chickens fed, baby or no. Effie Hanson described juggling: "We are milking 5 cows now and sometimes I help milk. It all depends on the baby if I can get away from her that long."[46] Lester Skjerven observed how women in his mother's generation managed haying: "They'd have the baby in the cradle at the end of the field and they'd make a round and come back and look after the baby. And go again." Grace Pearson explained her strategy: "I had that youngest girl. She was just a baby. I had to put her in a paper box then and set her on the barn floor when I watered the cattle. Of course, she cried at the top of her voice."

Toddlers required special attention as they could not be happily contained in a box. Barbara Levorsen recalled her neighbor's antics. "After the death of her brother and sister, Anne had no one to play with either, and like I, she took to roaming about, so her mother dressed her in red calico so she was easily seen, as Mama had done with me. Gunild's special fear was that she would fall into one of the abandoned wells that had never been filled in, and finally she did fall into one in the barnyard that she had been especially warned to keep away from."[47] Luckily, she was fine in spite of defying her mother's orders.

Women with lots of children had so many caregiving responsibilities they could do little outside. According to her children, because she was raising eight children, Swedish immigrant Jennie Anderson Carlson had her hands full in the house and thus never worked in the fields; that was the job of her husband, her daughters, and her sons. By the time she gave birth to her last child, the older children helped care for the younger ones. Similarly, Thor Peterson reported that his mother did not work in the fields in Norway or in North Dakota: "Well, I'm sure she helped. Especially when you got eleven kids, I don't think you'd be working out much." Older children's care for the little ones benefited the family as a whole. When Dagny Skurdell Bilden was born, "she was the seventh child, the fifth daughter, so she never lacked the attention of an older sister to rock or soothe her."[48] My maternal grandmother, Helene Haugen Kanten, needed a childcare strategy when she moved with her husband to Saskatchewan, because she anticipated working the fields. She brought along her husband's eight-year-old brother to care for the baby.

Adult relatives living in the household, on the property, or nearby also provided extensive assistance with childcare.[49] Grace Lambert described the system of caregiving in her family: her mother took care of the infant (presumably breast feeding) and did her work while her older kinswomen took care of the other children.

> On that homestead where my grandmother got killed by a lightning, when I was very small.... We had three old ladies: my grandmother, my dad's mother, and her mother, who was a very, very old lady.... We never lived in the nice frame house... that my dad built for the homestead. He had a log house there before, a great big one. And that's where these old ladies lived, and we the children, lived with them, but the baby stayed with my mother in the other house.[50]

Even with the major childrearing contributions of extended kin, grandmothers in particular, mothers continued to be important caregivers and symbolic figures. The centrality of mothers is poignantly recalled by adults who lost their mothers while young. Today, some single fathers raise their children, and even more single mothers do so. They are able to work for pay, if care for their children can be arranged. In the early twentieth century, as Patrick Langstaff put it, "They didn't have babysitters." There was a social understanding that if children did not have a mother, they needed someone—a housekeeper or a relative—to care for them.

Indeed, it was generally understood that most widowed fathers would be unable to care for young children, and those who had no one to come and help might place some or all of their children in other households. A couple of exceptional examples—when men ran the household and cared for young children themselves—stand out. Henry Mibebeya was a caring Dakota father, according to Carrie Pohl. "He is keeping house for himself and two little boys and does better than some of the Indian women as housekeeper. His windows were screened and the home fairly clean as well as himself and the little boys."[51] Because the home was the workplace, farming fathers were around young children a great deal; in fact, they spent more time with their children than most fathers do today, teaching them, playing with them, and working with them.[52] Instead of giving up his children for adoption or arranging for a housekeeper, Norwegian Knut Nelson hired a man to do the outside work so he could take care of the children. Community observations report approvingly on how well he was doing. Sigrid Gjeldaker Lillehaugen mentioned seeing Knut and the children at church: "They were dressed so nice and Knut is a good house mother. He washes and irons and mends clothes for himself and his children just as well as any mother."[53] But no one assumed he could take on all the work of farming and childcare by himself.

When children were old enough to help substantially, they made a reality of "family" farming. Dakota Grace Lambert fondly remembers working with her father: "My dad used to plow, plow the field, to put in his grain. He [had a couple] of horses, and I used to have to run alongside of him with a whip, to whip the horse so it could go. That was really happy times for me."[54] Several of the women recalled the pride of working side by side with their fathers. Lois Olson Jones's work history was shaped by her poor health as well as her age, gender, and family constellation. When she was eight, both she and her brother contracted whooping cough and scarlet fever. Her brother died. Her parents decided that in Lois's depleted state, "the way to get me back to health was to keep me out in the sun, and outdoors." It was a fate she did not mind. "I was always Dad's helper.... I always helped with the horses and went to the hayfield." Lois also found satisfaction in helping her grandfather with major responsibilities when she was twelve years old: "Grandpa lived with us.... In those days in order to harvest your crop you had a binder and it had to be pulled by horses or by a tractor or something, we were just getting into tractors in those years. And Grandpa would ride in the morning and the later part of the afternoon, but I could stand the heat, so I was the one who rode the binder from like 1 o'clock to 4 o'clock or so." In fact, Lois thrived on the farm and took comfort in her companionship with the animals.

Adulthood did not necessarily remove children from the family orbit, or its labor demands. Men were expected to keep close to their family of origin, which squelched their desire for autonomy. The burden bore especially heavily on those who were expected to take over the farm. In her study of an agricultural community, anthropologist Seena Kohl found: "Throughout childhood, the son works under the direction of his father, the boss of the enterprise. The relationship between father and son, therefore, has many of the features of the relationship between employer and hired hand."[55] Sons did the heavy work, while fathers did the planning and performed the lighter tasks. Relinquishing control in transition to retirement was a key generational shift that was often wrought with conflict. At this juncture, according to Kohl, marital partnerships were less important than those between parents and adult children.

Organizing Cooperatives

Embedded in a kin-based economy, North Dakota farmers relied on communal labor as well as extended family. In addition to informal labor exchange, they formally developed local cooperatives, turning their individual weakness into collective strength that mitigated hardship and sought to give them bargaining power in the market economy. After the decline of Populist Party in the 1890s, historian Mary Neth wrote, rather than fading away, "economic cooperatives continued to grow. Two organizations, the American Society of Equity (Equity) and the Farmers' Educational and Cooperative Union (Farmers' Union), continued to link local cooperatives into loose federations."[56] Both were founded in 1902 to wrest more control for farmers in agricultural markets that were largely controlled by corporations. They also tried to build a coalition between small farmers and urban workers. Equity in particular established cooperative grain elevators for storage, giving farmers more discretion over when and how to sell (see figure 41). According to Neth, "Cooperatives attempted to give a community of farmers greater power in the centralized economy of the late nineteenth and early twentieth centuries."[57] One Norwegian woman reflected on her husband's role in organizing for the American Society of Equity. "We both believed the organization was a good thing because it brought the farmers together to talk about markets and prices and newer methods of farming were discussed and rotation of crops was advocated. Pa liked this kind of work. He felt that he was helping his friends and neighbors preserve their interests and strengthen Dakota as a state."[58]

Helmer Dahlen, who farmed in a densely Norwegian area in Nelson County, recounted how in the early 1900s farmers were exploited by the businessmen who owned and ran the grain elevators. "They give you whatever they felt like, see." They did not abide by agreements that assigned greater value to higher qualities of grain. So Helmer's father joined some other farmers and "clubbed together and shipped a car load at a time" to market. In effect, they outmaneuvered the system that gave unfair advantages to owners of the elevators. Second-generation Norwegian Mamie

Larson explained that some farmers rebelled at their unfair treatment by dishonest businessmen in Sheyenne. "I can remember how the farmers used to haul their wheat into these here elevators.... They come in with a load and they would be maybe up to twenty bushels short on their loads, mind you.... Then finally the Farmers Union put in their own ... scale in town. So they could go and weigh it before they went in." With accurate scales and group mobilization against cheating, the farmers gained leverage.

Ralph E. Seastrand, a second-generation Swede, reported that the farmers around Sheyenne operated a cooperative grain elevator. "That was the first thing that they organized." He served on the Equity Elevator board for twenty-nine years. Elmer Tufte's (b. 1906) father, who had immigrated from Norway, "was one of the original ones that was in that Equity exchange" and was a big supporter of cooperatives. Equity also established grocery cooperatives to communalize some costs of capitalization and intervene in a market that shifted profits away from producers toward processors and retailers. The groceries did not prove as enduring as the elevators.

Some cooperative ventures began among kinship or ethnic groups, while others branched out across the locality. These networks of support established a base that in the 1910s galvanized an electoral movement. Those rooted in ethnicity created solidarity, but simultaneously deepened divides. Edd Johnson, a Swede, talked about his father's reluctance to join the Norwegian farmers' small-scale efforts at cooperation: "Dad didn't go into partnership with 'em, but a whole lot of Norwegians went together and got a threshing machine.... So they'd do a little short run, not very much to start out with." Farmers' call for state support in the form of crop insurance and grain elevators at railway terminals was based on their recognition that as a class they were unfairly absorbing the risks of capitalism and others were reaping profits at their expense. These experiences made them more receptive to the politics of the Nonpartisan League when it began organizing in 1915. The idea of a farmer-controlled economy had special appeal to Scandinavians, who brought a rural political culture rooted in cooperative efforts to intervene in markets and support family farming.

Harvest Time

Seasonal labor demands peaked at harvest time, which required crews of people who moved quickly and efficiently. When a crop was ready, particularly hay and wheat, it had to be harvested within a small window of time. If rain threatened, it had to be brought in quickly, since wet hay loses its nutritional value and wet wheat rots. "To harvest small grains, farm people cut the standing grain, bound and shocked or stacked it, and hauled it to the thresher."[59]

The urgency of the harvest placed greater demands on the community because everyone's crop ripened at about the same time. As a result, farmers had to share work with neighbors, hire others to assist them, or mechanize.[60] They regularly hired seasonal help, but haying and shocking (or "stooking," as gathering cut grain into sheaves and standing them up to dry in the field was locally called) and threshing grain needed larger crews of workers. Work crews would sweep through the countryside. The harvest brought together folks from different walks of life—factory workers from urban centers, farmworkers from the South, and unemployed laborers who followed the harvest across the Great Plains. This magnified inequalities, as prosperous farmers could purchase more machinery and hire more help. According to Neth, women acted as a reserve labor force that was mobilized during the harvest, as well as at planting time, to work in the fields.[61]

Many narrators described threshing as a time of fervent excitement, intense work, and great fun. A break from routine, it became "a vital ritual" that "symbolized sharing and the unity of the participants."[62] Patrick Langstaff recalled longing to join a threshing crew when he was just thirteen: "That was kind of an adventure.... Man, you wanted to go threshing!" Part of the excitement of threshing was the danger it involved. Thomas Pearson told an unhappy story about his uncle trying to repair a threshing machine. "He laid on the ground on the side there. And then...he was careless and got his arm caught in the rope that pulled him into the machine." His wife, Grace Pearson, acknowledged, "Oh, those threshing machines killed a lot of people."

Work crews were integrated; Indians, white settlers, urban migrants, and occasionally African Americans worked side by side. Patrick Langstaff, who grew up in Tokio, recalled: "We grew up together and we worked together.... There'd be Indian boys, everybody working on crews. You just got along together." Ambrose Littleghost's stepfather would hire white farm workers. When I asked Ingemund Peterson whether he had ever worked for a Dakota farmer, he answered: "No, but I worked together with them. Because, in the threshing, that was pret near all Indian.... In the first fall, 1915, me and a guy that used to work...he couldn't understand one word I said and I didn't understand [him]." Newly arrived from Norway, Ingemund found a common language only in work.

Threshing crews could include up to twenty workers, all of whom had to be fed as part of their pay. This obligation entailed lots of extra work for women of the household, who had to prepare three ample meals a day. Some crews traveled with a "cook car" staffed with women to prepare the food and equipped with a stove and cooking equipment. Lucy Russell reported cooking for twenty-four men whom her father employed as a traveling threshing crew. She had to make bread every day and "about seven pies for the noon meal.... But I got so I liked it." She enjoyed the press of the work, the collective efforts to bring in the crop, and the sociability that was part of the work and its aftermath. Someone helped her wash dishes and peel potatoes.

Cherrie Lane Wood also remembers threshing fondly, but for a different reason than most. As the wife of one of the most prosperous farmers on the reservation, she did less work than usual because additional help was hired: "I loved it, because we always had cooks...and that was my rest time....I had a good time then, just had to feed the kids." Cherrie's experience was unusual; only on large farms with a surplus of hired labor could the women of the household be excused from the extra demands of seasonal work. In over one hundred interviews, hers was the only account in which the harvest was not a labor emergency.

Lois Olson Jones recalled the threshing crew her father and brothers assembled and hired out. They lived just off the reservation in Ramsey County. "When they got as far as the Kirk Place, which is where they had to cross Devils Lake, and of course there was a road across there, it wasn't full of water like it is now, then they'd sound the whistles on the steam engine and then Grandma knew...the threshing machine was that close and they better start getting supper for the crew....They'd run into the garden...and dig potatoes." Lois commented, "I'm sure that they threshed for anybody that didn't have a machine that were on their way." But, did they do so if the farmers along the way were Indian?

Sparse records reveal that Dakotas were treated differently in neighboring white communities' systems of exchange. Indian superintendent Charles Ziebach reported in 1913: "The prospects for crops this year are not the best, owing to late spring and dry summer, but, there will be sufficient for immediate needs. A great deal of dissatisfaction is experienced among the Indians on account of having no means of threshing their grain."[63] He found that threshing rigs charged Indians "exorbitant prices." He insisted that the Indian Office provide equipment to ameliorate the problem: "Two suitable threshing machines should be furnished for this reservation."[64] The following year, Ziebach specified that "the Indians have been compelled to pay about twice as much for threshing as the white people are charged."[65] He reasoned that the price differential had less to do with outright bias and more to do with the location of Indian land: "The country is rough in places and the acreage is small and white threshers will not make long moves for small jobs. This has been overcome somewhat at times by having a machine locate[d] in the center of a community and having the Indians haul their grain to the machine, but on the whole the Indians are compelled to pay more for threshing per bushel than their white neighbors."[66] This issue did not surface in subsequent annual reports, so it is not clear whether Indians were given their own machine. Nonetheless, higher threshing prices created yet another barrier to successful Native farming.

Employment Divisions: Hired Men and Hired Girls

Since the region supported little industry, people worked out for other farmers. Farm labor opportunities increased over time, as did farm tenancy, particularly once the depression of the 1920s was underway. During the seasonal rush or times of acute need such as childbirth, even cash-poor farmers had to hire day laborers for inside or outside work. Lars R. Larson explained, "You generally got a girl that come and helped." Lois Olson Jones spoke of the huge labor demands: "When we got out here on this farm, we usually had a hired man but there were always more work to be done than what my dad and one hired man could do, or mother, too." Historian John D. Hicks explained the common arrangement in agricultural communities: "Neither the hired man nor the hired girl was thought of as an inferior; in many instances the hired man became a son-in-law, and the hired girl, a daughter-in-law."[67] This system of employment selected for homogeneity. Even those with sufficient resources to hire help pitched in alongside their hired hands.

Three challenges confronted those hiring labor: cost, availability, and quality. Farmers had to weigh the cost against their need for additional labor. As Sigrid Lillehaugen wrote in 1922, "Everybody has to hire, and hired men are expensive."[68] Poor farmers were not exempt from the adage: good hired help was often hard to find. Effie Hanson detailed her search for domestic assistance while she was pregnant in the spring of 1920. "I have not been so very well lately as my back hurts me all the time. Hope we get a boy this time. Anton thinks we have girls enough." She knew that once she gave birth she would be incapacitated for a while. The ideal hired girl would be energetic, versatile, and resourceful: "Have been looking for girls but never found any yet. Seems like they are getting married, what few they were. Have wrote to John's sister up by Regan for her oldest daughter but haven't got any answer yet. You know she stayed with Mrs. Hanson when she was so bad, [at] the last. She sure is a good girl if I do say it for John's niece. So quick to get around. Can harness horses, milk cows or most anything. She is 17 years old."[69] Later in the month Effie wrote again: "We haven't been able to locate a girl yet. Seem like they are hard to get. John…don't like to take a day off in the field and look for one but suppose if he has to he can do it."[70] She observed that young women were finding better-paying employment in the cities. "They all go to Bismarck this spring to work. All kinds of work there for girls."[71]

Hired men were more numerous but posed some of the same problems of adaptability. Notably, their behavior did not always meet the standards of the farmer who hired them. "One of the greatest problems in operating their farm, according to Johanna [Tvedt], was keeping the hired men in line. The men frequently procured the produce of the local moonshiners, often returning to the farm sick from its contents."[72] Gust A. Berg explained the logic of a farmer hiring himself out to other farmers: "See they were all poor guys, and…they were just working out to make enough money so they could make their payments." Gust's penetrating voice helped him make extra money by auctioneering and calling square dances; he kept working at odd jobs until he was ninety, long after he formally retired from farming. With eleven children when the family came from Norway, Peter Peterson sent all those who were old enough to work out. He continued to work as a day laborer into his old age, according to his sons Ingemund and Thor, including a long-term job as a sheepherder for a rancher near Sheyenne. Some men migrated to the lumber camps in Montana and Minnesota during the winter. Some women taught school in the winter and farmed in the summer.

Grace Lambert worked for some of the white families near her home on the reservation. For her neighbor, Mrs. Valinsky, "I used to go wash dishes for her and scrub the floor.…We all scrubbed the floors all the time because there was no linoleum" (see figure 42). Asked what it was like to work for a white family, she replied, "It was nice. I worked for…Mrs. Valinsky…during threshing time where they were getting the crop in. They have a lot of people that they feed, so they really do need help. That's all I did was stand there and go wash dishes. Heating water and hauling water.…So I used to work for these white people, but they were good to me."[73] Agnes Greene explained, "In the summertime you worked…for farms. The men, they worked for…farmers. Trying out here and there, but that was the only work they had."[74]

Children also worked on neighboring farms. Those from poorer families were sent out earlier, as their parents lacked the resources to feed them or take advantage of their labor. Second-generation Norwegian Einar Severson is a case in point. "After I was six, seven years old, I herded cattle for a neighbor that had a threshing outfit. I herded his cattle for two weeks and got 50 cents out of it. [Laughs.]" Young immigrant Hans Larsgaard (b. 1878) told of living with his Uncle Steim in Minnesota, while his father was working out and his mother, stricken by insanity, stayed behind in Norway. Hans recalls that his uncle was good to him, making sure he went to school but also sending him out to work. Like my own great-uncle, Hans began babysitting at the age of nine while the adults were working in the fields: "My first job was I took care of some children while the Mr. and Mrs. were stacking their grain. She was pitching and he was stacking. So I stayed with them two weeks and when that was over, I went to another place…where my uncle was working and herded cattle the rest of the fall, until Uncle Steim came and got brother and I and sister." The system of working out applied an apprenticeship model so young people accrued skills as well as money. Ella Dolbak worked as a hired girl when she deemed her mother was able to handle the farmwork at home without her: "I worked here and there.... I went and stayed with a relative of mine, that was a home ec[onomics] teacher from Norway. She taught me how to sew."

Organized Labor

From the perspective of hired men, they did not receive adequate pay, suffered from objectionable working and living conditions, and were subject to the arbitrary and often excessive authority of the farmer who hired them. Their low wages made it difficult to save enough money to buy land and farm independently. A hired man faced some of the same dilemmas as a hired girl, J. Olson Anders wrote: "He might be accepted as a 'member of the family'; but he was subject to call at any moment and had virtually no privacy."[75]

The high demand for harvest workers created an opportunity for them to organize for better working conditions and fair wages. Between 1900 and 1930, the Industrial Workers of the World (IWW, or "Wobblies") organized migrant farm laborers as well as industrial workers. Although historically labor unions have found it difficult to organize a mobile work force, the intense demand for labor gave them critical leverage.[76] In the North Dakota countryside, farmers were ambivalent about organized labor and suspicious of the militant tactics that made the IWW notorious among employers. If a farmer treated them unfairly, they were reputed to start fires or place booby traps in the fields that would disable farm machinery or even maim the farmer. Barbara Levorsen reported: "One fall there was much trouble in our neighborhood during threshing. Stones had been carefully concealed in the grain bundles, and in one instance a fork without a handle. When these objects came into the feeder they broke the feeder arms and teeth and brought about long and costly delays while repair parts were sought in towns near and far."[77] These acts of sabotage found a parallel in factories and among English farm laborers. Cherrie Lane Wood explained why her husband, who called labor activists "devils," had not hired any IWW-affiliated workers: "They're afraid of him. He wouldn't stand any nonsense from 'em." She explained, "Some of 'em came out and tried to hire on. He told 'em where to head it. I had that kind of old man." Had they pulled any funny business, she insisted, "He'd a shot 'em. He would've. So would I." And then she laughed. Her daughter-in-law, present at the interview, said, "She's not as vicious as she sounds." Cherrie, who liked being fierce, explained her position. "No, but I would have, if they'd a done anything to hurt the cows."

H. C. "Hugh" O'Connor (b. 1890), who had been similarly reluctant to contract with IWW workers, once hired a crew that denied being Wobblies. At the end of a week's work and after a few rounds of beer in town, Hugh discovered that all of the men, in fact, belonged to the union. He reasoned that they had been good workers and earned his respect, regardless of what organization they belonged to: "I said, 'By golly, *as long as a man is right, why not be right with him?*' I says. 'I ain't gonna try and make you fellas over or something.' Yeah. No. I had awful good luck with men" (O'Connor's emphasis). Maintaining good relations with hired men was a key to farmers' success. They had to treat workers fairly and toil alongside them. At bottom, while some expressed skepticism about organized labor, these folks admired work well done and would say so.

In contrast, many narrators commented on the limited usefulness of fabled teenage boys who were critical to a farm family labor force. The Olson siblings put some of the mythologized labor of teenagers in perspective. Joseph Olson explained: "No trouble with IWW or anything like that. They were all good.... We got some of the best men that you could ever get.... Better than the local help. The farmer would send his boys out. They were young. When they're young..." His sister, Frances Olson Krause (b. 1901), interrupted: "Well, they weren't getting anything out of it. Dad was going to make them pay the thresh bill." Joseph picked up the argument. "Sure, they didn't have any incentive.... That was the worst outfit you can get. Now if the grown men were to come, they'd have been ahead of the youngsters. They wanted to play around a lot, fool around. These other guys, they put in a day's work." These tensions emerged just when labor-intensive tasks intermingled with new technology. Some farmers continued using horses to plow their fields into the 1930s, while others made the transition to huge steam-powered outfits early in the 1910s. Teenage boys, who needed to be trained and had been a prized source of labor power in the nineteenth century, were coming to be more of a nuisance than an asset.[78]

SELF-PROVISIONING

The risks associated with commercial agriculture were mitigated by self-provisioning: growing vegetables, raising poultry, dairying, making things the family needed and using them to barter and trade, and purchasing as little as possible. In a cash-scarce economy, where consumer goods might have been available but were not affordable, women produced most of life's necessities. Importantly, as Joan Jensen found in the mid-Atlantic region, women exhibited ingenuity and resourcefulness in provisioning the household.[79] Economist Joann Vanek estimated that as late as 1924 rural families were producing 70 percent of their food.[80] They raised chickens for their eggs, meat, and feathers and cows for milk, butter, and cheese. A 1920 survey reported that 89 percent of rural women cared for poultry (see figure 43).[81] Giving concrete meaning to the ideal of farm family self-sufficiency, women grew vegetables, gathered whatever was growing wild, and preserved as much as possible. As Patrick Langstaff put it, "You only bought what you couldn't raise."

In a local economy that relied on the direct exchange of goods and services as much as cash, resourcefulness ensured adequate nutrition. Third-generation Norwegian Helmer Dahlen reflected on the virtue of frugality. "It just depends on how saving you could be." Being *saving* was the crucial factor. Some women were especially adept at making do, stretching food, and inventively utilizing the resources around them, which made the difference between getting by and going hungry. Women who were perceived as profligate faced harsh criticism from wagging female tongues. Cherrie Lane Wood told a story on herself, reflecting on her intended prudence but complete cluelessness: "When we was first down there, we couldn't afford all that stuff. Grandma give me a dozen eggs one time. That was a real treat to get hold of a dozen when you didn't have chickens.... I was so tickled, all of the things I was going to make with those dozen eggs. And I didn't know anything then, I was stupid as anything. Next morning I come and they was all busted open. Every one was frozen. [Laughs.] You know, a dozen eggs in the winter was quite a thing."

Some earned money through the sale or trade of products they made, and others provisioned through harvesting resources in the wild. Bjorne Knudson reported that his mother really liked to fish. Other women hunted or snared small wild game. Eunice Davison recalled an old Dakota woman, Mrs. Garfield, who lived alone next door to the Jetty family and would snare rabbits, skin them, and dry the meat. She also collected eggs from snake and bird nests for food. When asked about her father's hunting activities, May Gunning retorted that her mother was just as likely to bring in dinner. "She could handle a gun as good as any man. She'd go out and shoot...prairie chickens."[82] When asked if his family liked hunting and fishing, Mack Johnson (b. 1899) began talking about his mother. His wife interjected from the next room, "She was a regular naturalist." Mack Johnson chuckled. "She'd walk into woods with you, or out on the prairie, or anyplace, and she could tell you all the different kinds of bushes, trees, berries, everything like that. She was raised with the Indians." He attributed her outdoor skills to the fact that she grew up on a fort in Minnesota with Indian neighbors.

Vegetable Gardens

Providing meals for the family required growing, harvesting, and preserving vegetables. Women, who were mainly responsible for the one- to two-acre gardens, cultivated potatoes, sweet corn, squash, turnips, and cabbage with help from their daughters and younger sons. Second-generation Norwegian American Dagny Skurdell Bilden recalled: "Mother was an excellent gardener, and we always had a big garden, just east of the house. There was a well nearby, so when it was dry, we could irrigate."[83]

Gardening was a tradition that Dakota women continued on the reservation, one of the few Dakota customs encouraged by the Indian Office. In addition to providing vital foodstuffs, bountiful gardens were a great source of pride. Tribal member Eunice Davidson spoke with awe about her grandmother, Jenny Abraham, whose extensive garden yielded radishes and dill as well as hearty staples like corn and potatoes. Eunice observed that her grandmother's house was by the garden: she did not say that the garden was by the house. "My grandma loved a garden. She had ten children so they had to make every means so they could make it every year." Reflecting her proprietary sense of the garden, Jenny Abraham would call it "the woman's project," which made it exclusively her domain.

In making her rounds around the reservation, field matron Carrie Pohl observed the preparation, cultivation, tending, and harvesting of Dakota gardens. "Mrs. Little Wing and mother…keep chickens, ducks also pigs and is putting in a garden. Nearly all the Indian women are putting in gardens."[84] She visited Mrs. Holy Fruit and her son, Andrew Smith, whose household had boxes of dirt with sprouted cabbage and tomato shoots in anticipation of warmer weather and spring planting. Men as well as children joined women: "Mrs. John Belgard and her husband have put in two acres of garden."[85] Pohl approvingly recorded how elderly Lone Dog helped his wife: "They are good gardeners, they still have plenty of potatoes. The old lady's health has been poor for about a year. The old man chops wood for her and is kind to her."[86] In May 1915, she remarked that "Buffalo Jack's family have a good garden in; they tell me they have planted 35 bushels of potatoes."[87] Especially skillful, "Old Lady" Mazakahomni, as Pohl called her, evoked special praise because she "has the finest garden I have seen this summer."[88]

In the early twentieth century, preserving vegetables and fruits was the only way to have them to eat through most of the winter. Once prepared, they could be stored, divided, shared, and traded, as well as given away. While white women busied themselves with canning, Dakota women dried corn, wild fruit, and occasionally meat. When working out as a young woman, Grace Lambert learned to can from her white employers: "These ladies would can, which my mother never did. [Chuckle.] She never did can; she always dried things to keep.…But they made a lot of jelly, too, which was something my Ma never did either."[89] In her late summer rounds, Carrie Pohl observed that "many of the Indians are drying corn and fruit for the winter and have little time for house work." Like other kinds of harvesting, drying corn called upon entire families. "Found Mrs. [Wiyakawaste] is very poorly and she has complained all summer her trouble seems to be old age. Her husband and little son were drying corn for the winter." The same day she recorded, "Mrs. I[gnatius] F. Court is a fine housekeeper. She too was drying corn for the winter." Even Mrs. Waanatan, who had suffered a terrible accident, was "helping the family in drying corn."[90]

Domestic Arts

In the midst of the endless work and drudgery that farm making and farming required, women wrought beautifully crafted clothing and household goods. In retrospective accounts, narrators lavished praise on the handiwork of the skilled women in their families. Their home manufactures, both artistic and useful, generated gifts and offerings they exchanged within the community.[91]

Women sewed a great deal of their family's clothing, linens, and bedding, and also made household decorations. Agnes Greene recalled how her grandmother would sew moccasins using hand-rolled sinew for thread.[92] In contrast to earlier centuries, women purchased cloth and some clothing, such as overalls for their husbands. As she inventoried the furniture and tools in the Dakota households she visited, Carrie Pohl recorded a good number of sewing machines. Second-generation Norwegian Dagny Skurdell Bilden commented that her mother clothed her eleven children. "Mother knit all the socks and mittens, sewed the girls' dresses, school clothes for the boys and girls, plus shirts for her two brothers, even after they were married."[93]

Craft work varied by ethnic group as well as with individual aptitudes and inclinations. People admired the expertise that they interpreted as an ethnic specialization, such as Indian beadwork and Norwegian knitting. When asked whether other groups besides Norwegians knit, Amanda Skjerven (b. 1900) said, "I don't believe the Bohemians did it. Oh, they must have knitting too.... They're great people to work with hands, too. But I think they worked with feathers and such things more." Her husband, Lester Skjerven, interjected, "Yeah. They were more on poultry, I would say." Amanda explained that they raised geese and used them "for feathers. Feather ticking and feather pillows." Skillful work required properly stripping the feathers for use. "They have stripping bees here yet." She commented that no Bohemian household was without down quilts. "They're very good at poultry."

At the same time she made claim to a Norwegian skill, knitting wool, Amanda expressed special appreciation for her Norwegian mother-in-law's handiwork. While her husband was the primary focus of the interview, she continually piped up with admiring comments about his mother. "She spun *beautiful* yarn. Just beautiful. She was a perfectionist really.... A lot of them get little knots in it and everything, but ... hers was just as even and beautiful." In keeping with the ethic of the household economy, her father raised sheep and at one time had a flock of 200. Her mother-in-law processed wool: she "sheared it, washed it, carded it, and spun it, and dyed it." Boasting about her skills, Amanda asserted again, "She was a good knitter, wasn't she?" Lester concurred. Amanda elaborated: "Right after supper, that was. She didn't need any light, she could do that without. She could read and knit." Amanda said that "they never went" anywhere "without their knitting" (see figure 44). Lester enthusiastically explained women's remarkable ability to knit even while in motion. They kept the yarn "sitting there in their apron, kind of, and then they'd walk along, just knit as they were walking."

Dakota women's involvement with home manufacturing, primarily beaded goods and, later, star quilts, provided an important resource to families, exchanged for both goods and cash. Dakota women's beadwork was important for its cultural status as well as its economic value. In the pre-reservation era, Dakota women honored warriors by making them beaded clothing; in effect, their painstaking craft work recognized men's bravery and generosity.[94] Continuing this custom of publicly recognizing these virtues, Dakota women at Spirit Lake kept alive their craft well into the reservation period and boasted a number of master beadworkers. Agnes Greene followed in the tradition of her mother, who did quill work. Like earlier generations of native women, even after the Europeans brought glass beads to trade, she used porcupine quills to decorate moccasins. Women would chew the quills to make them pliable and dye them deep colors. "The beads was quicker than quills. But they still used quills." When I asked if her grandmother, who had also been a skilled quill worker, ever make things to sell to white people, she said, "No." She explained, "Mostly for the husband, for their father, like that. You just did it for yourselves."[95]

Generating Cash

In a cash-poor economy, men, women, and children found ways to bring resources into the household, as the single annual infusion of cash at harvest time never seemed to suffice. As a young girl of a different generation, Agnes Greene found a market for her work. At Fort Totten School, she learned new skills. "They taught us how to ... do beadwork, too, at school. Then, well, if you had time, you made belts. I made belts for my relatives and then I took one to the store, to Haslam Store, and I got $3.50 for it." Because local markets were limited, the students formed a club. Acting as their sales representative, a teacher found customers far from the reservation for the moccasins, birch bark baskets, billfolds, and dolls they made. "One day we'd get a check. Oh, that was something. [Laughs.]"[96]

Dakotas sold a variety of goods, from lumber to berries. As Native Americans, they were entitled to chop down trees on reservation land, so they sold them as fence posts and firewood. Bjorne Knudson recalled Dakotas selling from house to house around the reservation:

Like the older people now, they couldn't go out and chop good fence post, just for an example. Now a fence post should be at least five inches through to make a good post. So they'd chop poles which would be ... two or three inches across.

And they were no good for fence posts, but my mother she would always buy them anyway. And the common price on a fence post was ten cents a post. Well, if they come with a hundred posts, they'd have ten dollars. But they were old and feeble, kinda, and they couldn't chop good post. But my mother, she was that way, she just fed these people and done all she could for 'em.

Mamie Larson described Indians bringing cordwood to Sheyenne and, in turn, farmers going onto the reservation to buy wood. Others with fewer resources might make only occasional purchases. Thor Peterson said his family did not buy much from Indians, "'cause we couldn't afford to buy anything."

Every summer, Dakotas picked and sold wild berries. Agnes Greene recalled the satisfaction of generating cash: "Boy, when berry season came, you could sell berries. That's when you got money."[97] Hilda Redfox Garcia remembers the hard work of picking June berries all day long. Her mother would sell some, dry some, and can the rest for family use over the winter. As a child, Grace Lambert picked "whatever berries we have around here, like June berries, goose berries, currents, raspberries, choke cherries, plums."[98] Agnes Greene told a story about the profits one of her fellow tribal members made from selling June berries: "Like an old man, Wilfred Peoples, he lived right by Warwick.... When I was young, he was showing that little car and he had an old model T. ... And he said, 'That car's name is June.' After he sold June berries and bought it. [Laughs.] But he said in Indian, 'I named it June 'cause it's...' [Laughs.]"[99]

Many of the Norwegians in the area owned milk cows. Sigrid Gjeldaker Lillehaugen milked cows on her family farm, which meant she also fed them and watered them, mucked the barn, separated the cream from the milk, and often churned the butter.[100] Second-generation German Patrick Langstaff explained: "Milk cows, that was part of your livelihood; you always had your herd of milk cows. That was the one cash crop you could always depend on. [Laughs.] Grain you couldn't always depend on." His mother sold butter and eggs to the local store. Patrick continued: "They would buy the butter and the eggs, and then of course, you'd take the cash and...buy the store stuff. It was practically the same as barter. Only a little money changed, just a little bit, and then it went back out again. [Laughs.]"

In contrast, Dakotas did not engage in commercial dairying. In 1916, superintendent Ziebach wrote: "I find that the Indians do not take well to dairying, although many of them own cows and produce milk for their own use, but none is marketed."[101] He lamented the missed opportunity to generate income.

Women kept poultry as another source of small but steady income. Evelyn Jahr Greene's mother kept chickens, turkeys, and sheep. She would sell the wool from the sheep and sell turkeys at Thanksgiving and Christmas. Lois Olson Jones's mother "raised a thousand chicks. And then she cavenized the roosters." Not being raised on a farm myself, I had to ask what that meant. "You make them neuter!" she laughed. "And then they grow bigger. They grow 'til like ten pounds. . . . Almost like buying a turkey!" Her mother's industriousness turned into cash or highly valued commodities that were traded at the store. The poultry receipts enabled the family to pay the lawyer bills, for example. The birds had to be protected from predators in order to be profitable. Bjorne Knudson recalls his father setting a decoy and sitting in the barn, peering through a peephole, ready with his shotgun: "He'd shoot a coyote every once and a while."

* * * * *

Given the divergence between subsistence farming and industrialized, market-oriented agriculture, the bridges built by a common work life made coexistence possible. Scandinavian and Dakota women seemed immune to middle-class messages about the appropriate place of women as they fully engaged in the family economy. The independence they enjoyed was built on their deep involvement in agricultural work and on their capacity to make things and to fold childrearing into long work days. The system of flexible family and interdependent community labor helped these marginal farmers succeed in agriculture and establish autonomy from the larger culture.

FIGURE 1 Helene Haugen Kanten with family, 1902.

Like many families preparing to emigrate, the Haugens had their portrait taken in Christiania (Oslo), Norway, in 1902. Left to right, standing: Elling, Kjester, Aagodt, Helene; sitting: Inga, Christian, and Berthe. (Courtesy Hansen Family Private Collection.)

FIGURE 2 Ski jump on the Spirit Lake Reservation, 1936.

Norwegians brought skiing to the region and in the 1930s constructed a ski jump atop one of the reservation's highest hills. (Courtesy State Historical Society of North Dakota, Bismarck, 0056-004.)

FIGURE 3 Berthe Haugen's homestead shack, 2003.

This decaying, twelve-by-fourteen foot, two-story wooden structure overlooking the Sheyenne River was constructed as Berthe Haugen's residence on her homestead in 1906. Berthe planted the tree to the right of the shack, along with 599 others, as part of her improvement of the property. Photograph by Karen V. Hansen. (Courtesy Hansen Family Private Collection.)

FIGURE 4 Grace Lambert, 1976.

Grace Lambert was the only member of the Spirit Lake Nation who participated in the North Dakota Oral History Project. (Courtesy State Historical Society of North Dakota, Bismarck, 0032-IR-01-1.)

FIGURE 5 Visitors to powwow, Fort Totten, July 4, 1887.

White visitors gather to watch the annual Fourth of July powwow at Fort Totten, which featured Indian dancing. (Courtesy State Historical Society of North Dakota, Bismarck, 0420-0019.)

FIGURE 6 Sunka Ska, "White Dog"

Sunka Ska was a scout for the Sibley expedition of 1863 that searched for Dakotas who had killed white settlers during the U.S.—Dakota War. He lived at Spirit Lake, always wore a tomahawk in his belt, and often boasted of his collection of white men's scalps. He and an unidentified boy were included in a group portrait. (Courtesy Garcia Photo Collection, Tokio, ND.)

FIGURE 7 Two Dakota women, circa 1903–1916.

Two unidentified Dakota women pause for the photographer. (Courtesy Lake Region Heritage Museum, Cochburn Family Collection.)

FIGURE 8 Einar Severson, 1976.

In his oral history, Einar Severson told a story about his father rejecting the request of a traveling Dakota family to bury their deceased infant on the family farm. (Courtesy State Historical Society of North Dakota, Bismarck, 0032-NE-15.)

FIGURE 9 Indians traveling from Pembina to Fort Totten, 1910s.

At least two Native American families travel in horse-drawn wagons from Pembina to Fort Totten, gathering snakeroot and senega root, both used for medicinal purposes. (Courtesy North Dakota State University Archives-Institute for Regional Studies, Fargo, ND, rs006980).

FIGURE 10 Bridt and Knudt Fredrikson farm, 1911.

The huge barn and clapboard house of the Fredrikson family in Pekin, North Dakota, just east of Spirit Lake, confirmed that prosperity was possible. Editor Waldemar Ager published this image in *Kvartalskrift* along with a feature article assessing how Norwegian immigrants were doing in their western home. (Courtesy Fredrikson Family Collection.)

FIGURE 11 Ole Fredrikson, circa 1920.

Norwegian immigrant Ole Fredrikson was the brother of Knudt, who homesteaded in Nelson County and built that gargantuan barn. (Courtesy Fredrikson Family Collection.)

FIGURE 12 Marit Fredrikson, circa 1920.

Marit Fredrikson, who farmed with her husband, Ole, sits spinning wool. Many Norwegian women spun yarn and knitted sweaters, socks, and mittens. (Courtesy Fredrikson Family Collection.)

FIGURE 13 Bridt and Knudt Fredrikson family, 1901.

Bridt and Knudt Fredrikson pose with their children, Minne, Fridthjof, and baby Bella, in 1901. (Courtesy Fredrikson Family Collection.)

FIGURE 14 Man and woman haying with scythe, Norway, circa 1880–1890.

A man and woman in Norway cut hay using a scythe, while a younger woman stands near the drying racks. Their small farm, bounded by the fjord and mountains, has a shed made from an overturned boat. Photo by Swedish photographer Axel Lindahl, who documented the Norwegian countryside between 1880 and 1890. (Courtesy Norske Folkemuseum, Oslo, 9312-01157.)

FIGURE 15 James McLaughlin negotiating with Spirit Lake Dakotas, 1909.

U.S. Indian inspector James McLaughlin (front row, far right) returned to Spirit Lake many times to negotiate with the tribe. The room is filled with Dakotas. Front row, left: Suna Waanatan, son of the hereditary chief, unidentified woman, and agency officials. (Courtesy Denver Public Library, Western History Collection, Denver, CO, x-31650.)

FIGURE 16 Agnes and Warren Greene, 1942.

Wedding photo of Agnes and Warren Greene in front of St. Michael's Church, August 13, 1942. Photo taken by Father Dan, priest of St. Michael's. (Courtesy Garcia Photo Collection, Tokio, ND.)

FIGURE 17 Ignatius and Louisa Court, circa 1910.

Ignatius Court, Tamazakanhotanka ("His Loud Voiced Gun"), and his wife, Louisa Court, Itancanwin ("Boss/Chief Woman"). (Courtesy Garcia Photo Collection, Tokio, ND.)

FIGURE 18 Fort Totten main office, 1913.

This office was the bureaucratic headquarters of the Fort Totten Agency, where the superintendent met with tribal members and corresponded with the Commissioner of Indian Affairs in Washington, DC. (Courtesy State Historical Society of North Dakota, Bismarck, 970.637 T641 1913 p08.)

FIGURE 19 "Whole family" of Dakotas, circa 1903–1916.
Unidentified Dakota family sits in front of a tipi, with wagons and a house in the background. (Courtesy Lake Region Heritage Museum, Cochburn Family Collection.)

FIGURE 20 "Lest we forget": Woman in front of homestead shack, 1915.
A smiling woman stands in front of her homestead shack; "lest we forget" is written on the back. Note wash tub and rocking chair on display. (Courtesy State Historical Society of North Dakota, Bismarck, B0711-01.)

FIGURE 21 Kanten family, 1915.

Helene Haugen married Gilbert Kanten in 1910 and moved with his extended family to Saskatchewan, Canada. Here they pose with their children Ervin, Elsie, and baby Esther. (Courtesy Hansen Family Private Collection.)

FIGURE 22 Cherrie Lane Wood, 1976.

Cherrie Lane Wood, whose farmer husband became one of the largest landowners on the reservation by 1929, was interviewed for the North Dakota Oral History Project. (Courtesy State Historical Society of North Dakota, Bismarck, 0032-BE-17.)

FIGURE 23 Morton Anderson in Crary Bank, 1909.

Norwegian-American landowner Morton Anderson worked at the Crary Bank as a young man. He stands at the front teller window behind an unidentified man; W. J. Leahy is in the back window. (Courtesy Skurdall Family Collection.)

FIGURE 24 Bjorne Knudson, 1935.

Born to Norwegian immigrants and raised on the reservation, Bjorne Knudson found employment in Minnesota through a federal work program. He smiles jovially after planting six acres of corn. (Courtesy John Knudson Family Collection.)

FIGURE 25 Fort Totten Indian School, matron and students, 1896.

The female students and their white teacher at Fort Totten Indian School look surprisingly comfortable together. Photo by Herbert D. Cooper of Devils Lake. (Courtesy State Historical Society of North Dakota, Bismarck, D00663.)

FIGURE 26 Government Indian school, Fort Totten, 1907.

Groups of female students mill around the interior yard of the Fort Totten Indian School. A handwritten note bordering the image conveys news of an altercation after an athletic event: "We had a great time and great big fight too. The H[ilsboro High School] picked up there things and left the field. It was fierce for a while. . . . Lovingly, Lilian." (Courtesy North Dakota State University Archives, Fargo-Institute for Regional Studies, ND, rs003436.)

FIGURE 27 Rural school, Lakeview District, 1917 or 1918.

Children play outside the rural school, Lakeview District, in Lallie Township, Benson County. (Courtesy State Historical Society of North Dakota, Bismarck, 0032-BE-11-13.)

FIGURE 28 Ingemund Peterson and piglet, circa 1925.

Norwegian immigrant farmer Ingemund Peterson, who arrived on the reservation in 1915, poses with piglet. (Courtesy Peterson Family Private Collection.)

FIGURE 29 Theodore Jahr and unidentified fellow carpenter, Fort Totten, 1909.

Great-uncle of Evelyn Jahr Greene, Theodore Jahr (on the right, with unidentified man), found work as a carpenter at Fort Totten. He sent this photo as a postcard to his girlfriend in Minnesota. (Courtesy Brian Greene Private Collection.)

FIGURE 30 Warwick business district, circa 1905.

Once white homesteaders moved onto the reservation, two villages were planned. Main Street in Warwick was open for business even while under construction. (Courtesy State Historical Society of North Dakota, Bismarck, 2011-P-006-08.)

FIGURE 31 Lillian Wineman and friend, 1905.

Lillian Wineman, daughter of a Norwegian mother and German-Jewish father, claimed to be the first woman in Devils Lake to drive a car. (Courtesy State Historical Society of North Dakota, Bismarck, 0383-0007.)

FIGURE 32 Solomon Redfox and family with Reverend Ordahl, 1929.

The Redfox family camped at the dump ground near Binford, North Dakota. When Louise (Two Bear) gave birth, they recruited Lutheran minister Reverend M. B. Ordahl to baptize the infant. Left to right, standing: Solomon Redfox and Rev. M. B. Ordahl; sitting: June Marie Redfox (adopted); Mary (Mrs. Solomon) Redfox; Louise (Mrs. George) Redfox Two Bear, and infant; Ester Tipiwastewin ("grandmother"); a daughter of Ordahl; George Two Bear; and Archie Redfox, Sr. (Courtesy Garcia Photo Collection, Tokio, ND.)

FIGURE 33 Spirit Lake Indians dancing at Devils Lake Chautauqua, 1901.

Dakota women and men dance at the Chautauqua grounds north of Spirit Lake on Indian Day in 1901. (Courtesy State Historical Society of North Dakota, Bismarck, B0475.)

FIGURE 34 Spirit Lake Indian dancers, with U.S. flag flying, circa 1890.

Indian drum group and dancers at powwow, with non-Indian spectators in the background and U.S. flag flying, in 1901. (Courtesy State Historical Society of North Dakota, Bismarck, C1099.)

FIGURE 35 Norwegian Folk festival, circa 1930.

The costumes adorning these festival-goers were inspired by national Norwegian dress and fashioned with whatever people could find. The women wore white blouses and aprons, a few with breastplates, and the men wore white shirts, vests, and knickers. (Courtesy State Historical Society of North Dakota, Bismarck, 0075-0224.)

FIGURE 36 Helen Rutten and Cherrie Lane Wood, circa 1920.

Without a phone and separated by Devils Lake, friends Helen Rutten and Cherrie Lane Wood, longtime residents on the reservation, communicated in code by placing items on their clotheslines. (Courtesy Anderson Family Private Collection.)

FIGURE 37 Cherry Wood Monson, 1924.

Daughter of Cherrie Lane and Oscar Wood, Cherry Wood Monson grew up on her family's farm outside of Warwick on the reservation. She was two years old when this photo was taken in 1924. (Courtesy Anderson Family Private Collection.)

FIGURE 38 Fredrikson barn after the tornado, 1916.

In 1916, a tornado damaged the second story of the Fredrikson barn in Pekin, North Dakota, but missed the nearby house. (Courtesy Fredrikson Family Private Collection.)

FIGURE 39 Mr. and Mrs. Adolph Samuelson harvesting corn, 1909

Mr. and Mrs. Adolph Samuelson of Sheyenne harvest corn. Mrs. Samuelson, baby, and child pose in a buggy in their Sunday best. (Courtesy North Dakota State University Archives-Institute for Regional Studies, Fargo, ND, rs002737.)

FIGURE 40 Dakota woman working at the back of a wagon, circa 1903–1916.

An unidentified Dakota woman stands working at the back of a wagon. (Courtesy Lake Region Heritage Museum, Cochburn Family Collection.)

FIGURE 41 Great Western and Equity grain elevators, circa 1906–1912.

Equity Grain Elevator, on the right, was cooperatively owned by farmers. New Rockford, ND. (Courtesy North Dakota State University Archives-Institute for Regional Studies, Fargo, ND, rs006982.)

FIGURE 42 Grace Lambert and family,
circa 1939.

Charles, Grace, Vern, and Eugene Lambert.
(Courtesy Lambert Family Private Collection.)

FIGURE 43 Mrs. Martin Stahl feeding her poultry, 1922.

Mrs. Martin Stahl, of Pekin, North Dakota, feeding her poultry with a small child in tow. Most farms had a windmill to pump water. (Courtesy North Dakota State University Archives-Institute for Regional Studies, Fargo, ND, ua3322a.)

FIGURE 44 Norwegian woman knitting, circa 1880–1890.

Unidentified woman in Norway walks while knitting, with baby on her back and child with rake nearby, amidst agricultural activity. Photo by Swedish photographer Axel Lindahl, who documented the Norwegian country-side between 1880 and 1890. (Courtesy Norske Folkemuseum, Oslo, 9312-02408.)

FIGURE 45 Signing "declaration of allegience [*sic*]," 1913.

James McLaughlin is pressing the inked thumb of a Dakota man onto the page during a staged ritual at Fort Totten. Native people were asked to declare their allegiance to the U.S. government, abandon their Indian-ness, and embrace agriculture. Photo by Fredrick K. Dixon. (Courtesy Mathers Museum of World Cultures, Indiana University, 1962-08-3821.)

FIGURE 46 "Song of the Arrows," 1909.

"Song of the Arrows" was staged by photographer Joseph K. Dixon to dramatize Indians' shooting away traditional ways of life. Here, participants release their "last arrow" as part of this renunciation. He took this photo at the Crow Reservation in Montana with men he identified as members of the Blackfoot nation in 1909. Photo by Joseph K. Dixon. (Courtesy Mathers Museum of World Cultures, Indiana University, 1962-08-2006.)

FIGURE 47 Jennie Brown Cavanaugh, circa 1930.

Jennie Brown (Mrs. Frank) Cavanaugh, a farmer and the largest Dakota landowner, sits comfortably on her front porch. Photo taken by Clarence Itancan Longie. (Courtesy Garcia Photo Collection, Tokio, ND.)

FIGURE 48 Nancy Winona Mead, 1913.

Nancy Winona Mead's portrait was taken when Rodman Wanamaker's "Expedition of Citizenship to the North American Indian" visited Fort Totten in 1913. Photo by Fredrick K. Dixon. (Courtesy Mathers Museum of World Cultures, Indiana University, 1962-08-3814.)

FIGURE 49 Bernard Two Hearts, 1913.

Bernard Two Hearts, a farmer and litigant in the 1897 suit against the Benson County Board of Commissioners, posed in powwow regalia for the staged "shooting the last arrow" ritual at Fort Totten in 1913. Photo by Fredrick K. Dixon. (Courtesy Mathers Museum of World Cultures, Indiana University, 1962-08-3812.)

FIGURE 50 Mamie Larson, 1976.

Mamie Larson, an activist in the Nonpartisan League, participated in the North Dakota Oral History Project. (Courtesy State Historical Society of North Dakota, Bismarck, 0032-ED-17.)

FIGURE 51 Nonpartisan League picnic at Bye and Simonson farms, 1920.

Typical of Nonpartisan League picnics, this gathering, held on the adjacent farms of John Bye and John Simonson, brought families together for food, fun, and political discussion. Bye and Simonson were Norwegian immigrants whose homesteads were between Roseglen and Raub on the Fort Berthold Reservation in North Dakota. (Courtesy State Historical Society of North Dakota, Bismarck, 2009-P~1.)

FIGURE 52 Martin Fredrikson, Palmer Overby, Berdella Overby, and Bella Fredrikson, circa 1925. Martin and Bella were Fredrikson siblings and Palmer and Berdella were Overby siblings. The two families were neighbors, mixing friendship and occasionally romance. (Courtesy Fredrikson Family Collection.)

FIGURE 53 Gust A. and Annie Bostrom Berg, 1976.

Swedish American Gust A. Berg and his Swedish wife of fifty-five years, Annie Bostrom Berg, had lived at Spirit Lake Reservation since they married when they were interviewed by the North Dakota Oral History Project. (Courtesy State Historical Society of North Dakota, Bismarck, 0032-BE-15.)

FIGURE 54 Hans Larsgaard, 1976.

Norwegian immigrant, Hans Larsgaard of Nelson County, was interviewed by the North Dakota Oral History Project when he was 98 years old. (Courtesy State Historical Society of North Dakota, Bismarck, 0032-NE-14.)

FIGURE 55 Dakota leaders Suna Waanatan and Ignatius Court with President Franklin Delano Roosevelt at Fort Totten, 1934.

Suna Waanatan and Ignatius Court (left to right) stand next to the car transporting President Franklin Delano Roosevelt around Fort Totten two months after the passage of the Indian Reorganization Act, August 7, 1934. (Courtesy Garcia Photo Collection, Tokio, ND.)

PART THREE

The Divisions of Citizenship and the Grip of Poverty

7

Divergent Paths to Racialized Citizenship

FOR DAKOTA INDIANS and naturalized Norwegian immigrants, citizenship issues were deeply connected to land. Yet from their distinct vantage points, the avenues for political engagement pointed in different directions. Dakotas sought amends for their grievances against the U.S. government primarily in the courts, and Norwegians channeled their political voice through the ballot box.

In effect, Spirit Lake Dakotas took Congress at its word. The General Allotment Act of 1887 declared that, once allotted land, an Indian would be deemed a citizen: "Every Indian born within the territorial limits of the United States to whom allotments shall have been made under the provisions of this act, or under any law or treaty...is hereby declared to be a citizen of the United States, and is entitled to all the rights, privileges, and immunities of such citizens."[1]

In the early twentieth century, both Natives and newcomers used every available means to secure a place for themselves. They regarded land as an anchor against total dispossession and as a legitimate place on the continent. This chapter explores the ways in which Dakotas and Norwegian immigrants maneuvered through national debates about integration and adaptation into the American polity from their profoundly different legal positions. In particular, it chronicles how they interpreted and exercised their political citizenship.

A CONTESTED ELECTION

Even though Dakotas' main political antagonist was the U.S. government and their greatest political leverage resided in the federal courts, Dakotas at Spirit Lake acted upon their vision of full citizenship, which included the franchise. North Dakota held an election in November 1892, one week after the certification of tribal allotments. Interpreting the common-sense meaning of citizenship, Spirit Lake Dakotas showed up in force to vote.

According to the *Grand Forks Herald*, "Judge Standish made a flying trip to Devils Lake and other western points to head off the Indians who it was reported had made a grand charge 700 strong on the ballot boxes in the Fort Totten reservation on election day."[2] The inflammatory claim of a "grand charge" may have reflected how those manning the precinct at the fort perceived Dakotas' enthusiasm for voting, but it can hardly be considered a trustworthy account. There were only 485 adult men enrolled in 1890, along with 553 adult women.[3] While it is possible that Dakota women interpreted the Dawes Act as giving them the franchise as well—they were, after all, allotted land too—it is likely that the newspaper would have reported the even more spectacular event of Indian women demanding to vote when white women could not.[4] Needless to say, however much the general public supported "Indian reform," this assertion of political power was not what they had in mind. The enfranchisement of a large group of mostly illiterate people, as also occurred in the reconstruction South, stimulated reaction from white citizens who feared losing political power and being pressed to pay higher taxes with the expansion of public services and increased demands on the state.[5]

The small population of Spirit Lake Dakotas could not begin to affect statewide contests. Yet, because the majority of reservation land was concentrated in Benson County, Indians' votes were numerous enough to sway close elections. In that 1892 contest, Republican candidate Lars P. Havrevold, a naturalized Norwegian immigrant, won a seat in the state legislature by gaining Dakotas' votes. The losing candidate, James Michaels, disputed the results. Without Indian participation, he would have won by ten votes.[6] He took his case to court and challenged both the legitimacy of Havrevold's victory and the Indians' right to the franchise, arguing that Indians on the reservation should not have the power to decide an election. In adjudicating the case, Benson County sought testimony from officials at the U.S. Department of the Interior to clarify the right of Indians to vote.[7] The case immediately tested the meanings of citizenship under the Dawes Act.

Then, as now, states decided who was entitled to vote and how elections were conducted.[8] The 1884 case of *Elk v. Wilkins* pivoted on precisely this point. The U.S. Supreme Court upheld Nebraska's position that the Fourteenth Amendment did not apply to Native Americans. They were not citizens because they were not born on U.S. territory, but belonged to "alien nations, distinct political communities" within the boundaries of the United States. Even a man like John Elk, who had separated himself from his tribe and gone to live among whites, was not entitled to renounce his allegiance to his Native people; Indians were legally prohibited from becoming naturalized citizens.[9]

North Dakota's constitution, written in 1889 after the *Elk v. Wilkins* decision and the Dawes Act but before reservation land was allotted, specified that "civilized persons of Indian descent who shall have severed their tribal relations two years preceding such election" would be eligible to vote.[10] Here, as in many other states, "civilized" Indians were defined as those who owned land and were not governed by chiefs or tribal councils. These criteria were taken as measures of investment in the agricultural economy and independence from "foreign nations," that might be trying to shape U.S. politics. Legal scholar Jeanette Wolfley notes, "During the nineteenth century, opponents of Indian citizenship took the position that maintaining tribal ties was incompatible with citizenship, being 'civilized,' and voting in state elections."[11] Although in passing the Dawes Act the federal government rejected this position, states continued to interpret Indian citizenship in contradictory ways. In effect, North Dakota law linked citizenship to "civilization" and the rejection of historic ways of life.[12] Moreover, as Fredrick Hoxie explains, "The extension of citizenship to Indians did not alter their status as legal wards of the government. And the existence of the guardianship relation could limit their rights as citizens."[13]

After the dispute between Michaels and Havrevold, the state legislature took action to clarify conditions of the franchise and amended the state constitution in 1896. It explicated the meaning of Indian citizenship and its basis in landownership:

> No Indian or person of Indian descent who has not received a final patent conveying the title in free of lands allotted to him within the boundaries of this state... shall be deemed a qualified elector... or be entitled to the rights and privileges of an elector unless he was born within the limits of the United States, and has voluntarily taken up his residence within this State separate and apart from any tribe of Indians therein, and adopted the habits of civilized life, and is in no manner subject to the authority of any Indian chief or council or Indian agent of the United States.[14]

The pivotal clause involved the "final patent"—owning land in one's own name, free from federal guardianship. Allotment was a step toward individual landownership, but because of Indians' trust status, without a fee patent it did not convey outright ownership or signify an Indian's emancipation from wardship. Unhappy with the limits placed on tribal members' ability to vote, Dakotas went to court.

While the records of the Benson County legislative dispute were destroyed in a fire, several subsequent acts give us insight into how events unfolded. Dakotas petitioned to have a voting precinct at Fort Totten, but the Benson County commissioners refused. Seven Dakota men—Arthur Thompson, Frank Demarce, Alex Demarce,

Wakaksan, Canpaksan, Tawacinhehomni, and Bernard Two Hearts—pressed their claim, insisting that a precinct should be consistently open on the reservation so that they could exercise their "sovereign right of suffrage." The commissioners again refused. The *Bismarck Daily Tribune* reported white Benson County residents' concern about the potential power of Dakota voters to determine the outcome of local elections: "If they 'stand together' they can virtually control the politics of Benson county and the twentieth legislative district."[15] And indeed they did in 1892.

The lower court found in favor of Dakotas. Not willing to concede, the county commissioners appealed the decision and barred Dakotas from voting in the fall election of 1896.[16] In 1897, the North Dakota Supreme Court issued an opinion that upheld the lower court's decision, clarifying the issues of citizenship and jurisdiction implied in the recent amendment to the state constitution. The opinion refers to allotment as awarding "preliminary patents," not final ones. But from the court's perspective, those were sufficient to grant citizenship. According to the state supreme court's opinion, Dakotas "claim that they are citizens of the United States residing within the State of North Dakota, and amenable to all the laws, civil and criminal, of said state, and likewise entitled to all the privileges and immunities conferred by such laws upon other citizens of the United States resident within such state."[17] In effect, the court affirmed the Dakotas' interpretation of the law. That powerful opinion issued by North Dakota's highest court did not, however, forestall future disputes at the polls.

The important issue of legal jurisdiction over reservation land and inhabitants lingered. Did the reservation belong under the umbrella of the federal government or of the state? In its 1897 opinion, the North Dakota Supreme Court referred to the terms of agreement when Dakota Territory was divided into North Dakota and South Dakota. The two new states agreed to honor the treaties and contractual obligations of the United States as they then existed. Therefore, the North Dakota Supreme Court reasoned, the United States had the authority to make decisions regarding the disposition of land, but all other matters, including taxes, law enforcement, and the franchise, were to be decided by the state. This complex legal landscape created confusion since the terms of landownership were set by the federal government, but those terms affected the qualifications for the rights and responsibilities of citizenship determined by the state.

Comparing Dakotas and foreign-born Norwegians, both of whom had a tenuous foothold in the American polity, illuminates the racial stratification of citizenship and the assumptions that informed their actions as well as the processes that limited them. Federal policymakers and state-level politicians assumed that Scandinavians, like other northern Europeans, could readily be assimilated but that Indians must become "civilized" and "detribalized" in order to qualify for citizenship rights.

While the two groups faced some of the same challenges, Dakotas, like African Americans, encountered many more obstacles to full citizenship than Norwegians, who not only could be naturalized but were accepted as white. Dakotas' second-class citizenship was racialized, in parallel to that of African Americans.

Political citizenship gave Dakotas and Norwegian immigrants a means to exercise their political voice, but once conferred, it was not the rapid path to assimilation that social reformers and government officials imagined. At Spirit Lake, Dakotas and Norwegians both utilized the combination of landownership and citizenship not simply to adapt to American society but also to retain their hold on the land, resist the dominant culture, speak a language other than English, and challenge the economy that privileged big business and disadvantaged small producers.

As newly anointed citizens, Dakotas and naturalized Norwegians exercised the franchise. Their contrasting histories, population size, and legal status, however, pointed Indians primarily to the justice system and Norwegians to electoral politics. Not only were their numbers smaller, but Dakotas also met local resistance to their political participation, being turned away at the polls even after receiving sanction from the state's highest court.

DAKOTAS' PATH TO CITIZENSHIP

In spite of their status as domestic dependent nations, Indian tribes held a powerful means of leverage with the United States—treaty obligations—in addition to their rights specified in law. The federal logic of nation-to-nation relationships meant that Spirit Lake Dakotas could press Congress and the president to honor the government's commitments to their people. Because of a U.S. Court of Claims decision in 1881, they gained another federal forum for exposing and adjudicating their grievances against the United States.[18] According to Frederick Hoxie, a minor industry in Indian law sprang up during the late nineteenth century, including a significant number of indigenous attorneys. He observes that Indian leaders used "the court to air general indictments of government incompetence and deception."[19]

Sissetons and Wahpetons living on multiple reservations, including Spirit Lake, collectively sought redress for their treatment after the 1862 war; they mobilized to sue the United States in the Court of Claims to restore their annuities. In 1901 Congress approved their petition and passed "special jurisdictional legislation that would direct the court to hear their suits."[20] Sissetons and Wahpetons argued the annuities rightfully due them based on the 1851 Treaty of Traverse des Sioux had been wrongfully terminated. They claimed that despite their staunch loyalty to the United States in 1862, when some warriors scouted for U.S. generals and rescued many white residents and prisoners of war, they were treated as hostile enemies and promises made to them in the heat of war were subsequently abandoned. The hearings for the case solicited testimony from many of those scouts, who attested to the broken promises and devastating consequences.[21] "By confiscating their annuities and reservations Congress had left these friendly and innocent people homeless, to wander and suffer for lack of food and clothing in a high latitude," as William Folwell put it in his *History of Minnesota*.[22]

In 1904, after hearing the case, the Court of Claims dismissed their petition, arguing that the evidence presented was insufficient to differentiate who had maintained their loyalty to the United States from those who had taken up arms.[23] Sissetons and Wahpetons then took their case in two directions, appealing the Court of Claims decision before the U.S. Supreme Court and asking Congress to appropriate restored annuities. The U.S. Supreme Court decided against them in 1908, upholding the Court of Claims decision.[24] But they found political success with Congress. With support from Minnesota legislators, those closest to the history and most invested in assessing the outbreak and consequences of the war, in 1906, Congress passed appropriations with "set off payments" that recognized its wrongful action in 1863 and the veracity of the Sisseton-Wahpeton claims.

Consistent with its action in most Native American cases, the Court of Claims dismissed future cases, but Sissetons and Wahpetons did not give up. While they had more success adjudicating their issues in the North Dakota courts, they pressed forward, using the Court of Claims as a national venue for affirming their history and exposing the wrongs of the federal government.

The extent to which those designated "citizen Indians" exercised the franchise should be understood as the resolution of a fundamental tension between Dakotas' sense of entitlement and local whites' resistance to their full political participation. Despite the 1897 opinion upholding Indians' citizenship in North Dakota, the dispute over their ability to cast a ballot erupted again several years later in Eddy County, which also encompassed some reservation land. Dakota men there demanded a local precinct in 1900. The *Bismarck Daily Tribune* reported a confrontation in Jamestown:

Peter Blueshield and his attorneys were in the city last night to argue before the court the mandamus proceedings against the commissioners of Eddy county to establish a voting precinct upon that portion of the Fort Totten reservation in that county. There are about 13 civilized Indians residing in the three townships of the reservation that project into Eddy county and they want the privilege of voting this fall. Peter is a tall, well formed Indian and his brother Martin, John and Jacob Abrahamson, Jos. Jackson, [Samuel Akitena] and James C. Young are the plaintiffs in the suit. Jackson is said to be a fine accountant. All can speak English, have their several allotments, have severed their tribal relations and own considerable stock and farm machinery.[25]

From the perspective of the newspaper, these men's English proficiency, engagement in farming and commerce, and prepossessing appearance made a persuasive case. Four days later the *Bismarck Daily Tribune* reprinted the *New Rockford Volunteer*'s interpretation of the confrontation: "The refusal of the county board to establish a voting precinct for the Fort Totten Indians is because they fear the Indians will vote the Republican ticket. The board is democratic."[26] Like many American officeholders, the commissioners very possibly did seek to limit the voting rights of those who opposed the party in power. At this time, the Republicans were still considered the party of Lincoln, emancipation, and equal rights.

Thereafter, newspapers occasionally reported on voting patterns at Fort Totten. For example, the *Devils Lake Inter-Ocean* reported that of the 104 Indians who voted in the 1904 presidential election, 99 voted the straight Republican ticket, supporting the incumbent Theodore Roosevelt; four voted Democratic; and one voted for Eugene Debs, the Socialist Party candidate.[27] Annual reports to the Indian Office occasionally noted the number of tribal members who were "voters of the state," a number that precisely corresponded to the number of Dakota men twenty-one years of age and older.[28] Nonetheless, at various times Dakotas continued to face challenges when exercising their right to vote. A group living at the Standing Rock Reservation pressed the government on this issue. In 1920, the North Dakota Supreme Court decided *Swift v. Leach* in Dakotas' favor. In many realms, including the courts and the electoral process, Dakotas continued to struggle with their second-class citizenship and achieved some victories along the way.

Taxes, "Fee-Patent Indians," and Activist Mobilization

Another citizenship battle was fought over taxes. As the relationship between the United States and Indian people was framed in the Constitution, "Indians not taxed" were excluded from citizenship, enumeration, and political representation. In considering citizenship for black persons and recently freed slaves, Congress deliberated about whether Indians deserved a place in the Civil Rights Act of 1866. Refusing again to link Indian citizenship to property ownership, Congress explored the standing of Indians and how the constitutional framing related taxation to citizenship. Senators affirmed original intent by likening Indians, who they described as "wild, savage, and untamed," to " 'foreigners, as separate nations. We deal with them by treaty and not by law.' "[29] Ultimately, they inserted a phrase consistent with the Constitution—"excluding Indians not taxed"—into the bill, which was later incorporated into the Fourteenth Amendment. As scholar George Beck points out, Indians were considered virtual foreigners, members of "independent nations, to some extent, existing in our midst but not constituting a part of our population, and with whom we make treaties."[30] Henceforward, the category of "Indians taxed," as distinct from "Indians not taxed," was used interchangeably with citizenship and implied assimilation, or at least engagement in the formal economy.

To Dakotas, taxation loomed as a threat precisely because they foresaw how it could lead to land loss. In fact, to them it represented one of the more objectionable aspects of the Dawes Act. They argued that the treaty of 1867 stated that "they are entitled to their lands in severalty without subjecting them to taxation."[31] Not taxing Indian land had local consequences for precisely those services that taxes provided—schools, roads, and courts. To the white public, taxation epitomized taking responsibility for membership in the polity. Within a taxpayer's logic, entitlements to use public resources should be paired with contributions to the public good.[32]

As constructed in the land-in-severalty legislation, paying taxes and owning land were tied to competency. Initially, competence turned on the government's assessment of bloodedness, with "full blooded" Dakotas presumed to be "incompetent." Those judged "competent" to own the patent to their lands would then pay taxes. The Indian Office wielded the power of deciding who was competent, who could take title to their land, and who would pay taxes. After the Dead Indian Act of 1902 and the Burke Act of 1906, the issues of arbitrary decision making over a fee-simple title to land became more pressing and more confusing.

With citizenship and its attendant obligations and privileges constantly up for negotiation and land hanging in the balance, Congress was urged to clarify the citizenship status of Indians. It set out to resolve the messiness of the designation and the process by including a provision in the Omnibus Act of 1910 that established competency commissions. The goal was to establish a standardized process of assigning fee-simple titles to allotted Indians, taking the arbitrary decision-making power out of the hands of the Indian superintendent and the Commissioner of Indian Affairs. The rationale was that once native people had fee-simple titles they would be required to pay taxes on their land.

These commissions, which were to travel to reservations around the country making determinations, were designed to expedite full citizenship and hence facilitate tax paying. Frederick Hoxie outlines the contours of competency as it was debated and adjudicated within the Office of Indian Affairs: "'Competent' Indians had received some education or had some experience with whites and therefore could be expected to survive on their own. It was not necessary for a competent Indian to be the equal of his white neighbor, but only to be 'healthy' and a 'good laborer or other workman.' The incompetent were a 'mere waste element,' requiring constant supervision and support. Protection for the incompetent was justified by their backwardness."[33] Christine Zahn (b. 1901), a member of the Standing Rock Sioux, reflected on the message that "competency" so clearly conveyed to her: "I was just a kid, but I remember it said that we Indians were diseased and incompetent. That's why … it had to be held in trust. I never did forget that."[34] In doing research on land that had belonged to her grandmother that the family lost when she died, Eunice Davidson said, "In a lot of our probates … they declare them incompetent, or they say they couldn't read, mostly it was aiming at their language, not understanding or being able to write it, and they declared them incompetent because of that." She then points to the fact that it was in the early twentieth century, precisely at this moment and in these deliberations about competency, that "so many lost their land." Nationally, Hoxie finds Native American resistance and U.S. government intransigence: "Many Indians were uncooperative, but the next two years brought over two hundred thousand acres of trust land onto local tax rolls."[35] Ultimately, the sale of Indian lands, a newly stated goal of the Indian Office, became the mission of the commissions as well.

The public discussion of Indians' entitlements and obligations as citizens reflected an underlying unbridled resentment of Native people. In the context of the destruction of Native Americans' economic base and their confinement to reservations, this debate pointed to their lingering reliance on the government for basic necessities. Tax-paying residents of Benson County, including Scandinavian immigrants, viewed exemption from taxation as an unfair benefit accruing to Indians' dependent status. They interpreted treaty agreements that obliged the U.S. government to provide annuities and rations as welfare rather than as compensation for land that had been ceded or seized. In theory, taxation brought citizens into shared governance and created common public goods. Practically, tax revenue financed the building and improvement of roads, the public schools, and the county courts. White residents resented Native Americans' use of these services without commensurate contributions.

White residents recognized that taxing Indian land on the reservation would generate little additional funds for the county. In 1900, before white homesteaders had taken land on the reservation, the *Bismarck Daily Tribune* remarked that Indians' "personal property is so trifling in value that the cost of assessment and collection would exceed the returns."[36] In effect, as Dakotas were incorporated into the polity, whites' bitterness mounted in Benson County because reservation land was either exempt from taxation or had so little value that taxing it made only a minimal contribution to the county's tax coffers.

Furthermore, county costs rose with Indian citizenship because of increased demands placed upon the courts, the roads, and later the schools. As a result, Indian superintendent Charles Ziebach observed, "There is some prejudice against the Indian securing public school privileges and other recognition in state courts, owing to the fact that *he pays no taxes.*"[37] At Spirit Lake, only a small number of tribal members were "fee-patent" Indians (160 in 1913),[38] so the lack of taxes presumably refers to the low value of their property, while the rest of the tribe remained exempt from taxation. This disparity created a divisive wedge between Dakotas and Scandinavians, along with other whites. Contradictorily, whites were demanding that citizen Indians be held responsible for meeting the same obligations as whites and were angry that Indians were so poor. The substantial number of Native Americans who enlisted in the army during the Great War altered this discussion, although it did not recede entirely.[39] Offering one's life in defense of the country became a more profound measure of loyal citizenship.

Addressing these issues and a host of others in need of reform and providing a national voice representing Indian people, a group of educated Indians founded the Society of American Indians (SAI).[40] Along with other leaders in the SAI, such as Arthur C. Parker (Seneca) and Carlos Montezuma (Mohave Apache), Dakotas Zitkala-Ša and Charles Eastman sought to shape the national debate concerning pan-tribal issues and federal Indian policy. They informed the public about legislative agendas, and lobbied for the federal government to eliminate barriers so that Indians could succeed in American society while still retaining vital aspects of their ancestral cultures. The SAI published *American Indian Magazine* and sponsored national conventions to develop and debate legislation to improve the lives of Indian people.

The merits of citizenship were among the most hotly debated issues in the organization. In one of her many articles, Zitkala-Ša detailed her position: "Wardship is no substitute for American citizenship, therefore we seek his enfranchisement. The many treaties made in good faith with the Indian by our government we would like to see equitably settled. By a constructive program we hope to do away with the 'piecemeal legislation' affecting Indians here and there which has proven an exceedingly expensive and disappointing method."[41] Not all Indians embraced citizenship, and Hoxie observes that the franchise was not a primary focus either for Native activists or for the Indian Office's "'civilization' campaign."[42] Some saw the drive to citizenship as a thinly veiled attempt to strip Indians of their culture and their land. Mary Louise Defender Wilson commented that her grandparents found no use in fee-patenting at Standing Rock; in fact, she observed, most of those who attained citizenship in this way lost their land. But leading Spirit Lake tribal members, such as Chief Little Fish and Ignatius Court, embraced the privileges of citizenship and set an example of participating in the electoral system that they saw as a crucial dimension of political power.

Shooting the "Last Arrow"

In the 1910s—as the Indian Office was preoccupied by the business of assessing competency and promoting citizenship—land dispersal, art, and politics converged. Joseph K. Dixon, a Yankee photographer sponsored by the department store magnate, Rodman Wanamaker, used his art to create a symbolic break with the past, encourage citizenship among Native Americans, and generate a market for his work.[43] Like other photographers who documented indigenous peoples across the continent, Dixon traveled far and wide. Sanctioned by the government, Dixon and his traveling companion, James McLaughlin, then inspector with the Indian Office, staged a ceremony to symbolize the process of shedding Indian culture and embracing the virtues of U.S. citizenship. It dramatized the policy shifts underway and created an opportune occasion for photography.

With great fanfare, Dixon's 20,000-mile "Expedition of Citizenship to the North American Indian" made a stop at Fort Totten. In November 1913, tribal members, some dressed in full powwow regalia and others in their Sunday best, gathered in the Fort Totten square with Dixon and McLaughlin. The ceremony involved airing a speech recorded by President Woodrow Wilson, listening to McLaughlin deliver one of his own, raising a gargantuan U.S. flag, and signing a "declaration of allegiance [*sic*] to the United States Government" (see figure 45).[44] An iconic masculine image that Dixon staged earlier, the "song of the arrows," perfectly conveys the romantic "ideal" of the "noble savage," a photographic representation of historic Indian culture that Dixon asserted was marked for extinction (see figure 46).[45]

Perhaps more bizarre than this contrived and commercially invested but artistically driven event was the sequel staged by the Indian Office three years later. Commissioner of Indian Affairs Cato Sells—who, according to historian Francis Paul Prucha, was "obsessed with the idea of 'freeing' competent Indians from federal protection and supervision"[46]—devised a similar ritual with legal punch. Under Sells, who served as commissioner from 1913 to 1921, the Indian Office pushed fee patenting as a step toward full citizenship. This approach did not bother with preparation for civic engagement but rather focused on self-sufficient ownership of land.

Sells staged an Indian Office version of the "last arrow" spectacle, albeit without the photographs. Here, as in the 1913 pageant, Indians symbolically gave up hunting, part of their traditional way of life, and embraced the plow to signify sedentary farming. These ceremonies were performed at approximately eight reservations in 1916, including Fort Totten.[47] Once again, James McLaughlin was front and center.

Journalist Myrtle Wright reported on the inaugural event in South Dakota, which included the U.S. Secretary of the Interior, Franklin Lane, and Yankton Sioux: "Each Indian was called by his white name and then requested to tell his Indian name. As he responded to his name he was handed a bow and arrow and directed to shoot." By shooting the arrow, he indicated that he was leaving his Indian ways in the past. He was instructed to place his hand on the plow as Secretary Lane said, "This act means that you have chosen to live the life of the white man—and the white man lives by work. From the earth we all must get our living, and the earth will not yield unless man pours upon it the sweat of his brow. Only by work do we gain a right to the land or to the enjoyment of life."[48] The words were repeated with each candidate in turn. Participants were given a leather purse, a small flag, and "a golden-colored badge bearing the simple but glorious inscription: 'Citizen of the United States.'"[49] The event concluded with a tribute to the flag and a rousing rendition of "America." As Vine Deloria, Jr., astutely observes, "The ritual should be an adequate example of the utter failure of white society to comprehend the nature and meaning of culture."[50]

Like citizenship itself, the last-arrow ceremony was marked as masculine. In describing the process, Dakota elder Grace Lambert relayed her father's story about that day: "They made them shoot that arrow first, you remember? I suppose you have heard that." When I replied that I had, she continued. "Well, they said that all these selected men…that were capable of running a farm they figured. I don't know how they ever had that figuration, but they figured that these men here and their families could run a farm."[51] From the government's perspective, citizenship was fundamentally tied to private property, labor, and agriculture.[52] That men would be central to the ceremony was entirely in keeping with Dakota culture, in which men hunted and defended the tribe, kept bows and arrows, and negotiated treaties. It is no surprise that even Grace Lambert, one of Spirit Lake Dakotas' most eloquent and astute narrators, recounts the ceremony as a male affair.

Yet, I was surprised to discover, eight women stood alongside the eighteen men who shot the last arrow at Spirit Lake. After interviewing Grace Lambert, I returned to an article I had seen in the 1916 student newspaper, *The Fort Totten Review*. It listed the women who participated that day: Jennie Brown Cavanaugh, Jean Grawe, Lizzie Cavanaugh Lamereaux, Louisa Lohnes, Nancy Winona Mead, Inez Palmer Swartzlander, Maggie Strait, and Emma White.[53] Did they take the bow in hand and shoot an arrow? Without a more detailed account, it is difficult to know. With the exception of Vine Deloria, Jr., the many scholars, from Francis Prucha to Lucy Maddox, who have written about the last-arrow ceremonies, in either the Indian Office or the Wanamaker expedition version, have largely ignored their gendered dimension.[54]

Myrtle Wright's eyewitness account, the most detailed depiction of women I could locate, reported that the ceremony conferred "all the rights of suffrage, so far as compatible with the various state laws. Each woman was called by her white name and was tendered a work bag and a purse and instructed to hold them in her hand as the Secretary addressed her."[55] The purses, which were also given to men, symbolized prudent saving. As she noted, the gendered message about the place of women aligned with their subsidiary citizenship status.

In November 1916, white women did not have national suffrage, although they did have the right to vote in school elections in North Dakota. In fact, womanhood suffrage was a campaign issue in the elections that fall.[56] Yet eight Dakota women partook of the ceremony. Regardless of whether women shot the arrow, they sought autonomy for their people and for themselves. According to Prucha, however, "the Indians frequently did not welcome federal citizenship, and the effects of citizenship in the end were meager, for the actual situation of the Indians was changed very little."[57] What promise did these women imagine it would hold?

While no extant records speak to their personal motivations for participating, considering what is known about these women helps locate them in the community and provides some clues to their behavior. Although women were respected members of the tribe, they did not hold formal leadership positions and were not members of delegations that negotiated with the federal government. Importantly, all the women who participated that day were tribal members who had been allotted land. Jennie Brown Cavanaugh was a widow and, at sixty-one years, the eldest in the group; she was one of the most prosperous Dakota farmers on the reservation (see figure 47). As a landowner and farmer, she would have had strong incentives to exercise every legal means available to secure her grip on her land. She was born to a white father and a Dakota mother, and she married a white man, Frank Cavanaugh, the boss farmer for the reservation. After he died in 1915, she continued to run a successful farm enterprise. That year she owned a seven-room house, a 28' x 40' framed barn, 22 horses, 45 cattle, 22 hogs, 12 sheep, and lots of chickens, and had 400 acres under cultivation. She had given birth to twelve children, ten of whom were still living in 1916.[58] Singular in her approach to land, Jennie also bid on Indian land available for purchase.[59] By 1929, as a farmer in her own right, she owned 560 acres, becoming the largest landowner in the tribe.

All of the other seven women were married, three to white men and two to men who also shot the arrow. The youngest of the group, Louisa Lohnes, was twenty-five, had received six years of formal schooling, spoke English, and never had children. Inez Palmer Swartzlander was daughter to Elizabeth M. Faribault and Indian trader Frank Palmer. She was the great-granddaughter of Jean Baptiste Faribault (a French fur trader) and Pelagie Faribault, a Dakota woman related to Little Crow's band, who successfully held possession of Pikes Island at the intersection of the Mississippi and Minnesota (St. Peter's) Rivers in the early nineteenth century. Much to the chagrin of the expanding American empire and soldiers at Fort Snelling next door, she forced the U.S. government to pay for and recognize that the land "belonged to her and not her husband."[60]

Nancy Winona Mead was the only woman among them who consented to be photographed by Dixon in 1913, when she was forty-seven (see figure 48). We do know that she owned land in 1910 and that she still possessed her allotment in 1929. The story of her first marriage to Kaśdana, or Hair Cut, is a gruesome one. In the 1880s, as she traveled with her father (Two Bulls), her mother, two of her sisters, and her nephew to visit relatives on another reservation, Hair Cut made a fateful decision to show allegiance to James McLaughlin, who had forbidden tribal members to leave the reservation.[61] Evidently Hair Cut aspired to become a tribal policeman. In the middle of the night he used an ax to kill his father-in-law, his mother-in-law, and one of his sisters-in-law as they slept in a tipi. When Hair Cut's crimes were uncovered, he was jailed. Winona helped him escape, as the story goes, by smuggling a file to him in a cooked duck. According to the research of Louis Garcia, honorary tribal historian at Spirit Lake, Winona did so because she sought her own revenge. It was a family affair, not business of the state. Later, at the family's bidding, an unmarried man from the tribe was commissioned to kill Hair Cut. He found him in Pipestone, Manitoba, and shot him.[62]

Winona made a life for herself, remarrying several times. She gave birth to eight children, three of whom died in infancy. Thirty-five years after the violent tragedy in her family, she consented to be photographed by Dixon. Three years later she joined the other women in the citizenship ritual. With little evidence, we cannot know how a young woman who subverted U.S. law in order to claim Indian justice earlier in her life could later decide to leave behind symbolically her Indian-ness through a ceremony sponsored by the Indian Office.

Possible incentives for women's participation include a rejection of Indian Office control over their lives and a quest for autonomy regarding their land that one more gimmick might yield.[63] Ironically, submitting to a government ritual provided a means of rejecting government control. Perhaps the participants were proven, capable farm managers, as Grace Lambert implied. That was certainly true of Jennie Brown Cavanaugh. They may have been seeking the benefits of full landownership. Perhaps they shared the political perspective of the Society of American Indians and believed that citizenship was a path to economic, political, and cultural autonomy. Since half of them were related to non-Indians through descent and marriage, perhaps they were a self-selected group that was comfortable with integration and predisposed to the idea. According to Indian superintendent Ziebach's reports of 1910 and 1913, those who received fee patents had used their new status to obtain mortgages and purchase farm equipment, not to sell their land. Unquestionably, Dakota women had been disadvantaged in allotment and in their quest for full citizenship.

Many of the Dakota men who participated in the ceremony were active farmers with large acreages under cultivation. Since this ritual cast citizenship as rooted in private property and farming, it is logical that two of the four largest-scale male farmers on the reservation—John Lohnes and Robert Cavanaugh—participated.[64] William Leaf had previously applied to the Indian superintendent for a fee patent and had been turned down. Bernard Two Hearts, a prosperous farmer, had been one of the litigants pressing Dakotas' right to vote against the Benson County supervisors in 1892. Like Nancy Winona Mead and William Leaf, he had been photographed by Dixon in 1913 and had "shot the arrow" (see Figure 49). Perhaps he viewed this event as an opportunity. Four Dakota men who shot the arrow were related to women who participated that day. Two men were married to women who took part, and two others were sons of Jennie Cavanaugh. Some had kinship ties that linked them to white families in the Indian Office bureaucracy. Henry Buisson was the nephew of two former Indian agents, James McLaughlin and John Cramsie, who married his father's sisters. Half were under the age of forty, and all were married—many several times. Solomon Redfox had become a Congregational lay minister who had been educated at the Santee Normal Training School, where he learned to play the organ. Jacob Abraham had been one of the men to challenge the commissioners of Eddy County when he was denied access to the voting booth in 1900. He and Charley Belland belonged to the Bdecan Presbyterian Church.

In contrast to many indigenous peoples across the country, Dakotas at Spirit Lake seized upon the rhetorical promise of the Dawes Act. They participated in electoral politics by exercising their right to vote, asserting their citizenship, contesting its limitations, and indefatigably pressing their cases before the Court of Claims. Twenty-five years after allotment, a handful of tribal members participated in a ritual of citizenship that, given the change in laws, promised greater autonomy over their lives and land.

NORWEGIANS' PATH TO CITIZENSHIP

Immigrants and Indians, who entered the twentieth century with different legal statuses and contrasting histories, nonetheless had to decide which aspects of American society to accommodate, which to transform, and whether participation in the U.S. polity was worth the price.

Parallel to Dakotas, Norwegian Americans debated how to express Norwegian-ness and continue cultural and ancestral practices. Immigrants and their U.S.-born children deliberated the merits and dangers of blending into American society versus maintaining affiliation with Norway.[65] How much continuity and authenticity could be maintained in the U.S. context? These debates echoed the larger ones across North America during the Progressive Era as the country struggled to incorporate unprecedented numbers of immigrants into an economy and society that was fundamentally unequal but needed their cheap labor. Members of immigrant and indigenous groups were pressured to blend into the "melting pot," adopt capitalist and democratic values, embrace an American identity, speak English, and take their place in the expanding economy.

Many Norwegians, in contrast to more visible immigrant groups, rejected the dominant American ethos of abandoning their culture of origin and disappearing into the mainstream. They argued that the multiplicity of people who brought the best of their culture with them enriched civic life. Echoing the cultural pluralist positions of influential Norwegian American writers Ole Rølvaag and Waldemar Ager, a first-generation immigrant farmer, Rasmus Yri, forcefully justified his affinity with two countries in his unpublished memoir: "We hear so much about being 100 percent American. My contentions are that if one is ashamed or belittles his Fatherland, then he is not to be trusted in his adopted country."[66] From his perspective, his loyalty to his Norwegian ancestry enhanced his ability to contribute to the United States. Like Dakotas, Norwegian Americans debated the place of English and the desirability of Americanization.

Naturalization

Unlike Native Americans, immigrants could become naturalized citizens. Even with their ambivalence about the dominant culture and their continuing loyalty to their homeland, Norwegian immigrants became naturalized at extraordinarily high rates in North Dakota. By 1920, the year the Nineteenth Amendment granting women's suffrage, was ratified, 83 percent of Norwegian-born women in North Dakota had already become naturalized citizens. This figure compares to 52 percent of foreign-born women nationally and 79 percent of foreign-born women in North Dakota.[67] Swedish and Danish women also became naturalized at rates much higher than foreign-born women nationally: 76 percent and 68 percent, respectively, in North Dakota. Norwegian men, too, became citizens at a rate much higher than other immigrant men, although at a rate lower than women. In 1920, 75 percent of Norwegian men in North Dakota had been naturalized, compared to 47 percent of foreign-born men nationally.[68] Once women could vote and the census began collecting data on women separately, their naturalization rates slightly but consistently surpassed those of men.

Laws linking married women's citizenship status to that of their husbands shaped their nationality. Marrying a citizen altered women's status, whereas for men it did not. The 1855 Naturalization Act, the first piece of legislation that spoke to the citizenship rights of foreign-born women who married U.S. citizens, held that foreign-born women were automatically naturalized upon marriage to a U.S. citizen or when their husbands became naturalized. In effect, they received citizenship derivatively. The law structured incentives for them to marry men who were native-born or naturalized citizens or, perhaps, to push their husbands to be naturalized. A married foreign-born woman was unable to initiate the naturalization process. Like Indian people, she had no standing to apply for citizenship.[69]

The 1907 Expatriation Act added a twist by addressing the issue of women citizens who married foreign-born, non-naturalized men. Maintaining the idea that a married woman's citizenship status should be derivative, this law defined U.S.-born as well as foreign-born wives' citizenship by their husband's nationality.[70] According to the act, "any American woman who marries a foreigner shall take the nationality of her husband."[71] In effect, both U.S.-born and naturalized women were stripped of their citizenship by marrying noncitizen men. When the act was passed, women had not achieved the right to vote in North Dakota except in elections for the school board. Therefore, the law had little impact on voting, but it did matter in all other arenas of citizenship. With the passage of womanhood suffrage in North Dakota in 1917 and nationally in 1920, the law effectively disfranchised women citizens who married noncitizen men. Only in 1922, with the passage of the Cable Act separating women's status from their husband's, was women's autonomous citizenship restored.[72]

While Norwegian immigrants held fast to their ancestral identification and to their mother tongue, they recognized the importance of the franchise and an electoral voice. They took seriously their membership in the polity. The legal context of North Dakota fits the pattern that sociologist Irene Bloemraad describes as conducive to immigrant political participation because it did not erect systematic barriers to voting.[73] Importantly, I would add that land taking set in motion the process leading to citizenship. Homesteading required foreign-born persons to register their intention to be naturalized. Although homesteaders were not required to follow through and become citizens, many did. In effect, land provided the impetus as well as the avenue not only for migrating but also for switching citizenship. In giving new immigrants a stake in the country, naturalization laws gave them a potential political voice in the context of evolving racial-ethnic hierarchies.

The Nonpartisan League

The same year that Dakota women participated in the "last arrow" ceremony, Scandinavian women joined the widespread mobilization of the newly founded

Nonpartisan League (NPL). The name "nonpartisan" indicated a rejection of standard party politics and a critique of the corruption that was part and parcel of the two-party system. The NPL argued that the spoils system corrupted politicians of all stripes. Growing out of the movement of producer and consumer cooperatives, the American Society of Equity, the North Dakota Farmers Union, the Socialist Party, and the Grange, the NPL focused on agricultural issues: crop prices, profiteering middlemen, shipping and processing costs, and unscrupulous transactions that favored the buyer instead of the producer. In a call to support small farmers and limit the power of big business, the league appealed to American notions of democracy and fairness.[74] The nonpartisan group gathered momentum as it organized across the state and won the governorship and a plurality in the legislature in the fall election of 1916.

The NPL platform spoke directly to farmers' grievances. Among the most important was the call for state ownership of grain elevators, flour mills, and cold-storage plants. As Clare Hammonds and I have argued elsewhere, campaigns for the Nonpartisan League persuaded voters across the state to stand up for agrarian reform.[75] In an oral history interview, Lars Larson, whose father was a Leaguer, recalled: "They thought [there] was too much capitalistic control. Big business…had too much influence over prices.… They thought the farmer wasn't getting his fair share of what he should be getting." The platform also demanded state inspection of grain and grain storage, exemption of farm improvements from taxation, the public provision of hail insurance and, perhaps most controversial, the operation of nonprofit rural banks.[76] This platform aimed to correct the monopoly that middlemen, railroad corporations, and private elevator companies exercised and reduce the disadvantages of small producers.

The NPL sent paid organizers into a community to identify people who would become "boosters," introducing the organizer to others, signing up new members, and collecting dues. The NPL's communitarian values led them to recruit at the grassroots, going from farm to farm to discuss politics. They also organized outreach through picnics and community gatherings. This strategy was remarkably successful, and the NPL grew rapidly, not just in North Dakota but throughout the upper Midwest. In the first two years, membership grew to nearly 150,000 across thirteen states. By 1919 membership reached over 200,000,[77] almost half in Minnesota and North Dakota.[78] From 1915 to 1922 the NPL garnered a membership of over 40,000 in North Dakota alone.[79]

The league had a strong base among Scandinavians, especially Norwegians. While membership lists are difficult to come by, historian Kathleen Moum found that "at the grassroots level the Nonpartisan League was principally an organization of foreign-born farmers, particularly Norwegian immigrants."[80] Norwegians in North

Dakota were disproportionately farmers and disproportionately active in the NPL.[81] Their attachment to owning and cultivating land brought them into the political arena. Because local activism fixated on agricultural issues, they were drawn into electoral politics in their new country. Furthermore, membership was strongest in those sections of the state that had the largest Norwegian settlements.[82]

In her study of the NPL, Moum provides several possible explanations for the concentration of Norwegians in the league, which was especially clear in counties where wheat cultivation predominated. She suggests that Norwegian immigrants brought with them their political and class sensibilities—an antipathy toward arrogant merchants and townspeople and an affinity for cooperative association with neighbors. To this, historian H. Arnold Barton would add the "democratic, progressive, and forward looking" kind of nationalism of nineteenth-century Norway.[83] About 70 percent of Norwegian immigrants who arrived in the United States between 1884 and 1914 came from rural areas. That divide neatly separated farmers from business-people in towns and cities. Furthermore, Moum argues, the league relied heavily on existing social networks when organizing. Ethnic communities in geographically concentrated areas provided the basis for the radical movement.

A companion to ethnic solidarity—ethnic division—also surfaced as an obstacle to outreach and representation. In order to be effective, the league tried to bridge some historic rifts, especially between Norwegians and Swedes. I have found no evidence, however, that it reached out to Dakotas or other Native American farmers. Norwegians and Dakotas did not often socialize even when they were neighbors, and most did not belong to the same churches. Other than through shared labor and trade, they had few bases for affiliation. Nonetheless, Mary Louise Defender Wilson reported that her Dakota mother supported the NPL and had voted its ticket; she "just thought it was one that cared about what happened to people." Second-generation Norwegian Mamie Larson, an organizer herself, spoke to the success of the NPL in uniting Scandinavian groups: "They all seemed to be like one when it come to the League. Ya. Norwegians and Swedes alike, I guess. Well, we had Ole Olson among the Norwegians and we had some good men among the Swedes too, that were the pushers, see" (see figure 50).[84] By pushers, she meant the organizers. Members of other ethnic groups, especially Germans and Germans from Russia, were not as likely to join, although they too were farmers. During World War I, anti-immigrant and anti-German sentiment prompted people of German descent to avoid mobilizing as a community and attracting public attention. The radicalism of the NPL, too, was cast by some as anti-American, a risk that most Germans could not afford, even though after the war they joined in greater numbers.[85]

Initially, the NPL did not allow women members, yet women were at the heart of league organizing from its inception. Male heads of household joined on behalf of the whole family. Women were granted voting privileges in the NPL only by virtue of their relationship to men. While women had little formal access to the inner circles of the organization, they contributed in a number of important ways. Karen Starr highlights the conventionally gendered nature of their activism, including arranging rallies and preparing food for picnics as well as providing support at home when their husbands had to travel on league activities.[86] For example, second-generation Norwegian Gurine Moe took care of milking and feeding the chickens while her husband, Karl, went off to NPL meetings. "We the ladies…didn't have voting right.… The only thing we could vote for was the county school superintendent. So therefore I didn't take much interest. I wasn't the only one." Gurine described the core membership in her region: "It was the men. Oh, we fixed up some doings for it, had a dance down at that old hall. And then we brought eats and so forth. But that was just the social time." Although she minimized the importance of what she did, the NPL strategy depended upon large gatherings at which food and refreshment were essential, attracting entire families. Like the picnic co-hosted by John H. Bye and John Simonson on their adjoining homesteads, these events brought a multigenerational community together and provided a forum for communicating with current members, debating political issues, and recruiting new members (see figure 51).

As historian Kim Nielsen reminds us, "The 'farmer' was a family work unit; thus, the Nonpartisan League was a family activity in which women were involved as public advocates, organizers and picnic planners."[87] Norwegian women, like many other immigrant women, were deeply committed to family enterprises, so farm issues were their issues, and the NPL was the party of agrarian reform. Women voted their economic interests, which were rooted in their position as farm partners, independent farmers, and landowners. The Norwegian women who supported the league did not defy the gender norms of their community, although their behavior challenged those of the dominant society. They were furthering their own interest as well as that of their racial-ethnic group. Importantly, their political action was grounded in the value they placed on kinship and community, their centrality to networks of mutual aid, and the political incorporation process structured by the land taking. Among Norwegians, as with Dakotas, landownership was a vehicle for cultural continuity as well as citizenship and political participation.

A women's auxiliary was formed within the NPL in 1919. The movement for women's suffrage had redefined women's place in the polity, and in 1917 the state legislature, which was dominated by the league, passed womanhood suffrage. Activist farm women immediately sought to gain from their enfranchisement. Starting in 1920, the women's Nonpartisan clubs moved women into autonomous organizations and away from the centralized power of the NPL, providing women with new freedom to set their own agenda and address their distinctive needs. Nielsen presents evidence that these women's clubs went so far as to adopt a legislative agenda of their own that addressed a range of issues consistent with the feminist movement of the time, from protective labor legislation for women and children to the conditions of rural schools and even global disarmament.[88]

In addition to raising money, the auxiliaries ran their own candidates for public office and mobilized women to vote the NPL ticket. By 1921 there were more than 325 such organizations with more than 4,000 members.[89] Second-generation Norwegian Mamie Larson, longtime president of the women's auxiliary in Sheyenne, explained some immigrant women's hesitation to become active in politics: "There was so many that were so backward about their language that they didn't like to take part much.... But they were very helpful when it come to working, see. Very much so. Just so they didn't have to do any of the talking, or anything like that." Asked if it was difficult to mobilize women to vote, Mamie replied, "No, oh no. They'd go out and get 'em. They voted all right. They'd go to vote all right, when they found it was for their own good." In the north-central part of North Dakota, where the NPL was even stronger, Effie Hanson, also a second-generation Norwegian, wrote to a friend in November 1920: "We were all in to vote. And the Nonpartisans won we hear. What are you folks, or are you afraid to tell us. Well we will tell you the honest fact that we are Nonpartisans and not ashamed to admit it."[90] As a committed NPL member, she discussed the league's political prospects and electoral activities as fluently as she did grain prices on the open market, chores on the farm, and the well-being of her children. Interwoven into her perspective on her life as a partner farmer were commodity prices and farm politics. While Scandinavian women's activities in the league tended to be consistent with their gendered work, becoming political actors was a new departure.

The movement's message about regulating the market meant that the NPL, like many left-leaning organizations, had to defend its legitimacy to a broader U.S. public. From its inception it was accused of being "socialistic" and anti-American because of its stand against big business and in favor of a strong state role in the economy.[91] It opposed U.S. involvement in the war in Europe because, from its class perspective, "It is easier for the *real toiler* to see war in terms of toil and suffering than to see in it abstract rights and glorious adventure."[92] Historian Robert Morlan explained the NPL's logic about sharing the costs of war: "Conscription of men was clearly the most equitable method of raising an army, it said, and if that were just it seemed only logical that conscription of wealth was likewise the fairest means of financing."[93] Of course, it reasoned, no person or business should profit from war. For these positions the league was labeled "Bolshevik" and pilloried in the mainstream press and the political newspapers established to oppose it.[94] To its members, the league embodied the fundamental principles on which the country was founded. In its newspaper, *The Nonpartisan Leader*, one of its iconic political cartoons featured "democracy" as a woman, one hand resting on the arm of Uncle Sam, and the other pointing to North Dakota on a U.S. map. She declared, "Don't become discouraged—there is one bright spot where the people rule and we shall have real democracy in America—Your day is coming!"[95]

In this political environment, Norwegian immigrant and Nelson County resident Tosten Lillehammer grappled with the tensions between democratic principles, purported freedom of political affinity, and his community's fear of radicalism: "I believe there were many who felt that if there was to be a government by the people, it should be that not only in name but in practice as well, and that was my idea. That I had been a 'populist' perhaps had not been too bad, but if I went 'socialist,' people thought there must be '*ein skruve laus*' (a screw loose) in my upper story."[96] Left-wing activists and organizers were stigmatized as foreigners who did not belong in the United States. When the core of a movement was foreign-born, this fact gave rise to public debates about its appropriateness in U.S. politics. Longstanding hysteria about immigrant anarchists was bolstered by the revolution unfolding in the Soviet Union and the activism of European socialists and communists.

Just as they worked in the fields when most other ethnic women did not, Norwegian women in rural North Dakota, already tagged as foreign, were comfortable being different—cultural messages be damned. Their willingness to dissent from the mainstream marked their foreignness, even when they were U.S.-born. One second-generation Norwegian, Tom "Buck" Snortland, rebuffed the notion that NPL activists were outside the bounds of legitimate politics. "Obviously they were not dealing with radicals. Those old Norwegian fishermen were a long ways from radical." Snortland's parents had immigrated from a fishing community on the west coast of Norway; he was a member of the Farmers Union and ran for public office.

In practice, the NPL experienced the tensions of populist activism within competing interpretations of participatory democracy. Palmer Overby (see figure 52), a second-generation Norwegian farmer in Nelson County and ardent NPL supporter, articulated the reform dilemma:

> You come back to the same thing again, the farmers against the business. Any time you step on the business toes, why, you're a socialist. But you know one of the best things that hit North Dakota is that Mill, and the Bank of North Dakota. It isn't socialism in a way, but...it's run by the people. Socialism. [Chuckle.] And same way where...these cooperatives we have. They're supposed to be socialism from free enterprise. Well, we are in business. We are

in free enterprise because we own that business. Instead of one that owns it, a group of us owns it. We're not socialists; we're in the free enterprise.

His ruminations hit precisely on the paradoxes embedded in populist reforms advocated by the NPL. Workers owning businesses, such as grain elevators and flourmills, reshaped the market but did not supplant it. One of the longest-lived reforms instituted by the NPL is the state-owned Bank of North Dakota, which exists today, "promoting agriculture, commerce, and industry" by facilitating and financing economic development projects.[97]

The successes of the Nonpartisan League precipitated a backlash. Business interests organized the Independent Voters' Association (IVA) in 1918, winning control of the lower house of the state legislature, and passing a slate of anti-league measures in 1920, although the league maintained a majority in the state senate and kept the governorship. Most notably, the IVA led the campaign to recall the governor, Lynn Frazier, on grounds of financial mismanagement.[98] The damage to Frazier did not last much beyond his unseating in 1922, as he was elected to the U.S. Senate in the next political cycle and represented North Dakota for many years. The split between the NPL and the IVA created political space into which the Ku Klux Klan entered for several years in the mid-1920s. It ran on an anti-immigrant, anti-Communist, and anti-Catholic platform that appealed to white Protestants unsettled by the labor activism of the teens and the Nonpartisan League victories.[99] Its extreme tactics, secrecy, and violence provoked concerted resistance, including an anti-masking law that effectively drove the organization out of the state.[100] The NPL's political legacy reached at least into the 1950s. It eventually merged with the Democratic Party, although it did not regain control of state government after 1922.

Notably, in 1924 the U.S. Congress passed two major pieces of legislation relevant to unfolding relations between Dakotas, Norwegians, and the larger public. Responding to Native activists and addressing pervasive confusion, Congress passed the American Indian Citizenship Act, also known as the Snyder Act, granting full citizenship to all Indians regardless of their "bloodedness" or allotment status.[101] At the same time, tensions over patriotism, racial segregation, and social hierarchies consolidated "a broad alliance of cultural conservatives" that called for more restrictive immigration laws.[102] The dislocations of World War I, which left millions of refugees seeking a country and the Great Migration of southerners moving North, combined with technological developments that reduced industry's needs for cheap labor, as well as the social anxieties created by all of these trends, increased public support for restricting who could enter the country. By setting quotas for sending countries—privileging, first, Britons and, secondly, northern Europeans, discouraging eastern and southern Europeans, and prohibiting Asians—the Immigration Act of 1924, also known as the Johnson-Reed Immigration Act, created a "hierarchy of desirability" that determined which peoples were welcome and which were not, as well as how many would be allowed.[103] In combination with the American Indian Citizenship Act, it redefined the terms and contours of social and political engagement along and across the boundaries of race-ethnicity and, in the process, defined the United States as a white country.

EXERCISING POLITICAL VOICE: RESISTANCE AND PARTICIPATION

Native peoples as well as newcomers challenged the United States to live up to its promises. The U.S. assimilation project pushed for immigrants and Indians to disaffiliate from their heritage, but in North Dakota both groups continued unabashedly to express their distinctiveness from mainstream America. It was precisely that attachment to their ancestry and language and that refusal to accommodate to assimilationist expectations that made citizenship so valuable, even when it was racialized. In order to secure their rights, they battled in the courts and in the political arena.

For both Dakotas and foreign-born Norwegians, achieving citizenship and finding a way to exercise political voice were tied to owning land. The assimilation project was successful insofar as Spirit Lake Dakotas generally agreed to become landowners and citizens.[104] By taking allotments, they transitioned from commanding a vast territory to owning 80–160 acres of land as individuals. They came to accept that a specific plot of land could provide some security and support cultural continuity. As soon as the Dawes Act conferred limited citizenship upon them, Dakotas embraced the status, redefined it, and advocated for themselves so they could exercise the full range of their entitlements. They immediately encountered concerted resistance, but they persisted. The foreign-born, who were also subject to assimilation campaigns but were considered white, found an open door to naturalization. For them, the land-taking process—homesteading—required declaring their intention to naturalize and hence paved the way to citizenship. As those seeking to own land, Norwegians enthusiastically took advantage of this opportunity.

From Dakotas' perspective, the federal government's hypocrisy was on display, and they gained vindication and power from drawing attention to its violations of its founding philosophy, constitutional principles, and negotiated agreements. Indians across the country demanded that the federal government honor its treaties and deliver on its righteous claims of democracy. Those who were not citizens were not entitled to the freedoms guaranteed by the U.S. Constitution, including the right to political expression.[105] Those who were citizens, including those whose property ownership was ambiguous, had to fight for rights and entitlements. Most notably, after a small group of tribal members symbolically shot the last arrow, Dakota people still spoke their language, performed Indian dancing, and sued the federal government.

Although they shared an appreciation for citizenship and land, Dakotas and Norwegians did not develop a strong political alliance. Both groups tended to support Republican candidates until the advent of the NPL. Because Dakotas backed Norwegian-born Lars Havrevold in 1892, he became the state legislator from Benson County. Overt conflict rarely erupted. As landlords to Scandinavian farmers, Dakotas were less directly affected by the fluctuating market prices of wheat and flax. The commercial farmers' grievances taken up by the NPL were generally not their issues. No evidence I have come across suggests that Dakotas were involved in the Nonpartisan League or that the NPL took up Indians' causes against the government. Indians knew firsthand how corrupt public officials could be; they had no reason to think that big business would act any differently. But their involvement in the market was limited, and they learned soon after passage of the Dawes Act how easily their electoral action could be blocked, although Dakotas at Spirit Lake could and did affect Benson County elections. Moreover, tensions over taxation and financing public schooling divided the two groups. If Dakotas did not pay taxes, Norwegians reasoned, were they doing their part as citizens?

By the time whites were living on the reservation, Dakotas were voting, but their accusations of injustice were aimed largely at the federal government and the local representatives of the Indian Office. That is why Ambrose Littleghost could talk with fondness as well as ambivalence about white farmers, but scoff at the history of allotment. The Norwegians did not create allotment; they simply benefited from it. Dakotas recognized the difference. All adult men voted, but had Dakotas mobilized outside the bounds of conventional party politics, their actions would have been read as insurrection.

In contrast, Norwegians saw state government as a tool to counterbalance and restrain the market. For them, a focus on the farm economy built on a cooperative tradition, while shedding a critical light on the disadvantages to small farmers of the industrial organization of agriculture. Because they constituted a critical mass of the state's population and the laws of land taking opened the door to citizenship and the franchise, their political mobilization had a substantial impact. Recent immigrants to North Dakota could not vote if they did not become citizens. Those who did not have the resources to homestead land or who immigrated after all homestead land had been claimed did not have the same incentive to seek naturalization. As white immigrants, Norwegians could draw upon a race privilege denied to Dakotas.

Much to the chagrin of those who advocated that the U.S. become a melting pot, rural Norwegians who naturalized and joined the NPL did not exercise the kind of citizenship they had in mind. Indeed, Norwegian businessmen in towns and cities reviled them. The NPL Norwegians acted similarly to Dakotas in this regard. They maintained their distinctiveness and unapologetically held onto their cultural two-ness. Becoming American citizens did not mean they disavowed their heritage. Nor did it silence their criticisms of government or the market. Both groups found ways to participate in the polity without surrendering their ancestral identity.

8

A Fragile Hold on the Land

DAKOTAS HAD SURVIVED relocation and allotment, but dispossession continued. From a racially privileged and agriculturally advantaged position, Scandinavian landowners came to predominate at Spirit Lake. Living as wary neighbors on what had become an entangled enclave, both adapted to and resisted the capitalist economy and U.S. culture but remained attached to the land, rooted in kin networks, and committed to a rural way of life.

The plat maps of my great-grandmother's rural neighborhood—its racial-ethnic mosaic and its transformation over time—reveal in microcosm the larger arc of contraction, dispossession, and consolidation. In 1910, Berthe Haugen did not yet hold title, although she lived in the southwestern corner of section 13 (see map 5). By 1929, her name publicly inscribed her ownership. To her, land provided a place to live and a means of support in her old age. Like other Norwegian peasants, she considered land the essential source of sustenance. Once she proved up, she had something to bequeath her descendants, which in turn gave them an incentive to help her run her small farm. So Berthe Haugen counted her blessings when she took possession of her 160 acres overlooking the Sheyenne River. Her neighbors in the six-square-mile area of the reservation included nine Dakota, one Swedish, and sixteen Norwegian landowners. Two speculators also owned property in the area. The largest landowner, Henry W. Kiefer, a second-generation German, lived catty-corner across the road; by 1929, he had more than tripled his land holdings in this small district (see map 6).

Nineteen years later only seven of the original twenty-eight names on plats were the same: two were Dakota, three Norwegian (not including Berthe), and two large landowners (Henry W. Keifer and Fred R. Stevens). One new Swedish landowner had bought out several others. The Mutual Trust Life Insurance Company took

MAP 5 Berthe Haugen's rural neighborhood, 1910.

This six-square-mile section of Eddy Township (150N, R63W) on the north side of the Sheyenne River counted as Bertha Haugen's rural neighborhood. Her name is not recorded on the southwest corner of section 13 because she had not yet "proved up" her homestead and did not formally own it. (Courtesy State Historical Society of North Dakota, Bismarck.)

possession of 320 acres in section 13. In section 10, the State Treasurer made claim to a 200-acre chunk, possibly for unpaid taxes.

By 1929, Scandinavians owned more land within the bounded geographic space known as the Spirit Lake Dakota Reservation than Dakotas themselves. How do we comprehend the deepening dispossession of Dakotas and the endurance of some Scandinavians with modest holdings? What did these unfolding events and outcomes mean to those who continued to live on the reservation in 1929?

The fragility of landownership for Dakotas and Scandinavians was based on intersecting processes of accumulation and loss. Dakotas' grasp on land was undermined by the capricious control of the federal government, while Scandinavians were vulnerable to the market economy. As wards of the state, Dakotas were subject to the power exercised by the Indian Office over their resources, income, land, and everyday lives. It pursued a policy that accelerated the sale of Indian lands—undercutting Natives' efforts to retain land over generations (see document 2). While Scandinavians had autonomy as freeholders and naturalized citizens, they were susceptible to dramatic

MAP 6 Berthe Haugen's rural neighborhood, 1929.

The same six-square-mile section of Eddy Township (150N, R63W) looks very different in 1929. Berthe Haugen had title to her land in section 13, but many of her Dakota and Norwegian neighbors had sold and lost their land to speculators and banks. (Courtesy State Historical Society of North Dakota, Bismarck.)

fluctuations in prices brought by agricultural products and to unceasing pressures to enlarge and mechanize their farm operations. Some Dakotas, too, farmed for the market and ran the same risks; those who held the patent to their land could mortgage it and lose it to the banks or have it seized by the state for unpaid taxes. On the whole, however, in attempting to retain their place on the land and pass it on to the next generation, the two groups faced distinct but overlapping challenges.

A SCANDINAVIAN RESERVATION?

We might ask: Did disproportionate numbers of landowners turn Spirit Lake into a Scandinavian reservation? Scandinavians did not own the largest parcels of land, but collectively they surpassed all other racial-ethnic groups, including Dakotas. As non-Indians, Scandinavians had a freer legal status: they were not restricted in their movements and decision making by the federal government, and their daily lives were not monitored by agents of assimilation. The Fort Totten Agency had no

INHERITED AND NONCOMPETENT

INDIAN LANDS FOR SALE

Posted in the Office of the U. S. Indian School of Fort Totten, N. Dak.

BIDS OPENED OCTOBER 16, 1916.

No.	Subdivision	S.	T.	R.	Acres	Aprsmt.
1	NW ¼ SW ¼	17	152	66	40	$ 440.00
20	SE ¼ SW ¼	12	152	65	40	280.00
110	SE ¼ N E¼	20	152	64	40	600.00
129	SE ¼ NE ¼	29				
	W ½ NW ¼	28	151	62	120	1680.00
131	E ½ NW ¼	28	151	62	80	1120.00
	SE ¼ SW ¼	21	151	62	40	560.00
139	N ½ NW ¼	29	151	62	80	880.00
160	SW ¼	28	151	63	160	2080.00
163	S ½ SW ¼	11	151	65	80	800.00
171	SW ¼ NW ¼	27				
	N ½ SE ¼	28	152	64	120	1920.00
	Lot 1 (NE ¼ SE ¼) and					
	Lot 2 (SE ¼ SE ¼)	33	153	64	27.90	195.30
180	NW ¼ NW ¼	27	152	64	40	480.00
195	N ½ NE ¼	9	152	64	80	960.00
221	Lots 4 & 5 (S½ NW¼)	18	152	64	52.30	400.00
	Lots 12 & 13 (S½SW¼)	7	152	64	22.68	176.00
249	Lot 7 (SE¼ NE¼)	12	152	65	24.50	170.00
275	Lot 2 (SE¼ SE¼)	35	151	64	39.12	480.00
279	Lot 4 (SE¼ NW¼) and					
	Lot 5 (SW¼ NW¼)	22	152	65	33.93	271.44
297	SW ¼ SE ¼	18	152	66	40	640.00
309	S ½ NE ¼	24	152	67	80	900.00
340	SW¼ NE¼ and					
	SE ¼ NW ¼	12	151	65	80	1120.00
341	W ½ NW ¼	12	151	65	80	1200.00
379	N ½ NE ¼	17				
	(leased to Dec. 31, 1917)					
	SE ¼ SE ¼	8	150	64	120	1680.00
390	Lot 2 (NW¼ NE¼)	5	151	62	19.40	140.00
426	SE ¼ NE ¼	23	151	63	40	480.00
458	SW ¼ SE ¼	2	151	65	40	480.00
506	N W¼ NW ¼	17	152	65	40	100.00
520	S ½ NW ¼ and					
	NW ¼ NW ¼	12	152	66	120	1440.00
526	Lots 3 & 4 (NW¼)	5	152	64	34.82	348.00
	(leased to Aug. 6, 1917)					
532	N ½ NW ¼	26	151	63	80	1120.00
558	NW ¼ SW ¼ and					
	SW ¼ NW ¼	21	152	63	80	1840.00
559	S W¼ NW ¼	18	152	63	40	560.00
566	SW ¼ NE ¼ and					
	NW ¼ SE ¼	15	151	64	80	800.00
591	SW ¼ SE ¼	28	152	66	40	480.00
593	SW ¼ NE ¼ and					
	NE ¼ SW ¼	33	152	66	80	560.00
613	SW ¼ NW ¼	36	153	64	40	320.00
612	NW ¼ SE ¼	31	153	63	40	400.00
635	E ½ NW ¼	4	150	64	80.12	1120.00
636	SW ¼ SW ¼	34	151	64	40	400.00
639	W ½ SE ¼ and					
	Lot 1 (NE¼SE¼) and					
	Lot 2 (SE¼ SE¼)	14	151	64		
	Lot 2 (SW¼ SW¼)	13	151	64	158.09	1580.00
644	NW ¼ SW ¼ and					
	Lot 3 (SW ¼ NW ¼)	24	151	64	72.70	727.00
678	N ½ NE ¼	29	151	63	80	1360.00
680	SE ¼ SW ¼	20	151	65	40	480.00
690	E ½ NW ¼	24	152	66	80	1200.00
	W ½ SW ¼	24	152	66	80	640.00
725	SE ¼ SE ¼	6	151	64	40	480.00
727	Lot 4 (NW ¼ NW ¼) and					
	E ½ NW ¼	1	150	65	120.26	1380.00
	NE ¼ NW ¼	31	151	64	40	480.00
72[illegible]	SE ¼ SW ¼	28	152	66	40	400.00
749	Lot 1					
	N ½ NE ¼ and					
	NE ¼ NW ¼	11	152	66	160	1600.00
760	N ½ SE ¼	13	152	65	80	640.00
766	NE ¼ SW ¼	24	152	65	40	320.00
770	SW ¼ NE ¼	30				
	SE¼ NW¼, SE¼ NE¼					
	and SE ¼ SE ¼	19	152	64	160	1280.00
811	Lot 6 (NE¼ NE¼)	31				
	Lot 5 (W ½ NW ¼)	32	150	64	64.26	771.12
819	Lot 3 (NW¼ SE¼)	36	153	64	39.70	400.00
820	SE ¼ SW ¼	26	153	64	40	400.00
829	SW ¼ NE ¼ and					
	SE ¼ NW ¼	30	151	65	80	1200.00
839	Lot 5 (SW¼ NW¼), E½					
	NW¼ & NW¼ NW¼	27	151	65	157.10	1571.00
850	NW ¼ SW ¼	16	150	62	40	480.00
875	E ½ NE ¼ and					
	NW ¼ NE ¼	25	152	65	120	960.00
878	N ½ NW ¼	33	152	64	80	800.00
886	SE ¼ NE ¼	14	152	63	40	400.00
898	W ½ SE ¼	28	151	62	80	800.00
908	W ½ NW ¼	9	151	64	80	960.00
913	Lot 2 (SE ¼ NE ¼)					
	and N ½ NW ¼	32	152	64	108.53	1085.00
915	SW ¼ NW ¼ and					
	NW ¼ SW ¼	1	151	64	80	1000.00
949	NW ¼ NE ¼ and					
	NE ¼ NW ¼	34	151	64	80	1200.00
954	NE ¼ SW ¼	7	151	64	40	520.00
955	SW ¼ SW ¼	6	152	64	40	320.00
	SW ¼ NE ¼	3	151	65	40	400.00
958	S ½ SW ¼	9	150	64		
	N ½ NW ¼	16	150	64	160	2560.00
967	NW ¼ SE ¼	23	152	65	40	320.00
971	Lot 6 (SW¼), Lot 7					
	(SW¼ SE¼)NW¼SE¼	27	151	65	94.36	943.00
997	Lot 1 (NE¼ NE¼)	2	151	65	44.41	440.00
1014	Lot 8 (NW ¼ SW ¼) and					
	SW ¼ SW ¼ and					
	Lot 7 (NE¼ SW¼)	22	152	64	92	1250.00
1029	[illegible] ½ NE ¼ and					
	NE ¼ NW ¼	20	151	64	120	1920.00
1060	Lot 3 (NW ¼ NW ¼)	5	152	65	44.66	535.20
1088	S ½ SW ¼	1	151	66	80	1040.00
1090	NW ¼ SE ¼	23	152	66	40	400.00
1107	NW ¼ NW ¼	31	152	66	40	600.00
1112	Lot 7 (NE ¼) and					
	NE ¼ NE ¼	28	151	65	78.20	782.00
1138	NW ¼	33	151	63	160	2400.00
1145	SW ¼ NE ¼	33	151	63	40	600.00
1154	S ½ SW ¼	23	153	67	80	1040.00
1175	Lots 13 and 12 (SE¼)	4				
	Lot 6 (SW ¼)	3	149	64	93.20	840.00
1190	W ½ SE ¼	24	151	63	80	1200.00
1205	Lot 3 (NW¼ SE¼)	16	152	63	37.90	450.00
	BIDS OPENED NOVEMBER 16, 1916.					
151	SE ¼ NE ¼	34				
	NW ¼ SW ¼	35	152	63	80	1440.00
168	W ½ SE ¼	20	150	64	80	1360.00
200	NW ¼ NE ¼	36	153	64	40	400.00
210	S ½ SE ¼	30	152	64	80	640.00
218	N ½ NE ¼	28	151	63	80	1800.00
	(leased to Dec. 31, 1916)					
281	SW ¼ NW ¼	28	151	64	40	600.00
288	Lot 3 (SE ¼)	10	152	65	27.95	139.75
	SE ¼ SE ¼	18	152	66	40	600.00
314	NW ¼ NW ¼ and					
	NE ¼ NW ¼	36	152	67	80	2000.00
332	N ½ of NW ¼	17	151	63	80	1600.00
	(leased to Dec. 31, 1916)					
449	Lot 4 (NE ¼ NW ¼)	17				
	Lot 12 (SE¼ SW¼)	8	152	64	34.70	277.00
	SE ¼ SE ¼	30				
	Lot 10 (SE¼ SW¼)					
	Lot 11 (SW¼ SW¼)	29				
	Lot 6 (NE¼ NE¼)	31	151	65	125.44	1505.28
567	SW ¼ SE ¼	29				
	W ½ NE ¼ and					
	NE ¼ SE ¼	32	153	65	160	1440.00
571	N ½ NW ¼	29	152	66	80	2000.00
	(leased to Mar. 1, 1917)					
622	SE ¼ SW ¼	21	152	66	40	480.00
	NW ¼ NE ¼	21	152	66	40	320.00
	E ½ NE ¼	20	152	66	80	2000.00
	(leased to Dec. 31, 1916)					
785	NW ¼ SE ¼	31	151	66	40	680.00
	(leased to Dec. 31, 1916)					
855	S ½ NE ¼	27	152	63	80	1440.00
879	NW ¼ SW ¼	36	152	67	40	600.00
919	Lots 5&6 (W½SE¼)	19	152	66	55.16	827.40
942	Lot 2 (NE ¼ NE ¼)	11	150	65	14.55	145.50
	E½ NW¼ (less 1.0125					
	acres sold for school site	8	150	64	78.9875	1422.00
	(leased to Dec. 31, 1916)					
946	SE ¼ NE ¼	7				
	(leased to Dec. 31, 1916)					
	SW ¼ NW ¼	8	152	66	80	2000.00
	NE ¼ SW ¼	11	152	66	40	320.00
984	W ½ NE ¼ and					
	Lot 5 (NE¼NE¼) and					
	Lot 6 (SE¼ NE¼)	31	152	63	154.40	2316.00
990	SW ¼ SE ¼	23	151	64	40	600.00
	W ½ NE ¼	23	151	64	80	800.00
1089	NW¼ SE¼ (leased 1916)	19	151	64	40	640.00
	SE ¼ SW ¼ and					
	SW ¼ SE ¼	17	151	64	80	1120.00
1186	S ½ NW ¼	1	151	63	80	2000.00
	(leased to Dec. 31, 1916)					
1198	SW ¼ NW ¼ and					
	NW ¼ SW ¼	35	152	65	80	960.00
547	Lot 9 (SE ¼ NE ¼)					
	and NE ¼ NE ¼	24	150	63	57.70	850.00
	Lot 4 (SW ¼ SW ¼)	18	150	62	41.03	1000.00

NOTICE TO BIDDERS.

All inherited and noncompetent Indian lands are advertised for sale under the rules and regulations approved by the Secretary of the Interior Oct. 12, 1910. Successful bidders or purchasers will receive a patent in fee from the government for Indian lands purchased.

Only sealed bids will be considered. In submitting a bid the bidder will give the number of allotment, as indicated by the foregoing schedule, the description of the land, the price per acre, and total amount. Each bid must be accompanied by a duly certified check on some solvent bank, payable to C. M. Ziebach, Superintendent, for ten per cent (10 per cent) of the amount offered, as a guarantee of the bidders faithful performance of his proposition If the bid shall be accepted and the bidder shall, within thirty (30) days after due notice, fail to comply with the terms of his bid, such check will be forfeited to the owner of the land, less the cost of advertising, etc. No bids for less than appraised value as given in the foregoing schedule will be considered. The right is reserved to reject any or all bids. All bids for Indian lands at the above sale must be in the Office not later than 5:00 o'clock P. M. of the date set for the opening of bids, and will be received any time up to that date. Bids will be opened 6 P. M. of the date set for the opening of bids. Bidders are invited to be present in this Office at the opening of bids, and the same invitation is extended to everybody interested All cost in connection with the conveying of Indian lands, and advertising, must be paid by the purchasers

UNITED STATES INDIAN SCHOOL,
FORT TOTTEN, NORTH DAKOTA.
C. M. ZIEBACH, Superintendent.

DOCUMENT 2 Indian lands for sale, 1916.

This poster lists the sections of Indian land for sale, with their acreage and appraised price. Posted in the office of the Fort Totten Indian School, it details procedures for submitting sealed, competitive bids for purchase. Signed by C. M. Ziebach, Indian superintendent. (Courtesy Great Plains Regional Archives, National Archives and Records Administration, Kansas City, MO.)

TABLE 8.1 Race-Ethnicity and Landownership by Gender, Spirit Lake Dakota Reservation, 1910 and 1929

Race-Ethnic Group	1910 Total Acreage	1910 Number of Landowners	1910 Number of Women Landowners	1910 Women as % of Landowners	1929 Total Acreage	1929 Number of Landowners	1929 Number of Women Landowners	1929 Women as % of Landowners
Dakota	99,038	1003	379	38%	49,009	586	204	35%
Scandinavian	48,359	325	43	13%	70,931	340	82	24%
Yankee*	21,135	129	14	11%	30,648	151	33	22%
German	10,838	58	7	12%	21,049	81	16	20%
Other foreign-born	12,827	63	7	11%	14,564	51	8	16%
Unidentified ethnicity**	14,539	115	28	24%	16,466	139	47	34%
Total	203,736	1693	480	28%	202,667	1348	390	29%

Yankee is the term I use to describe those born in the United States whose parents were also born in the United States. Referring to them as "native-born of native parentage," as the federal census does, confuses those who are Native American Indian and those who are not.

**This residual category encompasses those names not identified through Bureau of Indian Affairs tribal enrollment lists or U.S. manuscript censuses. We presume that some are Native American Indians and others are Yankees or immigrants.

jurisdiction over them, which complicated its mission to manage Indian people and reservation land. Tribal members still lived there, in approximately similar numbers as at the time the land was allotted, but they did so on many fewer acres.

Landowning: Dispossession and Displacement

By 1929, the total acreage owned by Dakotas had been cut in half to 49,009 acres, compared to the 70,931 acres owned by Scandinavians (see table 8.1). The expansion of Scandinavians' land base, predicated upon the contraction of Dakotas', is visible when comparing the GIS map of 1929 landownership to the map of unallotted lands in 1904 (see map 7).

For Dakotas, the decline in total acres owned amounted to dramatic dispossession that found a parallel in other reservations across the country.[1] The Indian Office's efforts to increase Indian fee patents resulted in more land sales and consequently a reduced collective land base and smaller average acreage.[2] In 1929, superintendent W. R. Beyer documented that "less than ten percent of the Indians receiving a fee patent have retained their lands."[3]

Barely twenty-five years after the reservation was opened to white homesteading and twenty years after it was platted, not only did Dakotas own less total acreage,

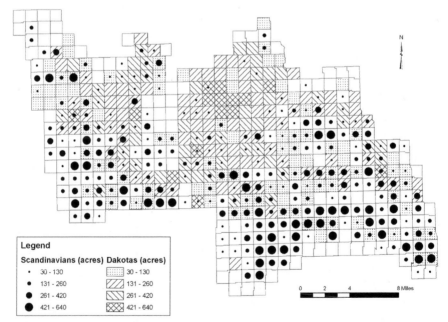

MAP 7 GIS Map of Dakota and Scandinavian landownership, 1929.

Map of landownership by Dakotas and Scandinavians in 1929 reveals the expansion of Scandinavian landowning and the contraction of Dakota landowning since 1910. Map generated using Geographic Information Systems (GIS), with a database developed from plat maps.

but also fewer Dakotas owned land and, on average, individual landowners held fewer acres than before. While Dakota landowners continued to be more numerous than Scandinavians, the numbers owning land had declined by approximately forty percent. And by design of allotment, none of the land on the reservation was owned by Spirit Lake Dakotas as a tribe.

Like other successful white farmers across the country, Scandinavians were consolidating their land holdings. By 1929, a more established, smaller group of Scandinavians owned more land in larger parcels; they had increased their holdings to an average of 208.6 acres. While this change represents growth as well as endurance, by regional standards those owning land on the reservation were still smallholders. As latecomers who were poorer and had fewer opportunities to expand their holdings, their median acreage was less than half the average farm size in North Dakota as a whole, which was 500 acres in 1930.[4]

A gendered story lies behind these patterns of landownership and dispossession. Across the country, disparities between men's and women's landownership were growing.[5] Significantly, the female proportion of the tribe contracted precipitously: by 1929, women were reduced to 46 percent of enrolled members. The lopsided death rate signals the brutal impact of allotment and poverty on Native women. On the reservation, Dakota women held onto their land. Their average acreage reached relative parity with men: in 1929, Dakota women owned an average 82.6 acres to Dakota men's 84.2. This equivalence signals gender equality in inheritance: women comprised 38 percent of Dakota landowners in 1910, and 35 percent in 1929.

In contrast, among Scandinavians and all other racial-ethnic groups, consistent with national trends, the gender gap in landownership widened. Notably, the largest inequality in acreage owned was between Yankee women—identified by Elaine Lindgren as the most active homesteaders elsewhere in North Dakota—and Yankee men. Strikingly, women who shared farm labor with men—who adopted the "we" perspective, especially Norwegian immigrants and Dakotas—tended to establish greater equity in landowning. They were more closely connected to the land, invested more of their labor and resources in land, were more likely to be farmers and not just farm partners, and were motivated to own and cultivate it. Importantly, men of their racial-ethic group were poorer and had fewer resources than those in other white groups.[6]

A glimpse at the handful of people who were the largest landowners reveals that racial-ethnic dynamics intertwined with gender. By 1929, ten people had accumulated more than 1,000 acres on the reservation—nine white men and one white woman. Of the white men, three were Scandinavian—two Swedish farmers (Herman Anderson and Edwin Jacobson) and one Norwegian banker turned real estate investor, Morton Anderson. None of the white women who owned land on a large scale was Scandinavian, and none was a farmer. Those white women who owned more than 500 acres, like men, tended to be business proprietors; they were either in partnership with their husbands or in business in their own right.[7]

In one dramatic exception to this pattern, Dakota tribal member Jennie Brown Cavanaugh, who owned 560 acres, was a farmer. Through allotment, purchase, and inheritance, she had become the largest landowner in the tribe. After her husband died in 1915, she continued to run her farm and accumulate land. Cavanaugh had many children who lived to adulthood, including a daughter and several sons who also farmed. Her marriage to the boss farmer of the reservation probably reflected a similarity in class position, and unquestionably enhanced her ability to thrive in agriculture while he was alive. Nonetheless, after he died she continued to farm, on her own and with her children, and to use land to her advantage.

Overall, by 1929, a larger proportion of the reservation land was owned by white women—Scandinavian women included. In fact, they owned more than twice as much acreage as in 1910. By 1929, 24 percent of Scandinavian landowners were women (compared to 13 percent in 1910), and their average holdings had risen to 144.8 acres. Some of the increase can be explained by women like Berthe Haugen, who claimed homestead land early but proved up their claims after 1910. Widowhood conferred land on some women; others resolutely purchased land whenever they could.

Because homesteading and land purchase came at the expense of Dakotas, the transfer from previous landowners to the new beneficiaries was immediate, direct, and visible. The dispossessed lived in community with the dispossessors—witnessing their use of the land and their customary habits, suffering their affronts, and interacting with them, at least occasionally at harvest time or in town.

The Indian Office and Oversight of Indian Land

The prosperity and inflation of the postwar period were followed by a dramatic regional downturn that lasted through the late 1920s. The high wheat prices that enticed people into farming had inflated land values and elevated the cost of consumer goods, which was felt acutely in the cash-poor local economy. Starting in 1923, annual rainfall declined and, with a few exceptions, stayed below normal for almost two decades. As the region got progressively drier, weeds reclaimed formerly cultivated land and the lake continued to shrink. The development of the West through homesteading backfired environmentally as the vast transformation of land disrupted the Great Plains ecosystem, creating a disaster of epic proportion. Crop failures became more frequent, and deflation reduced grain prices by half. Both trends accelerated the protracted economic slide into the national depression.[8] In 1930, superintendent Gray reported: "Crops were a disappointment on the greater part of the reservation on account of drought. Prices were also low on different small grain crops so that no profit was made by the Indian farmers who raised small grain."[9] Gray noted that alfalfa and sweet clover were still growing well—ideal for dairy cows, of which Dakotas had few and Scandinavians had many. Drought made adequate nutrition and potable water more difficult to come by and heightened fatigue and despair.

At precisely the same moment the Indian Office was implementing policies to reduce Indian landownership, commercial agriculture required bigger farms and more machinery. Smallholders and family farmers were being squeezed. Those who owned land had to cultivate more acres and mechanize their operation. Each step of raising livestock or growing crops on a large scale required machinery and capital. Historian Mary Neth succinctly summarized the economic calamity: "In rural America, the development of industrial capitalism directly collided with a family-based labor system."[10] This reorganization displaced many people, "including farmers on small farms, tenants, hired workers, and unpaid women and youths."[11] The contraction of opportunities created an exodus of the rural population as whites of all ethnicities left for urban centers in search of jobs. Given little choice, Dakotas remained on the reservation.

The Indian Office continued to push farming at a time when even some Norwegian landowning farmers—who had endured because of their racial-ethnic privilege, legal autonomy, and agricultural background—were themselves becoming dispirited. In his 1929 memoir, Ole Lima reflected on the dubious merits of his way of life in the southeastern corner of North Dakota:

> Fall came, and I had to start farming again. This has been a poor business, since the prices fell. If one can live decently, as well as manage taxes, insurance, and other expenses without increasing one's debt, one must consider himself fortunate. But indeed one has to hang on. Toiling early and late—16 to 17 hours a day. As the years pile up, there is rheumatism and helplessness besides. Certainly it can be truly said that he who envies the farmer knows not what he does.[12]

Even Norwegians, who were celebrated for their commitment to and skill at farming, were reassessing its viability as a livelihood. Clearly this man was aging and dejected, tired of constant failures and low yields. His prospects only worsened as drought and depression gripped North Dakota.

Because of Dakotas' continuing wardship (except those with fee patents), their relation to their individually owned property was mediated by the federal government. Dakotas continued to be subjected to Washington's constant changes of policy and its arbitrary paternalistic power.[13] The government's unwillingness to appropriate sufficient funds to provide the resources and training needed to prosper in farming undermined the efforts that Indians themselves made. The policy of selling Indian land and undercapitalizing their agricultural endeavors while pushing a farming agenda made a mockery of the Indian Office's assertion that it sought to improve Native people's lives and promote their economic independence.

The flip side of the paradoxical relationship between Indians and land was that individual Dakotas who sold or lost land could still live on the reservation, albeit as landless persons. Dakota elder Agnes Greene reflected on the meaning of "reservation" for Indians as opposed to white homesteaders: "The farmers were poor too. They didn't have nothing. And they were worse off, because if they didn't keep up their payments, well, the banks took their land and they had to get off, *go*. Where the Indians is, they stayed here. They had reservation to live on."[14] Her statement captures one of the ironies of being Indian: while the government constricted Dakotas' movements and subordinated their culture, the reservation held the power of place and connoted belonging in ways that it could not for white settlers. The reservation harbored their families and rooted their relationships. While they continued to visit family members in the United States and Canada, Spirit Lake was home. For Dakotas, hardship could bring dispossession but no longer meant regional displacement.

In contrast, Scandinavians unable to forge a livelihood and unable or unwilling to hold on to unproductive land could and did leave the region, heading west or north in search of jobs and other Scandinavian communities. Losses in farming extended beyond crops to young children, partners, employment, resources, and land. Some were poised with skills—adaptability, knowledge of farming, financial reserves, literacy, facility with the law—to take advantage of the system and others' misfortunes. Others had social capital—good relations with bankers, a robust kin network, legal advantage, political voice, and community support—and racial privilege that helped translate motivation and labor into viability and improvement rather than hardship and despair. In fact, oral and community histories, like all retrospective accounts, are shaped by those who remained, however discouraged, and managed to hold tightly to their land.

Even as they retained the right as Indians to stay on the reservation, Dakotas incurred losses that differed in scale and dimension from homesteaders' experiences of failure. However precarious their economic circumstances, Scandinavians' collective survival was never threatened.

SCANDINAVIANS' LAND LOSS AND THE CHALLENGE OF INTERGENERATIONAL TRANSMISSION

Scandinavians' fragile hold on the land stemmed primarily from their position as farmers and their relationship to agricultural markets. When they struggled as they so often did, the ability of their kin and ethnic communities to provide a safety net also suffered. This system of agriculture, like that in the U.S. South, did not allow farm laborers and tenant farmers to accumulate much capital. Banks became increasingly central to the farm enterprise. While Scandinavians saw a positive role for state government, including the newly established state bank, to help farmers, they had to wait out the depression of the 1920s for federal help. When President Franklin D. Roosevelt took office, his administration began providing relief.

Familiar with the dismal prospects for early twentieth-century farmers, I was surprised by an article in the 1908 *Warwick Weekly Sentinel* that celebrated Gust S. Berg's homesteading success. Berg boasted that in North Dakota good fortune and prosperity was easy.[15] Indeed, his trajectory seemed an instance of the fulfillment of the American promise. And then, from the oral history interview with Gust A. and Annie Berg, his son and daughter-in-law, I learned more about the aftermath of that optimistic moment. In 1888, Gust S. and Marie Berg left Sweden with two small sons and headed for Illinois. Soon they had another son and then a daughter. Digging deeper, I found that their fortune turned when their two-year-old daughter contracted diphtheria and died. In 1893, in the wake of her next birth, Marie died, and her infant son quickly followed her.

A year later, with his remaining three small children in tow, Gust S. married Hilda Olson, who had recently arrived from Sweden. They continued building a family, and before long their table was surrounded by children. They decided to try their luck in North Dakota. While working in a harness shop in Lakota, Gust S. got another break: His name was drawn in the land-taking lottery at Fort Totten, and he claimed 160 acres near Warwick. His eldest son, Albert, took land right near him. Another son, Edward, bought the adjacent 20 acres. They launched their modest version of a family landowning dynasty, something that never would have been possible for them in Sweden or Illinois.

Unfortunately, Gust S. did not especially like North Dakota. His older children, too, preferred Illinois. His son, Gust A., reported that the family would have moved back had they been able to afford it. With thirteen children to feed, Gust S. expanded his holdings by purchasing an additional 80 acres from the neighboring "Olson woman."[16] Still, he and his family struggled financially.

Gust S.'s success proved only temporary. What choices did they have? The postwar economic downturn hit hard. Even with the ideal family labor force and cheap land, Gust could not keep up with payments on his mortgage. By about 1921, his son Gust A. took it over. "I bought it for $30 an acre. And the bank in Warwick. I bought from my dad, and he was broke. I had to buy on time, see. I had no money to pay for it."

In 1929, when Gust S. Berg died of pneumonia at the age of 58, his dream had completely unraveled. He was penniless and landless. His sons had trouble scraping together ten dollars to pay for his burial.[17] Even with some property and remarkable fecundity, enduring success eluded him. The bankers, whom North Dakota farmers always mistrusted, lurk in the Berg family narrative as shady, possibly unscrupulous characters. It is only when Annie Berg, Gust A.'s wife, revealed that her father-in-law, Gust S., was virtually illiterate and therefore easy to swindle that the story fills out. When she added that he "drank quite a bit," we realize that Gust S.'s misfortune may have had more layers than first appeared.

If a farmer's legacy resides in progeny as well as land, then Gust S. Berg's life does not look as bleak as it might have just before he died. Many of his children grew to adulthood, bought land, married, had their own children, and made a life for themselves on the land. Indeed, Gust A. Berg, who took over his father's note and later managed to pay the burial fees, stayed on the reservation, farming all his life and amassing 307 acres by the time he retired (see figure 53). In his life partner, Annie, he met his match. Remaining in good health, Gust A. worked at odd jobs until the age of 90 and lived to be 102 years old.

While financing farm expansion, mortgages created a cycle of debt that left landowners vulnerable. Their involvement can be measured in the rising proportion of farm families with mortgages.[18] After Gust A. Berg had purchased 80 acres of land on the reservation and married Annie Bostrom, newly arrived from Sweden, they borrowed in order to sustain their operations:

GUST BERG: "We had seed loans and feed loans."
ANNIE BERG: "And cattle loans."
GUST BERG: "Yeah, barnyard loans."
ANNIE BERG: "And they even come and wanted loan on my few chickens out there. And I told 'em, 'You want me, too?' [Chuckle.] I was young then."

When cash was needed, mortgages, however risky, became the vehicle for expansion. Although Annie Berg's name did not appear on the deed to the land, her labors produced the assets that generated much-needed cash income and, when the bank required a guarantee, served as collateral for a loan.

But inability to make payments threatened foreclosure and loss of land. Banks could call in a mortgage for a single missed payment on the grounds that it deemed the farm insolvent, or they could refuse to give one. A raft of foreclosures struck the entire region. In March 1923, Effie Hanson, who lived near Minot, wrote: "It sure is fierce the hard times. There are quite a few sold mortgaged stock & used the money for fuel & clothing. The bankers don't like that a tall [and they] tried to scare the farmers but most are too wise for the bankers. So the bankers had to keep their mouth shut."[19] That she and her husband were ardent anti-capitalist Nonpartisan Leaguers did not exempt them from having to borrow money from those for whom Effie expressed heartfelt antipathy.

By 1929, as a consequence of farmers' inability to meet debt payments, the acreage owned by banks and private companies on the reservation had increased tenfold, to 17,910 acres. Ignatius Court, a leader of Spirit Lake Dakota people, no longer had his allotment. "I lost it by foreclosure,"[20] he declared. He and his wife lived on forty acres given to him by his aunt, but he did not farm it. Rather, he pieced together a living by acting as an interpreter, taking odd jobs, and leasing his land. Even Morton Anderson, a second-generation Norwegian banker and land manager, lost most of his considerable land holdings. In 1928 he and his wife mortgaged their land in Minco Township; in 1935 the Bank of North Dakota foreclosed on it. According to James Skurdall, by 1941, Anderson owned only three lots and their house in Warwick, which they auctioned off before they moved permanently to Seattle.

Scandinavians' migrations echoed their *vanderinger* history; the economic downturn of the 1920s and inhospitable conditions for farming prompted many to move on, while others relocated in local orbits. Thor Peterson attributed his family's repeated moves to his parents' poverty: "Seems like we moved for every year.... Tried to find a better place. [Chuckle.] We usually got a poorer place than we had before." Like the Holbrooks in Tillie Olsen's *Yonnondio*, some families' moves were precipitated by a failed crop. In North Dakota, as in Scandinavia, not all children inherited land, so many had to "travel." Indeed, some returned to Scandinavia: return migration rates ranged from 19 percent of Swedes to 25 percent of Norwegians in the period between 1880 and 1930.[21] Poverty and marginality prompted people to keep moving.[22] But as the Berg family story shows, poverty could also inhibit mobility. Oral accounts highlight the importance of social capital—kinship and friendship in particular—in decisions about where to live. Some distressed survivors stayed where they had support.

Farm making as well as farming required long-term endurance. Gust S. Berg's troubles exposed how precarious the transmission of land to the next generation could be. It required fortuitous timing and a bit of luck—cheap land at below-market prices at the expense of Dakota Indians and an able partner willing to share the labor. Historian Barbara Handy-Marchello outlines farmers' multigenerational outlook: "Farm families expected to prosper through generations linked to each other by their work and presence on the land."[23] While she found that a land-keeping ethic existed across groups, it seems to have been stronger among immigrants from agricultural societies. It took years, even decades, for homesteaders to develop a farm. Their achievement could be measured only over time with family succession and increased yield. Gust S.'s path might have been smoother if he had mastered reading and writing in English. Drink, the scourge of Western communities, undermined many a well-intentioned farmer, sapping energy, precious capital, good judgment, and the personal discipline needed for the long haul. But the weather and world commodity prices had to be on your side as well. The road to failure could be just as long and uncertain as the path to success.

To remain economically viable, farms had to be kept in the family and operations had to be expanded gradually. Scandinavians understood that farm development was an intergenerational process, and they devoted themselves to passing land to descendants.[24] As historian Mary Neth put it, "Family members' return for their labor came not through an individual wage, but through a share of the living the farm provided and an assurance that the farm would be a resource for the family's future."[25] Second-generation Norwegian Wilma J. Pierson (b. 1928) observed the farm succession in Benson County. "You'll find that all through the community here, where the son is on the homestead." That generational endurance was evident in the Forde family's ability to hold onto some land for a century. One of the Forde brothers, Nils, farmed near Hamar. While he still owned land in 1929, "that was sold later on," according to Norman Forde. But the extended family also owned land in Nelson County. "My folks passed away...that's now my nephews'; they're farming it. My youngest brother's boys."

Parental assistance to adult children was a critical factor in farm succession. Upward mobility may have been the American dream, but many Scandinavian families had more modest goals. When Thomas Pearson credited his father with helping him get started, he told a familiar tale. His dad held title to a homestead: "He didn't have much land either. Then I bought this 40 [acres] from my dad. That's why I got started. I didn't have no money [to] lay down on it. He had a little loan on that 40, so I took that over." Taking over the payments enabled Thomas to get a foothold. Recognizing the power of assistance from kin, Lois Olson Jones discussed the importance of living near her family: "Because how would you ever get established...unless you had a cow and so on?" Sharing labor and being given such essentials as livestock were as important as owning land. Lois knew that staying near her family would make the difference between getting by and suffering during hard times. Narrators recounted the many ways their parents helped them establish their own households. Ruth and Helmer Dahlen married in 1929 and began farming in 1932. Helmer reported, "In the first year we only had four cows." Ruth chimed in, "Yeah, to start with." Helmer continued, "I got some cows from my dad and she got some from her dad. And then we farmed next door to my father-in-law and we used his machinery. We just bought a few horses. So we got along for a couple years."

At another stage in life, long-term family succession ensured some reciprocity and old-age security, although it required adult children to stay in the vicinity.[26] Lois Olson Jones reported that her parents helped out her Grandpa Olson during the 1920s, when depression and drought first hit North Dakota. In her account, caregiving intertwined with the land. "In 1926, my grandmother died out here on the farm. So that meant that somebody had to come and live with Grandpa...and everybody else had established themselves somewhere else. Mother was the logical one to come home." The intergenerational problem of caring for a widower, who was unused to being by himself and unable to care for a house and work the farm at the same time, was solved by sharing a household. Because the farm needed to be tended along with Grandpa Olson, this kind of exchange over the life course amounted to what sociologist Sonya Salamon has called a land-keeping strategy.[27] The move, however, involved multiple financial liabilities. "This farm, by the time mother and Dad came onto it, to live with Grandpa, was heavily in debt....Dad and mother accepted all this debt." Eventually, the Federal Land Bank foreclosed on the farm. Lois described that action's enduring impact: "I've been afraid of Federal Land Bank all my life. Because they were going to take the farm.... And they did. They took *lots* of farms." Around 1935, her parents were able to start buying the farm back. The process of recovery took more than a decade. Lois prized continuity on the land: "We still have it and we farm it, yet...because Dad farmed it, and Grandpa lived with us. Then...my husband and I farmed it for Dad, and when he passed on, why, we farmed for Mother."

Land superseded individual concerns; indeed, keeping and cultivating it rose above the immediate needs of a nuclear family. Land became a family legacy—provided that control could be retained over generations. Lois Olson Jones said, "I don't know what ties us to the land but I still think it's security." Landlessness meant vulnerability. Adult children stood to inherit the land as long as their parents did not lose it, which meant taking increasing responsibility for the farm and assisting parents in financial trouble. Their actions were neither purely self-serving nor narrowly self-sacrificial. An unspoken challenge was the prospect of taking care of poor and propertyless parents if they lost the land. The Olsons followed a cultural logic of keeping the land for the long haul. As a place and a resource, land minimized the risky unknowns of the future. In the multigenerational long term, it hedged against cyclical scarcity and the devastations of illness or old age.[28]

Yet creeping in between the cheerful remembrances of ancestral resourcefulness are sagas in which adult children must intervene to save the land and resurrect the family legacy. These accounts were told reluctantly, not triumphantly. In the past, as it does today, American culture linked "providing" with adult masculinity. Losing land meant failure to provide. Recovering the family's land sometimes involved rescuing the father's reputation and sense of self. When interviewer Larry Sprunk asked Edd Johnson if his father gave him money to help him get started, he got an unusually forthright answer: "No. No. We helped him to pay off the debt. Then we had everything paid for."

These stories are rooted in a matter-of-fact shame that acknowledges hard times. Hans Larsgaard's kin exemplified what could happen in that precarious generational transition, particularly in the context of economic disaster (see figure 54). In 1905, he took over his father's farm in Aneta in Nelson County. "I bought it under conditions that I pay his debts. So it cost me a little over $4,000 for two quarters. That's the way I started. That's just when I got married in '05, then I took the farm over." Then, in the 1930s, on the brink of losing it himself, his daughter paid the overdue taxes on the land. As he had done, his daughter acted to keep the land in the family. He was able to buy it back from her later, when the rain starting falling and the land began to yield once again.[29]

But it was not always possible to save face for fathers. Evelyn Jahr Greene's parents did not have much to lose. Her second-generation Norwegian father had homesteaded thirty-six acres on the reservation, an economic toehold, but not much of a farm. Since he had grown up landless, impoverished, and motherless, owning any land seemed a major accomplishment. He and his wife had a two-room house, three children, and a few animals. That was their life until the hardships of the Great Depression caught up with him. After losing "everything" in 1937, Evelyn said, "My father was not motivated" to do anything. She never knew him to work again. Fortunately for the family, her mother "wouldn't quit." She turned to domestic service to earn a living, cooking for others, cleaning, and even painting houses. She was not Norwegian, and she did not aspire to own land. "It was just to have a place to live." But the cumulative losses depleted Evelyn's father.

North Dakota was a rural state with an agricultural economy. In 1930, ten years after a majority of the population in the United States had become urban, 83 percent of the state's residents lived in rural areas.[30] Norwegians, more than any other Euro-American immigrant groups, including other Scandinavians, had a proclivity for nonurban living and tended to stay in ethnic communities for generations. Above all, Norwegians sustained a striking and enduring commitment to agriculture. Father William Sherman's classic study, *Prairie Mosaic: An Ethnic Atlas of Rural North Dakota*, reveals distinct ethnic clustering as late as 1965.[31] His historically informed demographic analysis reveals that some areas that were heavily Norwegian in 1914 had become even more so by 1965. Once constructed, Norwegian neighborhoods tended to retain the next generation to a greater degree than other ethnic concentrations did.

Danes, Swedes, and other European immigrants were more likely to assimilate, leave agriculture, and move away from ethnic settlements. Torben Grøngaard

Jeppesen has found that, in comparison to other Scandinavians, Norwegians exhibited a greater propensity to live near others with the same cultural heritage, making choices about where to live and what land to buy or sell on that basis. After the first couple of generations, the Danes, by contrast, moved away to places with more job opportunities and better agricultural prospects.[32] Swedes, never as numerous and more inclined to assimilate, rapidly migrated to urban centers.[33] Norwegians passed up those opportunities in favor of staying in rural communities near their kin and co-ethnics. Displaying a proclivity for rural living, Norwegians consolidated into communities that persisted, even on the Spirit Lake Dakota Indian Reservation.

DAKOTAS' UNREMITTING QUEST FOR AUTONOMY

Dakotas' intergenerational transmission of land was endangered, not a transparent or easily accessible process. Although their personal and tribal autonomy was at stake, they had the federal government as well as the market standing in their way. These challenges made holding onto the land across generations more important, yet more precarious. Decisions about the disposition of land were not made by the entire group, but the tribe felt the communal consequences of individual actions.

In explaining the logic of inheritance, Hilda Redfox Garcia reflected on her father's and mother's successful strategies in acquiring land and passing it on to the next generation. Hilda reported, "My dad would buy land and so, we all got land. All of us. He made sure of that. That's why I said we were all around him, and we were all in our...own property." She had twelve siblings and step-siblings, although some of them had predeceased her. She likened her father's land-buying strategy to nesting: "like they will say, 'the hen and all her chicks all around her'—well, I guess that's the way we were with our dad and mom." Her mother had her own allotment, which she gave to one of Hilda's sisters, for reasons she found logical and justifiable: "My sister is partially sighted. When she was small, she had an eye infection, and they put something in her eyes that damaged it, so...she can see, she can get around, but it's not like us; we can see. So [my mom] said, 'She's always gonna be needing help,' she said. So she gave it all to her—all her land—so she gets lease money or whatever."

Multiple paradoxes stymied Dakota people. The Indian Office espoused a rhetoric that belied its policies and practices. It designated the reservation as a place uniquely belonging to Dakotas, but then unleashed changes that would inexorably dispossess them. With characteristic paternalism it professed a commitment to Indians' economic independence but consistently exercised arbitrary control and provided too few resources for farming, rendering them ever more dependent on the government. One successful result of Native activism, the Indian Citizenship Act of 1924, clarified national suffrage for Indian people, but it exempted some states from its provisions. Moreover, voting offered only a partial remedy to the issues that confronted Native Americans. The act did not grant them control over trust monies and land management.

Dakotas were acutely aware of these contradictions. As members of a federally recognized tribe described as "a domestic dependent nation," they put an accent on "nation" and sought to escape "dependency." They continued to press the United States to enforce its own laws, practice due process, honor its negotiated agreements, and grant them discretion over their rightful resources. Superintendent Samuel Young disparagingly observed, "They are headstrong and determined. They remark that the land is theirs and the money is theirs and that they should have the right to do as they please in the matter of selling their lands and using their money."[34] Clearly Dakotas were seeking self-determination; they insisted that they should have the power to decide matters relevant to their lives and livelihood—including how to use their land—for themselves.

They continued to pursue recognition of past treaties and compensation for federal violations of their terms. After 1906, when Congress reinstated the contractually agreed-upon annuities specified in the Treaty of 1851, Dakotas were inspired by a renewed sense of possibility and sought legal redress. The government's many unmet treaty obligations remained pressing. In 1916, Sissetons and Wahpetons again successfully persuaded Congress to recognize their legal standing and authorize another case to be argued in the U.S. Court of Claims. Dakotas charged fraud and misrepresentation on the part of the federal government in treaty negotiations in 1851 and 1857 and contended that they had been pressured into ceding lands that were not rightly their own but belonged to other Native peoples. In 1923 the Court of Claims ruled that it had no authority under the law to adjudicate fraud or misrepresentation "unless expressly authorized by Congress so to do." Sissetons and Wahpetons appealed to the Supreme Court, which in 1928 upheld the Court of Claims decision.[35]

The same year the Supreme Court decision was handed down, many families continued to make an effort to become self-sufficient in agriculture. In addition to using land for pasture, 209 Indian families at Spirit Lake were farming an average of about 45 acres each. But many farms did not yield an adequate livelihood. Moreover, as the income generated from agriculture declined, jobs as farm laborers for non-Indians as well as Dakotas disappeared.[36] There were no alternative industries on the reservation. As white farmers struggled, they were less able to pay the rent on their leases, so Dakota leaseholders also suffered.

Two generations after their defeat in war, while being simultaneously mythologized and despised in the dominant U.S. culture, Dakotas continued to find ways to adapt to their situation. Dakota men had long been unable to fulfill the masculine warrior ideal, although women found more gender continuity as cultivators and gatherers. Dakotas held onto the value of generosity as a measure of valor and dignity. They treated money and farm machinery the way they had historically treated other possessions: if you had them, you shared. People of standing redistributed their resources to those in greater need. The overwhelming challenge of making a living and feeding a family in a depressed economy during a drought that obliterated not just crops but all food that grew wild, including game, made this cultural logic of sharing even more essential for group survival. But within an agricultural system that required reinvestment of accumulated capital and ever-increasing expanses of land, redistribution further undermined their viability as farmers. The premium Dakotas placed on helping the less fortunate operated in tension with their efforts to provide for their own well-being.

Education also had paradoxical effects. The earlier logic of reform had vested Indian assimilation in the promise of gendered schooling. While boarding schools were geared toward turning Indian boys into farmers and girls into skilled farm wives, they also taught English proficiency and literacy. By 1930, the divide between educated young people and older, less literate Indians was not falling along the lines whites had predicted. Superintendent Gray reported: "The best farmers here are the ones who had very little schooling. The returned student expects more wages from the white farmers, and will not stay on the job."[37] In fact, the younger people's attitude was consistent with that of white youth across the Midwest who recognized the limited opportunities agriculture offered, moved to urban centers, and found other ways to make a living. Unlike Indians, who encountered severe racial discrimination and outright exclusion when they sought jobs off the reservation, Scandinavians and other Euro-Americans could easily obtain jobs elsewhere.

Reversing the optimism about integration expressed a generation earlier, Indian Office bureaucrats recognized the unintended deleterious consequences of coexistence, which historian Francis Prucha called the "white problem."[38] The sale of alcohol was never allowed on the reservation, and Prohibition had criminalized making as well as selling it. As liquor was hard to come by, those who sought drink would go fourteen miles north to the town of Devils Lake. Some turned to desperate measures, such as drinking canned heat (Sterno) or denatured alcohol. Superintendent Grey blamed the problem on the baneful influence of lower-class non-Indians: "a crowd of low down whites infesting that city."[39] Rather than the imagined uplift, authorities were faced with the stark possibility of Indians' assimilation to American lower-class culture.

Enduring structural poverty, the result of punitive policies that cultivated dependency, continued to create severe health problems for Dakotas.[40] Dakotas and agents had been demanding a hospital for decades before one was finally built. During an epidemic of whooping cough in 1927, the superintendent "estimated that the deaths among smaller children will be twice as large as the number of births."[41] A national survey of reservation conditions, the 1928 *Meriam Report*, praised Fort Totten for its relative success in stemming the incidence of trachoma, but the unconscionably high tuberculosis rate continued to ravage the tribe and revealed the prevalence of inadequate nourishment and overcrowded housing conditions. Infants and young children were the most vulnerable to outbreaks of disease, with demographically as well as personally catastrophic consequences. Dakota tribal member Fred Lawrence described the devastation inflicted by tuberculosis: "My boy was sick and now I lost all my family by T.B., my wife and seven children and that is the only boy I got left."[42] By 1933, the survey of conditions at Fort Totten reported 73 cases of active and arrested TB and added that "seventy-five percent of the population may be classified as contacts."[43]

The agency dispensed meager rations even in times of hardship and acute need. The Indian Office increased its procurement of milk cows for Indian families in order to bolster children's nutrition, however. The much-reviled superintendent John Hammitt reported that in 1929 he spent $1.06 per month per person on rations, which bought "beans, pork, sugar, flour, baking powder, hard bread, and sometimes rice."[44] Such paltry and intermittent supplies did not adequately nourish those Dakotas who had little else.

Concerned about the multitude and severity of problems such as land loss, poverty, and ill health, in 1929 the subcommittee of the Senate Committee on Indian Affairs launched a national study of conditions on reservations. The local hearings were convened by senators Burton K. Wheeler (Democrat) of Montana and Lynn Frazier (Republican) of North Dakota, who chaired both the committee and subcommittee. As the former NPL governor, Senator Frazier believed in fighting corruption in government, while Wheeler had litigated successfully against giant corporations in court, bringing a history of commitment to social justice and powerful skills in interrogation.[45]

On Saturday, July 20, 1929, tribal members pressed into the Benson County courthouse in Minnewaukan to give testimony about their concerns and the consequences of their lack of autonomy: the inability to make sound decisions about land and resources, unresolved treaty issues, unconscionably high levels of tuberculosis on the reservation, corporal punishment of their children in the white-run boarding school, and multiple charges of misconduct against the sitting Indian superintendent, John Hammitt.

The testimony brought before the committee was emblematic of problems that dogged Dakota people. Martin Strait, a laborer and interpreter who had shot the "last arrow" in 1916, took the stand to represent Moses Smith, who was ill and unable to attend. Smith's complaint centered on the impossibility of clearing title to his land, which had been mortgaged. He wanted to pay off the mortgage so as not to endanger his children's inheritance, but because of the lack of transparency in the Fort Totten administrative office he could not get a straight answer on the status of his land or his account. An Oberon bank held the mortgage, but the superintendent would not clarify the situation, which prevented him from paying off the encumbering loan. Here was an illuminating instance of a Dakota man wanting to follow the law and protocol so as to ensure the intergenerational transmission of his land. Rather than facilitating his sound efforts, the administration created seemingly insurmountable obstacles.

Another stalwart farmer and "patent-in-fee Indian," who had been a litigant in the 1897 case against Benson County and later participated in the citizenship ritual, Bernard Two Hearts, registered a complaint against superintendent Hammitt for his maltreatment of an elderly Dakota woman. She wanted to visit her brother in Cannon Ball, on the Standing Rock Sioux Indian Reservation. She had sold her allotment, as she had nobody to help her take care of it. When Senator Frazier asked, "Did anyone take care of her on the reservation?" Bernard Two Hearts answered, "They used to take care of her but no one could get along with the old lady." She requested $50 from her trust account, which, like everyone else's, was under the control of the superintendent. So Bernard had intervened on her behalf. "I went and talked with Mr. Hammitt and he wanted to give her a purchase order for $20 and she walked from the office and she was crying." He said that Mr. Hammitt "refused to give her $50" from her account. To remedy this egregious wrong, a sympathetic young man offered to transport her and bankroll the trip to see her brother. But "the car broke down west of Cheyenne [*sic*] and they put her on the train and sent her to Cannon Ball and she had bad cold and pneumonia and died of that."[46] Clearly, Bernard Two Hearts laid the woman's tragic death at the feet of Hammitt and objected to the superintendent's arbitrary micromanagement of trust expenditures. Not only did the woman have to request permission to use funds that rightfully belonged to her, but the superintendent had the power to deny her the amount she requested and determine what form the funds would take.

A week after these hearings, Dakotas held a council and composed a letter to the Senate subcommittee that eloquently called for autonomy, justice, and due process. Remarkably, a sizable proportion of its 163 signatories were women. The female names listed on the letter indicate not only that women had grievances (which men presented at the hearing), but also that they fully participated in the post-hearing council deliberations. The letter deftly built upon ideological principles of the U.S. legal system. It centered on issues of inheritance and how heirship was determined and by what process Indian Office decisions could be challenged and appealed:

SIRS: Come now the four tribes of Sioux Indians residing on said reservation, viz, Sissetons, Whapetons [*sic*], Yanktons, and Cutheads, this date in council assembled, and respectfully show unto your honors the following:

1. That decrees of heirship in any estates of deceased Indians have been entered by the department and the same are erroneous in that heirs entitled to participate in the distribution of estates have been omitted and in some instances persons not heirs have been decreed to be such, all to the loss and damage of the rightful heirs.

2. That in many instances where the estate consisted of money such money has been distributed (a) to only part of the heirs, or (b) to persons not heirs in fact, and such moneys can not now be recovered and paid to the rightful heirs.

3. That in the handling of said estates the department acted as trustee of an express trust, the said Indians having no voice in the selection of such trustee, and such trustee has paid trust funds to parties not entitled thereto.

4. That the heirs who have suffered such loss and damage are without any plain, speedy, or adequate remedy at law in that, among other things, such Indians have no funds to prosecute their claims; that to prosecute such claims would take years of litigation; that the burden of such litigation should not be thrown upon them where a trustee has violated the duties of the trust; that the amount due to many individuals would not warrant litigation; and in this their remedy at law is not adequate or equitable.

5. That there should be an act of Congress appropriating a sum of money for the purpose of reimbursing heirs whose moneys have been wrongfully disbursed by the said trustee, and the said trustee should not be permitted to invoke any statute of limitations. That many Indians now living on said reservation are justly entitled to funds belonging to estates of deceased Indians and they have no funds to enable them to assert and establish their lawful claims. That a competent lawyer should be sent to said reservation with power to examine all claims against the estates of deceased Indians, to examine all decrees of heirship heretofore entered, to take testimony and make findings to support amended decrees of heirships, all to the end that justice be done to excluded heirs and to heirs whose moneys have been improperly disbursed by said trustee.[47]

The list of the names of the signatories who "respectfully submitted" this petition begins with "Suna (his x mark) Waanatan," the eldest son of Chief Waanatan, who had been an important tribal leader and a member of numerous delegations to Washington representing Dakotas.

Substantively, the airing of Dakota issues in the hearings and the letter challenged the systematic denial of access to rightful resources. The petition called out the ineptitude of the Indian Office and contested the limits on Dakotas' decision-making power. It condemned the Indian Office's violation of its stated goals and procedures for determining heirs. Further, it pointed out that there was no recourse for aggrieved parties to remedy either the procedure or the outcomes produced by an incompetent and, perhaps, malevolent bureaucracy. It urged congressional action to rectify the systemic wrongs created by careless or intentional errors and inadequate oversight.

Through legal processes—the courts and public hearings—Dakotas continued to battle the government over its duplicity and unmet promises. This petition, like the Sisseton-Wahpeton cases in the U.S. Court of Claims, reveals the Dakotas' sophisticated approach to using the means available to air publicly their grievances. As a nation that had diplomatic relations with the United States, they made efforts at negotiation, and when those failed, they pressed on. As Frederick Hoxie points out, persistence paid off—not necessarily in legal victories but in creating opportunities to bring Native peoples' issues to public attention and to point out the hypocrisy of the U.S. government.[48]

On the basis of the overwhelming evidence presented at the hearings, Senator Wheeler, who succeeded Frazier as chair of the committee, went on to sponsor the Wheeler-Howard Act of 1934, also known as the Indian Reorganization Act. This landmark legislation ended the allotment process and created a means for tribes to acquire land.[49] Cast as the "Indian New Deal," it was supported by President Franklin Delano Roosevelt, who visited Fort Totten in August 1934, two months after the bill passed (see figure 55).

* * * * *

From dissimilar structural positions, Scandinavians and Dakotas, even those who shared farming as an occupation and livelihood, were affected differently by political and economic processes. Because their tenuous hold on the land was threatened by different forces, they had unique political targets. Dakotas' grasp on land was undermined by the capricious control of the federal government, while Scandinavians were vulnerable to the vicissitudes of the market economy.

As strangers who had become ambivalent acquaintances, living side by side for twenty-five years, Dakotas and Scandinavians had learned something of each other's ways of life. Both braved the transition from farm making to farming that required at least occasional reliance on each other. Dakota farming families contended with severe weather and fluctuating markets, just as Scandinavian farmers did, but they also had to contend with a federal government that consistently thwarted their efforts through undercapitalization, interference with autonomous decision making, and disruption of their ability to bequeath land to their children. The combination of the government's malfeasance and its dual goals of selling Indian land and amalgamating the Indian population meant that retaining land and achieving agricultural sustainability were possible for only a minority.

Land did not guarantee freedom from poverty. Nonetheless, never owning it or losing it created deeper privation and made relocation more likely. Eventually it became clear that, contrary to prevalent predictions, Indians endured the destructive cultural and economic onslaught and proved they had a place in the twentieth century. Never challenged as fundamentally, Scandinavians were at Spirit Lake to stay and, if possible, to thrive.

Conclusion: Strangers No More

IN THE EARLY twentieth century, dispossession swept the land on the southern shores of Spirit Lake out of the collective hands of one people and into the family hands of another. One hundred years later, nature took back that land from all parties, heedless of history or identity. Devils Lake has been rising for two decades, ceaselessly flooding its banks and reclaiming everything in its path. Reaching a peak of 1,454.3 feet in June 2011, the volume of water had increased more than sevenfold. In 1993 the lake covered 44,230 acres; eighteen years later, it covered 211,300 acres.[1] The reservation and its neighboring towns and farms to the west and east are inundated with water. Year after year, roads get built higher and higher, but they lead to fewer places as farmland disappears, homes are lost, lives are submerged, and dreams vanish. Dakotas' choices of elevated land, which seemed so foolish to the agricultural eye in 1890, now seem wise.

In the face of nature's power, all else is dwarfed and humbled. Yet in the wake of the flood, human communities remain, striving to make meaning of their lives. Here the might of natural forces yields to the quiet authority of memory, voice, and reflection.

SILENCES AND HISTORICAL MEMORY

The history Scandinavians tell about themselves does not include the social cost of land taking on the reservation. Norwegians like my great-grandmother did not come to be settler colonialists or to usurp the place of others. They deeply resented having been colonized by Danes and Swedes and could not conceive of themselves as occupying an oppressive position in a foreign country. As newcomers, immigrants were searching desperately for a place to remake home: they were steered into the reservation enterprise by forces largely beyond their control and outside their ken. With their vivid memory of the suffering endured in Norway and Sweden and the sacrifices made during migration, they judged themselves and their descendants worthy of the land. They began a process of land taking that would continue for decades, hunkered down on their farms, and made the United States their permanent home. At the same time, Norwegians especially resisted cultural assimilation and held fast to their mother country. But this cultural "two-ness" did little to slow down the expansion of their individual and aggregate holdings.

Scandinavians were not unique in the fundamental dynamics of their land taking. Because Americans are almost entirely of immigrant descent, the forebears of all non-Native people have played some role, direct or indirect, in indigenous dispossession. Yet most historical narratives fail to confront this fact, and most Americans do not wrestle with its far-reaching consequences. The migration maps in U.S. textbooks show bold arrows arcing across the continent and targeting the Northern Plains. I now see how my great-grandmother's flight along one of those trajectories fortuitously landed her in North Dakota at precisely the moment when homesteading was allowed at Spirit Lake. As a result, she and her daughters were able to forge a new life here. Like many of their immigrant counterparts, they were content to let the sordid details of the past dissolve into a convenient haze of foggy memories. They dwelt on the present and the future, as land takers often do, and rarely probed the past or questioned laws that privileged them while disadvantaging others.

Many people now concede that the U.S. government dealt with Indian peoples unconscionably throughout the process of state building and imperial expansion, but recognition of the nature and effect of these policies has no more effect now than it did one hundred years ago. It does not prompt current government leaders or individual land holders to make apologies, propose reparations, or give back land. In the face of the outrage of dispossession, Scandinavians past and present have eluded the thorny past by misremembering it or by living uncomfortably with their personal or ancestral culpability.

In that resounding silence, a few Scandinavian narrators spoke up and struggled with the problem. At the end of the twentieth century, some members of the second generation, such as Bjorne Knudson, and my grandmother, Helene Haugen Kanten, drew me into their moral quandaries. They reflected on why the government pursued the land taking and probed the meaning of their own unwitting but active participation in the process. Helene worried about having stolen land from Native Americans. Just because homesteading on the reservation was legal did not relieve whites of their responsibility. Bjorne, having lived on the reservation all his life, critically evaluated what happened. "Well that's where I think they done a mistake. They let this land out to the white people to homestead or buy it or do anything....I think they should have kept the white people off the reservation entirely." Despite these misgivings, looking back with regret did little to change things. Though troubled by her mother's actions and its consequences, my grandmother did not become a Native rights advocate or abandon her Norwegian chauvinism.

Some find a kind of belated reckoning in the current Devils Lake flood. The 500 acres owned by Bjorne Knudson before he died are now completely under water, uncompensated by disaster relief. His well-laid plans to bequeath his farm to his children have left them land in title only, and saddled them with an unrelieved burden of property taxes they must pay, lest they lose it altogether. Agnes Greene reveled in the irony of the flooding and its costs to the U.S. government. When her grandparents were forced to relocate from Stump Lake onto the reservation, they were promised compensation. "The government was going to *pay* them for that land. They never got nothing. They died thinking they were going to get paid." As Devils Lake has overflowed into nearby Stump Lake and threatens to spill over into the Sheyenne River, public agencies have had to invest enormous resources into managing the evolving environmental and economic disaster. Agnes remarked, "That's why that water's going over there; and I'm always praying the water's going over there. I'm so glad for my grandparents....[Laughs.]"[2] More than a century after the government reneged on its agreement to compensate her family, it is paying vast sums in a futile attempt to stem the tide. Her sense of Mother Nature's sweeping retribution was sweet: she saw the flood as restoring a natural order that her grandparents would have applauded.

Among Dakotas, government repression that intended to sever Native children from their ancestors, cultural practices, and language contributed to the vast silence. Grace Lambert attested to the government's success in interrupting cultural transmission. "See, I made up my mind when I used to be abused, I am *never* teaching my children to talk Indian."[3] Later, as Eunice Davidson said, older people simply could not bear to speak of what had happened, because it was so painful. She recalled what her grandmother told her: " 'We couldn't speak our language, couldn't dance,' she said, 'and that was very hurtful.' " Taking her grandmother's message to heart, Eunice expressed the need not to feel resentment or anger, not to dwell upon earlier times, but "to remember, so it never goes back to that again."

My first, serendipitous visit to North Dakota became a long journey through the forested mountains of Norway, the rolling farmlands of Denmark, and archives across the United States, that irresistibly pulled me back, again and again, to Spirit Lake. Before that initial trip to the reservation I had reveled in an idealized "Vikings on the prairie" version of my family saga. The bracing recognition of my grandmother's ethical dilemma spurred me to grapple with my troubled inheritance.

As a child of immigrants from rural western Canada, I feel the power of connection to these specific places and people, however disconcerting the particulars. I have come to see my family story less as an idiosyncratic set of ordeals and heroic acts, and more as a part of a collective process of migration, resettlement, and displacement. Actions, events, and choices that once seemed random revealed themselves as the harsh result of global forces that dislocated peasants and dispossessed Native peoples. Through my search for the missing pieces of this intricate puzzle, I have come to understand how profoundly those two processes were intertwined. At the same time, these narratives of people I have come to admire and cherish have been the source of so much of my learning. In this way, my sense of history has become both more and less personal, both more and less about judgment and justice, both more and less *certain*.

THE POWER OF PLACE IN THE AFTERLIFE OF DISPOSSESSION

The reservation, a designated area not chosen but assigned, became a legally defined and socially symbolic place with real power in Indian people's lives. Over generations, allotments and homesteads provided a foundation on which to build physical and metaphorical homes where kin lived, visitors gathered, and memories were recounted. As Mary Louise Defender Wilson said of another Dakota reservation, "For some of us, if it weren't for those allotted lands, we wouldn't really have any connection to Standing Rock." When I asked if she meant connection through owning land, she replied, "No, I mean by having a feeling that we belong here."

Ironically, it was the private ownership of land that allowed her to feel that way; this transformation of the Dakota approach to legal property rights led to a new medium of affiliation. Within a dominant economic and political system rooted in private property, this change was of no small consequence. Reflecting on the allotment process and its aftermath, Mary Louise said that owning private property made a difference to her ancestors: "I think they were grateful to have a place where they could always be.... Let's face it, they were harassed in their own aboriginal area. At least my mother's people were. And made to come over here to Standing Rock. So that when they had an area that was theirs, where they could always be and stay; well then, I think they liked that."

Dakotas had to shift from revering and protecting land as a communal resource to holding on to it as private owners and preserving it over generations. Eunice

Davidson relayed the perspective of her Dakota grandmother: "She always made that remark that the land was one of the greatest gifts. That's what it was to her, a gift, she said.... When you give something to an Indian, back then and now, that's really a gift you get, and you really cherish it." Through this transition from allotment to landowning alongside whites, keeping the land was in tension with selling it. Short-term needs were dire, and legal processes often conspired against Indian people's retention of the land. Scandinavians, in contrast, drew on a very different ancestral legacy that dovetailed more readily with U.S. agrarian capitalism: own the land and sacrifice everything else to pass it down over generations.

Since they arrived, both Dakotas and Scandinavians made claim to the land by constructing home. Sociologist Alfred Schuetz acknowledged that while home is hard to define, it is powerful and "emotionally evocative": it means "the family, the sweetheart, the friends; it means a beloved landscape, 'songs my mother taught me', food prepared in a particular way, familiar things for daily use, folkways, and personal habits—briefly, a peculiar way of life composed of small and important elements, likewise cherished."[4] A home signifies safety and the conditions for intimacy, not just a locus for later nostalgia. When land is home, many refuse to part with it.

Land was also fundamental to cultural continuity. Immigrants and Dakotas sought out people who spoke their language, made their favorite foods, and told jokes they understood.[5] In everyday life, seasonal celebrations, and sacred rituals, Dakotas hosted powwows and dances that expressed their communal identity. Norwegians held dances of their own and stopped work to celebrate Norway's Constitution Day on May 17. They consolidated their scattered holdings into enduring neighborhood clusters, reaffirmed kinship bonds, resisted mainstream politics, and remained stubbornly rural.

Spirit Lake was a place of defiant persistence, regardless of ancestry or culture. Neither group followed the road to assimilation planned by government officials and reformers. Jointly and separately, Dakotas and Scandinavians found ways to subvert Americanization efforts targeting them. Grace Lambert harkened to one of the great Dakota chiefs, Sitting Bull: "He told his grandchildren, he says, 'My grandchildren, the white people are here to teach you.' He says, 'But listen, and look. Whatever is good, pick it up; whatever is no good, don't.' And I think that he was right."[6]

For Dakotas and Norwegians, the quest for citizenship has been mistakenly interpreted as a form of assimilation. In fact, each used land and citizenship as a base to make radical claims against the government and economic system. They decidedly did not seek incorporation into the mainstream. Maintaining their cultural uniqueness was essential to them.

Landowning was a similar source of power. However marginalized Indians and immigrants were socially, economically, and geographically, owning reservation land conferred clout. Paradoxically, instead of disrupting Dakotas' anchor in Indian community and culture, individual landownership strengthened it. Homesteading land at Spirit Lake set Norwegians on a path to naturalization and secured them a place in North America.

People of both cultures expressed a stubborn attachment to the soil, whether they regard it as munificent or capricious. For some, the land represented Mother Earth, the bountiful provider, or the fruitful product of their ancestors' toil. For many—sometimes the very same people—land was "the Nature," as Norwegians put it, a vastness utterly indifferent to humans' fate. Never seeing nature as benign, and fully cognizant of the irony in his characterization, Phillip John Young said to me, arms outstretched overlooking the coulees and wetlands of Spirit Lake, "This is my McDonalds."

DO GOOD FENCES MAKE GOOD NEIGHBORS?

The encounter was a process, not a moment. Over time, social interactions transformed this curious space—a contact zone of strangers caught in multiple contradictions—into an enclave of wary, yet inextricably entangled neighbors.[7]

As the encounter became routinized, everyday exchanges became ordinary and predictable, less fraught with anxiety. The habits and actions of "the other" became familiar. Second-generation Swede Blenda Carlson said, "We just took the Indians for granted." The generation born to the original white settlers simply assumed coexistence. Yankee Cherry Wood Monson grew up on the reservation and learned about Dakota culture by associating with Natives. "Living among the Indians was natural and not thought about when we were young." After moving to California to teach, she was surprised that people wondered about her growing up as a non-Indian on a reservation. "If you are reared near an old board fence you accept that as something everyone has in their backyard. When someone asks the history of the old board fence, you have to scratch your head and think about it." When people and situations are no longer strange, they become comprehensible and expected. Dakotas tolerated the presence of white farmers, Scandinavians included, and naturalized neighbors became part of their lives.

The shared geographic space was divided by a gaping social chasm. Physical integration went hand in hand with social segregation. Between the two groups we find simmering resentment, judgment, and mistrust, although without the violence of 1862. Exceptional cases of mutuality created opportunities for "border crossings," as did occasional intermarriage and intertwined kinship. Mutual aid enabled women in the nexus of networks to establish increasing levels of economic interdependence.

While coexistence did not translate into empathy or political cooperation, proximity ameliorated past conflicts.

Dakotas and Scandinavians also crossed boundaries through learning about one another and expressing mutual respect. Teaching breeds understanding, according to Grace Lambert, but only for people who want to learn. Eventually, she had a change of heart, no longer refusing to instruct her children in order to spare them the pain she suffered, but tutoring anyone, Dakota or not, who was interested in the language and culture. What are the conditions for this kind of transformation and social repair? The pipe carrier for the tribe, Ambrose Littleghost, understood the importance of trying to speak a few words of someone else's language and the power of trying to bridge cultures. He would say, "Takk!" (Thanks!) to his Norwegian neighbors.[8] His approach, at least late in his life, was based on the belief that people share more than they differ and that respecting differences builds a common ground. Eunice Davidson called this "the healing process," which over generations would allow the suffering to cease.

Despite parallel social lives and mutually exclusive ceremonial remembrances, Scandinavians and Dakotas recognized each other, however grudgingly. This taken-for-grantedness betokened an unarticulated acknowledgment. In contrast to the dominant culture, Scandinavians living on the reservation could not erase Dakota people, either from their recollections or from their contemporary lives. Residence on the reservation rendered inescapable both the reality of dispossession and the continued existence of Native people. To Dakotas, Scandinavians living on the reservation became an everyday phenomenon, familiar if not well known, whose very ordinariness and localness made them unlike others.

THE LANDOWNING ADVANTAGE

Dakotas and Scandinavians came to own land through different processes. While the notion of private property was imposed on Dakotas, over time they adapted and embraced the idea of ownership. Scandinavians brought this core ideal with them. It motivated them to homestead in North Dakota, where conditions, however difficult, were better than those in the old country, and it gave them a clear advantage in the U.S. economic system.

Reformers and some government officials envisioned allotment for Indians as a stopgap against the hemorrhage of dispossession, while others saw it as an opportunity to terminate Indian claims on the land. In a country where land equals wealth, landownership, even of relatively small parcels, confers some power. Larger land holdings translated into more resources, greater political voice, and increased economic well-being. While landownership did not necessarily lead to prosperity, those who had access to this key resource did better than those who did not; owning little or no land led to impoverishment and further displacement. In an era during which the safety net was local, social, and noninstitutional, people without land were more vulnerable to hunger and cold. As the basic means of production, land provided not only a refuge but also a base from which to work against poverty. By mixing their labor with land, women in particular were able to combine childrearing and full-time income-producing work, giving them flexibility and some autonomy in organizing their lives.

The end of my story, the year 1930, is a useful place to pause and take stock, but it is hardly a stopping point. Contemplating the period that followed, we are left with compelling questions. Dakotas experienced a communal catastrophe, as Scandinavians and others continued to expropriate their land—legally, incrementally, inexorably. Many Scandinavians left the reservation, moving to the Pacific Northwest, to the Canadian plains, or to urban centers in search of jobs and land; others remained. Among Native people, although individual land loss continued, the tribe once again became a major landowner, following the passage of the Indian Reorganization Act in 1934. Hilda Redfox Garcia observed, "Nowadays, I don't think anybody has any land, 'cause they sold it all to the tribe." In the twenty-first century, the Spirit Lake Dakota Nation has become the primary owner and purchaser of land, rendering Dakotas' formal attachment to the land, once again, manifestly communal.

In the entangled enclave of this Indian reservation, the everyday lives of Dakotas and Scandinavians conjoined infrequently through friendship and kinship, occasionally with mutual aid, and consistently through land, labor, and trade. No longer enemies, these strangers became wary neighbors. As a group, Dakotas were foreigners, alien noncitizens on the continent of their birth, living in a country and a society not of their choosing. Also foreigners, Scandinavians dug in deeply at Spirit Lake while holding fast to their ancestral identity. Despite state-engineered, legally codified racial stratification and clashing cultural logics, these vastly different peoples achieved a degree of peaceable coexistence. Throughout their shared and separate history, the land on which they have coexisted has both defined the boundaries between them, and held them together.

By bringing the annals of these two groups together into the same frame, I sought to ascertain Dakotas' and Scandinavians' effects on each other and to sound how deeply their lives have been connected. Entering into this project, I expected mutual incomprehension. I was surprised by moments of recognition, relationship, and transcendence of prejudice. Those I spoke with, like some of those interviewed forty years before, often tended to be both brutally frank truth-tellers and cultural mediators who wanted to understand, connect, and facilitate dialog. A certain feistiness, trenchant candor, and hope of achieving a more abiding coexistence were often a part of their generous approach to sharing what they knew. I extend this book as an offering to them—and to all those who are similarly intrigued or troubled and want to learn more about this tangled past.

Appendixes

Appendix A

―――

1851   Treaty of Traverse des Sioux between United States and Dakotas

1857   Dakota warriors led by Inkpaduta attack, capture, and kill white settlers near Spirit Lake, Iowa

1858   Land Cessions Treaty between United States and Sissetons and Wahpetons

1861   Outbreak of U.S. Civil War

1862   Homestead Act passed (May)
       U.S.–Dakota War breaks out (August)

1863   Congress abrogates treaty agreements with all Dakotas
       Massacre at Whitestone Hill (September)
       Thirty-eight Dakotas executed—largest mass hanging in U.S. history (December)

1965   Civil War ends; President Lincoln assassinated

1867   Devils Lake Sioux Indian Reservation and Fort Totten Military Fort established

1876   Battle at Little Bighorn

1887   General Land Allotment Act, also known as the Dawes, or Severalty, Act

1889   State of North Dakota admitted to the United States

1890   Massacre at Wounded Knee

1891   Fort Totten Indian Boarding School established

1901   Spirit Lake Dakotas sign agreement to allow white homesteading on reservation

1902   Dead Indian Land Act

1904   Presidential proclamation and congressional approval of 1901 agreement
       Land lottery for homesteading on reservation land
       First white settlers begin moving onto the reservation

1905   Norway gains independence from Sweden

1906　Burke Act amends Dawes Act by ending trust status of Indian land for allottees who obtain fee-simple titles and are granted citizenship

1907　Expatriation Act—Section 3 revokes citizenship of women married to foreign nationals

1910　Omnibus Act creates competency commissions

Spirit Lake Reservation first platted

1911　Society of American Indians founded

1914　War begins in Europe

1916　Nonpartisan League sweeps North Dakota state legislature and wins governorship

1917　North Dakota passes womanhood suffrage

United States enters the war in Europe

1918　Germany surrenders; peace declared

1919　Prohibition begins—Eighteenth Amendment to the U.S. Constitution

1920　National womanhood suffrage ratified—Nineteenth Amendment to U.S. Constitution

1922　Cable Act restores women's right to citizenship based on country of birth

1924　American Indian Citizenship Act, also known as the Snyder Act

Immigration Act of 1924, also known as the Johnson-Reed Act

1929　Stock market crashes; nationwide Great Depression begins

1933　Prohibition ends—repeal of the Eighteenth Amendment

1934　Indian Reorganization Act, also known as the Wheeler-Howard Act, ends allotment of reservation land

ORAL HISTORY INTERVIEW SUBJECTS

Name	Birth Year	Birthplace	Ethnicity or Tribal Affiliation and Enrollment	Immigrant Generation	Year of Interview	Source
Adams, Mr.	?	[Dakota Territory]	Dakota (Sisseton-Wahpeton)	—	1968	AIRP, 161
Adams, Mrs.	1886	Dakota Territory	Dakota (Sisseton-Wahpeton)	—	1968	AIRP, 161
Alberts, Alvina	1912	North Dakota	Dakota (Spirit Lake)	—	1993	IBSOHP
Alex, Christine	1922	North Dakota	Dakota (Spirit Lake)	—	1993	IBSOHP
Belgarde, Peter	1944	North Dakota	Dakota (Spirit Lake)	—	1993	IBSOHP
Berg, Annie Bostrom (Mrs. Gust A.)	1899	Sweden	Swedish	first	1976	NDOHP, 55A
Berg, Gust A.	1889	Illinois	Swedish	second	1976	NDOHP, 55A

Name	Birth Year	Birthplace	Ethnicity or Tribal Affiliation and Enrollment	Immigrant Generation	Year of Interview	Source
Blue, Harriet Parshall	1905	Nebraska	Dakota (Sisseton), English	—	1971	AIRP, 774
Blue, Helen Williams (Mrs. Norman)	1909	South Dakota	Dakota (Sisseton-Wahpeton)	—	1968	AIRP, 164
Blue, Norman	1905	South Dakota	Dakota (Sisseton-Wahpeton)	—	1968	AIRP, 164
Carlson, Blenda	1930	North Dakota	Swedish	second	1999	author interview
Carlson, Linnea	1935	North Dakota	Swedish	second	1999	author interview
Carlson, Mauritz	1948	North Dakota	Swedish	second	1999	author interview
Casper, Emma Beckstrand	1886	Sweden	Swedish	first	1976	NDOHP, 55B
Cree, Charles	1895	North Dakota	Turtle Mountain Band of Chippewa	—	1977	NDOHP, 833A&B
Dahlen, Helmer	1899	North Dakota	Norwegian	third	1976	NDOHP, 677B and 678A&B

Name	Birth	State	Heritage		Year	Source
Dahlen, Ruth (Mrs. Helmer)	1904	North Dakota	Norwegian	second	1976	NDOHP, 677B and 678A&B
Davidson, David	1944	North Dakota	Norwegian	third	2008	author interview
Davidson, Eunice Abraham (Mrs. David)	1951	North Dakota	Dakota (Spirit Lake)	—	2008	author interview
Deloria, Ella	1888	South Dakota	Dakota (Standing Rock Sioux)	—	1969	AIRP, 386
Demarce, Berthe	1911	North Dakota	Dakota (Spirit Lake)	—	1993	IBSOHP
Dolbak, Ella M.	1880	Minnesota	Norwegian	second	1976	NDOHP, 50A&B
Eastman, Mae Ellen	1898	South Dakota	Dakota (Mdewakanton, Santee Sioux)	—	1971	AIRP, 754
Eastman, Oliver	1904	South Dakota	Dakota (Santee, Sisseton-Wahpeton)	—	1971	AIRP, 768
Eliason, Stanley B.	1939	North Dakota	Norwegian	second	2005	author interview
Estvold, Arthur	1888	Minnesota	Norwegian	second	1976	NDOHP, 676A&B
Estvold, Ella (Mrs. Arthur)	1895	Minnesota	Norwegian	second	1976	NDOHP, 676A&B

Name	Birth Year	Birthplace	Ethnicity or Tribal Affiliation and Enrollment	Immigrant Generation	Year of Interview	Source
Fjeld, Julius O.	1884	Dakota Territory	Norwegian	second	1975	NDOHP, 1029A&B
Forde, Norman	1914	North Dakota	Norwegian	third	2006	author interview
Forde, Oscar T.	1895	North Dakota	Norwegian	third	1975	NDOHP, 157A&B
Frank, Marie Olson	1889	North Dakota	Norwegian	second	1976	NDOHP, 748B & 749A&B
Garcia, Hilda Redfox (Mrs. Louis)	1945	South Dakota	Dakota (Spirit Lake)	—	2005	author interview
Garcia, Louis R.	1940	New York	Spanish, Irish	second	2005	author interview
Goodbird, Titus	1890	South Dakota	Dakota (Sisseton-Wahpeton)	—	1969	AIRP, 433
Goranson, Carl E.	1911	North Dakota	Swedish	second	1976	NDOHP, 51A&B
Greene, Agnes	1915	North Dakota	Dakota (Spirit Lake)	—	1993; 1999	IBSOHP; author interview

Name	Birth year	Place	Ethnicity	Generation	Year	Source
Greene, Evelyn Jahr	1935	North Dakota	Norwegian, Yankee	third	2009	author interview
Gunning, Joe	1891	Wisconsin	Yankee	—	1976	NDOHP, 305A&B
Gunning, May Nunn (Mrs. Joe)	1887	Dakota Territory	Irish	second	1976	NDOHP, 305A&B
Hansen, Eleanor Barrett	1914	Alberta, Canada	English	second	1998	author interview
Hansen, Esther Kanten	1915	Saskatchewan, Canada	Norwegian	second	1979; 1995	author interview
Henrickson, Ida M.	1893	North Dakota	Norwegian	second	1976	NDOHP, 315A&B
Hilbert, Annie	1896	North Dakota	Hungarian-German	second	1976	NDOHP, 314A&B
Howe, Clarence Irving	1897	Minnesota	Yankee	—	1976	NDOHP, 52A&B
Jensen, Clarence Loyal	1899	North Dakota	Norwegian	second	1976	NDOHP, 52A&B
Jensen, Elward "Baw"	1894	North Dakota	Norwegian	second	1976	NDOHP, 52A&B

Name	Birth Year	Birthplace	Ethnicity or Tribal Affiliation and Enrollment	Immigrant Generation	Year of Interview	Source
Jensen, Lillian Hovland (Mrs. Clarence)	1902	North Dakota	Norwegian	second	1976	NDOHP, 52A&B
Johnson, Edd	1886	North Dakota	Swedish	second	1976	NDOHP, 307A&B
Johnson, W. H. "Mack"	1899	Minnesota	Norwegian, Scottish, French	third	1976	NDOHP, 44A&B
Jones, Lois Olson	1918	North Dakota	Swedish, Irish, Swiss	third	2005	author interview
Kanten, Helene Haugen	1891	Norway	Norwegian	first	1977	author interview
Kanten, Shirley	1914	Minnesota	Norwegian	second	1997	author interview
Kennedy, Alvin H.	1897	Minnesota	Irish, Scottish, Canadian, German	second	1976	NDOHP, 318A&B
Kills in Sight, George	1897	South Dakota	Lakota (Rosebud Brule Sioux)	—	1971	AIRP, 767
Knudson, Bjorne	1911	North Dakota	Norwegian	second	1999	author interview

Name	Birth	Place	Ethnicity	Generation	Year	Source
Knudson, Margaret Dahlen (Mrs. Nels)	1905	North Dakota	Norwegian	third	1976	NDOHP, 685A
Knudson, Nels	1888	Norway	Norwegian	first	1976	NDOHP, 685A
Krause, Frances Olson	1901	North Dakota	Norwegian	second	1976	NDOHP, 53A&B
Lambert, Grace M. Young	1909	North Dakota	Dakota (Spirit Lake)	—	1976; 1993; 1999	NDOHP, 1101A&B; IBSOHP; author interview
Langstaff, Patrick	1915	North Dakota	German, Irish, Dutch	second	1999	author interview
Larsgaard, Hans	1878	Norway	Norwegian	first	1976	NDOHP, 684A
Larson, Evelyn M. (Mrs. Lars R.)	1907	North Dakota	Norwegian, Swedish	second	1976	NDOHP, 45A&B
Larson, Lars. R.	1895	Norway	Norwegian	first	1976	NDOHP, 45A&B
Larson, Mamie Vik	1884	North Dakota	Norwegian	second	1976	NDOHP, 320A&B

Name	Birth Year	Birthplace	Ethnicity or Tribal Affiliation and Enrollment	Immigrant Generation	Year of Interview	Source
Little, Elsie Kanten	1913	Saskatchewan, Canada	Norwegian	second	2000	author interview
Littleghost, Ambrose	1932	North Dakota	Dakota (Spirit Lake)	—	2005	author interview
Lovejoy, Naomi	1909	[South Dakota]	Dakota (Yanktonai—"Cut-Head")	—	1968	AIRP, 317
Mann, E. Earl	1887	Dakota Territory	Yankee	—	1976	NDOHP, 745A&B
Manning, Erland Reed "E. R."	1900	North Dakota	Norwegian, Canadian	second	1975	NDOHP, 317A&B
McDonald, Demus	1945	North Dakota	Dakota (Spirit Lake)	—	1993	IBSOHP
Mikkelson, Hope Baker	1909	North Dakota	Scotch-Irish, English	—	1999	author interview
Moe, Gurine Lokken	1890	North Dakota	Norwegian	second	1976	NDOHP, 679A&B
Monson, Cherry Wood	1922	North Dakota	Yankee	—	1999	author interview
Moore, Grace Eastman	1886	Dakota Territory	Dakota (Mdewakanton, Flandreau Santee)	—	1971	AIRP, 685

Name						
Mosbaek, Amy J. Polst	1923	North Dakota	German	third	2005	author interview
Nelson, Carolina Henrickson	1888	Sweden	Swedish	first	1976	NDOHP, 49B
Nordhaugen, Orris G.	1901	North Dakota	Norwegian	third	1976	NDOHP, 42A&B
O'Brien, Florence Kanten	1921	Saskatchewan, Canada	Norwegian	second	1997	author interview
O'Connor, H. C. "Hugh"	1890	North Dakota	Irish	second	1976	NDOHP, 313A&B
Olson, Joseph	1894	Minnesota	Norwegian	second	1976	NDOHP, 53A&B
Olson, Richard	1899	Minnesota	Norwegian	second	1976	NDOHP, 53A&B
Overby, Berdella	1903	North Dakota	Norwegian	second	1976	NDOHP, 687A&B
Overby, Palmer	1894	North Dakota	Norwegian	second	1976	NDOHP, 687A&B
Pearson, Grace (Mrs. Thomas)	1903	North Dakota	Norwegian	second	1976	NDOHP, 685B, 686A&B

Name	Birth Year	Birthplace	Ethnicity or Tribal Affiliation and Enrollment	Immigrant Generation	Year of Interview	Source
Pearson, Thomas	1894	North Dakota	Norwegian	second	1976	NDOHP, 685B, 686A&B
Peiler, Gladys Jorgenson	1916	North Dakota	Norwegian	second	2005	author interview
Peterson, Ingemund	1894	Norway	Norwegian	first	1999	author interview
Peterson, Thor	1913	Norway	Norwegian	first	1999	author interview
Pierson, Ralph	1899	North Dakota	Swedish, Norwegian	second	1976	NDOHP, 43A&B
Pierson, Wilma J. Larson Kvenild	1928	North Dakota	Norwegian	second	1976	NDOHP, 43A&B
Ravnsborg, Solvig Olson	1888	Norway	Norwegian	first	1976	NDOHP, 682A&B
Red Star, Henry	1880	Dakota Territory	Sisseton	—	1969	AIRP, 434
Reeves, Frank Elgin "Jack"	1918	North Dakota	Yankee	—	2005	author interview
Rendahl, Lester J.	1912	North Dakota	Norwegian	third	1976	NDOHP, 48B & 49A

Name	Year	Place	Ethnicity	Generation	Interview	NDOHP
Rossing, Johan	1895	Minnesota	Norwegian	second	1976	NDOHP, 306A
Rue, Carl	1895	North Dakota	Norwegian	second	1976	NDOHP, 316A
Rue, Ellen Sandvik (Mrs. Carl)	1897	Norway	Norwegian	first	1976	NDOHP, 316A
Russell, Lucy	1883	Indiana	Yankee	—	1976	NDOHP, 47B, 48A
Seastrand, Ralph E.	1901	North Dakota	Swedish	second	1976	NDOHP, 315A&B
Seckinger, Clifford	1907	North Dakota	German, Irish	third	1976	NDOHP, 311A&B
Seckinger, John C.	1896	North Dakota	German, Irish	third	1976	NDOHP, 311A&B
Serumgard, Harold	1898	North Dakota	Norwegian	second	1976	NDOHP, 747A&B
Severson, Einar	1892	North Dakota	Norwegian	second	1976	NDOHP, 648B
Skjerven, Amanda (Mrs. Lester)	1900	Nebraska	Norwegian	second	1976	NDOHP, 680A&B
Skjerven, Lester	1895	North Dakota	Norwegian	second	1976	NDOHP, 680A&B

Name	Birth Year	Birthplace	Ethnicity or Tribal Affiliation and Enrollment	Immigrant Generation	Year of Interview	Source
Skurdall, James A.	1942	Washington	Norwegian	third	2009	author interview
Smestad, Juel G.	1921	North Dakota	Norwegian	second	2006	author interview
Snortland, Tom "Buck"	1917	North Dakota	Norwegian	second	1975	NDOHP, 920B
Stedman, Charles	1900	North Dakota	Yankee	—	1976	NDOHP, 319A&B
Stedman, Collie (Columbine H.) Christianson (Mrs. Charles)	1908	Colorado	Norwegian	second	1976	NDOHP, 319A&B
Stensli, Marte Holen	1970	Norway	Norwegian	first	2006	author interview
Sullivan, Agnes Lorrick (Mrs. James)	1900	South Dakota	Canadian	second	1976	NDOHP, 310A&B

Name						
Sullivan, James	1899	third	Irish	Iowa	1976	NDOHP, 310A&B
Thal, Alfred A.	1899	second	German Jewish	North Dakota	1977	NDOHP, 689B, 690A&B
Tharalson, Marie J. Palmer	1895	second	German, Yankee	North Dakota	1977	NDOHP, 761A&B
Tufte, Elmer	1906	second	Norwegian	North Dakota	1976	NDOHP, 46A&B
Wakeman, Jess	1882	—	Dakota (Santee, Mdewakantan)	Dakota Territory	1971	AIRP, 755
Wakeman, Keith	1922	—	Dakota (Santee, Lower Yanktonai)	South Dakota	1971	AIRP, 825
Weston, Jeanette Red Wing	1883	—	Dakota (Mdewakanton)	Dakota Territory	1971	AIRP, 726
Weston, Virgil	1915	—	Dakota (Mdewakanton)	[South Dakota]	1971	AIRP, 726
Wilcox, Eleanor	1915	—	Yankee	North Dakota	1998	author interview
Williams, Johnson	1928	—	Dakota (Flandreau-Sisseton, Mdewakanton)	[South Dakota]	1968	AIRP, 165

Name	Birth Year	Birthplace	Ethnicity or Tribal Affiliation and Enrollment	Immigrant Generation	Year of Interview	Source
Wilson, Mary Louise Defender	1930	North Dakota	Dakota (Ihanktonwanna), Hidatsa	—	2011	author interview
Wineman, Lillian	1888	Dakota Territory	Norwegian, German Jewish	second	1976	NDOHP, 748A
Wood, Cherrie Lane (Mrs. O. B.)	1886	Dakota Territory	Yankee	—	1976	NDOHP, 56A&B
Young, Phillip John	1944	North Dakota	Dakota (Spirit Lake)	—	2005	author interview
Zahn, Christine (Mrs. Robert)	1901	[South Dakota]	Dakota (Standing Rock Sioux)	—	1969	AIRP, 359
Zahn, Robert	1900	North Dakota	Dakota (Standing Rock Sioux)	—	1969	AIRP, 359

Notes and Abbreviations

Brackets around birthplaces indicate informed guesses. AIRP = American Indian Research Project, Institute of American Indian Studies, South Dakota Oral History Center, Vermillion. IBSOHP = Indian Boarding Schools Oral History Project, Fort Totten, ND. NDOHP = North Dakota Oral History Project, State Historical Society of North Dakota, Bismarck.

NOTES

PREFACE

1. Dhooleka Sarhadi Raj, "Ignorance, Forgetting, and Family Nostalgia: Partition, the Nation State, and Refugees in Delhi," *Social Analysis* 44, no. 2 (2000): 30–55.

2. Agnes Greene, interview by author (Fort Totten, ND: 1999), audio recording. This is the first of over one hundred interviews I quote from in the book. Hereafter, see Appendix B, "Oral History Interview Subjects," for a complete inventory of the 128 recorded oral histories. With only two informants do I regularly reference audio interviews—Agnes Greene and Grace Lambert—because they gave multiple interviews.

3. Robert H. Lowie, "Dance Associations of the Eastern Dakota," *Anthropological Papers of the American Museum of Natural History* 11 (1913): 101–42.

4. Anderson cites Louis Garcia as the source of these stories about him. Laura L. Anderson, ed., *Being Dakota: Tales and Traditions of the Sisseton and Wahpeton* (St. Paul: Minnesota Historical Society Press, 2003), 33, fn 73. Oneroad's relatives described Oneroad as being aware of the federal government's and the Presbyterian church's "official ban against possessing religious artifacts as well as promoting the stories and instructions from the former way of life" (33).

5. Stephen R. Riggs, *A Dakota-English Dictionary*, ed. James Owen Dorsey (1890; repr., St. Paul: Minnesota Historical Society Press, 1992), 508–509.

6. Daniel Mendelsohn, *The Lost: A Search for Six of Six Million* (New York: Harper Perennial, 2006), 252.

7. Ibid.

8. Tillie Olsen, *Tell Me a Riddle* (New York: Dell Publishing, 1956), 95.

9. Willa Cather, *My Ántonia* (1918; repr., Peterborough, Ontario: Broadview Press, 2003).
10. Cherry Wood Monson, personal communication, August 4, 2005.

INTRODUCTION

1. Although the largest group of Indians at Spirit Lake was Dakotas, the Turtle Mountain Band of Chippewas and others also lived there. I use the terms *Native American* and *Indian* interchangeably when referring to larger groups, relying on the colloquial language common to the reservation.

2. Some scholars have been documenting North American encounters for decades. More recently some are calling for a theoretical understanding of the intertwined processes of immigration and Native dispossession. See, for example, Colin G. Calloway, ed., *Dawnland Encounters: Indians and Europeans in Northern New England* (Hanover, NH: University Press of New England, 1991); Colin G. Calloway, Gerd Gemünden, and Susanne Zantop, eds., *Germans and Indians: Fantasies, Encounters, Projections* (Lincoln: University of Nebraska Press, 2002); Gunlög Fur, *A Nation of Women: Gender and Colonial Encounters among the Delaware Indians* (Philadelphia: University of Pennsylvania Press, 2009); Gunlög Fur, "Indians and Immigrants—Entangled Histories" (unpublished manuscript, 2013); Timothy J. Kloberdanz, "In the Land of Inyan Woslata: Plains Indian Influences on Reservation Whites," *Great Plains Quarterly* 7 (1987): 69–82; Jean M. O'Brien, *Dispossession by Degrees: Indian Land and Identity in Natick, Massachusetts, 1650–1790* (New York: Cambridge University Press, 1997); George J. Sanchez, "Race, Nation, and Culture in Recent Immigration Studies," *Journal of American Ethnic History* 18 (Summer 1999): 66–84.

3. Ingrid Semmingsen, *Norway to America: A History of the Migration*, trans. Einar Haugen (Minneapolis: University of Minnesota Press, 1978), 99; Theodore C. Blegen, *Norwegian Migration to America: The American Transition* (1940; repr., New York: Haskell House, 1969); Jon Gjerde, *From Peasants to Farmers: The Migration from Balestrand, Norway to the Upper Middle West* (New York: Cambridge University Press, 1985).

4. I distinguish between settlers of European ancestry and Scandinavians. Importantly, Scandinavians were not Anglo-Saxon and did not identify as Anglo-American. Fur, "Indians and Immigrants," 9. Framing them as "off-whites" lacking the privileges of power and economic strength is essential to understanding their social location in the North Dakota context. However "hyper-white" (Linda Haverty Rugg's term) Scandinavians might appear in the twenty-first century, in the early twentieth century Norwegians especially were seen as foreign, alien, inferior, and radical. Because I see the social construction of race-ethnicity as structuring inequality in law, policy, economics, and everyday practices, I interchangeably use the term *white* to refer to non-Indian people.

5. Betty A. Bergland, "Norwegian Immigrants and 'Indianerne' in the Landtaking, 1838–1862," *Norwegian-American Studies* 35 (2000): 319–50; Odd S. Lovoll, *Norwegian Newspapers in America: Connecting Norway and the New Land* (St. Paul: Minnesota Historical Society Press, 2010); Orm Øverland, "Skandinaven and the Beginnings of Professional Publishing," *Norwegian-American Studies* 31 (1986): 187–214.

6. Frederick E. Hoxie, "Retrieving the Red Continent: Settler Colonialism and the History of American Indians in the U.S.," *Ethnic and Racial Studies* 31 (2008): 1163.

7. Allison M. Dussias, "Squaw Drudges, Farm Wives, and the Dann Sisters' Last Stand: American Indian Women's Resistance to Domestication and the Denial of their Property Rights," *North Carolina Law Review* 77 (1998–1999): 637–729; Sherry L. Smith, "Beyond Princess and Squaw: Army Officers' Perceptions of Indian Women," in *The Women's West*, ed. Susan Armitage and Elizabeth Jameson (Norman: University of Oklahoma Press, 1987), 63–75. On perceptions of Native women, see Patricia C. Albers and Beatrice Medicine, eds., *The Hidden Half: Studies of Plains Indian Women* (Washington, DC: University Press of America, 1983).

8. What is called "the new Western history," which focuses on the interactions of diverse peoples in the regions that became the western United States, has partially remedied this problem. See, for example, Patricia Nelson Limerick, *Legacy of Conquest: The Unbroken Past of the American West* (New York: W.W. Norton, 1987). Nonetheless, most studies of intercultural contact in the Midwest and Great Plains focus on the period from initial encounters until the mid-nineteenth century. An important exception is Joan M. Jensen, *Calling This Place Home: Women on the Wisconsin Frontier, 1850–1925* (St. Paul: Minnesota Historical Society Press, 2006). For a discussion of how Scandinavian immigrants figure into this history, see Fur, "Indians and Immigrants."

9. I call those people who had lived in the United States for several generations "Yankees." This term does not mean that they came from New England; rather, it is equivalent to what the U.S. Census Bureau called "native born of native parentage." In centering this study on Native Americans, I find the application of "native born" to European Americans absurd as well as confusing. Scandinavians often referred to English-speaking people as "Yankees." Dakotas occasionally referred to the English-speaking as "American," a term that reflects their nation-building project, as Michael Witgen so astutely points out. Michael Witgen, "Imagining Colonialism: The United States, the Native New World, and the Fantasy of an Unsettled Continent," paper presented at the Native American and Indigenous Studies Association, Uncaseville, CT, June 4–6, 2012.

10. Hoxie, "Retrieving the Red Continent."

11. Jean M. O'Brien, *Firsting and Lasting: Writing Indians Out of Existence in New England* (Minneapolis: University of Minnesota Press, 2010).

12. As Claudio Saunt so elaborately demonstrates, those distinctions also pitted the groups against each other in the Creek communities of the south. *Black, White, and Indian: Race and the Unmaking of an American Family* (New York: Oxford University Press, 2005). Also see David A. Chang, *The Color of the Land: Race, Nation, and the Politics of Landownership in Oklahoma, 1832–1929* (Chapel Hill: University of North Carolina Press, 2010); and Martha Hodes, "Fractions and Fictions in the United States Census of 1890," in *Haunted by Empire: Geographies of Intimacy in North American History*, ed. Ann Laura Stoler (Durham, NC: Duke University Press, 2006), 240–70.

13. O'Brien, *Firsting and Lasting*, xvi.

14. Patrick Wolfe, "Settler Colonialism and the Elimination of the Native," *Journal of Genocide Research* 8 (December 2006): 400.

15. Ibid., 387.

16. Generations of historians and sociologists have amassed mounds of evidence of the labors of working women—factory workers, farmers and agricultural laborers, and servants—whose sweaty toil belied this bourgeois representation and proved essential to their families' well-being. Mignon Duffy, *Making Care Count: A Century of Gender, Race, and Paid*

Care Work (New Brunswick, NJ: Rutgers University Press, 2011); Jensen, *Calling This Place Home*; Jacqueline Jones, *Labor of Love, Labor of Sorrow: Black Women, Work, and the Family from Slavery to the Present*, rev. and updated ed. (New York: Basic Books, 2010); Alice Kessler-Harris, *Gendering Labor History* (Urbana: University of Illinois Press, 2006); Theda Perdue, ed., *Sifters: Native American Women's Lives* (New York: Oxford University Press, 2001).

17. Homestead Act of 1862, 37–64, 37th Cong. 2d sess. (May 20, 1862).

18. Frederick E. Hoxie, *This Indian Country: American Indian Activists and the Place They Made* (New York: Penguin, 2012).

19. *Papers Relating to Talks and Councils Held with the Indians in Dakota and Montana Territories in the Years 1866–1869* (Washington, DC: Government Printing Office, 1910), 100. I appreciate Mark Diedrich's footnote that led me to this speech. Mark Diedrich, *Dakota Oratory: Great Moments in the Recorded Speech of the Eastern Sioux, 1695–1874* (Rochester, MN: Coyote Books, 1989), 96.

20. General Allotment Act, 49th Cong., 2d sess. (February 8, 1887).

21. Tonia M. Compton, "Proper Women/Propertied Women: Federal Land Laws and the Gender Order(s) in the Nineteenth-Century Imperial American West" (Ph.D. diss., University of Nebraska, 2009), chapter 4; Rose Stremlau, *Sustaining the Cherokee Family: Kinship and the Allotment of an Indigenous Nation* (Chapel Hill: University of North Carolina Press, 2011).

22. Amendment to the Dawes Act, 51st Cong., 2d sess. (February 28, 1891). Although, as Barbara Handy-Marchello points out, the Homestead Act included single women, no small leap in gendered law at that historical moment. Barbara Handy-Marchello, "Women and the Homestead Law: Standing Equal before the Law of the Land," presented at "Lincoln Legacy: The Homestead Act," 20th Annual Governor's Conference on North Dakota History, Bismarck, ND, November 8, 2008. The issue of married women had been critical for tribal members, as in Alice Fletcher's negotiation with Omahas over their allotments. This amendment also increased the acreage allotted to children to 80 acres.

23. D. S. Otis, *The Dawes Act and the Allotment of Indian Lands* (Norman: University of Oklahoma Press, 1973).

24. Frederick E. Hoxie, *A Final Promise: The Campaign to Assimilate the Indians, 1880–1920* (Lincoln: University of Nebraska Press, 1984), 26.

25. Otis, *The Dawes Act and the Allotment of Indian Lands*, 15. Otis is quoting from Secretary of the Interior Carl Schurz.

26. John W. Cramsie, Report of Devil's Lake Agency, *Annual Report of the Commissioner of Indian Affairs (hereafter ARCIA)* (1889), 143. Cramsie had translated the text of the Dawes Act into Dakota and circulated it so that people could read it and understand what it entailed.

27. Wolfe, "Settler Colonialism and the Elimination of the Native," 397.

28. Irene Bloemraad, Anna Korteweg, and Gokce Yurdakul, "Citizenship and Immigration: Multiculturalism, Assimilation, and Challenges to the Nation-State," *Annual Review of Sociology* 34 (2008): 154.

29. Ibid.; Evelyn Nakano Glenn, *Unequal Freedom: How Race and Gender Shaped American Citizenship and Labor* (Cambridge, MA: Harvard University Press, 2002).

30. Naturalization Act of 1790, 103, 1st Cong., 2d sess. (March 26, 1790). Alexander Keyssar, *The Right to Vote: The Contested History of Democracy in the United States*, rev. ed. (New York: Basic Books, 2009), 48; Jeanette Wolfley, "Jim Crow, Indian Style: The

Disenfranchisement of Native Americans," *American Indian Law Review* 16 (1991): 167–202. According to Lucy Maddox, "Carlos Montezuma liked to say in his speeches and publications, that Indians would be much better off if they could be put on boats and then allowed to reenter the country as immigrants, with the same treatment and entitlements as new arrivals from abroad." Lucy Maddox, *Citizen Indians: Native American Intellectuals, Race, and Reform* (Ithaca, NY: Cornell University Press, 2005), 75.

31. Gary Clayton Anderson, *Kinsmen of Another Kind: Dakota-White Relations in the Upper Mississippi Valley, 1650–1862* (St. Paul: Minnesota Historical Society Press, 1997), 275.

32. Odd S. Lovoll, *The Promise of America: A History of the Norwegian-American People* (Minneapolis: University of Minnesota Press, 1984).

33. Ibid.; Semmingsen, *Norway to America*.

34. Mary Louise Pratt, *Imperial Eyes: Travel Writing and Transculturation* (New York: Routledge, 1992), 6.

35. Charles A. Eastman (Ohiyesa), *From the Deep Woods to Civilization: Chapters in the Autobiography of an Indian* (1916; repr., Lincoln: University of Nebraska Press, 1977), 152–53.

36. Diedrich, *Dakota Oratory*, 85. He is citing Alexis Andre to Bishop Alexander Tache, December 29, 1863, Belleau Collection, Provincial Archives of Manitoba (Winnepeg).

37. According to Mary Louise Defender Wilson, an elder of Dakota and Hidatsa background and an accomplished storyteller, some bands never did surrender and submit to reservation life. They continued to move around, although they had relatives at Spirit Lake and Standing Rock.

38. Michael Omi and Howard Winant, *Racial Formation in the United States: From the 1960s to the 1990s* (New York: Routledge, 1994), 56, emphasis in original.

39. Alfred Schuetz, "The Stranger: An Essay in Social Psychology," *American Journal of Sociology* 49 (May 1944): 499. In his exploration of the idea, Schuetz focused on immigrants, intentionally excluding groups with, as he put it, "different levels of civilization," such as Hurons who were taken from the Great Lakes to Europe in the seventeenth century. He claims that such cases would require more explanation using his theoretical frame.

40. Nick J. Enfield, "The Theory of Cultural Logic: How Individuals Combine Social Intelligence with Semiotics to Create and Maintain Cultural Meaning," *Cultural Dynamics* 23 (2011): 35–64. Enfield is not speaking of cross-cultural encounters, and I do not agree with his entire definition. On this point, however, I think his approach is useful.

41. Paul Rabinow and William M. Sullivan, "The Interpretive Turn: A Second Look," in *Interpretive Social Science: A Second Look*, ed. Paul Rabinow and William M. Sullivan (Berkeley: University of California Press, 1987), 7. Rabinow and Sullivan clarify that meaning by saying that culture "does not present itself neutrally or with one voice" (7).

42. An emergent literature on cultural logics within anthropology and literary studies attempts to define them. For example, see Edward F. Fischer, *Cultural Logics and Global Economies: Maya Identity in Thought and Practice* (Austin: University of Texas Press, 2001).

43. Harold Garfinkel, *Studies in Ethnomethodology* (Englewood Cliffs, NJ: Prentice-Hall, 1967), 4.

44. Omi and Winant, *Racial Formation in the United States*, 60.

45. Schuetz, "The Stranger," 502.

46. Ibid.

47. O'Brien, *Firsting and Lasting*; Hoxie, *This Indian Country*.

48. O'Brien, *Dispossession by Degrees*; O'Brien, *Firsting and Lasting*; Alan Trachtenberg, *Shades of Hiawatha: Staging Indians, Making Americans, 1880–1930* (New York: Hill and Wang, 2004).

49. Hoxie uses the term *insistent* in surveying two centuries of Indian legal action against the United States. Hoxie, *This Indian Country*. In *A Final Promise*, he also makes the argument that marginality had its benefits for maintaining indigenous practices.

50. Nazli Kibria, *Becoming Asian Americans: Second-Generation Chinese and Korean American Identities* (Baltimore, MD: Johns Hopkins University Press, 2002).

51. Stephen Cornell and Douglas Hartmann, *Ethnicity and Race: Making Identities in a Changing World*, 2nd ed. (Thousand Oaks, CA: Pine Forge Press, 2007), 25.

52. Ibid., 35.

53. Maxine Baca Zinn, "Family, Feminism, and Race in America," in *Families in the U.S.: Kinship and Domestic Politics*, ed. Karen V. Hansen and Anita Ilta Garey (Philadelphia, PA: Temple University Press, 1998), 33–40.

54. Lynn Abrams, *Oral History Theory* (New York: Routledge, 2010).

55. For 1929, I was able to identify 90 percent of the 1,348 landowners. It is important to note that the racial designations on the census form are sometimes fiction, designed to suit the needs of the government and/or census taker at the time. Hodes, "Fractions and Fictions." See Claudio Saunt's work for an example of how the census got manipulated and worked over. *Black, White, and Indian*, especially chapter 8, 157ff.

56. Grace Lambert, interview by author (Fort Totten, ND, 1999), audio recording.

57. As a respected, authoritative elder in her tribe, she made efforts to record her version of what she has come to believe. Lambert, interview by author (Fort Totten, ND, 1999), audio recording. In addition to the archive of her papers at the State Historical Society of North Dakota, she agreed to be interviewed for the NDOHP in 1976, to be interviewed by me, and to collaborate with Cherry Monson in writing a book about her childhood: Grace Lambert and Cherry Monson, *Dakota Hoksiyopa Wan: "A Dakota Child"* (Warwick, ND: privately published, 2001). For a discussion of contradictory accounts of history, see Waziyatawin Angela Wilson, *Remember This! Dakota Decolonization and the Eli Taylor Narratives* (Lincoln: University of Nebraska Press, 2005).

58. Einar I. Haugen, "Norwegians at the Indian Forts on the Missouri River during the Seventies," *Norwegian-American Studies and Records* 6 (1931): 102.

59. I cite in notes those interviews that I read as transcripts (AIRP and the Indian Boarding Schools Oral History Project, or IBSOHP), but refer readers to appendix B, "Oral History Interview Subjects," for reference to those audio oral histories (NDOHP and my own).

60. Fifty-two of the NDOHP oral histories were with Scandinavians, as were twenty of those I conducted.

61. Eric R. Wolf, *Europe and the People without a History* (Berkeley: University of California Press, 1982); O'Brien, *Firsting and Lasting*.

62. Judith Stacey, "Can There Be a Feminist Ethnography?" in *Women's Words: The Feminist Practice of Oral History*, ed. Sherna Gluck and Daphne Patai (New York: Routledge, 1991), 111–19; Donna Haraway, "Situated Knowledges: The Science Question in Feminism and the Privilege of Partial Perspective," *Feminist Studies* 14 (Autumn 1988): 575–99. Also see Beatrice Medicine, *Learning to Be an Anthropologist and Remaining "Native"* (Urbana: University of Illinois Press, 2001).

CHAPTER 1

1. Lambert, interview by author (Fort Totten, ND, 1999), audio recording.

2. Charles A. Eastman (Ohiyesa), *The Soul of the Indian: An Interpretation* (1911; repr., Lincoln: University of Nebraska Press, 1980), 105.

3. Cherrie Lane Wood and Cherry Wood Monson, *Thanks for the Cornfield* (Warwick, ND: privately published, 1980), 101.

4. Frederick E. Hoxie, *Parading through History: The Making of the Crow Nation in America, 1805–1935* (New York: Cambridge University Press, 1995).

5. He explained that historically regalia was worn over painted bare skin, but the practice changed to wearing long underwear in the nineteenth century, when "Victorian women were shocked to see naked Indians." Garcia, e-mail communication, December 13, 2012.

6. W. Raymond Wood, "An Introduction to the History of the Fur Trade on the Northern Plains," *North Dakota History* 61, no. 3 (1994): 2.

7. Russell Thornton, "Native American Demographic and Tribal Survival into the Twenty-first Century," *American Studies* 46, no. 3/4 (2005): 23; *American Indian Holocaust and Survival: A Population History since 1492* (Norman: University of Oklahoma Press, 1987).

8. Hyde, *Empires, Nations, and Families*; Van Kirk, *Many Tender Ties*.

9. Thornton, *American Indian Holocaust and Survival*, 36, 31.

10. Ibid., 91.

11. Wood, "An Introduction to the History of the Fur Trade."

12. Louis Garcia, "Where Is Aspen Island?" *A Message from Garcia: The History and Culture of the Spirit Lake Dakota*, no. 6 (Tokio, ND: privately published, 2000).

13. Anderson, *Kinsmen of Another Kind*.

14. Gary Clayton Anderson and Alan R. Woolworth, eds., *Through Dakota Eyes: Narrative Accounts of the Minnesota Indian War of 1862* (St. Paul: Minnesota Historical Society Press, 1988), 20.

15. Anderson, *Kinsmen of Another Kind*, chapter 11.

16. Ibid., 240. The embedded quote, which refers to Dakotas' anger at the surveyors, is from Rev. Alexander Berghold, *The Indians' Revenge, or Days of Horror, Some Appalling Events in the History of the Sioux* (San Francisco, CA: P. J. Thomas, 1891), 43.

17. Anderson, *Kinsmen of Another Kind*, 240. Louis Garcia informed me that "Red Iron Mazasa" is a common mistranslation of the Dakota *mazas'a,* which means "sounding iron." He says it probably refers to "*mazawakan,* a gun going off, or a blacksmith pounding on his anvil." Garcia, personal communication, December 13, 2012.

18. Ibid.

19. Anderson and Woolworth, *Through Dakota Eyes*.

20. Court of Claims of the United States, "Sisseton and Wahpeton Bands of Dakota or Sioux Indians v. The United States: Evidence for Claimant," no. 22524 (1901–1907), 192. Elsewhere in the manuscript, Waanatan is spelled without the dashes. But this is how it appeared in the transcript.

21. Anderson, *Kinsmen of Another Kind*; Court of Claims of the United States, "Sisseton and Wahpeton Bands of Sioux Indians v. The United States: Evidence for Claimant."

22. Greene, interview by author (Fort Totten, ND, 1999), audio recording.

23. J. Michael McCormack, "Soldiers and Sioux: Military Life among the Indians at Fort Totten," in *Fort Totten: Military Post and Indian School, 1867–1959*, ed. Larry Remele (Bismarck: State Historical Society of North Dakota, 1986), 10.

24. Lambert, interview by author (Fort Totten, ND, 1999), audio recording. Anderson and Woolworth, *Through Dakota Eyes*. Also see Anderson, *Kinsmen of Another Kind*, 253.

25. Marion P. Satterlee, "Outbreak and Massacre by the Dakota Indians in Minnesota in 1862," in *Outbreak and Massacre by the Dakota Indians in Minnesota in 1862*, ed. Don Heinrich Tolzmann (1925; repr., Westminster, MD: Heritage Books, 2001), 125–28.

26. Louis Garcia, "Forde Township," *A Message from Garcia,* no. 33 (Tokio, ND: privately published, 2004). In 1857, White Lodge was involved in an effort to bring Inkpaduta to justice for the murders at Spirit Lake, Iowa. After that time, according to Garcia, White Lodge had "become hostile to the civilization movement and joined in the Minnesota War of Rebellion" (3); see also Anderson, *Kinsmen of Another Kind*, 217. This earlier series of events is commonly called the Spirit Lake Massacre, even though the murders did not occur at Spirit Lake, Iowa, but rather at Lake Okoboji, Iowa, and Jackson, Minnesota.

27. Arthur P. Rose, *An Illustrated History of Jackson County, Minnesota* (Jackson, MN: Northern History Publishing Company, 1910), 106.

28. Like many other whites, Oscar misunderstands the meaning of *powwow,* interpreting a gathering for a council of Indians as a dangerous precursor to war.

29. Rose, *An Illustrated History of Jackson County*, 93–109. Rose spells the family name "Fohre," which may have been how it sounded to his ear at the time he did research, particularly since the Fordes no longer lived in Belmont Township.

30. Garcia, "Forde Township."

31. Kenneth Carley, *The Sioux Uprising of 1862* (St. Paul: Minnesota Historical Society Press, 1961), 65; Anderson, *Kinsmen of Another Kind*, 276; Carol Chomsky, "The United States-Dakota War Trials: A Study in Military Injustice," *Stanford Law Review* 43, no. 1 (1990): 13–98.

32. Clair Jacobson, *Whitestone Hill: The Indians and the Battle* (LaCrosse, WI: Pine Tree Publishing, 1991), 89. Assessing available sources—primarily military reports and the diary of a soldier who fought there—Jacobson estimates that there were between 300 and 600 lodges, amounting to about 3,500 Indians. On the U.S. side, there were more than 2,000 soldiers.

33. William Watts Folwell, *A History of Minnesota*, rev. ed., 4 vols. (St. Paul: Minnesota Historical Society Press, 1956–1969), 2:279.

34. Jacobson, *Whitestone Hill*, 100. Jacobson is citing Sully's official report (560–61), in which Sully records the Indian perspective.

35. Folwell, *A History of Minnesota*, 2:279.

36. Elwyn B. Robinson, *History of North Dakota* (Lincoln: University of Nebraska Press, 1966), 101.

37. Folwell, *A History of Minnesota*, 2:280, emphasis in original, spelling and punctuation as in the original. Folwell is quoting from the Brown Papers. Samuel J. Brown's father had formerly been an Indian agent to Dakotas and his mother was Franco-Dakota; he and his family were prisoners during the 1862 conflict. He subsequently became a scout for General Sibley. Anderson and Woolworth, *Through Dakota Eyes*, 70.

38. Folwell, *A History of Minnesota*, vol. 2. These figures are based on Sully's reports.

39. Ibid., 2:279.

40. Mark Diedrich, *Mni Wakan Oyate: A History of the Sisituwan, Wahpeton, Pabaksa, and Other Dakota That Settled at Spirit Lake, North Dakota* (Fort Totten, ND: Cankdeska Cikana Community College Publishing, 2007).

41. "Destitution of Sioux Indians," Ex. Doc 76, House of Representatives, 40th Congress, 2nd sess., January 7, 1868, 5.

42. Ibid.

43. See propaganda brochure of the Dakota Territory Department of Immigration and Statistics, "The Year of Statehood, 1889, Dakota: Official Guide, Containing Useful Information in Handy Form for Settlers and Homeseekers, Concerning North and South Dakota" (Aberdeen, Dakota : F. H. Hagerty, 1889).

44. Kendric Charles Babcock, "The Scandinavian Element in American Population," *American Historical Review* 16, no. 2 (1911): 302.

45. Robinson, *History of North Dakota*, 284.

46. Richard White, *Railroaded: The Transcontinentals and the Making of Modern America* (New York: W. W. Norton, 2011).

47. Zitkala-Ša, *American Indian Stories* (1921; repr., Lincoln: University of Nebraska Press, 2003), 47.

48. Ibid., 93.

49. Ibid.

50. Ibid., 94.

51. Louis Garcia, personal communication, August 8, 2006. Garcia says that White Dog acted as a scout for General Sibley. "He may have had Indian scalps from inter-tribal warfare." Personal communication, December 18, 2012.

52. Barbara Levorsen, *The Quiet Conquest: A History of the Lives and Times of the First Settlers of Central North Dakota* (Hawley, MN: Hawley Herald, 1974), 26.

53. Daniel R. Mandell, *Tribe, Race, History: Native Americans in Southern New England, 1780–1880* (Baltimore, MD: Johns Hopkins University Press, 2008).

54. Levorsen, *The Quiet Conquest*, 25.

55. Alan Trachtenberg, *Shades of Hiawatha: Staging Indians, Making Americans, 1880–1930* (New York: Hill and Wang, 2004). Also see the collected works of Edward Curtis.

56. Susan Bernardin et al., *Trading Gazes: Euro-American Women Photographers and Native North Americans, 1880–1940* (New Brunswick, NJ: Rutgers University Press, 2003).

57. See Levorsen, *The Quiet Conquest*, 26.

58. Barbara Handy-Marchello, *Women of the Northern Plains: Gender and Settlement on the Homestead Frontier, 1870–1930* (St. Paul: Minnesota Historical Society Press, 2005), 77.

59. Orm Øverland, "Intruders on Native Ground: Troubling Silences and Memories of the Land-Taking in Norwegian Immigrant Letters," in *Transnational American Memories*, ed. Udo J. Hebel (Berlin: Walter de Gruyter, 2009), 80.

60. Levorsen, *The Quiet Conquest*, 93.

61. John H. Waugh, "Report of Devil's Lake Agency," *ARCIA* (1891), 318.

62. Mark Diedrich, with Louis Garcia, *Little Fish: Head Chief of the Dakota on the Fort Totten Reservation* (Rochester, MN: Coyote Books, 2009), 74. Diedrich is quoting Little Fish's testimony from the councils.

63. Charles A. Eastman (Ohiyesa), *From the Deep Woods to Civilization: Chapters in the Autobiography of an Indian* (1916; repr., Lincoln: University of Nebraska Press, 1977); Mary K. Whelan, "Dakota Indian Economics and the Nineteenth-Century Fur Trade," *Ethnohistory* 40, no. 2 (1993): 246–76.

64. Zitkala-Ša, *American Indian Stories*, 137.

65. Agnes Reiten Hared, *The Naked Prairie: Pioneer Life in North Dakota* (New York: Vantage Press, 1992), 9.

66. Ellen Mattson Roach, "The Early Days at Sheyenne," in *History of the Sheyenne Area, 1883–1976* (Sheyenne, ND: Sheyenne Bicentennial Commission, [1976]), 5.

67. Whelan, "Dakota Indian Economics and the Nineteenth-Century Fur Trade." Also see Mrs. Mary Eastman, *Dahcotah; or Life and Legends of the Sioux around Fort Snelling* (1849; repr., Minneapolis, MN: Ross & Haines, Inc., 1962).

68. Anderson, *Kinsmen of Another Kind.*

69. Handy-Marchello, *Women of the Northern Plains*, 111. Odd S. Lovoll finds the same thing among Norwegians in central Minnesota. *Norwegians on the Prairie: Ethnicity and the Development of the Country Town* (St. Paul: Minnesota Historical Society Press, 2006).

70. Ibid.

71. Eastman (Ohiyesa), *The Soul of the Indian*, 100.

72. Judge William L. Gipp, "Oral History," *North Dakota History* 43, no. 2 (1976): 82.

73. Johnson Williams, interview by Vijay B. Gupta (1968), AIRP, transcript 165, 26–27.

74. Zitkala-Ša, *American Indian Stories*, 161–62.

75. Eastman (Ohiyesa), *The Soul of the Indian*, 99–100.

76. Ibid., 88.

77. Greene, interview by author (Fort Totten, ND: 1999), audio recording; Grace Lambert, interview by Robert Carlson (1976), NDOHP, audio recording, 1101A&B.

78. Louis Garcia was told this information by former tribal chairman Elmer White. Personal communication, December 18, 2012.

Chapter 2

1. J. Olson Anders, "From Selbu to the Dakota Prairie: Recollections of Frontier Life on the Middle Border" (1960), Special Collections, Chester Fritz Library, University of North Dakota, Grand Forks, 6.

2. Svanau Yri Horne and Beverly Kraus Horne, *Reminiscing with Svanau*, State Historical Society of North Dakota, 1992, 14.

3. Handy-Marchello, *Women of the Northern Plains*, 28.

4. Waldemar Ager, *"Blandt Norske Nybyggere"* (Among Norwegian settlers), *Kvartalskrift*, 8th ed. (Eau Clare, WI: Reform Press, 1912), 16–19.

5. Ibid.

6. Ibid.

7. Wallace Stegner, *Wolf Willow: A History, a Story, and a Memory of the Last Plains Frontier* (New York: Viking, 1962).

8. Semmingsen, *Norway to America*, 117.

9. For example, novelist Aagodt Raaen poignantly portrays the ways her father's alcoholism ravaged the family. Aagot Raaen, *Grass of the Earth* (1950; repr., St. Paul: Minnesota Historical Society Press, 1994). See especially Handy-Marchello's introduction to the reprint edition.

10. Duane Rodell Lindberg, *Men of the Cloth and the Social-Cultural Fabric of the Norwegian Ethnic Community in North Dakota* (New York: Arno Press, 1980).

11. Semmingsen, *Norway to America*, 99.

12. Lovoll, *Norwegians on the Prairie*, 182.

13. Dag Blanck, "Constructing an Ethnic Identity: The Case of the Swedish-Americans," in *The Ethnic Enigma: The Salience of Ethnicity for European-Origin Groups*, ed. Peter Kivisto (Philadelphia, PA: Balch Institute Press, 1989), 137.

14. Semmingsen, *Norway to America*, 33.

15. Carlton C. Qualey, *Norwegian Settlement in the United States* (New York: Arno Press and the New York Times, 1970). Qualey makes clear the fever originated with the land boom from 1879 to 1886 (163).

16. Claude S. Fischer and Michael Hout, *Century of Difference: How America Changed in the Last One Hundred Years* (New York: Russell Sage Foundation, 2006). As an example, see Stegner's account of his father in *Wolf Willow*.

17. Semmingsen, *Norway to America*, 113.

18. O'Brien, *Firsting and Lasting*, 84.

19. Mark R. G. Goodale and Per Kare Sky, "A Comparative Study of Land Tenure, Property Boundaries, and Dispute Resolution: Case Studies from Bolivia and Norway," *Journal of Rural Studies* 17 (2001): 187.

20. Levorsen, *The Quiet Conquest*, 3.

21. Ibid.

22. Ibid.

23. Some areas in Sweden and Denmark had partible inheritance. See Øyvind Østerud, *Agrarian Structure and Peasant Politics in Scandinavia: A Comparative Study of Rural Response to Economic Change* (Oslo, Norway: Universitetsforlaget, 1978).

24. Goodale and Sky, "A Comparative Study of Land Tenure," 188.

25. Gunhild Setten, "Farmers, Planners, and the Moral Message of Landscape and Nature," *Ethics, Place, and Environment* 4, no. 3 (2001): 225, fn 1.

26. Ibid., 225. The law was changed in 1974 to allow for eldest daughters to inherit under the same conditions.

27. Terje Mikael Hasle Joranger, "The Migration of Tradition: Land Tenure and Culture in the U.S. Upper Mid-West," *European Journal of American Studies* 2 (2008): document 3, Online since 10 November 2008. Available: http://ejas.revues.org/3252. [July 6, 2009.]

28. Tosten Mikkelsen Lillehaugen, "Tosten Mikkelsen Lillehaugen's Autobiography," *Lillehaugen Family Treasures* (Greenbush, MN: Theresse Lundby, 1917), 11.

29. Ibid., 12.

30. Ibid. This equalizing statement is typically Norwegian.

31. Ibid.

32. Semmingsen, *Norway to America*, 112.

33. Ibid.

34. David M. Katzman, *Seven Days a Week: Women and Domestic Service in Industrializing America* (New York: Oxford University Press, 1978), 49. Irish-born (60.5 percent) and German-born (42.6 percent) women were also likely to be employed in domestic work, but proportionately less so than Scandinavians.

35. Semmingsen, *Norway to America*, 32.

36. Jon Gjerde, *From Peasants to Farmers: The Migration from Balestrand, Norway to the Upper Middle West* (New York: Cambridge University Press, 1985). That tolerance varied geographically.

37. Kendric Charles Babcock, "The Scandinavian Element in American Population," *American Historical Review* 16, no. 2 (1911): 304.

38. Johanna Tvedt, "Interview by Mark Olson" (1971), North Dakota Institute for Regional Studies, Fargo, 3.

39. Semmingsen, *Norway to America*, 105.

40. Although I have not found evidence of formal contracts, this arrangement seemed fairly common and bound the emigrant to the employer for a year, the amount of labor equivalent to the price of a ticket. It is reminiscent of the redemption exchange of colonial labor contracts. Sharon V. Salinger, *"To Serve Well and Faithfully": Labor and Indentured Servants in Pennsylvania, 1682–1800* (New York: Cambridge University Press, 1987). This arrangement is apt to have been informal and not recorded because "contract labor"—that is, bringing in workers who were bound to an employer—was forbidden by immigration authorities as part of the anti-Chinese measures.

41. Ibid.

42. Russell Thornton, *American Indian Holocaust and Survival: A Population History since 1492* (Norman: University of Oklahoma Press, 1987).

43. U.S. Bureau of the Census, *Indian Population in the United States and Alaska, 1910* (Washington, DC: Government Printing Office, 1915).

44. Elwyn B. Robinson, *History of North Dakota* (Lincoln: University of Nebraska Press, 1966), 284.

45. Wallace Stegner, *The Sense of Place* (Madison, WI: Silver Buckle Press, 1986).

46. James A. Skurdall, *Skurdall-Skurdell-Skurdahl: Emigrants from Sør-Fron to Dakota Territory: A Norwegian-American Family History* (Decorah, IA: Anundsen Publishing Co., 1999).

47. Cherry Wood Monson et al., *Warwick Memories* (Warwick, ND: privately published, 2002), 204.

48. Anders, "From Selbu to the Dakota Prairie," 9.

49. Carrie Young, *Nothing to Do but Stay: My Pioneer Mother* (Iowa City: University of Iowa Press, 1991), 98.

50. Qualey, *Norwegian Settlement in the United States*, 169.

51. Willa Cather, *O Pioneers!* (1913; repr., Lincoln: University of Nebraska Press, 1992), 153.

52. Ibid.

53. Ole E. Rølvaag, *Giants in the Earth: A Saga of the Prairie*, trans. Lincoln Colcord and the Author (New York: Harper & Brothers, 1927).

54. Handy-Marchello, *Women of the Northern Plains*, 79.

55. Ibid., 81.

56. Örnulv Ödegaard, "Emigration and Insanity: A Study of Mental Disease among the Norwegian-born [*sic*] Population of Minnesota," *Acta Psychiatrica et Neurologica*, Supplementum I (1932): 11–190.

57. Martha Lima, letter 41 (August 26, 1894), Letters of Martha Lima, 1893–1900, Norwegian-American Historical Association, Northfield, MN.

58. Øyvind T. Gulliksen, *Twofold Identities: Norwegian-American Contributions to Midwestern Literature* (New York: Peter Lang, 2004), 197.

59. Ibid.

60. Handy-Marchello, *Women of the Northern Plains*, 80. Interestingly, the rest of the trilogy seems to have had virtually no effect on widespread conceptions of women in

Norwegian-American culture. In the wake of Per Hansa's death, Beret finds enormous success as a widowed head of household, raising her children and running the farm. Indeed, her intelligence, steadfastness, and willingness to experiment with new technologies combined with her religiosity to make her one of the most respected farmers in the community.

61. My efforts to learn more about those institutionalizations have been foiled by a fire that destroyed records in Washington and the needle-in-the-haystack character of searching for John, a man not in control of his faculties, across the continent. The 1890 *Report on Indians Taxed and Indians not Taxed* at Spirit Lake points to the respect for the insane among Dakotas: "These people were never known to harm any person who was idiotic or weak-minded, believing such a person to be under the direct care and supervision of the Great Spirit. Under no circumstances would they allow harm to befall such a person if they could prevent it." U.S. Bureau of the Census, *Report on Indians Taxed and Indians Not Taxed in the United States (Except Alaska)* (Washington, DC: Government Printing Office, 1890), 514.

62. North Dakota State Hospital, Jamestown, ND. Record for John O. Beck, admitted September 22, 1911, died August 3, 1928. Karen V. Hansen Private Family Collection.

63. Cherrie Lane Wood and Cherry Wood Monson, *Thanks for the Cornfield* (Warwick, ND: privately published, 1980), 3.

CHAPTER 3

1. Frederick Hoxie, *A Final Promise: The Campaign to Assimilate the Indians, 1880–1920* (1984; repr., Lincoln: University of Nebraska Press, 2001), xviii.

2. Lambert, interview by author (Fort Totten, ND, 1999), audio recording. John W. Cramsie, "Devil's Lake Agency, Dakota," *ARCIA* (1886), 57. Cramsie's comments appear to be a deliberate reference to the Dred Scott decision (1857), which observed that in contemporary society "no black man, slave or free, has any rights which a white man was bound to respect." *Dred Scott v. Sandford* 60 U.S. 393 (1856).

3. Thomas Biolsi, *Organizing the Lakota: The Political Economy of the New Deal on the Pine Ridge and Rosebud Reservations* (Tucson: University of Arizona Press, 1992), 23.

4. Frederick E. Hoxie, *A Final Promise;* Francis Paul Prucha, *The Great Father: The United States Government and the American Indians* (Lincoln: University of Nebraska Press, 1984).

5. Mari Sandoz writes that land "was held for tribal use and for posterity. Sale of land to the Sioux meant sale of the use." Mari Sandoz, *These Were the Sioux* (New York: Hastings House, 1961), 105. William Cronon writes of the clash between Indians and colonists in New England: "Conceptions of land tenure mimicked systems of ecological use." *Changes in the Land: Indians, Colonists, and the Ecology of New England* (1983; repr., New York: Hill and Wang, 2003), 72.

6. Charles A. Eastman (Ohiyesa), *From the Deep Woods to Civilization: Chapters in the Autobiography of an Indian* (1916; repr., Lincoln: University of Nebraska Press, 1977), 159.

7. James McLaughlin, *My Friend the Indian* (1910; repr., Lincoln: University of Nebraska Press, 1989), 67. For a full discussion, see Francis Paul Prucha, *American Indian Policy in Crisis: Christian Reformers and the Indian, 1865–1900* (Norman: University of Oklahoma Press, 1976).

8. McLaughlin, *My Friend the Indian*; Frederick E. Hoxie, *This Indian Country*, 202.

9. Louis L. Pfaller, *James McLaughlin: The Man with an Indian Heart* (Richardton, ND: Assumption Abbey Press, 1992), xi.

10. Louis Garcia, "Who Are the Cut-Heads?" *A Message from Garcia*, no. 4 (Tokio, ND: privately published, 2000). Mary Louise Defender Wilson spoke of Indian children McLaughlin was reported to have brought from Minnesota to Spirit Lake after the 1862 war, a reason for greater respect. There were also those who held him responsible for the death of Sitting Bull, as it was under his watch that the mighty chief was killed. Louis Garcia informed me that Dakotas called the Indian agent Ateyapi (Father), while the president of the United States was called Tunkasina (Grandfather), "because they expected them to look after them like relatives would." Personal communication, December 18, 2012.

11. Cramsie, "Report of Devil's Lake Agency," *ARCIA* (1889), 146.

12. For example, in 1887, he made an impassioned moral and legal plea. "I, therefore, in the name of justice and the Sioux of Devil's [*sic*] Lake, ask that Congress be requested to reimburse these Indians for the land erroneously taken from them, and to which they are under treaty justly entitled." "Devil's Lake Agency, Dakota," *ARCIA* (1887), 27.

13. Cramsie, "Report of Devil's Lake Agency," *ARCIA* (1889), 146.

14. Cramsie, "Devil's Lake Agency, Dakota," *ARCIA* (1887), 54.

15. Ella Cara Deloria, *The Dakota Way of Life* (Rapid City, SD: Mariah Press, 2007), 25.

16. For example, according to Louis Garcia, Waanatan II "lived near the St. Michael Mission. Red Shield, Jr,. and his Pabaksa band also came to Spirit Lake and settled in the Crow Hill District." Garcia, "Who Are the Cut-Heads?" As an administrative center on a military reserve smack dab in the middle of the reservation, that land was unavailable for Indian settlement.

17. Cramsie, "Devil's Lake Agency, Dakota," *ARCIA* (1887), 33.

18. Cramsie, "Report of Devil's Lake Agency," *ARCIA* (1888), 41.

19. Cramsie, "Report of Devil's Lake Agency," *ARCIA* (1889), 143.

20. Ibid.

21. Board of Indian Commissioners, *Twenty-First Annual Report of the Board of Indian Commissioners, 1889* (Washington, DC: Government Printing Office, 1890), 8.

22. Cramsie, "Report of Devil's Lake Agency," *ARCIA* (1889), 143.

23. Ibid., 144.

24. Cramsie's annual report does not enumerate the other protestations, but it is clear there were more. Ibid.

25. Although, as Louis Garcia puts it, the payment of $1.25 per acre "was not a cash payment, but was to be spent on horses, cows, plows, harness, materials and labor to repair over 200 homes." Louis Garcia, "Wild Horses for Land," *A Message from Garcia*, no. 5 (Tokio, ND: privately published, 2000). Garcia points out that the horses provided in payment were actually wild mustangs, absolutely useless for farming purposes, hardly a good faith effort on the part of the U.S. government to provide what Dakota farmers needed. As Garcia sums it up, "It was another get-rich scheme at the expense of the Indian." This action was part of a pattern of the government's practice of bait and switch. It promised monies to Dakota people for a land cession. And rather than give money to them directly, it used funds to fill in the regular budget of the Indian Office, without the approval of Dakotas.

26. U.S. Bureau of the Census, *Report on Indians Taxed and Indians Not Taxed*, 513.

27. Ibid., 514.

28. Ibid. The allotting agent completed and signed "certificates of selection" that specified the tribal member's name and the location of his or her land. "Certificates of Selection," file 46, RG 75/A003/B038/C002//E035, National Archives and Records Administration, Central Plains Region, Kansas City, MO.

29. John H. Waugh, "Report of Devil's Lake Agency," *ARCIA* (1892), 350.

30. Ralph Hall, "Report of Devils Lake Agency," *ARCIA* (1894), 217. Although most tribal members were allotted in 1890 and 1891, some were allotted as late as 1920; Louis Garcia Papers, Chester Fritz Library Special Collections, University of North Dakota, Grand Forks, ND.

31. Greene, interview by author (Fort Totten, ND, 1999), audio recording.

32. Deloria, *The Dakota Way of Life*, 23; Patricia C. Albers, "The Regional System of the Devil's Lake Sioux: Its Structure, Composition, Development, and Functions" (Ph.D. diss., University of Wisconsin-Madison, 1974). The importance of kinship is consistent with Native peoples' choices at other reservations. For example, see Emily Greenwald, *Reconfiguring the Reservation: The Nez Perces, Jicarilla Apaches, and the Dawes Act* (Albuquerque: University of New Mexico Press, 2002); Bonnie Lynn-Sherow, *Red Earth: Race and Agriculture in Oklahoma Territory* (Lawrence: University of Kansas Press, 2004); Rose Stremlau, *Sustaining the Cherokee Family: Kinship and the Allotment of an Indigenous Nation* (Chapel Hill: University of North Carolina Press, 2011).

33. Greene, interview by author (Fort Totten, ND, 1999), audio recording.

34. Greenwald interprets patterns of land ownership to indicate agency on the part of allottees, *Reconfiguring the Reservation*. Cf. Tonia M. Compton, "Proper Women/Propertied Women." Studies of Nez Perce give insight into the well-documented allotment process, which included the high-profile figure of Alice C. Fletcher as allotting agent and Jane Gay as photographer to capture a visual record. E. Jane Gay, *With the Nez Perces: Alice Fletcher in the Field, 1889–1892*, ed. Frederick E. Hoxie and Joan T. Mark (Lincoln: University of Nebraska Press, 1981); Margaret D. Jacobs, *White Mother to a Dark Race: Settler Colonialism, Maternalism, and the Removal of Indigenous Children in the American West and Australia, 1880–1940* (Lincoln: University of Nebraska Press, 2009).

35. Waugh, "Report of Devil's Lake Agency," *ARCIA* (1892), 350. This approach to having different kinds of land, rather than a single consolidated plot, was also common to Norway—pasture in the high mountains, forests for gathering wood, and a small garden.

36. Lambert, interview by author (Fort Totten, ND, 1999), audio recording. Ralph Hall, "Report of Devil's Lake Agency," *ARCIA* (1893), 230.

37. F. O. Getchell, "Annual Report, 1902," Records of the Fort Totten Indian Agency (hereafter RFTIA), 10.

38. U.S. Bureau of the Census, *Report on Indians Taxed and Indians Not Taxed*, 512. Few records speak to the tribal response and internal deliberations, unlike the Nez Perce whose allotment records reveal a great deal. Gay, *With the Nez Perce*; Compton, "Proper Women/Propertied Women." Like many things about the allotment process, the order of selection is somewhat mysterious. Allotments were not assigned in alphabetical order, by age, or by district, although gender and marital status played a role. Wives of allotted men were allotted last. Waugh, "Report of Devil's Lake Agency," *ARCIA* (1892), 350. As Louis Garcia pointed out, "Some important chief like Waanatan, his number is #384. See, there was 383 people that got a piece of land before he did. Which, traditionally you could say, he hung back to let the people get

their land. I don't know. There's probably a thousand questions there." Unreferenced quotes like this one comes from the author's interview with Garcia; see Appendix B.

39. Louis Garcia, "Ignatius Court," *A Message from Garcia*, no. 46 (Tokio, ND: privately published, 2010).

40. F. O. Getchell, September 16, 1902, "Copies of letters sent to the Commissioner of Indian Affairs," RFTIA.

41. "No provision was made at the time of allotment for making wills." James O. Fine, "An Analysis of Factors Affecting Agricultural Development on the Fort Totten Indian Reservation" (Master's thesis, University of North Dakota, 1951), 35.

42. Dead Indian Act of 1902, ch.888, 32 Stat.245, 32nd Cong 1st sess. (May 27, 1902).

43. Ibid.

44. F. O. Getchell, "Annual Report, 1903," RFTIA, 8.

45. Ibid., 11–12.

46. John H. Waugh, "Report of Devil's Lake Agency," *ARCIA* (1891), 317.

47. Ella Cara Deloria, interview by Bea Medicine (1969), AIRP, transcript 386, 18; Janet L. Finn, "Walls and Bridges: Cultural Mediation and the Legacy of Ella Deloria," in *Women Writing Women: The Frontiers Reader*, ed. Patricia Hart and Karen Weathermon, with Susan H. Armitage (Lincoln: University of Nebraska Press, 2006), 175–98.

48. Elaine Goodale Eastman, *Sister to the Sioux: The Memoirs of Elaine Goodale Eastman*, ed. Kay Graber (1978; repr., Lincoln: University of Nebraska Press, 1985), 70.

49. Lambert, interview by Robert Carlson (1976), NDOHP, audio recording, 1101A&B.

50. For debates at the Congress of Indian Educators held in St. Louis, Missouri, June 1904, see Estelle Reel, *Report of the Superintendent of Indian Schools* (Washington, DC: Government Printing Office, 1904), 43.

51. Daniel F. Littlefield, Jr., and Lonnie E. Underhill, "Renaming the American Indian: 1890–1913," *American Studies* 12, no. 2 (1971): 33–45; Lonnie E. Underhill and Daniel F. Littlefield, Jr., *Hamlin Garland's Observations of the American Indian, 1895–1905* (Tucson: University of Arizona Press, 1976); Raymond Wilson, *Ohiyesa: Charles Eastman, Santee Sioux* (Urbana: University of Illinois Press, 1983). Comments made in interviews indicate that disputes involving Eastman carried over to Indian people's reaction to his involvement in the renaming project. Harriet Blue, interview by Herbert Hoover (1971), AIRP, transcript 774. At Spirit Lake many tribal members were enrolled under English names as well as their Dakota names long before 1905, so it is not clear how usage changed after Eastman's visit to the reservation.

52. Zitkala-Ša, *American Indian Stories,* 159.

53. Ibid., 163.

54. Ibid., 164.

55. Anderson, *Being Dakota*, 88–90.

56. Lambert, interview by author (Fort Totten, ND, 1999), audio recording.

57. In many religious traditions, healers would give a new name to a seriously ill person in order to signify a new spirit that was less vulnerable to an untimely death.

58. Philip J. Deloria, *Playing Indian* (New Haven, CT: Yale University Press, 1998).

59. Cathleen D. Cahill, *Federal Fathers and Mothers: A Social History of the United States Indian Service, 1869–1933* (Chapel Hill: University of North Carolina Press, 2011).

60. Lambert, interview by Robert Carlson (1976), NDOHP, audio recording, 1101A&B.

61. Greene, interview by author (Fort Totten, ND, 1999), audio recording.

62. Louis Garcia, "Left Bear," *A Message from Garcia,* no. 48 (Tokio, ND: privately published, 2008); "Waanatan's Pipe and Tobacco Bag," *Whispering Wind* (May/June 2010): 4–6.

63. This point was particularly sticky for a time, as Dakotas turned to the Benson County court system to handle their charges and disputes. As citizens, they saw themselves as entitled to use the judicial system; however as non–taxpayers, they were resented by white residents of the county because of their demands on the court system.

64. Cramsie, "Devil's Lake Agency, Dakota, 1886," 54.

65. Cramsie, "Devil's Lake Agency, Dakota, 1887," 28.

66. F. O. Getchell, " Report of Devil's Lake Agency," *ARCIA* (1898), 221.

67. Hall, "Report of Devil's Lake Agency," *ARCIA* (1893), 229.

68. F. O. Getchell, "Report of Agent for Devil's Lake Agency," *ARCIA* (1901), 296. For a discussion of contemporary debates about vaccinations, see Michael Willrich, *Pox: An American History* (New York: Penguin, 2012).

69. Available: http://www.mayoclinic.com/health/tuberculosis/DS00372/DSECTION= causes. [January 26, 2013].

70. David S. Jones, *Rationalizing Epidemics: Meanings and Uses of American Indian Mortality since 1600* (Cambridge, MA: Harvard University Press, 2004), 145.

71. Charles M. Ziebach, "Annual Report, 1913," RFTIA, 5.

72. Carrie Pohl, "Report of Homes Visited, 1905–1927" (hereafter RHV), National Archives and Records Administration, Central Plains Region, Kansas City, MO. Pohl gives numerous examples, including Mrs. Jennie Black (September 25, 1913) and Mrs. Anton Longie (July 23, 1914). A few even rented their homes to white farmers to use as granaries while they continued to live in them.

73. Cahill, *Federal Fathers and Mothers*; Lisa E. Emmerich, " 'Right in the Midst of My Own People': Native American Women and the Field Matron Program," *American Indian Quarterly* 15, no. 2 (1991): 201–16; Rebecca J. Herring, "The Creation of Indian Farm Women: Field Matrons and Acculturation on the Kiowa-Comanche Reservation, 1895–1906," in *At Home on the Range: Essays on the History of Western Social and Domestic Life,* ed. John R. Wunder (Westport, CT: Greenwood Press, 1985), 39–56; Wendy Wall, "Gender and the 'Citizen Indian,' " in *Writing the Range: Race, Class, and Culture in the Women's West,* ed. Elizabeth Jameson and Susan Armitage (Norman: University of Oklahoma Press, 1997), 202–29. For a discussion of the general fear of disease and unease about the massive influx of foreigners, and reformers' efforts to improve household sanitation and public health, see Barbara Ehrenreich and Deirdre English, *For Her Own Good: 100 Years of Experts' Advice to Women* (New York: Anchor Press, 1978); Susan Strasser, *Never Done: A History of American Housework* (New York: Pantheon Books, 1982).

74. Herring, "The Creation of Indian Farm Women," 42.

75. Laurence F. Schmeckebier, *The Office of Indian Affairs: Its History, Activities and Organization* (Baltimore, MD: Johns Hopkins University Press, 1927), 251.

76. Herring, "The Creation of Indian Farm Women," 44; Schmeckebier, *The Office of Indian Affairs,* 251. Also see Jacobs, *White Mother to a Dark Race*; Jane E. Simonsen, *Making Home Work: Domesticity and Native American Assimilation in the American West, 1860–1919* (Chapel Hill: University of North Carolina Press, 2006).

77. Stephanie Bryson and Karen V. Hansen, "Satisfactory Accommodations: Cleanliness, Culture, and Compromise in the Fort Totten Field Matron Program, 1913–1915," presented at the meetings of the American Sociological Association, San Francisco, CA, 2004. I am deeply grateful to Stephanie Bryson for her research assistance and her insightful analysis of Carrie Pohl as a transitional figure. The field nurse program was established in 1924. See Nancy Reifel, "American Indian Views of Public Health Nursing," *American Indian Culture and Research Journal* 23, no. 3 (1999): 143–54.

78. Pohl, RHV, May 22, 1914. Surely she never would have done that to a white woman, although in this context she did not monitor non-Indian women.

79. Pohl, RHV, January 12, 1914.

80. Pohl, RHV, August 12, 1913.

81. According to the Meriam report, trachoma was the second most common disease on Indian reservations. Lewis Meriam, *The Problem of Indian Administration* (Baltimore, MD: Johns Hopkins University Press, 1928), 208. Contagion between whites and Indians was so extensive that it was impossible to identify the original source. Pohl, RHV. By interviewing Lakotas in South Dakota, public health historian Nancy Reifel was able to assess people's reaction to the reservation public-health nurse, the successor to the field matron. "The personal character of the nurse was critical in determining how well the Indians accepted her services." Reifel, "American Indian Views," 147. Lakotas had a positive assessment of healers who were "dedicated to helping people, responsive to the people, and respectful." Sources do not reveal how Dakotas felt about Carrie Pohl's departure in 1915, or how they greeted the public-health nurses who arrived a decade later.

82. Pohl, RHV, May 11, 1914.

83. Pohl, RHV, May 21, 1913.

84. Robinson, *History of North Dakota*, 181, emphasis added.

85. Congressional Agreement, 58th Cong., 2d sess., 1904, 84.

86. Getchell, "Annual Report, 1902," RFTIA, 4.

87. Land Allotment Act of 1904, 179, 58th Cong., 2d sess., April 27, 1904.

88. *Sheyenne Star*, April 4, 1904.

89. Theodore Roosevelt, "A Proclamation by the President of the United States of America," in *Indian Affairs: Laws and Treaties* 3, no. 32 June 2, 1904, 33 Stat., 2368, compiled and ed. Charles J. Kappler (Washington: Government Printing Office, 1913).

90. *Sheyenne Star*, May 19, 1904.

91. Monson et al., *Warwick Memories*, 256.

92. "Winners in Ft. Totten Land Lottery," *Sheyenne Star*, September 1, 1904. For reasons perhaps related to their awareness of what homesteading might entail, one-fifth of the people whose numbers were selected in the first draw of the lottery did not show up immediately to claim their land. *Sheyenne Star*, October 13, 1904.

93. Monson et al., *Warwick Memories*, 32.

94. H. Elaine Lindgren, *Land in Her Own Name: Women as Homesteaders in North Dakota* (Fargo: North Dakota Institute for Regional Studies, 1991), 201.

95. Erling N. Sannes, "'Free Land For All': A Young Norwegian Woman Homesteads in North Dakota," *North Dakota History* 60, no. 2 (1993): 27, emphasis in original.

96. Ibid., 28.

97. *Sheyenne Star*, May [25], 1905.

98. Monson et al., *Warwick Memories*, 186.

99. Charles Davis, "Annual Report, 1905," RFTIA, 5.

100. Land Allotment Act of 1904, 179, 58th Cong., 2d sess., April 27, 1904. Also see chapter 2, "The Land and the Law," in Lindgren, *Land in Her Own Name*.

101. Handy-Marchello, *Women of the Northern Plains*, 55.

102. For a discussion of what some of those payments to the tribe translated into, see Louis Garcia, "Wild Horses for Land."

103. *Sheyenne Star*, May [25], 1905.

104. *Warwick Weekly Sentinel*, January 2, 1908. For a discussion of challenged and relinquished claims, see Mary Burtzloff, "Dutiful Daughters, Sisters, Wives, and Mothers: The Female Homesteader and the Role of the Family," presented at the "Homesteading Reconsidered" conference, Center for Great Plains Studies, Lincoln, NE, 2007.

105. Berthe Haugen, homestead entry no. 935760, June 17, 1912.

106. James A. Skurdall, personal communication, February 11, 2009.

107. John D. Hicks, "The Western Middle West, 1900–1914," *Agricultural History* 20, no. 2 (1946): 74.

108. Available: http://www.nps.gov/home/faqs.htm. [January 31, 2013.] Compton finds the success rate higher for women than men in the township she studied in Kansas. Compton, "Proper Women/Propertied Women," 204–205.

109. Rachel Bella Calof, "My Story," in *Rachel Calof's Story: Jewish Homesteader on the Northern Plains*, ed. J. Sanford Rikoon (Bloomington: Indiana University Press, 1995).

110. Also see Calof, "My Story"; Karen V. Hansen, "Historical Sociology and the Prism of Biography: Lillian Wineman and the Trade in Dakota Beadwork, 1893–1929," *Qualitative Sociology* 22, no. 4 (1999): 353–68; Sophie Trupin, *Dakota Diaspora: Memoirs of a Jewish Homesteader* (Lincoln: University of Nebraska Press, 1984).

111. Cherrie Lane Wood and Cherry Wood Monson, *Thanks for the Cornfield* (Warwick, ND: privately published, 1980), 26.

112. Ibid., 39.

113. John C. Hudson, *Plains Country Towns* (Minneapolis: University of Minnesota Press, 1985). His name is also spelled "Stoltz."

114. Handy-Marchello, *Women of the Northern Plains*, 24.

115. Eunice Davidson Private Family Collection. He lost the land due to unpaid taxes, according to Eunice.

116. James A. Skurdall Private Family Collection, Warranty Deed No. 47863, Allottee No. 141.

117. James A. Skurdall Private Family Collection, Benson County land documents.

118. Board of Indian Commissioners, *Report of the Board of Indian Commissioners to the Secretary of the Interior, 1906* (Washington, DC: Government Printing Office, 1906), 18.

119. Sean J. Flynn, "Western Assimilationist: Charles H. Burke and the Burke Act," *The Midwest Review* 11 (Spring 1989): 1–15.

120. The Dakota allotments that had been passed on to the next generation through inheritance did not appear as divided in the 1910 plat maps, upon which this analysis is based. This means that the total acreage is correct, but the average land holdings are somewhat inflated. If "Dead Indian Land" were indeed sold, the plat maps would record the new owner, and the reduction would be computed in the average acreage.

CHAPTER 4

1. Mary Neth, *Preserving the Family Farm: Women, Community and the Foundations of Agribusiness in the Midwest, 1900–1940* (Baltimore, MD: Johns Hopkins University Press, 1995), 84.

2. Mr. and Mrs. Norman Blue, interview by Vijay Gupta (1968), AIRP, transcript 164, 21.

3. Mark Diedrich, *Mni Wakan Oyate: A History of the Sisituwan, Wahpeton, Pabaksa, and Other Dakota that Settled at Spirit Lake, North Dakota* (Fort Totten, ND: Cankdeska Cikana Community College Publishing, 2007).

4. The Fish and Wildlife Service website for Sully's Hill National Game Preserve (Available: http://www.fws/gov/sullyshill. [January 30, 2013]) does not mention why Sully was honored; it says only that he and his troops never came to meet the cavalry who had camped out on this high hill.

5. Stegner, *The Sense of Place*. This kind of ethnocentric arrogance has provoked angry responses. See, for example, Elizabeth Cook-Lynn, *Why I Can't Read Wallace Stegner and Other Essays* (Madison: University of Wisconsin Press, 1996).

6. Louis Garcia, "Shin Bone Lake and Warwick," *A Message from Garcia*, no. 26 (Tokio, ND: privately published, 2006). Garcia specifies the name in Dakota: Bde Tacupa Ota (literally, Much Buffalo-Marrow Lake).

7. Notice she uses a strong language of objectification: "they grew around there."

8. Wood and Monson, *Thanks for the Cornfield*.

9. Ibid. 56. I have corrected the spelling of Wambdikuwa (Chasing Eagle).

10. Brenda J. Child, *Boarding School Seasons: American-Indian Families, 1900–1940* (Lincoln: University of Nebraska Press, 2000).

11. Wilbert H. Ahern, "'To Kill the Indian and Save the Man': The Boarding School and American Indian Education," in *Fort Totten: Military Post and Indian School, 1867–1959*, ed. Larry Remele (Bismarck: State Historical Society of North Dakota, 1986), 37. In the same volume, also see Merlan E. Paaverud, Jr., "Swimming with the Current: Education at the Fort Totten Indian School," 44.

12. John H. Waugh, "Report of Devil's Lake Agency," *ARCIA* (1891), 317.

13. F. O. Getchell, "Annual Report, 1902," RFTIA, 9. He worried that the head of the school, Charles Davis, would yield to the complaint. He strongly disapproved of Davis's administration, charging him with ineffectiveness in disciplining Dakota boys and catering to "the half breed element of the Turtle Mountain reservation." He saw the Turtle Mountain Band of Chippewas as having educational opportunities in the local district schools off the reservation and insisted that the rightful mission of the Fort Totten Indian School was educating the "unresponsive full blood Sioux of this reservation." "Annual Report, 1903," RFTIA, 10–11. From his perspective, the Grey Nuns had been very successful teaching Dakota students.

14. Getchell, "Annual Report, 1903," RFTIA, 10.

15. Ibid. White as well as Indian boys would disappear from rural schools across the Midwest when the season came to help on the farm.

16. Charles Davis, "Annual Report, 1905," RFTIA, 6–7.

17. The searing issues raised by the imposition of the assimilation project on children are explored with nuance and eloquence in many excellent studies. Child, *Boarding School Seasons*.

18. Bertha Demarce, interview by Rhonda Weiss (1993), IBSOHP, audio tape and transcript, 28.

19. Seven interviews were conducted with alumni of the Fort Totten Indian School; the narratives seem consistent with those found by other scholars of Indian boarding schools. See Paaverud's discussion of Dakotas' boycott of the school in the 1890s and continued resistance to enrolling their children, "Swimming with the Current," 44–48. Also see David Wallace Adams, *Education for Extinction: American Indians and the Boarding School Experience, 1875–1928* (Lawrence: University Press of Kansas, 1995); Child, *Boarding School Seasons*; Jacobs, *White Mother to a Dark Race*; K. Tsianina Lomawaima, *They Called It Prairie Light: The Story of Chilocco Indian School* (Lincoln: University of Nebraska Press, 1994); Jon Reyhner and Jeanne Eder, *American Indian Education: A History* (Norman: University of Oklahoma Press, 2004); Margaret Connell Szasz, *Education and the American Indian: The Road to Self-Determination since 1928*, 3rd ed. (Albuquerque: University of New Mexico Press, 1999); Myriam Vučković, *Voices from Haskell: Indian Students between Two Worlds, 1884–1928* (Lawrence: University Press of Kansas, 2008); Kim Cary Warren, *The Quest for Citizenship: African American and Native American Education in Kansas, 1880–1935* (Chapel Hill: University of North Carolina Press, 2010).

20. Demus McDonald, interview by Luci Grosz (1993), IBSOHP, audio tape and transcript, 8.

21. He went on to be a fierce advocate of education and served many years on the board of Cankdeska Cikana Community College at Spirit Lake.

22. Peter Belgarde, interview by Shannon Cameron (1993), IBSOHP, audio tape and transcript, 5.

23. Alvina Alberts, interview by Timber Moser (1993), IBSOHP, audio tape and transcript, 19.

24. Ibid., 16.

25. Ibid., 22.

26. Ibid., 19–20.

27. Lambert, interview by Robert Carlson (1976), NDOHP, audio recording, 1101A&B.

28. Charles M. Ziebach, "Annual Report, 1916," RFTIA, 7. The cervical lymph nodes in the neck would swell in response to infection.

29. Ibid., 8.

30. Ibid., 9.

31. Agnes Greene, interview by Susan Sevitts (1993), IBSOHP, audio tape and transcript, 18.

32. Belgarde, interview by Shannon Cameron (1993), IBSOHP, audio tape and transcript, 13.

33. Zitkala-Ša, *American Indian Stories*, 69.

34. Ahern, " 'To Kill the Indian and Save the Man,' " 37.

35. Teacher's report, April 23, 1907, Benson County Superintendent of Schools records, Minnewaukan, ND, 1885-1929.

36. Charles M. Ziebach, "Annual Report, 1910," RFTIA, Education Division—Schools Section, n.p. Jean M. O'Brien incisively discusses the government's double-talk about "authentic" Indians. *Firsting and Lasting*; also see Eva Marie Garroutte, *Real Indians: Identity and the Survival of Native America* (Berkeley: University of California Press, 2003). Three years later Ziebach acknowledged, "A small number of the mixed blood Indians attend the public schools, for which no tuition charge is made." Charles·M. Ziebach, "Annual Report, 1913," RFTIA, Narrative Section III—Schools, n.p.

37. Lambert, interview by author (Fort Totten, ND, 1999), audio recording.

38. Greene, interview by author (Fort Totten, ND, 1999), audio recording. Lambert, interview by Robert Carlson (1976), NDOHP, audio recording, 1101A&B.

39. Semmingsen, *Norway to America,* 93.

40. Ada Engen, "Interview," *North Dakota History* 44 (Fall 1977): 37.

41. Charles M. Ziebach, "Annual Report, 1914," RFTIA, Narrative Section I, Law & Order, n.p.

42. Einar Haugen, "Planning for a Standard Language in Modern Norway," *Anthropological Linguistics* 35 (1993): 110.

43. Integrated Public Use Microdata Series (IPUMS), Minnesota Population Center, University of Minnesota, North Dakota English Language proficiency by birthplace, 1910. The group with the highest proportion reporting that they did not speak English (57 percent) was the Russian born, who in this case were Germans from Russia.

44. Handy-Marchello, *Women of the Northern Plains,* 108–109.

45. Levorsen, *The Quiet Conquest.* Also see Theodore C. Blegen, *Norwegian Migration to America*; Gjerde, *From Peasants to Farmers*; Odd S. Lovoll, *Norwegians on the Prairie.*

46. Lori Ann Lahlum, "'Everything was Changed and Looked Strange': Norwegian Women in South Dakota," *South Dakota History* 35 (Fall 2005): 189–216.

47. Lindberg, *Men of the Cloth and the Social-Cultural Fabric of the Norwegian Ethnic Community in North Dakota*; Semmingsen, *Norway to America.* Orm Øverland astutely points out that "the most important factor in the rapid decline of the use of Norwegian" was "the sudden drop in immigration." Orm Øverland, *The Western Home: A Literary History of Norwegian America* (Northfield, MN: Norwegian-American Historical Association, 1996), 326.

48. Øyvind T. Gulliksen, "*Assimilasjonsprosessen i Waldemar Agers Paa veien til smeltepotten,*" in *Norwegian-American Essays, 2001,* ed. Knut Djupedal, Harry T. Cleven, Ingeborg Kongslien, and Dina Tolfsby (Oslo: NAHA-Norway, 2001), 183–205; Odd S. Lovoll, ed. *Cultural Pluralism versus Assimilation: The Views of Waldemar Ager* (Northfield, MN: Norwegian-American Historical Association, 1977); Ole E. Rølvaag, *Concerning Our Heritage,* trans. Solveig Zempel (Northfield, MN: Norwegian-American Historical Association, 1998).

49. Carrie Young, *Nothing to Do but Stay,* 140–41.

50. Levorsen, *The Quiet Conquest,* 106.

51. Jon Gjerde, "Transatlantic Linkages: The Interaction between the Norwegian American and Norwegian 'Nations' during the Century of Migration, 1825–1920," *Immigrants and Minorities* 20 (2001): 25.

52. Øyvind T. Gulliksen, *Twofold Identities: Norwegian-American Contributions to Midwestern Literature* (New York: Peter Lang, 2004), 9. Gjerde, in "Transatlantic Linkages," described the resulting affiliation as a "Norwegian 'nation' in the United States" (23). In contrast, Gulliksen called the dual attachments postnational, claiming that the "successful adoption of two cultures, rather than two countries, reframes the meaning of nation-state" (3). Both scholars astutely observed the reconstitution of migrants' national identities in the process of international relocation. See Karen V. Hansen and Ken Chih-Yan Sun, "Localizing Transnational Norwegians: Exploring Nationalism, Language, and Labor Markets in Early Twentieth Century North Dakota," *Norwegian-American Essays* 13 (2011): 73–107.

53. Lambert, interview by author (Fort Totten, ND, 1999), audio recording.

54. Among the "interesting people" anthropologist Robert Lowie reported meeting on reservations were "squaw men and innkeepers, veterans of the wars against hostile Indians who had decided to settle near the scenes of their past adventures, painters, photographers, traders, and missionaries." Robert H. Lowie, *Robert H. Lowie, Ethnology: A Personal Record* (Berkeley: University of California Press, 1959), 95. "Squaw men" were "white men who had married Indian women and lived as members of the tribe." Prucha, *American Indian Policy in Crisis*, 213.

55. "Two Villages to Be Started," *Sheyenne Star*, April 28, 1904.

56. Ziebach, "Annual Report, 1910," RFTIA, Land Division—Contract Section, n.p.

57. Rølvaag, *Concerning Our Heritage.*

58. *Warwick Weekly Sentinel*, April 9, 1908.

59. Davis, "Annual Report, 1905," RFTIA, 6.

60. Handy-Marchello, *Women of the Northern Plains*, 110.

61. Hudson, *Plains Country Towns*; Louis Garcia, "McDonald the Mail Carrier," *A Message from Garcia*, no. 15 (Tokio, ND: privately published, 2002).

62. Louis Garcia, personal correspondence, February 23, 1999. Garcia explains that *koda* is a man's greeting; women would say *han,* "hello."

63. Lambert, interview by Robert Carlson (1976), NDOHP, audio recording, 1101A&B.

64. Ibid.

65. Harriet Blue's oral history with AIRP includes a reading of a letter her father wrote to her and her sisters about their tribal history. In it, he mentions that those in the family who went to Canada after the 1862 war developed a love of black tea. Interview by Herbert Hoover (1971), AIRP, transcript 774, 29.

66. Without complete store records, it is not possible to determine whether this was a deliberate strategy.

67. Eugene Nielsen, *Oberon, N.D., 1884–1990: "Echoes of the Past"* (Fargo, ND: Richtman's Printing and Packaging, 1991).

68. Levorsen, *The Quiet Conquest*, 98–99.

69. Prucha, *American Indian Policy in Crisis*, 32.

70. For a discussion of the importance of religion for immigrants, see R. Stephen Warner, "Work in Progress toward a New Paradigm for the Sociological Study of Religion in the United States," *American Journal of Sociology* 98 (1993): 1044–93.

71. Ziebach, "Annual Report, 1913," RFTIA, Statistical Section II, Law & Order, 4. Also see Anderson, *Being Dakota.*

72. Anne B. W. Effland, Denise M. Rogers, and Valerie Grim, "Women as Agricultural Landowners: What Do We Know about Them?" *Agricultural History* 67 (1993): 235–61. The government used the terminology of *leasing*, as did Dakotas, but the white farmers talked about *renting*.

73. Thomas Biolsi finds that for Lakotas at Pine Ridge and Rosebud, leasing was deeply appealing—it was the most profitable use of the land. *Organizing the Lakota*, 13.

74. Neth, *Preserving the Family Farm*, 72. "Economic studies published in the late 1930s and early 1940s argued that tenancy was a more efficient way for a farmer to get a return for his labor and his capital investment. With similar capital resources, a tenant could earn a much larger income than a farm owner, they argued" (72).

75. Howard A. Turner, *The Ownership of Tenant Farms in the North Central States* U.S. Department of Agriculture Bulletin No. 1433, 1926.

76. Congress passed amendments in 1891 to enable the leasing of allotment that belonged to old or disabled Indians. In 1894, the exceptions were broadened to include "inability," which threw open the door to leasing land that Indians did not want or were unable to cultivate. Hoxie, *A Final Promise*.

77. Ibid., 158.

78. Charles Ziebach, August 10, 1906, Letters to Commissioner of Indian Affairs, Book No. 5, May 7, 1906–January 24, 1907, National Archives and Records Administration, Central Plains Region, Kansas City, MO.

79. Sonya Salamon and Vicki Lockhart, "Land Ownership and the Position of Elderly in Farm Families," *Human Organization* 39 (1980): 324–31.

80. Anthropologist Patricia Albers finds, "The growing practice of leasing land had an unanticipated advantage for some Dakota women. Those who were divorced and widowed could accrue direct cash benefits from lands in their name." Patricia Albers, "Autonomy and Dependency in the Lives of Dakota Women: A Study in Historical Change," *Review of Radical Political Economics* 17 (1985): 121. She also reports that "Dakota men often respected their wives' prior claims on these funds."

81. Hilda Redfox Garcia talks about chinking as an autumn activity: "My uncle used to have a loghouse.... Just before fall or whatever, my mom would say, 'We got to go over to Auntie's and help her *wospa*,' it means to plaster your house for the winter.... 'Cause some of it would start falling off. So we go over there, she would've had a big, like, trough.... And then we would have to cut up the hay.... And they get that clay at a special place, they would have to haul it. So I remember I used to like to do that, just liked to go and help them do that. To me it was fun."

CHAPTER 5

1. Following a similar logic, we might predict that Thanksgiving would also have been an important national holiday on the reservation. According to numerous accounts, Norwegians did not understand the concept of Thanksgiving, and it took many years before they observed it. On the other hand, Christian Dakotas "always observed Thanksgiving Day," according to Louis Garcia. Personal communication, December 20, 2012 and November 30, 1998.

2. Nancy F. Cott, "Marriage and Women's Citizenship in the United States, 1830–1934," *American Historical Review* 103, no. 5 (1998): 1440.

3. Harriet Watts Birkeland, "John Birkeland and the Watts Family," in *Our Heritage: Sheyenne Area, 1883–1980*, ed. Sheyenne Historical Society (Altona, Manitoba: D. W. Friesen & Sons, Ltd., 1980), 385.

4. Lucy Maddox, "Politics, Performance and Indian Identity," *American Studies International* 40, no. 2 (2002): 9.

5. Louis Garcia helped shed light on this through conversation and the Louis Garcia Papers, Chester Fritz Library Special Collections, University of North Dakota, Grand Forks. See Tisa Wenger, *We Have a Religion: The 1920s Pueblo Indian Dance Controversy and American Religious Freedom* (Chapel Hill: University of North Carolina Press, 2009); and "Indian Dances and the Politics of Religious Freedom, 1870–1930," *Journal of the American Academy of Religion* 79 (2011): 850–878.

6. Clyde Ellis, "'The Sound of the Drum Will Revive Them and Make Them Happy,'" in *Powwow*, ed. Clyde Ellis, Luke Eric Lassiter, and Gary H. Dunham (Lincoln: University of Nebraska Press, 2005), 11.

7. Wenger, "Indian Dances and the Politics of Religious Freedom."

8. Lambert, interview by author (Fort Totten, ND, 1999), audio recording, emphasis added. Superintendent Charles Ziebach observed in 1916 that although dances were well attended, in his judgment, "a great number of them go simply for the purpose of visiting with their neighbors, as these halls are common meeting places where they pass occasional evenings." Charles M. Ziebach, "Annual Report, 1916," RFTIA, 2–3. According to Wenger, many superintendents across the country adopted this position. Wenger, "Indian Dances and the Politics of Religious Freedom."

9. Alfred Schuetz, "The Homecomer," *American Journal of Sociology* 50, no. 5 (1945): 371.

10. Neth, *Preserving the Family Farm*, 82. Also see Michèle Lamont and Virág Molnár, "The Study of Boundaries in the Social Sciences," *Annual Review of Sociology* 28 (2002): 167–95; Andreas Wimmer, "The Making and Unmaking of Ethnic Boundaries: A Multilevel Process Theory," *American Journal of Sociology* 113 (January 2008): 970–1022.

11. Mandell, *Tribe, Race, History*, 3.

12. Samuel Young, "Annual Report, 1919," RFTIA, 4.

13. Charles M. Ziebach, "Annual Report, 1913," RFTIA, Narrative Section I—Law & Order, n.p. The Sun Dance, in which young men pierced their skin with leather thongs, tied themselves to a central pole, and danced beyond the point of exhaustion, was seen as "barbaric" and harmful to their health. It was also seen as threatening to whites and the federal government, since the dancers were proclaiming themselves warriors. Wenger, "Indian Dances and the Politics of Religious Freedom."

14. See the Mathers Museum's Wanamaker collection of World War I documents that includes interviews with Native American veterans and photographs of some of them. From Fort Totten, Burning Earth, Red Star, and Iron Necklace were among those listed in the Name Index.

15. Louis Garcia, "Grass Dance Warrior Society," *A Message from Garcia*, no. 2 (Tokio, ND: privately published, 2000).

16. Louis Garcia, "Lone Buffalo Club," *A Message from Garcia*, no. 1 (Tokio: privately published, 2000).

17. Garcia, "Grass Dance Warrior Society."

18. Eldon E. Snyder, "The Chautauqua Movement in Popular Culture: A Sociological Analysis," *Journal of American Culture* 8, no. 3 (1985): 79–90. The peak year was 1924.

19. *Chautauqua Program 1907*, N page, cited in Judy R. Peterson Ryan, "Chautauqua in Devils Lake, North Dakota: An Historical Study of the Organization, the Facilities, and the Programs" (Master's thesis, University of North Dakota, 1990), chapter 4. Presumably the "war dance" billing was part of the exoticizing of the event; Dakotas did not typically perform war dances at powwows. Tepee is the original spelling.

20. *Grand Forks Herald*, July 8, 1910. Lambert, interview by author (Fort Totten, ND, 1999), audio recording.

21. Greene, interview by author (Fort Totten, ND, 1999), audio recording.

22. Ibid.

23. Ryan, "Chautauqua in Devils Lake," 83. Two decades later Norwegians sponsored an extravaganza (in Minneapolis) to observe 100 years since the arrival of the "sloopers," and permanent settlement in North America. April R. Schultz, *Ethnicity on Parade: Inventing the Norwegian American through Celebration* (Amherst: University of Massachusetts Press, 1994). At this juncture, Norwegian independence was the impetus for national recognition and discussion.

24. Omi and Winant, *Racial Formation in the United States*, 59.

25. Echoing these issues of social mapping, Raj finds that the subjects of her study of the South Asian diaspora regularly queried, "Where are you from?" Perhaps it served as a friendlier or more polite version of the same question; they located their interlocutor and sought ethnic solidarity. Dhooleka Sarhadi Raj, *Where Are You From? Middle Class Migrants in the Modern World* (Berkeley: University of California Press, 2003).

26. Studies of North Dakota consistently find the enduring imprint of race-ethnicity over generations, shaping concentrations of land holdings, language use, political opinion and voting behavior, religious observance, and the gendered division of labor. Handy-Marchello, *Women of the Northern Plains;* Robert L. Morlan, *Political Prairie Fire: The Nonpartisan League, 1915–1922* (1955; repr., St. Paul: Minnesota Historical Society Press, 1985); William C. Sherman, *Prairie Mosaic: An Ethnic Atlas of Rural North Dakota* (Fargo: North Dakota Institute for Regional Studies, 1983).

27. Lambert, interview by author (Fort Totten, ND, 1999), audio recording.

28. Melissa L. Meyer, *The White Earth Tragedy: Ethnicity and Dispossession at a Minnesota Anishinaabe Reservation* (Lincoln: University of Nebraska Press, 1994).

29. Karen V. Hansen and Mignon Duffy, "Mapping the Dispossession: Scandinavian Homesteading at Fort Totten, 1900–1930," *Great Plains Research* 18, no. 1 (2008): 67–80. It was possible for the census information to be just as wrong as family stories, or for census takers to use their own misguided judgment in assessing veracity. Conceivably, Bjorne's grandparents had lived in Sweden as workers while maintaining Norwegian culture and identity. This would have been while Sweden still ruled Norway, before 1905 independence, and therefore they would not have been crossing international borders.

30. The aggressiveness of Germany in launching the Great War in Europe stimulated hostility to and disdain of German-speaking peoples in the United States, leading some people of German descent to conceal their ancestry. See Chang, *The Color of the Land*, and Saunt, *Black, White, and Indian,* for discussions of census manipulations of racial categories.

31. Greene, interview by author (Fort Totten, ND, 1999), audio recording.

32. Greene, interview by author (Fort Totten, ND, 1999), audio recording, emphasis added.

33. Levorsen, *The Quiet Conquest*, 106.

34. Ibid., 105.

35. Philip J. Anderson and Dag Blanck, eds., *Norwegians and Swedes in the United States: Friends and Neighbors* (St. Paul: Minnesota Historical Society Press, 2012). Anthropologist Robert Lowie observed, "Despite the pan-Scandinavian movement, efforts to unite Swedes and Norwegians in church activities ended in dismal failure. Even in glee-clubs it was impossible to attain cooperation." Robert H. Lowie, "An Anthropologist Looks at Scandinavia" (1952), Robert Harry Lowie Papers, 1872–1968, Bancroft Library, University of California, Berkeley, 6.

36. Young, *Nothing to Do but Stay*, 152, emphasis added.

37. Wood and Monson, *Thanks for the Cornfield*, 86–87.

38. For a discussion of fur trade society and the role of kinship, see Anne F. Hyde, *Empires, Nations, and Families: A New History of the North American West, 1800–1860* (Lincoln: University of Nebraska Press, 2011); Sylvia Van Kirk, *Many Tender Ties: Women in Fur-Trade Society, 1670–1870* (Norman: University of Oklahoma Press, 1980).

39. Charles Eastman's marriage to Elaine Goodale was one prominent exception. Elaine Goodale Eastman, *Sister to the Sioux*. Also see Katherine Ellinghaus, *Taking Assimilation to Heart: Marriages of White Women and Indigenous Men in the United States and Australia, 1887–1937* (Lincoln: University of Nebraska Press, 2006); and Jacobs, *White Mother to a Dark Race*.

40. Deloria, *The Dakota Way of Life*.

41. John C. Hudson, "The Study of Western Frontier Populations," in *The American West*, ed. Jerome O. Steffen (Norman: University of Oklahoma Press, 1979), 55.

42. Semmingsen, *Norway to America*, 132. Also see Dag Blanck, "Friends and Neighbors? Patterns of Norwegian-Swedish Interaction in the United States," in *Norwegians and Swedes in the United States: Friends and Neighbors*, ed. Philip J. Anderson and Dag Blanck (St. Paul: Minnesota Historical Society Press, 2012), 5–20; Hudson, *Plains Country Towns*; Torben Grøngaard Jeppesen, *Dannebrog on the American Prairie: A Danish Colony Project in the 1870s—Land Purchase and the Beginnings of a Town*, trans. James D. Iversen (Odense, Denmark: Odense City Museums, 2000); William C. Sherman et al., eds., *Plains Folk: North Dakota's Ethnic History* (Fargo: North Dakota Institute for Regional Studies, 1988). Only after the 1924 legislation shutting off the influx of new potential mates from the "old country" did intermarriage increase.

43. Blanck, "Friends and Neighbors?" 16.

44. Prucha, *The Great Father*. Before this legislation passed, Indian trader Frank Palmer inherited his wife's land, according to an oral history by his daughter. Elizabeth M. Faribault Palmer, who was Dakota, died in childbirth in 1887.

45. Monson et al., *Warwick Memories*, 145.

46. Samuel Young, "Annual Report, 1920," RFTIA, section III, 5.

47. W. R. Beyer, "Annual Report, 1927," RFTIA, Narrative Section III—Schools, 2.

48. Ibid.

49. Michael Witgen, *An Infinity of Nations: How the Native New World Shaped Early North America* (Philadelphia: University of Pennsylvania Press, 2012).

50. For example, Carrie Pohl, RHV, August 25, 1913.

51. See Stoler, *Haunted by Empire*.

52. Viviana Zelizer, *Pricing the Priceless Child: The Changing Social Value of Children* (New York: Basic Books, 1985). Also see Linda Gordon, *The Great Arizona Orphan Abduction* (Cambridge, MA: Harvard University Press, 1999). At that time a child might become an "orphan" by losing his or her mother; people did not assume that widowed fathers could care for their small children. And they recognized that a single woman would have a hard time financially supporting her children, although remarriage could "solve" that problem.

53. Louis Garcia, "The Scorned Suitor," *A Message from Garcia*, no. 39 (Tokio, ND: privately published, 2006). Irish Mike was sent back to white society as a teenager where he tried but failed to fit in. So he returned to the reservation and married an Indian woman, Tohanzi,

or "Her Shade," who was part black and part Indian. They had three children, Julia, Claude, and Joseph. "Mike Irish," as he was designated in tribal enrollment records and the census, wore Indian clothing and received an allotment. His daughter, Julia Irish, was reputed to be a healer with buffalo powers that enabled her to tell the future (3).

54. Later, when social service agencies took Native children out of their communities and placed them in foster homes or adopted them out, the issue became contentious. Jacobs, *White Mother to a Dark Race.*

55. Skurdall, *Skurdall-Skurdell-Skurdahl,* 76. "Dropsy" was the swelling that resulted from excess fluid retention, as commonly happened with congestive heart failure and rheumatic heart disease.

56. Seena B. Kohl, *Working Together: Women and Family in Southwestern Saskatchewan* (Toronto, Ontario: Holt, Rinehart and Winston, 1976), 30–31.

57. Neth, *Preserving the Family Farm,* 2.

58. Knut Hamsun, *Growth of the Soil* (1917; repr., New York: Penguin, 2007), 279.

59. Cyrene Bakke Dear, "Besta: A Story of North Dakota Pioneers," *Grand Forks Herald,* November 19, 1950–February 4, 1951.

60. Lambert, interview by author (Fort Totten, ND, 1999), audio recording.

61. Ibid.

62. Patricia C. Albers, "Sioux Women in Transition: A Study of Their Changing Status in Domestic and Capitalist Sectors of Production," in *The Hidden Half: Studies of Plains Indian Women,* ed. Patricia C. Albers and Beatrice Medicine (Washington, DC: University Press of America, 1983), 175–234.

63. Rosabeth Moss Kanter, *Men and Women of the Corporation* (New York: Basic Books, 1977), 6.

64. Patricia Albers, "Autonomy and Dependency in the Lives of Dakota Women: A Study in Historical Change," *Review of Radical Political Economics* 17, no. 3 (1985): 124. Albers notes that the social networks of giving "linked the Dakota at Devils Lake to Indian people from neighboring communities in Canada and the United States" (125).

65. Albers and Medicine, *The Hidden Half;* Deborah Fink, *Agrarian Women: Wives and Mothers in Rural Nebraska, 1880–1940* (Chapel Hill: University of North Carolina Press, 1992); Rauna Kuokkanen, "Indigenous Economies, Theories of Subsistence, and Women: Exploring the Social Economy Model for Indigenous Governance," *American Indian Quarterly* 35 (2011): 215–40; Jane Marie Pederson, *Between Memory and Reality: Family and Community in Rural Wisconsin, 1870–1970* (Madison: University of Wisconsin Press, 1992); Perdue, *Sifters;* Nancy Shoemaker, ed., *Negotiators of Change: Historical Perspectives on Native American Women* (New York: Routledge, 1995); Rose Stremlau, *Sustaining the Cherokee Family.*

66. Greene, interview by author (Fort Totten, ND, 1999), audio recording.

67. Lambert, interview by author (Fort Totten, ND, 1999), audio recording.

68. Wood and Monson, *Thanks for the Cornfield,* 57.

69. Ibid., 58.

70. Alberts, interview by Timber Moser (1993), IBSOHP, audio tape and transcript, 8.

71. James Skurdall, personal communication, September 16, 2008.

72. Eugene Nielsen, *Oberon, N.D., 1884–1990: "Echoes of the Past"* (Fargo, ND: Richtman's Printing and Packaging, 1991), 295.

73. Monson et al., *Warwick Memories*.

74. Neth, *Preserving the Family Farm*, 18.

75. Compton, Tonia M. "Proper Women/Propertied Women: Federal Land Laws and the Gender Order(s) in the Nineteenth-Century Imperial American West." (Ph.D. diss., University of Nebraska, 2009), 236–238.

76. Three important studies refer to the land women own, but do not analyze the gendered variations in land ownership among Native women: Emily Greenwald, *Reconfiguring the Reservation*; Meyer, *The White Earth Tragedy*; and Stremlau, *Sustaining the Cherokee Family*.

77. H. Elaine Lindgren, "Ethnic Women Homesteading on the Plains of North Dakota," *Great Plains Quarterly* 9, no. 3 (1989). In her study of nine counties, Lindgren found that women claimed an average of 12 percent of homesteads. *Land in Her Own Name*, 53. The averages ranged between 6 and 20 percent. In five of the townships in the counties she studied, women filed claims for between 30 and 32 percent of the homesteads. Only two townships out of the 300 she studied had no women filers. Lindgren argues that homesteading varied little by ethnicity, but rather by chronology. More women homesteaded later, especially after 1900. None of the counties she studied included reservation land. Although women of all ethnic groups homesteaded, Lindgren found that Anglo-Americans claimed the most homesteads in the settlement period following 1900; Norwegians did so only "moderately." "Ethnic Women Homesteading," 162.

78. Howard A. Turner, *The Ownership of Tenant Farms in the North Central States*, U.S. Department of Agriculture Bulletin No. 1433, 1926, 26.

79. Hansen and Duffy, "Mapping the Dispossession." Notably, other groups of immigrants and native-born landowners included even smaller proportions of women.

80. Turner, *The Ownership of Tenant Farms in the North Central States*, 26. The study surveyed ten counties in southeastern North Dakota and an adjacent county in South Dakota. The 1920 study of rented farms revealed that, on average, men owned more land than women: 374.6 acres compared to 232 acres. In their general study of land ownership in the United States, Anne B. W. Effland, Denise M. Rogers, and Valerie Grim found that in 1946 men owned about one-third more acreage than women; women's parcels were consistently smaller. Effland, Rogers, and Grim, "Women as Agricultural Landowners," 245.

CHAPTER 6

1. Charles M. Ziebach, "Annual Report, 1916," RFTIA, 13.

2. *Tolna Tribune*, August 10, 1916, 1.

3. *Devils Lake Journal*, August 10, 1916.

4. Aagodt Beck was granted an absolute divorce from John Beck (misspelled "Back") on April 28, 1916, Ramsey County District Court. Aagodt Beck and Ole Borgerson, certificate of marriage, April 29, 1916, Ramsey County, North Dakota, Karen V. Hansen Private Family Collection.

5. Cherry Wood Monson, *Forde Acres* (Warwick, ND: Brenorsome Museum, 1975), 22.

6. Grey Osterud, *Putting the Barn before the House: Women and Family Farming in Early Twentieth-Century New York* (Ithaca, NY: Cornell University Press, 2012).

7. Seena B. Kohl, *Working Together: Women and Family in Southwestern Saskatchewan* (Toronto, Ontario: Holt, Rinehart and Winston, 1976), 88. Kohl finds that sibling relationships were quite variable and, in adulthood, became optional. For the settlement period, at least, I disagree. Siblings often arrived together and collaborated, making land taking possible. Kohl finds that among the second generation, the older siblings took responsibility for the younger ones and had authority over them. Kohl also gives many examples of brothers working together where both inherit equally "and attempt to operate jointly." In this configuration, conflicts are inevitable (89). Also see Sonya Salamon, "Sibling Solidarity as an Operating Strategy in Illinois Agriculture," *Rural Sociology* 47, no. 2 (1982): 349–68.

8. Charles M. Ziebach, "Annual Report, 1910," RFTIA, Narrative Education Division— Industries Section, n.p., emphasis added.

9. Ibid.

10. Biolsi, *Organizing the Lakota*, 3.

11. Ibid.

12. John D. Hicks, "The Western Middle West, 1900–1914," *Agricultural History* 20, no. 2 (1946): 69.

13. Handy-Marchello, *Women of the Northern Plains*.

14. Ibid., 4. Also see Fink, *Agrarian Women*; Joan M. Jensen, *Promise to the Land: Essays on Rural Women* (Albuquerque: University of New Mexico Press, 1991); Nancy Grey Osterud, *Bonds of Community: The Lives of Farm Women in Nineteenth-Century New York* (Ithaca, NY: Cornell University Press, 1991).

15. Young, *Nothing to Do but Stay*, 50.

16. Theresse Nelson Lundby, Kristie Nelson-Neuhaus, and Ann Nordland Wallace, eds., *Live Well: The Letters of Sigrid Gjeldaker Lillehaugen* (Minneapolis, MN: Western Home Books, 2004), 14–15.

17. Frances Wold, "The Letters of Effie Hanson, 1917–1923: Farm Life in Troubled Times," *North Dakota History* 48, no. 1 (1981): 26. For a more elaborate discussion of the "we" perspective, see Karen V. Hansen, "Land Taking at Spirit Lake: The Competing and Converging Logics of Norwegian and Dakota Women, 1900–1930," in *Norwegian American Women: Migration, Communities, and Identities*, ed. Betty A. Berglund and Lori Ann Lahlum (St. Paul: Minnesota Historical Society Press, 2011), 211–45.

18. This assertion is a direct counter to the invisibility of women farmers. Carolyn E. Sachs, *The Invisible Farmers: Women in Agricultural Production* (Totowa, NJ: Rowman & Allanheld, 1983). As sociologist Anita Ilta Garey observes in contemporary families, women "attempt to call attention to or emphasize" their performance. She focuses specifically on mothering activities that often go ignored. Anita Ilta Garey, "Maternally Yours: The Emotion Work of 'Maternal Visibility,'" in *At the Heart of Work and Family: Engaging the Ideas of Arlie Hochschild*, ed. Anita Ilta Garey and Karen V. Hansen (New Brunswick, NJ: Rutgers University Press, 2011), 172.

19. Neth, *Preserving the Family Farm*; Sonya Salamon and Ann Mackey Keim, "Land Ownership and Women's Power in a Midwestern Farming Community," *Journal of Marriage and the Family* 41, no. 1 (1979): 109–19.

20. Osterud, *Bonds of Community*; Osterud, *Putting the Barn before the House*.

21. Handy-Marchello, *Women of the Northern Plains*, 53, 58.

22. Pohl, RHV, June 15, 1914.

23. Lambert, interview by author (Fort Totten, ND, 1999), audio recording.

24. Patricia C. Albers and Beatrice Medicine, "The Role of Sioux Women in the Production of Ceremonial Objects: The Case of the Star Quilt," in *The Hidden Half: Studies of Plains Indian Women*, ed. Patricia C. Albers and Beatrice Medicine (Washington, DC: University Press of America, 1983), 123–40; Deloria, *The Dakota Way of Life*.

25. Mr. and Mrs. Norman Blue, interview by Vijay Gupta (1968), AIRP, transcript 164, 5, spelling as in original.

26. Lambert, interview by author (Fort Totten, ND, 1999), audio recording.

27. Many foraging peoples revered meat, but consumed most of their calories from the roots, berries, and vegetables that women gathered. See M. Kay Martin and Barbara Voorhies, *Female of the Species* (New York: Columbia University Press, 1975).

28. Hilde Bjorkhaug and Arild Blekesaune, "Masculinisation or Professionalisation of Norwegian Farm Work: A Gender Neutral Division of Work on Norwegian Family Farms?" *Journal of Comparative Family Studies* 38 (2007): 423–34.

29. Svanau Yri Horne and Beverly Kraus Horne, *Reminiscing with Svanau* (Bismarck, ND: State Historical Society of North Dakota, 1992). What work women and children did varied regionally, as did the major crops and dominant industries. Norwegian women were typically responsible for the milking. Some married Norwegian men claimed that since milking was not men's work in Norway, they would refuse to do it in the United States. Barbara Handy-Marchello, "The 'Main Stay': Women's Productive Work on Pioneer Farms," *North Dakota History* 63 (1996): 17–27; L. DeAne Lagerquist, *In America the Men Milk the Cows: Factors of Gender, Ethnicity, and Religion in the Americanization of Norwegian-American Women* (Brooklyn, NY: Carlson Publishing, 1991).

30. Barbara Levorsen, *The Quiet Conquest: A History of the Lives and Times of the First Settlers of Central North Dakota* (Hawley, MN: Hawley Herald, 1974).

31. Handy-Marchello, *Women of the Northern Plains*. Neth included German women as well, working "most consistently at what might be considered male labor, participating in barnyard and field work." *Preserving the Family Farm*, 25.

32. Albers and Medicine, "The Role of Sioux Women in the Production of Ceremonial Objects"; Bonnie Thornton Dill, *Across the Boundaries of Race and Class: An Exploration of Work and Family among Black Female Domestic Servants* (New York: Garland, 1994); Jacqueline Jones, *Labor of Love, Labor of Sorrow: Black Women, Work, and the Family from Slavery to the Present*, rev. and updated ed. (New York: Basic Books, 2010).

33. Semmingsen, *Norway to America*, 133.

34. Katherine M. Weist, "Beasts of Burden and Menial Slaves: Nineteenth Century Observations of Northern Plains Indian Women," in *The Hidden Half: Studies of Plains Indian Women*, ed. Patricia C. Albers and Beatrice Medicine (Washington, DC: University Press of America, 1983), 29–52. Nancy Shoemaker makes the observation that indigenous women had a great deal of autonomy and freedom of movement with first contact. In the process of imposing a cultural frame of female dependency and domesticity, Europeans viewed that freedom to engage in labor as an affront. "Introduction," in *Negotiators of Change*.

35. Albers and Medicine, *The Hidden Half*; Cahill, *Federal Fathers and Mothers*; Colette A. Hyman, *Dakota Women's Work: Creativity, Culture, and Exile* (St. Paul: Minnesota Historical Society Press, 2012); Perdue, *Sifters*; Shoemaker, *Negotiators of Change*.

36. According to Handy-Marchello, "The amount of field work women did depended on the age and sex of their children. If there were boys old enough to work effectively in the fields, women and girls seldom had to do heavy work, except perhaps during harvest." *Women of the Northern Plains*, 61.

37. Young, *Nothing to Do but Stay*, 66.

38. Pohl, RHV, May 26, 1914.

39. Lambert, interview by Robert Carlson (1976), NDOHP, audio recording, 1101A&B.

40. Pohl, RHV, May 14, 1914.

41. Pohl, RHV, June 3, 1914.

42. Elizabeth Hampsten, *Settlers' Children: Growing Up on the Great Plains* (Norman: University of Oklahoma Press, 1991); Zelizer, *Pricing the Priceless Child*.

43. Pearson's emphasis. Hampsten's powerful book, *Settlers' Children*, documents the many ways that children suffered for being critical laborers in the family economy.

44. Karen V. Hansen and Grey Osterud, "Landowning, Dispossession, and Land Use among Dakota and Scandinavian Women at Spirit Lake, 1900–1929," unpublished manuscript, 2013.

45. Valerie Grim, "'Tryin' to Make Ends Meet': African American Women's Work on Brooks Farm, 1920–1970," in *Unrelated Kin: Race and Gender in Women's Personal Narratives*, ed. Gwendolyn Etter-Lewis and Michèle Foster (New York: Routledge, 1996), 27–28; Kohl, *Working Together*.

46. Wold, "The Letters of Effie Hanson," 25.

47. Levorsen, *The Quiet Conquest*, 72.

48. Skurdall, *Skurdall-Skurdell-Skurdahl*, 117.

49. Albers and Medicine, *The Hidden Half*; Deloria, *The Dakota Way of Life*; Stremlau, *Sustaining the Cherokee Family*.

50. Lambert, interview by Robert Carlson (1976), NDOHP, audio recording, 1101A&B.

51. Pohl, RHV, July 7, 1914.

52. Donald J. Hernandez, "Children's Changing Access to Resources: A Historical Perspective," in *Families in the U.S.: Kinship and Domestic Politics*, ed. Karen V. Hansen and Anita Ilta Garey (Philadelphia, PA: Temple University Press, 1998), 201–15.

53. Lundby, Nelson-Neuhaus, and Wallace, *Live Well*, 122.

54. Lambert, interview by Robert Carlson (1976), NDOHP, audio recording, 1101A&B.

55. Kohl, *Working Together*, 58.

56. Neth, *Preserving the Family Farm*, 131.

57. Ibid., 130. Progressive-era reformers during World War I and the 1920s saw farm organizing as "dangerous" (105).

58. Dear, "Besta."

59. Neth, *Preserving the Family Farm*, 150.

60. Ibid., 23.

61. Ibid., 31.

62. Ibid., 149.

63. Charles M. Ziebach, "Annual Report, 1913," RFTIA, Section IV—Industries, n.p.

64. Ibid.

65. Charles M. Ziebach, "Annual Report, 1914," RFTIA, Section IV—Industries, n.p.

66. Ibid.

67. Hicks, "The Western Middle West," 69.

68. Lundby, Nelson-Neuhaus, and Wallace, *Live Well*, 124.

69. Wold, "The Letters of Effie Hanson," 31.

70. Ibid., 32.

71. Ibid.

72. Tvedt, "Interview by Mark Olson," 5.

73. Lambert, interview by author (Fort Totten, ND, 1999), audio recording.

74. Greene, interview by author (Fort Totten, ND, 1999), audio recording.

75. Anders, "From Selbu to the Dakota Prairie," 5.

76. Hudson, *Plains Country Towns*.

77. Levorsen, *The Quiet Conquest*, 57.

78. Zelizer, *Pricing the Priceless Child*.

79. Jensen, *Promise to the Land*.

80. Joanne Vanek, "Time Spent in Housework," *Scientific American* (November 1974): 116–20.

81. Neth, *Preserving the Family Farm*, 19–20. Neth considers the study numbers conservative. See Theda Perdue's discussion of Cherokee women as "sifters" and economic producers.

82. The prairie chicken is a large grouse, and its survival is now threatened because of the loss of its tall-grass prairie habitat.

83. Skurdall, *Skurdall-Skurdell-Skurdahl*, 77.

84. Pohl, RHV, May 18, 1914.

85. Pohl, RHV, May 25, 1914.

86. Pohl, RHV, April 2, 1915.

87. Pohl, RHV, May 6, 1915.

88. Pohl, RHV, June 22, 1914.

89. Lambert, interview by author (Fort Totten, ND, 1999), audio recording.

90. Pohl, RHV., September 15, 1913.

91. Hyman, *Dakota Women's Work*.

92. Greene, interview by author (Fort Totten, ND, 1999), audio recording.

93. Skurdall, *Skurdall-Skurdell-Skurdahl*, 77.

94. Albers, "Autonomy and Dependency in the Lives of Dakota Women."

95. Greene, interview by author (Fort Totten, ND, 1999), audio recording.

96. Anthropologist Patricia Albers argues: "Although much of this work was geared toward home consumption, many women created goods to sell or trade in neighboring white communities. The earnings from this work were meager, but they did provide Dakota women and their families with sources of income partially independent of federal control." "Autonomy and Dependency in the Lives of Dakota Women," 119. Albers also notes that like household goods, women's earnings were independent of the control of men. Hyman, *Dakota Women's Work*; Greene, interview by author (Fort Totten, ND, 1999), audio recording.

97. Greene, interview by author (Fort Totten, ND, 1999), audio recording.

98. Lambert, interview by author (Fort Totten, ND, 1999), audio recording.

99. Greene, interview by author (Fort Totten, ND, 1999), audio recording.

100. Lundby, Theresse Nelson, Kristie Nelson-Neuhaus, and Ann Nordland Wallace, eds. *Live Well: The Letters of Sigrid Gjeldaker Lillehaugen*. Minneapolis, MN: Western Home Books, 2004.

101. Ziebach, "Annual Report, 1916," RFTIA, Industry, 14.

CHAPTER 7

1. General Allotment Act, ch. 119, SS6, 24 Stat 388, 390, Section 6.

2. *Grand Forks Herald,* November 20, 1892, reporting from the *Nelson County Observer.*

3. U.S. Bureau of the Census, *Report on Indians Taxed and Indians Not Taxed,* 509.

4. Women may have accompanied men to the polls, as black women did during Reconstruction when they, along with black men, were newly granted citizenship. Elsa Barkley Brown, "Mapping the Terrain of Black Richmond," *Journal of Urban History* 21, no. 3 (1995).

5. Heather Cox Richardson, *West from Appomattox: The Reconstruction of America after the Civil War* (New Haven, CT: Yale University Press, 2007).

6. *Grand Forks Herald,* January 17, 1893. On September 23, 1896, the *Bismarck Daily Tribune* reported 113 Dakota cast votes in 1892, 100 of which went to Republicans.

7. *Grand Forks Herald,* December 21, 1892.

8. Because the legal criteria for voting were determined by states, there was large variation across the continent in whether Indians could vote and how their citizenship status was interpreted. Alexander Keyssar notes, "Several states moved to disfranchise all Indians, or Indians 'not taxed,' or members of specific tribes, while others expressly limited suffrage to citizens or to 'civilized Indians' who were 'not a member of any tribe.'" *The Right to Vote: The Contested History of Democracy in the United States,* rev. ed. (New York: Basic Books, 2009), 48. Wolfley enumerates the five primary criteria states used to disfranchise Indians: "(1) failure to sever tribal ties makes Indians ineligible; (2) 'Indians not taxed'; (3) Indians are under guardianship; (4) reservation Indians are not residents; and (5) tribal sovereignty precludes participation in state and local governments." "Jim Crow, Indian Style," 182. Monroe E. Price, *Law and the American Indian* (Indianapolis, IN: Bobbs-Merrill, 1973), 229–37, originally outlined these categories.

9. *Elk v. Wilkins,* 112 U.S. 94 (1884).

10. 1889 North Dakota Constitution, Art. 5, Sec. 121.

11. Wolfley, "Jim Crow, Indian Style," 190.

12. Keyssar, *The Right to Vote.*

13. Hoxie, *A Final Promise,* 236.

14. Keyssar, *The Right to Vote,* 363.

15. This list of names corrects the misspellings in the official court records. Louis Garcia, personal communication, December 20, 2012; *Bismarck Daily Tribune,* September 25, 1896. Stephen Skowronek argues that in the late nineteenth century government primarily consisted of the courts and the parties. In this context, pursuing justice through a main avenue of state authority was quite rational. *Building a New American State: The Expansion of National Administrative Capacities, 1877–1920* (New York: Cambridge University Press, 1982).

16. *Bismarck Daily Tribune,* September 15, 1896, and February 28, 1897.

17. North Dakota Supreme Court Opinion, *State ex rel. Tompton v. Denoyer,* 6 N. Dak. 586, 72 N. W. 1014 (1897), 3,.

18. Hoxie, *This Indian Country.* Hoxie explains that although the court was established in 1855, it excluded Indians until the Choctaws filed and won their suit.

19. Ibid., 209.

20. This complex procedure is detailed by Hoxie, ibid., 207.

21. For example, Tan-tan-yan-do-wan, Good Singer, who lived at Lake Traverse, and Daniel Paul, who was a scout for General Sibley in 1863. Court of Claims of the United States,

"Sisseton and Wahpeton Bands of Dakota or Sioux Indians v. The United States: Evidence for Claimants" no. 22524 (1901–1907), 230–245.

22. William Watts Folwell, *A History of Minnesota*, rev. ed., 4 vols. (St. Paul: Minnesota Historical Society Press, 1956–1969), 2:418.

23. Ibid., 2:434. Prucha says, "By 1947 nearly two hundred Indian claims had been filed with the Court of Claims, but only twenty-nine received awards, most of the rest were dismissed on technicalities." *The Great Father*, 1018.

24. *United States v. Sisseton and Wahpeton Indians* 208 U.S. 561 (1908). In writing the decision for the court, Justice Holmes expressed unusual vitriol toward the Indians and a lack of sympathy for their case. Perhaps this stems from the fact that he served in the Union Army in 1862, and may have seen the Dakotas' assault on the United States as an act of betrayal. Indian Appropriations Act of June 21, 1906, ch. 3504, 34 Stat. 325.

25. *Bismarck Daily Tribune*, August 27, 1900. I corrected the misspelled name, "Simel Atkitena."

26. *Bismarck Daily Tribune*, September 1, 1900.

27. *Devils Lake Inter-Ocean*, November 25, 1904.

28. In 1916, for example, it was 290. Charles M. Ziebach, "Annual Report, 1916," RFTIA, Statisical Section V—Industries, 15.

29. George Beck, "The Fourteenth Amendment as Related to Tribal Indians: Section I, 'Subject to the Jurisdiction Thereof' and Section II, 'Excluding Indians Not Taxed,'" *American Indian Culture and Research Journal* 28, no. 4 (2004): 42, 38.

30. Ibid., 41. This phrase appears in section 2, which deals with how representatives are to be apportioned among states on the basis of their population.

31. John W. Cramsie, "Report of Devil's Lake Agency," *ARCIA* (1889), 143.

32. This set of issues forced fierce debates in urban areas where working-class non–property owners made demands for public services but paid no property taxes, which funded those services. See, for example, the Tilden Commission in New York City in the 1870s. I appreciate the input from Carmen Sirianni who brought this to my attention.

33. Hoxie, *A Final Promise*, 177.

34. Christine Zahn and Robert Zahn, interview by Bea Medicine (1969), AIRP, transcript 359, 15.

35. Hoxie, *A Final Promise*, 176.

36. *Bismarck Daily Tribune*, January 29, 1900.

37. Charles M. Ziebach, "Annual Report, 1916," RFTIA, 12, emphasis added.

38. "Total number of patents in fee issued during fiscal year 1913," in Charles M. Ziebach, "Annual Report, 1913," RFTIA, 51. Mary Louise Defender Wilson observed that those tribal members at Standing Rock who obtained fee patents were the ones who had gone to boarding schools and were also the first ones to lose their land.

39. Susan Applegate Krouse, *North American Indians in the Great War* (Lincoln: University of Nebraska Press, 2007).

40. Frederick E. Hoxie, "Comment on Citizenship and Property Rights," presented at the American Historical Association meetings, San Diego, CA, January 7, 2010; and "Introduction: American Indian Activism in the Progressive Era," in *Talking Back to Civilization: Indian Voices from the Progressive Era*, ed. Frederick E. Hoxie (Boston, MA: Bedford/St. Martins, 2001); Maddox, *Citizen Indians*.

41. Zitkala-Ša, *American Indian Stories*, 187. The male pronoun was commonly used, even by women writers talking about women.

42. According to Frederick Hoxie, "Native Americans did not vote in large numbers." Hoxie finds that voting was not very widespread. "Even the most fervent reformers argued that suffrage was a privilege the Indian might forego." *A Final Promise*, 231.

43. Maddox, *Citizen Indians*. Also see Trachtenberg, *Shades of Hiawatha*, chapter 5.

44. Russel Lawrence Barsh, "An American Heart of Darkness: The 1913 Expedition for American Indian Citizenship," *Great Plains Quarterly* 13 (1993): 91–115.

45. Ibid.; Lucy Maddox, "Politics, Performance and Indian Identity," *American Studies International* 40, no. 2 (2002): 7–36; Trachtenberg, *Shades of Hiawatha*.

46. Prucha, *The Great Father*, photos following 686.

47. Hoxie, *A Final Promise*, 180; Pfaller, *James McLaughlin*, 339; Myrtle Wright, "A Ritual for Citizenship," *The National Magazine* (October, 1916–March 1917): 331.

48. "A Ritual for Citizenship," 331.

49. Ibid.

50. Vine Deloria, Jr., ed., *Of Utmost Good Faith* (New York: Bantam, 1971), 141–42.

51. Lambert, interview by author (Fort Totten, ND, 1999), audio recording. Note that she recognizes the importance of families in running a farm.

52. Glenn, *Unequal Freedom*; Hoxie, *A Final Promise*.

53. *Fort Totten Review*, November 1, 1916. The *Review*, published by students at the Fort Totten Indian School, listed one woman as Jean Grawe. According to Louis Garcia she was the daughter of Frank Palmer and married a man named Fred Grawe, but that spelling may not be correct. Personal communication, 3 January 2013. Women were included in other ceremonies also. Pfaller, *James McLaughlin*.

54. Prucha, *The Great Father*; Maddox, *Citizen Indians*. Although, in his 1971 collection and analysis of important documents in American Indian history, Vine Deloria, Jr., incorporates the protocol for the government ceremony, including the participation of women. *Of Utmost Good Faith*, 142–43.

55. Wright, "A Ritual for Citizenship," 332. Pfaller, who writes about these rituals as a biographer of James McLaughlin, quotes a Missoula, Montana, reporter about the pronouncement when awarding women a purse: "The money that you gain from your labor must be wisely kept." Secretary Lane did not record the women's part of the ritual in his notes. *James McLaughlin*, 338.

56. When the elected members of the Nonpartisan League took office in 1917, they immediately awarded suffrage to female citizens.

57. Prucha, *The Great Father*, 686.

58. Louis Garcia Papers, Charles Fritz Library Special Collections, UND.

59. Land sale cards, folder no. 8, 1913–1925, RG 75/A003/B038/C002//E035, National Archives and Records Administration, Central Plains Region, Kansas City, MO.

60. Catherine Denial, "Pelagie Faribault's Island: Property, Kinship, and the Meaning of Marriage in Dakota Country," *Minnesota History* 62 (Summer 2010): 50.

61. McLaughlin, *My Friend the Indian*, 52–58. McLaughlin calls him One Elk, but based on oral recollections Louis Garcia identifies him as Hair Cut. Louis Garcia, "Murder at Bad Butte," *A Message from Garcia*, no. 40 (Tokio, ND: privately published, 2009). Also see Pfaller, *James McLaughlin*, 47–48.

62. Garcia, "Murder at Bad Butte." That is the reported story; Garcia invites others to investigate further.

63. Evidence at Lake Traverse reveals that Dakota farmers wanted to move off the reservation and tried to do so, but Indian Office officials prevented them. Elwin E. Rogers, *For God and Land: Brown Earth, a Dakota Indian Community, 1876–1892* (Sioux Falls, SD: Pine Hill Press, 2002).

64. The 1918 annual reports lists the five largest acreages under cultivation by individual Indians—Jennie Cavanaugh (400 acres) and four men: John Lohnes (475 acres), Felix Dance Eagle (319 acres), James Lohnes (200 acres), and George Cavanaugh (200 acres). Samuel Young, "Annual Report, 1918," RFTIA, Statistical Section V—Industries, 26.

65. Øyvind T. Gulliksen, *"Assimilasjonsprosessen i Waldemar Agers,"* Odd S. Lovoll, ed., *Cultural Pluralism versus Assimilation: The Views of Waldemar Ager* (Northfield, MN: Norwegian-American Historical Association, 1977); Rølvaag, *Concerning Our Heritage.*

66. Svanau Yri Horne and Beverly Kraus Horne, "Reminiscing with Svanau," 14. Other immigrant groups could and did make a similar claim.

67. Norwegian women in Minnesota, Wisconsin, and Iowa—other states of dense Norwegian settlement—also had high naturalization rates, but not quite as high as those in North Dakota. Clare Hammonds and Karen V. Hansen, "Women's Citizenship, Political Mobilization, and the Nonpartisan League in North Dakota, 1900–1925," presented at the Rural Women's Studies Association meetings, September 14–17, Bloomington, IN, 2009. The differences between midwestern states are small, so they may not be statistically significant. The Swedish women in Iowa have virtually comparable rates. See Integrated Use Microdata Series: PUMS data. Available: http://usa.ipums.org/usa/. [September 15, 2009].

68. The men followed the same pattern in other midwestern states (such as Minnesota and Wisconsin), but at slightly lower rates than women. U.S. Bureau of the Census, *Statistical Abstract of the United States, 1920* (Washington, DC: Government Printing Office, 1921). The small number of immigrant women who married U.S. citizens before 1922 became citizens automatically, while immigrant men doing the same did not.

69. Candice Lewis Bredbenner, *A Nationality of Her Own: Women, Marriage, and the Law of Citizenship* (Berkeley: University of California Press, 1998), 42.

70. Ann Marie Nicolisi, " 'We Do Not Want Our Girls to Marry Foreigners': Gender, Race, and American Citizenship," *National Women's Studies Association Journal* 13, no. 3 (2001): 1–21.

71. Expatriation Act of 1907, 59th Cong. 2nd sess. (March 2, 1907), Sect. 3.

72. Bredbenner, *A Nationality of Her Own;* Nancy F. Cott, *Public Vows: A History of Marriage and the Nation* (Cambridge, MA: Harvard University Press, 2000); Linda K. Kerber, *No Constitutional Right to Be Ladies: Women and the Obligations of Citizenship* (New York: Hill and Wang, 1998).

73. Irene Bloemraad, "Citizenship Lessons from the Past: The Contours of Immigrant Naturalization in the Early 20th Century," *Social Science Quarterly* 87, no. 5 (2006): 927–53.

74. Herbert Earle Gaston, *The Nonpartisan League* (New York: Harcourt, 1920).

75. Hammonds and Hansen, "Women's Citizenship, Political Mobilization, and the Nonpartisan League."

76. Gaston, *The Nonpartisan League;* Morlan, *Political Prairie Fire.*

77. Gaston, *The Nonpartisan League.*

78. Morlan, *Political Prairie Fire*.

79. In a state with a total population of 646,872 in 1920, this is a large proportion of adult voters.

80. Kathleen Moum, "The Social Origins of the Nonpartisan League," *North Dakota History* 53 (1986): 19.

81. Torger Anderson Hoverstad, *The Norwegian Farmers in the United States* (Fargo, ND: Hans Jervell Publishing Co., 1915). Historian Daron Olson disagrees with the conclusions drawn by others such as Moum and Morlan that the League was disproportionately Norwegian. Daron W. Olson, "Norwegians, Socialism and the Nonpartisan League in North Dakota, 1904–1920: How Red Was Their Protest?" (Master's thesis, University of North Dakota, 1993).

82. Michael Paul Rogin, *The Intellectuals and McCarthy: The Radical Specter* (Cambridge, MA: MIT Press, 1967). Historian Daron Olson argues that Norwegians were also involved in the opposition Independent Voters Association. "Norwegians, Socialism and the Nonpartisan League."

83. Moum, "The Social Origins of the Nonpartisan League," 22; H. Arnold Barton, "Norwegians and Swedes in America: Some Comparisons," in *Norwegians and Swedes in the United States: Friends and Neighbors*, ed. Philip J. Anderson and Dag Blanck (St. Paul: Minnesota Historical Society Press, 2012), 23.

84. Ole H. Olson was elected lieutenant governor in 1932, and when Governor William Langer was indicted two years later Olson became the governor of North Dakota.

85. Morlan, *Political Prairie Fire*, 109; Walter Nugent, *Progressivism: A Very Short Introduction* (New York: Oxford University Press, 2010).

86. Karen Starr, "Fighting for a Future: Farm Women of the Nonpartisan League," *Minnesota History* (1983): 255–62.

87. Kim E. Nielsen, "'We All Leaguers by Our House': Women, Suffrage, and Red-Baiting in the National Nonpartisan League," *Journal of Women's History* 6, no. 1 (1994): 35.

88. Ibid.

89. Ibid.

90. Wold, "The Letters of Effie Hanson," 34.

91. Gaston, *The Nonpartisan League*; Morlan, *Political Prairie Fire*.

92. Gaston, *The Nonpartisan League*, 175, emphasis added.

93. Morlan, *Political Prairie Fire*, 110–11.

94. *The Red Flame* and the Independent Voters' Association's *Independent* were key opposition papers. Gaston, *The Nonpartisan League*; Morlan, *Political Prairie Fire*; Nielsen, "'We All Leaguers by Our House.'"

95. This political cartoon was drawn by John Miller Baer, the league's "cartooning Congressman," according to Morlan. *Political Prairie Fire*, xvii. The 1919 cartoon is now on Digital Horizons. Available: http://digitalhorizonsonline.org/cdm4/item_viewer.php?CISOROOT=/ndsu-npl&CISOPTR=1&CISOBOX=1&REC=13. [February 24, 2013].

96. Tosten Mikkelsen Lillehaugen, "Tosten Mikkelsen Lillehaugen's Autobiography," in *Lillehaugen Family Treasures* (Greenbush, MN: Theresse Lundby, 1917), 19.

97. Available: http://banknd.nd.gov/about_BND/history_of_BND.html. [January 26, 2013].

98. Scott Ellsworth, "Origins of the Nonpartisan League" (Ph.D. diss., Duke University, 1982); Morlan, *Political Prairie Fire*.

99. Trevor M. Magel, "The Political Effect of the Ku Klux Klan in North Dakota" (Master's thesis, University of Nebraska, 2011).

100. Linda Grathwohl, "The North Dakota Anti-Garb Law: Constitutional Conflict and Religious Strife," *Great Plains Quarterly* 13, no. 3 (1993): 187–91.

101. On the Indian Act of 1924, see Keyssar, *The Right to Vote*.

102. Aristide R. Zolberg, "Immigration Control Policy: Law and Implementation," in *The New Americans: A Guide to Immigration since 1965*, ed. Mary C. Waters and Reed Ueda, with Helen B. Marrow (Cambridge, MA: Harvard University Press, 2007), 29. Conservatives included Republicans, Southern Democrats, and organized labor. Zolberg argues that "the measure was designed to enlarge the British quota while concomitantly reducing the German, Irish, and Scandinavian allotments, and even more drastically reducing the quotas granted to more recent arrivals," namely southern and eastern Europeans. "Matters of State: Theorizing Immigration Policy," in *The Handbook of International Migration: The American Experience*, ed. Charles Hirschman, Philip Kasinitz, and Josh DeWind (New York: Russell Sage Foundation, 1999), 75.

103. Mae M. Ngai, *Impossible Subjects: Illegal Aliens and the Making of Modern America* (Princeton, NJ: Princeton University Press, 2004), 7.

104. I appreciate the observation made by Fred Hoxie at the 2010 American Historical Association meetings in San Diego, CA. Hoxie, "Comment on Citizenship and Property Rights." As he explains the logic, "It would seem that 'tribal' people would not do that" (1).

105. Witness, for example, the high-profile trial and deportation of Emma Goldman and Alexander Berkman in 1919. Candace Falk, *Love, Anarchy, and Emma Goldman* (New Brunswick, NJ: Rutgers University Press, 1990).

CHAPTER 8

1. For example, Chang, *The Color of the Land*; Meyer, *The White Earth Tragedy*; Wishart, *An Unspeakable Sadness*.

2. The total area of allotted lands that belonged to fee-patented Dakotas was 13,304, a little more than a quarter of total Dakota acreage. D. C. Gray, "Annual Summary, 1929," RFTIA, n.p. The average size of their land holdings had shrunk to 83.6 acres, at a time when more acreage was needed for a farm enterprise to be economically viable. The plat maps do not account for the fragmentation of allotments, which also impeded cultivation.

3. W. R. Beyer, "Annual Report, 1927," RFTIA, Industries, 3. Despite the contradictions between his observation and the stated policy, he still recommended giving patents to everyone speaking English. Taking stock in the summer of 1929, superintendent Gray reported that 600 allotments, amounting to approximately half of the original, were still held completely or partly in trust. The Indian Office's agenda of issuing fee patents had resulted in 151 Dakotas—either original allottees or their heirs—holding land independently. From Mary Louise Defender Wilson's perspective at Standing Rock, those who got fee patents sold their land.

4. Handy-Marchello, *Women of the Northern Plains*, 26. There are many more ranches in the western part of the state, as there is less rain and the land is more conducive to livestock grazing than to cultivation. This difference in size can be partly explained by federal land policies

that enabled individuals to homestead 160 acres and add to their holdings by tree claims and preemption. In effect, homesteaders could claim up to 480 acres of land at below-market prices. In contrast, on the reservation, after homesteading or allotment a person could acquire more land only through purchase or inheritance and little land was available.

5. Effland, Rogers, and Grim, "Women as Agricultural Landowners."

6. This pattern has a parallel in contemporary wage differentials across racial-ethnic groups. Women of color earn more relative to men of color than white women do relative to white men. This can be explained partly by the fact that men of color earn lower wages. Theresa Amott and Julie Matthaei, *Race, Gender, and Work: Multi-Cultural Economic History of Women in the United States* (Boston, MA: South End Press, 1996).

7. James A. Skurdall Private Family Collection; Cherry Wood Monson, Betty Loe Westby, Cherrie Lane Monson Anderson, and Stella Rasmusson Papachek, *Warwick Memories* (Warwick, ND: privately published, 2002); U.S. Bureau of the Census, Manuscript Census, 1910, 1920, 1930.

8. Hudson, *Plains Country Towns*; Neth, *Preserving the Family Farm*; W. R. Beyer, "Annual Report, 1923," RFTIA, Narrative Section 4—Industries, 8; Timothy Egan, *The Worst Hard Time: The Untold Story of Those Who Survived the Great American Dust Bowl* (New York: Houghton Mifflin, 2006); National Climatic Data Center website. Available: http://www.ncdc.noaa.gov/. [January 25, 2013.]

9. D. C. Gray, "Annual Report, 1930," RFTIA, Narrative Section II—Industries, 1.

10. Neth, *Preserving the Family Farm*, 3.

11. Ibid., 5.

12. Ole D. Lima, "My Coming to America and My Experiences Here," (1929) in Ole Lima Papers, Norwegian-American Historical Association, Northfield, MN. His comments reflect a moment late in his life when he was widowed, lonely, and not well. For more about his life, see Hampsten, *Settlers' Children*, chapter 7.

13. Hoxie, *A Final Promise*; Hoxie, *This Indian Country*; Prucha, *The Great Father*.

14. Greene, interview by author (Fort Totten, ND, 1999), audio recording.

15. Monson et al., *Warwick Memories*, 330, reprints clips from the *Warwick Weekly Sentinel*.

16. Presumably this refers to Ida Olson, the aunt of Lois Olson Jones.

17. The issue of insufficient money to pay for coffins surfaces in Dakota testimonies at the 1929 hearings. Paying for a respectable burial was no easy task for poor people.

18. The land boom contributed to the increase in debt. According to economist L. J. Norton, mortgage debt tripled from 1910 to 1925; North Dakota was no exception to the regional pattern. L. J. Norton, "The Land Market and Farm Mortgage Debts, 1917–1921," *Journal of Farm Economics* 24, no. 1 (1942): 1973.

19. Wold, "The Letters of Effie Hanson," 42.

20. U.S. Senate, Subcommittee of the Committee on Indian Affairs, *Survey of Conditions of the Indians in the United States: Hearings before a Subcommittee of the Committee on Indian Affairs*, S. Rep. No. 71-1 (July 18, 20, 1929), 3237.

21. Mark Wyman, *Round-Trip to America: The Immigrants Return to Europe, 1880–1930* (Ithaca, NY: Cornell University Press, 1993), 10–12. Multiple reasons contributed to those return rates, economic failure among them, and the return rates were concentrated between 1910 and 1935 for Norwegians. Knut Djupedal, "Tales of America," *Western Folklore* 49 (1990): 178.

22. For a discussion of "shifting workers," see Jacqueline Jones, *The Dispossessed: America's Underclasses from the Civil War to the Present* (New York: Basic Books, 1992).

23. Handy-Marchello, *Women of the Northern Plains*, 28.

24. Ibid.; Sonya Salamon and Shirley M. O'Reilly, "Family Land and Development Cycles among Illinois Farmers," *Rural Sociology* 44, no. 3 (1979): 525–42.

25. Neth, *Preserving the Family Farm*, 18.

26. Hudson, "The Study of Western Frontier Populations." Hudson's study of the Historical Data Project found high rates of proximate residence of "pioneer offspring." He finds that 50.4 percent of Norwegian adult children lived in the same county as their parents, and another 10.1 percent lived in another North Dakota County (58). Only Germans from Russia had a higher rate of intergenerational proximate residence.

27. Sonya Salamon and Vicki Lockhart, "Land Ownership and the Position of Elderly in Farm Families," *Human Organization* 39, no. 4 (1980): 324–31.

28. See John C. Caldwell, "The Wealth Flows Theory of Fertility Decline," in *Determinants of Fertility Trends: Theories Reexamined; Proceedings of a Seminar Held in Bad Homburg*, ed. Charlotte Höhn and Rainer Mackensen (Liège, Belgium: Ordina Editions, 1982); John C. Caldwell, "Toward a Restatement of Demographic Transition Theory," *Population and Development Review* 2, no. 3/4 (1976): 339.

29. Hans stayed on the farm until 1950, and by that time had five and a half quarters, completely paid off. At that point he sold the farm to Karl, the only son who stayed in the area; the other eight Larsgaard children had moved away.

30. Handy-Marchello, *Women of the Northern Plains*, 26.

31. William C. Sherman, *Prairie Mosaic: An Ethnic Atlas of Rural North Dakota* (Fargo: North Dakota Institute for Regional Studies, 1983).

32. Jeppesen, *Dannebrog on the American Prairie*.

33. Dag Blanck, "Constructing an Ethnic Identity: The Case of the Swedish-Americans," in *The Ethnic Enigma: The Salience of Ethnicity for European-Origin Groups*, ed. Peter Kivisto (Philadelphia, PA: Balch Institute Press, 1989); Philip J. Anderson and Dag Blanck, eds., *Swedes in the Twin Cities: Immigrant Life and Minnesota's Urban Frontier* (Uppsala, Sweden: Uppsala University Library, 2001).

34. Samuel Young, "Annual Report, 1919," RFTIA, Narrative Section IV—Industries, 12.

35. *Sisseton and Wahpeton Bands of Sioux Indians v. United States* 277 U.S. 424(1928).

36. John S. R. Hammitt, "Annual Report, 1928," RFTIA, Statistical Section III—Industries, 17. According to anthropologist Patricia Albers, "By the 1920s, land no longer supported most Dakota at Devil's Lake, either on a cash or productive basis. Increasingly, Dakota families were forced to survive on wage-labor and federal relief." "Autonomy and Dependency in the Lives of Dakota Women," 121.

37. Gray, "Annual Summary, 1929," RFTIA, Narrative Section II—Industries, 5.

38. Francis Paul Prucha, *Indian Policy in the United States: Historical Essays* (Lincoln: University of Nebraska, 1981).

39. Gray, "Annual Report, 1930," RFTIA, Narrative Section I—Law and Order, 1. There is a long and much-debated history of Indian's overuse of and addiction to alcohol. See, for example, Beatrice Medicine, *Learning to Be an Anthropologist and Remaining "Native"* (Urbana: University of Illinois Press, 2001); Gray, "Annual Report, 1930," RFTIA, Narrative Section I—Law and Order, 2.

40. According to the report, the 957 enrolled members at Fort Totten had a per capita *earned* income of $101. Total per capita income for tribal members was $165. Meriam, *The Problem of Indian Administration*, 456, 452.

41. Beyer, "Annual Report, 1927," RFTIA, Health, section 1.

42. U.S. Senate, *Survey of Conditions of the Indians*, 1929, 3253–54.

43. U.S. Senate, Subcommittee of the Committee on Indian Affairs, *Survey of Conditions of the Indians in the United States: Hearings before a Subcommittee of the Committee on Indian Affairs*, 73–1, October 12–16, 1933, 16447.

44. U.S. Senate, *Survey of Conditions of the Indians*, 1929, 3227.

45. Ronald Briley, "Lynn J. Frazier and Progressive Reform: A Plodder in the Ranks of a Ragged Regiment," *South Dakota History* 7, no. 4 (1977): 438–54.

46. U.S. Senate, *Survey of Conditions of the Indians*, 1929, 3233–34.

47. Ibid., 3212–13.

48. Hoxie, *This Indian Country*.

49. Prucha, *The Great Father*.

CONCLUSION

1. Available: http://www.swc.state.nd.us/4dlink9/4dcgi/GetContentPDF/PB-206/Fact%20 Sheet.pdf. [January 27, 2013.] The geological records reveal that over the last 4,000 years, water levels have been even higher.

2. Greene, interview by author (Fort Totten, ND, 1999), audio recording.

3. Lambert, interview by Robert Carlson (1976), NDOHP, audio recording, 1101A&B.

4. Alfred Schuetz, "The Homecomer," *American Journal of Sociology* 50 (March 1945): 369–76.

5. Jon Gjerde, "Chain Migrations from the West Coast of Norway," in *A Century of European Migrations, 1830–1930*, ed. Rudolph J. Vecoli and Suzanne M. Sinke (Urbana: University of Illinois Press, 1991), 158–81.

6. Lambert, interview by Robert Carlson (1976) NDOHP, audio recording, 1101A&B.

7. I am grateful to Gunlög Fur for so astutely capturing the notion of entanglement.

8. To my unaccustomed ear, his soft voice seemed to be saying, "Takksalot." My informants assure me that no such word exists in Norwegian, but it would make perfect sense, however invented, as Norwegian-American English for "thanks a lot."

BIBLIOGRAPHY

———

ARCHIVAL SOURCES

Bancroft Library, University of California, Berkeley
    Robert Harry Lowie Papers, 1872–1968
Benson County Superintendent of Schools records, Minnewaukan, ND
    Teachers' Reports, 1885-1929
Chester Fritz Library, Special Collections, University of North Dakota, Grand Forks, ND
    J. Olson Anders. "From Selbu to the Dakota Prairie: Recollections of Frontier Life on the Middle Border" (1960)
    Louis Garcia Papers, 1967–
Eunice Davidson Private Family Collection
Institute of American Indian Studies, South Dakota Oral History Center, Vermillion
    American Indian Research Project (AIRP): interviews (transcripts)
Integrated Public Use Microdata Series (IPUMS), Minnesota Population Center, University of Minnesota
James A. Skurdall Private Family Collection
Karen V. Hansen Private Family Collection
Mathers Museum of World Cultures, Indiana University, Bloomington
    Wanamaker Collection. Images of Native Americans
    Wanamaker Collection. World War I Documents
North Dakota Institute for Regional Studies, NDSU Libraries, North Dakota State University, Fargo
    Dear, Cyrene Bakke, "Besta: A Story of North Dakota Pioneers," 1950-51
    Institute Photograph Collections
    Tvedt, Johanna, interview by Mark Olson, 1971

Norwegian-American Historical Association, Northfield, MN
  Lima, Martha. Letters of Martha Lima. Cooperstown, ND
  Lima, Ole D. "My Coming to America and My Experiences Here." Ole Lima Papers
State Historical Society of North Dakota, Bismarck
  1915 North Dakota State Census
  1925 North Dakota State Census
  Fort Totten Indian Reservation Census, 1885-1905, 1910-1939
  Horne, Svanau Yri, and Beverly Kraus Horne. *Reminiscing with Svanau*
  Indian Boarding Schools Oral History Project (IBSOHP): interviews (audio recordings and
    transcripts)
  North Dakota Oral History Project (NDOHP): interviews (audio recordings) and photographs
National Archives and Records Administration, Central Plains Region, Kansas City, MO
  Annual Reports of Indian agents and superintendents, 1902–1930
  Letters to Commissioner of Indian Affairs, land sale cards, certificates of selection.
  Records of the Fort Totten Indian Agency (RFTIA). RG 75/A003/B038/C002//E035
  "Report of Homes Visited, 1905-1927," (RHV) Carrie Pohl, Field Matron
National Archives at Boston, Waltham, MA
  U.S. manuscript census records, 1890-1930

GOVERNMENT DOCUMENTS

Annual reports of the Board of Indian Commissioners. Washington, DC: Government Printing
  Office.
Board of Indian Commissioners, *Report of the Board of Indian Commissioners to the Secretary of
  the Interior, 1906*. Washington, DC: Government Printing Office, 1906.
———. *Twenty-First Annual Report of the Board of Indian Commissioners, 1889*. Washington,
  DC: Government Printing Office, 1890.
Commissioner of Indian Affairs. *Annual Reports of the Commissioner of Indian Affairs (ARCIA)*.
  Commissioner of Indian Affairs, 1886–1894, Washington, DC.
Court of Claims of the United States. "Sisseton and Wahpeton Bands of Dakota or Sioux Indians
  v. The United States: Evidence for Claimant." No. 22524, 1901–1907.
Dakota Territory Department of Immigration and Statistics. *The Year of Statehood, 1889,
  Dakota: Official Guide, Containing Useful Information in Handy Form for Settlers and
  Homeseekers, Concerning North and South Dakota*. Aberdeen, Dakota: F. H. Hagerty, 1889.
*Papers Relating to Talks and Councils Held with the Indians in Dakota and Montana Territories in
  the Years 1866–1869*. Washington, DC: Government Printing Office, 1910.
Reel, Estelle. *Report of the Superintendent of Indian Schools*. Washington, DC: Government
  Printing Office, 1904.
Roosevelt, Theodore. "A Proclamation By the President of the United States of America," *Indian
  Affairs: Laws and Treaties* 3, no. 32 June 2, 1904, 33 Stat., 2368. Compiled and ed. Charles
  J. Kappler. Washington: Government Printing Office, 1913.
Turner, Howard A. *The Ownership of Tenant Farms in the North Central States*. U.S. Department
  of Agriculture Bulletin No. 1433, 1926.
U.S. Bureau of the Census. *Indian Population in the United States and Alaska, 1910*. Washington,
  DC: Government Printing Office, 1915.
———. *Report on Indians Taxed and Indians Not Taxed in the United States (except Alaska)*. Vol.
  11. Washington, DC: Government Printing Office, 1890.

U.S. Congress. Amendment to the Dawes Act, 51st Cong., 2d sess., February 28, 1891.

U.S. Senate, Subcommittee of the Committee on Indian Affairs. *Survey of Conditions of the Indians in the United States: Hearings before a Subcommittee of the Committee on Indian Affairs,* 71–1, July 18, 20, 1929. Washington, DC: Government Printing Office, 1931.

———. *Survey of Conditions of the Indians in the United States: Hearings before a Subcommittee of the Committee on Indian Affairs,* 73–1, October 12–16, 1933. Washington, DC: Government Printing Office, 1934.

Newspapers—North Dakota

Bismarck Daily Tribune
Devils Lake Inter-Ocean
Devils Lake Journal
Fort Totten Review
Grand Forks Herald
Nelson County Observer
Sheyenne Star
Tolna Tribune
Warwick Weekly Sentinel

Published Sources

Abrams, Lynn. *Oral History Theory.* New York: Routledge, 2010.

Adams, David Wallace. *Education for Extinction: American Indians and the Boarding School Experience, 1875–1928.* Lawrence: University Press of Kansas, 1995.

Ager, Waldemar. "*Blandt Norske Nybyggere.*" [Among Norwegian settlers]. In *Kvartalskrift.* 8th ed., 16–19. Eau Clare, WI: Reform Press, 1912.

Ahern, Wilbert H. " 'To Kill the Indian and Save the Man': The Boarding School and American Indian Education." In *Fort Totten: Military Post and Indian School, 1867–1959,* ed. Larry Remele, 23–42. Bismarck: State Historical Society of North Dakota, 1986.

Albers, Patricia. "Autonomy and Dependency in the Lives of Dakota Women: A Study in Historical Change." *Review of Radical Political Economics* 17, no. 3 (1985): 109–34.

———. "The Regional System of the Devil's Lake Sioux: Its Structure, Composition, Development, and Functions." Ph.D. diss., University of Wisconsin-Madison, 1974.

———. "Sioux Women in Transition: A Study of Their Changing Status in Domestic and Capitalist Sectors of Production." In *The Hidden Half: Studies of Plains Indian Women,* ed. Patricia C. Albers and Beatrice Medicine, 175–234. Washington, DC: University Press of America, 1983.

———, and Beatrice Medicine, eds. *The Hidden Half: Studies of Plains Indian Women.* Washington, DC: University Press of America, 1983.

———, and Beatrice Medicine. "The Role of Sioux Women in the Production of Ceremonial Objects: The Case of the Star Quilt." In *The Hidden Half: Studies of Plains Indian Women,* ed. Patricia Albers and Beatrice Medicine, 123–40. Washington, DC: University Press of America, 1983.

Amott, Theresa, and Julie Matthaei. *Race, Gender, and Work: Multi-Cultural Economic History of Women in the United States.* Boston, MA: South End Press, 1996.

Anderson, Gary Clayton. *Kinsmen of Another Kind: Dakota-White Relations in the Upper Mississippi Valley, 1650–1862.* 1984. Reprint, St. Paul: Minnesota Historical Society Press, 1997.

———, and Alan R. Woolworth, eds. *Through Dakota Eyes: Narrative Accounts of the Minnesota Indian War of 1862*. St. Paul: Minnesota Historical Society Press, 1988.

Anderson, Laura L. "Introduction." In *Being Dakota: Tales and Traditions of the Sisseton and Wahpeton* by Amos E. Oneroad and Alanson B. Skinner, 3-53. St. Paul: Minnesota Historical Society Press, 2003.

Anderson, Philip J., and Dag Blanck, eds. *Norwegians and Swedes in the United States: Friends and Neighbors*. St. Paul: Minnesota Historical Society Press, 2012.

———, and Dag Blanck, eds. *Swedes in the Twin Cities: Immigrant Life and Minnesota's Urban Frontier*. Uppsala, Sweden: Uppsala University Library, 2001.

Babcock, Kendric Charles. "The Scandinavian Element in American Population." *American Historical Review* 16, no. 2 (January 1911): 300–310.

Baca Zinn, Maxine. "Family, Feminism, and Race in America." In *Families in the U.S.: Kinship and Domestic Politics*, ed. Karen V. Hansen and Anita Ilta Garey, 33–40. Philadelphia, PA: Temple University Press, 1998.

Barsh, Russel Lawrence. "An American Heart of Darkness: The 1913 Expedition for American Indian Citizenship." *Great Plains Quarterly* 13 (Spring 1993): 91–115.

Barton, H. Arnold. "Norwegians and Swedes in America: Some Comparisons." In *Norwegians and Swedes in the United States: Friends and Neighbors*, ed. Philip J. Anderson and Dag Blanck, 21–34. St. Paul: Minnesota Historical Society Press, 2012.

Beck, George. "The Fourteenth Amendment as Related to Tribal Indians: Section I, 'Subject to the Jurisdiction Thereof' and Section II, 'Excluding Indians Not Taxed.'" *American Indian Culture and Research Journal* 28, no. 4 (2004): 37–68.

Berghold, Rev. Alexander. *The Indians' Revenge, or Days of Horror, Some Appalling Events in the History of the Sioux*, ed. Don Heinrich Tolzmann. 1891. Reprint, Roseville, MN: Edinborough Press, 2007.

Bergland, Betty A. "Norwegian Immigrants and 'Indianerne' in the Landtaking, 1838–1862." *Norwegian-American Studies* 35 (2000): 319–50.

Bernardin, Susan, Melody Graulich, Lisa MacFarlane, and Nicole Tonkovich. *Trading Gazes: Euro-American Women Photographers and Native North Americans, 1880–1940*. New Brunswick, NJ: Rutgers University Press, 2003.

Biolsi, Thomas. *Organizing the Lakota: The Political Economy of the New Deal on the Pine Ridge and Rosebud Reservations*. Tucson: University of Arizona Press, 1992.

Birkeland, Harriet Watts. "John Birkeland and the Watts Family." In *Our Heritage: Sheyenne Area, 1883–1980*, ed. Sheyenne Historical Society, 385–86. Altona, Manitoba: D. W. Friesen & Sons, Ltd., 1980.

Bjorkhaug, Hilde, and Arild Blekesaune. "Masculinisation or Professionalisation of Norwegian Farm Work: A Gender Neutral Division of Work on Norwegian Family Farms?" *Journal of Comparative Family Studies* 38, no. 3 (Summer 2007): 423–34.

Blanck, Dag. "Constructing an Ethnic Identity: The Case of the Swedish-Americans." In *The Ethnic Enigma: The Salience of Ethnicity for European-Origin Groups*, ed. Peter Kivisto, 134–52. Philadelphia, PA: Balch Institute Press, 1989.

———. "Friends and Neighbors?: Patterns of Norwegian-Swedish Interaction in the United States." In *Norwegians and Swedes in the United States: Friends and Neighbors*, ed. Philip J. Anderson and Dag Blanck, 5–20. St. Paul: Minnesota Historical Society Press, 2012.

Blegen, Theodore C. *Norwegian Migration to America: The American Transition*. 1940. Reprint, New York: Haskell House, 1969.

Bloemraad, Irene. "Citizenship Lessons from the Past: The Contours of Immigrant Naturalization in the Early 20th Century." *Social Science Quarterly* 87, no. 5 (December 2006): 927–53.

———, Anna Korteweg, and Gokce Yurdakul. "Citizenship and Immigration: Multiculturalism, Assimilation, and Challenges to the Nation-State." *Annual Review of Sociology* 34 (2008): 153–79.

Bredbenner, Candice Lewis. *A Nationality of Her Own: Women, Marriage, and the Law of Citizenship.* Berkeley: University of California Press, 1998.

Briley, Ronald. "Lynn J. Frazier and Progressive Reform: A Plodder in the Ranks of a Ragged Regiment." *South Dakota History* 7, no. 4 (Fall 1977): 438–54.

Brochmann, Grete, and Knut Kjeldstadli. *A History of Immigration: The Case of Norway 900–2000.* Oslo: Universitetsforlaget, 2008.

Brown, Elsa Barkley. "Mapping the Terrain of Black Richmond." *Journal of Urban History* 21, no. 3 (March 1995): 296–346.

Bryson, Stephanie, and Karen V. Hansen. "Satisfactory Accommodations: Cleanliness, Culture, and Compromise in the Fort Totten Field Matron Program, 1913–1915." Presented at the American Sociological Association meetings, San Francisco, CA, August 14–17, 2004.

Burtzloff, Mary. "Dutiful Daughters, Sisters, Wives, and Mothers: The Female Homesteader and the Role of the Family." Presented at the "Homesteading Reconsidered" conference, Center for Great Plains Studies, Lincoln, NE, May 17–19 2007.

Cahill, Cathleen D. *Federal Fathers and Mothers: A Social History of the United States Indian Service, 1869–1933.* Chapel Hill: University of North Carolina Press, 2011.

Caldwell, John C. "Toward a Restatement of Demographic Transition Theory." *Population and Development Review* 2, no. 3/4 (Sept.–Dec. 1976): 321–66.

———. "The Wealth Flows Theory of Fertility Decline." In *Determinants of Fertility Trends: Theories Re-examined; Proceedings of a Seminar Held in Bad Homburg*, ed. Charlotte Höhn and Rainer Mackensen, 169–88. Liège, Belgium: Ordina Editions, 1982.

Calloway, Colin G., ed. *Dawnland Encounters: Indians and Europeans in Northern New England.* Hanover, NH: University Press of New England, 1991.

———, Gerd Gemünden, and Susanne Zantop, eds. *Germans and Indians: Fantasies, Encounters, Projections.* Lincoln: University of Nebraska Press, 2002.

Calof, Rachel Bella. "My Story." In *Rachel Calof's Story: Jewish Homesteader on the Northern Plains*, ed. J. Sanford Rikoon, 1–97. Bloomington: Indiana University Press, 1995.

Carley, Kenneth. *The Sioux Uprising of 1862.* St. Paul: Minnesota Historical Society Press, 1961.

Cather, Willa. *My Ántonia.* 1918. Peterborough, Ontario: Broadview Press, 2003.

———. *O Pioneers!* 1913. Reprint, Lincoln: University of Nebraska Press, 1992.

Chang, David A. *The Color of the Land: Race, Nation, and the Politics of Landownership in Oklahoma, 1832–1929.* Chapel Hill: University of North Carolina Press, 2010.

Child, Brenda J. *Boarding School Seasons: American-Indian Families, 1900–1940.* Lincoln: University of Nebraska Press, 2000.

Chomsky, Carol. "The United States-Dakota War Trials: A Study in Military Injustice." *Stanford Law Review* 43, no. 1 (November 1990): 13–98.

Compton, Tonia M. "Proper Women/Propertied Women: Federal Land Laws and the Gender Order(s) in the Nineteenth-Century Imperial American West." Ph.D. diss., University of Nebraska, 2009.

Cook-Lynn, Elizabeth. *Why I Can't Read Wallace Stegner and Other Essays.* Madison: University of Wisconsin Press, 1996.

Cornell, Stephen, and Douglas Hartmann. *Ethnicity and Race: Making Identities in a Changing World*. 2nd ed. Thousand Oaks, CA: Pine Forge Press, 2007.

Cott, Nancy F. "Marriage and Women's Citizenship in the United States, 1830–1934." *American Historical Review* 103, no. 5 (December 1998): 1440–74.

———. *Public Vows: A History of Marriage and the Nation*. Cambridge, MA: Harvard University Press, 2000.

Cronon, William. *Changes in the Land: Indians, Colonists, and the Ecology of New England*. 1983. Reprint, New York: Hill and Wang, 2003

Deloria, Ella Cara. *The Dakota Way of Life*. Rapid City, SD: Mariah Press, 2007.

Deloria, Philip J. *Playing Indian*. New Haven, CT: Yale University Press, 1998.

Deloria, Vine, Jr. 1969. *Custer Died for Your Sins: An Indian Manifesto*. Reprint, Norman: University of Oklahoma Press, 1988.

———. ed. *Of Utmost Good Faith*. New York: Bantam, 1971.

Denial, Catherine. "Pelagie Faribault's Island: Property, Kinship, and the Meaning of Marriage in Dakota Country." *Minnesota History* 62 (Summer 2010): 48–59.

Diedrich, Mark. *Dakota Oratory: Great Moments in the Recorded Speech of the Eastern Sioux, 1695–1874*. Rochester, MN: Coyote Books, 1989.

———. *Mni Wakan Oyate: A History of the Sisituwan, Wahpeton, Pabaksa, and Other Dakota That Settled at Spirit Lake, North Dakota*. Fort Totten, ND: Cankdeska Cikana Community College Publishing, 2007.

———, with Louis Garcia. *Little Fish: Head Chief of the Dakota on the Fort Totten Reservation*. Rochester, MN: Coyote Books, 2009.

Dill, Bonnie Thornton. *Across the Boundaries of Race and Class: An Exploration of Work and Family among Black Female Domestic Servants*. New York: Garland, 1994.

Djupedal, Knut. "Tales of America." *Western Folklore* 49 (April 1990): 177–89.

Duffy, Mignon. *Making Care Count: A Century of Gender, Race, and Paid Care Work*. New Brunswick, NJ: Rutgers University Press, 2011.

Dussias, Allison M. "Squaw Drudges, Farm Wives, and the Dann Sisters' Last Stand: American Indian Women's Resistance to Domestication and the Denial of Their Property Rights." *North Carolina Law Review* 77 (1998–99): 637–729.

Eastman (Ohiyesa), Charles A. *From the Deep Woods to Civilization: Chapters in the Autobiography of an Indian*. 1916. Reprint, Lincoln: University of Nebraska Press, 1977.

———. *The Soul of the Indian: An Interpretation*. 1911. Reprint, Lincoln: University of Nebraska Press, 1980.

Eastman, Elaine Goodale. *Sister to the Sioux: The Memoirs of Elaine Goodale Eastman*. Ed. Kay Graber. 1978. Reprint, Lincoln: University of Nebraska Press, 1985.

Eastman, Mrs. Mary. *Dahcotah; or, Life and Legends of the Sioux around Fort Snelling*. 1849. Reprint, Minneapolis, MN: Ross & Haines, Inc., 1962.

Effland, Anne B. W., Denise M. Rogers, and Valerie Grim. "Women as Agricultural Landowners: What Do We Know About Them?" *Agricultural History* 67 (Spring 1993): 235–61.

Egan, Timothy. *The Worst Hard Time: The Untold Story of Those Who Survived the Great American Dust Bowl*. New York: Houghton Mifflin, 2006.

Ehrenreich, Barbara, and Deirdre English. *For Her Own Good: 100 Years of Experts' Advice to Women*. New York: Anchor Press, 1978.

Ellinghaus, Katherine. *Taking Assimilation to Heart: Marriages of White Women and Indigenous Men in the United States and Australia, 1887–1937*. Lincoln: University of Nebraska Press, 2006.

Ellis, Clyde. "'The Sound of the Drum Will Revive Them and Make Them Happy.'" In *Powwow*, ed. Clyde Ellis, Luke Eric Lassiter, and Gary H. Dunham, 3–25. Lincoln: University of Nebraska Press, 2005.

Ellsworth, Scott. "Origins of the Nonpartisan League." Ph.D. diss., Duke University, 1982.

Emmerich, Lisa E. "'Right in the Midst of My Own People': Native American Women and the Field Matron Program." *American Indian Quarterly* 15, no. 2 (Spring 1991): 201–16.

Enfield, Nick J. "The Theory of Cultural Logic: How Individuals Combine Social Intelligence with Semiotics to Create and Maintain Cultural Meaning." *Cultural Dynamics* 23 (2011): 35–64.

Falk, Candace. *Love, Anarchy, and Emma Goldman*. New Brunswick, NJ: Rutgers University Press, 1990.

Fine, James O. "An Analysis of Factors Affecting Agricultural Development on the Fort Totten Indian Reservation." Master's thesis, University of North Dakota, 1951.

Fink, Deborah. *Agrarian Women: Wives and Mothers in Rural Nebraska, 1880–1940*. Chapel Hill: University of North Carolina Press, 1992.

Finn, Janet L. "Walls and Bridges: Cultural Mediation and the Legacy of Ella Deloria." In *Women Writing Women: The Frontiers Reader*, ed. Patricia Hart and Karen Weathermon, with Susan H. Armitage, 175–98. Lincoln: University of Nebraska Press, 2006.

Fischer, Claude S., and Michael Hout. *Century of Difference: How America Changed in the Last One Hundred Years*. New York: Russell Sage Foundation, 2006.

Fischer, Edward F. *Cultural Logics and Global Economies: Maya Identity in Thought and Practice*. Austin: University of Texas Press, 2001.

Flynn, Sean J. "Western Assimilationist: Charles H. Burke and the Burke Act." *The Midwest Review* 11 (Spring 1989): 1–15.

Folwell, William Watts. *A History of Minnesota*. 1921–1930. Rev. ed. 4 vols. Reprint, St. Paul: Minnesota Historical Society Press, 1956–1969.

Fur, Gunlög. *A Nation of Women: Gender and Colonial Encounters among the Delaware Indians*. Philadelphia: University of Pennsylvania Press, 2009.

———. "Indians and Immigrants—Entangled Histories." Unpublished manuscript, 2013.

Garcia, Louis. "Forde Township." *A Message from Garcia: The History and Culture of the Spirit Lake Dakota*, no. 33. Tokio, ND: privately published, 2004.

———. "Grass Dance Warrior Society." *A Message from Garcia: The History and Culture of the Spirit Lake Dakota*, no. 2. Tokio, ND: privately published, 2000.

———. "Ignatius Court." *A Message from Garcia: The History and Culture of the Spirit Lake Dakota*, no. 46 Tokio, ND: privately published, 2010.

———. "Left Bear." *A Message from Garcia: The History and Culture of the Spirit Lake Dakota*, no. 48. Tokio, ND: privately published, 2008.

———. "Lone Buffalo Club." *A Message from Garcia: The History and Culture of the Spirit Lake Dakota*, no. 1. Tokio: privately published, 2000.

———. "McDonald the Mail Carrier." *A Message from Garcia: The History and Culture of the Spirit Lake Dakota*, no. 15. Tokio, ND: privately published, 2002.

———. "Murder at Bad Butte." *A Message from Garcia: The History and Culture of the Spirit Lake Dakota*, no. 40. Tokio, ND: privately published, 2009.

———. "Shin Bone Lake and Warwick." *A Message from Garcia: The History and Culture of the Spirit Lake Dakota*, no. 26. Tokio, ND: privately published, 2006.

———. "The Scorned Suitor." *A Message from Garcia: The History and Culture of the Spirit Lake Dakota*, no. 39. Tokio, ND: privately published, 2006.

——. "Waanatan's Pipe and Tobacco Bag." *Whispering Wind* (May/June 2010): 4–6.

——. "Where Is Aspen Island?" *A Message from Garcia: The History and Culture of the Spirit Lake Dakota*, no. 6. Tokio, ND: privately published, 2000.

——. "Who Are the Cut-Heads?" *A Message from Garcia: The History and Culture of the Spirit Lake Dakota*, no. 4. Tokio, ND: privately published, 2000.

——. "Wild Horses for Land." *A Message from Garcia: The History and Culture of the Spirit Lake Dakota*, no. 5. Tokio, ND: privately published, 2000.

Garey, Anita Ilta. "Maternally Yours: The Emotion Work of 'Maternal Visibility.'" In *At the Heart of Work and Family: Engaging the Ideas of Arlie Hochschild*, ed. Anita Ilta Garey and Karen V. Hansen, 171–79. New Brunswick, NJ: Rutgers University Press, 2011.

Garfinkel, Harold. *Studies in Ethnomethodology*. Englewood Cliffs, NJ: Prentice-Hall, 1967.

Garroutte, Eva Marie. *Real Indians: Identity and the Survival of Native America*. Berkeley: University of California Press, 2003.

Gaston, Herbert Earle. *The Nonpartisan League*. New York: Harcourt, 1920.

Gay, E. Jane. *With the Nez Perces: Alice Fletcher in the Field, 1889–1892*. Ed. Frederick E. Hoxie and Joan T. Mark. Lincoln: University of Nebraska Press, 1981.

Gipp, Judge William L. "Oral History." *North Dakota History* 43, no.2 (Spring 1976): 80–83.

Gjerde, Jon. "Chain Migrations from the West Coast of Norway." In *A Century of European Migrations, 1830–1930*, ed. Rudolph J. Vecoli and Suzanne M. Sinke, 158–81. Urbana: University of Illinois Press, 1991.

——. *From Peasants to Farmers: The Migration from Balestrand, Norway to the Upper Middle West*. New York: Cambridge University Press, 1985.

——. "Transatlantic Linkages: The Interaction between the Norwegian American and Norwegian 'Nations' during the Century of Migration, 1825–1920." *Immigrants & Minorities* 20 (2001): 19–35.

Glenn, Evelyn Nakano. *Unequal Freedom: How Race and Gender Shaped American Citizenship and Labor*. Cambridge, MA: Harvard University Press, 2002.

Goodale, Mark R. G., and Per Kare Sky. "A Comparative Study of Land Tenure, Property Boundaries, and Dispute Resolution: Case Studies from Bolivia and Norway." *Journal of Rural Studies* 17 (2001): 183–200.

Gordon, Linda. *The Great Arizona Orphan Abduction*. Cambridge, MA: Harvard University Press, 1999.

Grathwohl, Linda. "The North Dakota Anti-Garb Law: Constitutional Conflict and Religious Strife." *Great Plains Quarterly* 13, no. 3 (Summer 1993): 187–91.

Greenwald, Emily. *Reconfiguring the Reservation: The Nez Perces, Jicarilla Apaches, and the Dawes Act*. Albuquerque: University of New Mexico Press, 2002.

Grim, Valerie. "'Tryin' to Make Ends Meet': African American Women's Work on Brooks Farm, 1920–1970." In *Unrelated Kin: Race and Gender in Women's Personal Narratives*, ed. Gwendolyn Etter-Lewis and Michèle Foster. 123–38. New York: Routledge, 1996.

Gulliksen, Øyvind T. *"Assimilasjonsprosessen i Waldemar Agers Paa Veien Til Smeltepotten."* In *Norwegian-American Essays, 2001*, ed. Knut Djupedal, Harry T. Cleven, Ingeborg Kongslien, and Dina Tolfsby, 183–205. Oslo: NAHA-Norway, 2001.

——. *Twofold Identities: Norwegian-American Contributions to Midwestern Literature*. New York: Peter Lang, 2004.

Hammonds, Clare, and Karen V. Hansen. "Women's Citizenship, Political Mobilization, and the Nonpartisan League in North Dakota, 1900–1925." Presented at the Rural Women's Studies Association meetings, Bloomington, IN, September 24, 2009.

Hampsten, Elizabeth. *Settlers' Children: Growing up on the Great Plains.* Norman: University of Oklahoma Press, 1991.

Hamsun, Knut. *Growth of the Soil.* 1917. Reprint, New York: Penguin, 2007.

Handy–Marchello, Barbara. "The 'Main Stay': Women's Productive Work on Pioneer Farms." *North Dakota History* 63, no. 2 & 3 (1996): 17–27.

———. "Women and the Homestead Law: Standing Equal before the Law of the Land." Presented at "Lincoln Legacy: The Homestead Act" 20th Annual Governor's Conference on North Dakota History, Bismarck, ND, November 7–8, 2008.

———. *Women of the Northern Plains: Gender and Settlement on the Homestead Frontier, 1870–1930.* St. Paul: Minnesota Historical Society Press, 2005.

Hansen, Karen V. "Historical Sociology and the Prism of Biography: Lillian Wineman and the Trade in Dakota Beadwork, 1893–1929." *Qualitative Sociology* 22, no. 4 (1999): 353–68.

———. "Land Taking at Spirit Lake: The Competing and Converging Logics of Norwegian and Dakota Women, 1900–1930." In *Norwegian American Women: Migration, Communities, and Identities,* ed. Betty A. Berglund and Lori Ann Lahlum, 211–45. St. Paul: Minnesota Historical Society Press, 2011.

———, and Mignon Duffy. "Mapping the Dispossession: Scandinavian Homesteading at Fort Totten, 1900–1930." *Great Plains Research* 18, no. 1 (Spring 2008): 67–80.

———, and Grey Osterud, "Landowning, Dispossession, and Land Use among Dakota and Scandinavian Women at Spirit Lake, 1900–1929." Unpublished manuscript, 2013.

———, and Ken Chih-Yan Sun. "Localizing Transnational Norwegians: Exploring Nationalism, Language, and Labor Markets in Early Twentieth Century North Dakota." *Norwegian-American Essays* 13 (2011): 73–107.

Haraway, Donna. "Situated Knowledges: The Science Question in Feminism and the Privilege of Partial Perspective." *Feminist Studies* 14 (Autumn 1988): 575–99.

Hared, Agnes Reiten. *The Naked Prairie: Pioneer Life in North Dakota.* New York: Vantage Press, 1992.

Haugen, Einar I. "Norwegians at the Indian Forts on the Missouri River during the Seventies." *Norwegian-American Studies and Records* 6 (1931): 89–121.

———. "Planning for a Standard Language in Modern Norway." *Anthropological Linguistics* 35 (1993): 109–23.

Hernandez, Donald J. "Children's Changing Access to Resources: A Historical Perspective." In *Families in the U.S.: Kinship and Domestic Politics,* ed. Karen V. Hansen and Anita Ilta Garey, 201–15. Philadelphia, PA: Temple University Press, 1998.

Herring, Rebecca J. "The Creation of Indian Farm Women: Field Matrons and Acculturation on the Kiowa-Comanche Reservation, 1895–1906." In *At Home on the Range: Essays on the History of Western Social and Domestic Life,* ed. John R. Wunder, 39–56. Westport, CT: Greenwood Press, 1985.

Hicks, John D. "The Western Middle West, 1900–1914." *Agricultural History* 20, no. 2 (April 1946): 65–77.

Hodes, Martha. "Fractions and Fictions in the United States Census of 1890." In *Haunted by Empire: Geographies of Intimacy in North American History*, ed. Ann Laura Stoler, 240–70. Durham, NC: Duke University Press, 2006.

Hoverstad, Torger Anderson. *The Norwegian Farmers in the United States*. Fargo, ND: Hans Jervell Publishing Co., 1915.

Hoxie, Frederick E. *A Final Promise: The Campaign to Assimilate the Indians, 1880–1920*. Lincoln: University of Nebraska Press, 1984.

———. "Comment on Citizenship and Property Rights." Presented at the American Historical Association meetings, San Diego, CA, January 7, 2010.

———. "Introduction: American Indian Activism in the Progressive Era." In *Talking Back to Civilization: Indian Voices from the Progressive Era*, ed. Frederick E. Hoxie, 1–29. Boston, MA: Bedford/St. Martins, 2001.

———. *Parading through History: The Making of the Crow Nation in America, 1805–1935*. New York: Cambridge University Press, 1995.

———. "Retrieving the Red Continent: Settler Colonialism and the History of American Indians in the U.S." *Ethnic and Racial Studies* 31 (2008): 1153–67.

———. *This Indian Country: American Indian Activists and the Place They Made*. New York: Penguin, 2012.

Hudson, John C. *Plains Country Towns*. Minneapolis: University of Minnesota Press, 1985.

———. "The Study of Western Frontier Populations." In *The American West*, ed. Jerome O. Steffen, 35–60. Norman: University of Oklahoma Press, 1979.

Hyde, Anne F. *Empires, Nations, and Families: A New History of the North American West, 1800–1860*. Lincoln: University of Nebraska Press, 2011.

Hyman, Colette A. *Dakota Women's Work: Creativity, Culture, and Exile*. St. Paul: Minnesota Historical Society Press, 2012.

Jacobs, Margaret D. *White Mother to a Dark Race: Settler Colonialism, Maternalism, and the Removal of Indigenous Children in the American West and Australia, 1880–1940*. Lincoln: University of Nebraska Press, 2009.

Jacobson, Clair. *Whitestone Hill: The Indians and the Battle*. LaCrosse, WI: Pine Tree Publishing, 1991.

Jameson, Elizabeth, and Susan Armitage, eds. *Writing the Range: Race, Class, and Culture in the Women's West*. Norman: University of Oklahoma Press, 1997.

Jensen, Joan M. *Calling This Place Home: Women on the Wisconsin Frontier, 1850–1925*. St. Paul: Minnesota Historical Society Press, 2006.

———. *Promise to the Land: Essays on Rural Women*. Albuquerque: University of New Mexico Press, 1991.

Jeppesen, Torben Grøngaard. *Dannebrog on the American Prairie: A Danish Colony Project in the 1870s—Land Purchase and the Beginnings of a Town*. Trans. James D. Iversen. Odense, Denmark: Odense City Museums, 2000.

Jones, David S. *Rationalizing Epidemics: Meanings and Uses of American Indian Mortality since 1600*. Cambridge, MA: Harvard University Press, 2004.

Jones, Jacqueline. *The Dispossessed: America's Underclasses from the Civil War to the Present*. New York: Basic Books, 1992.

———. *Labor of Love, Labor of Sorrow: Black Women, Work, and the Family from Slavery to the Present*. Rev. and updated ed. New York: Basic Books, 2010.

Joranger, Terje Mikael Hasle. "The Migration of Tradition: Land Tenure and Culture in the U.S. Upper Mid-West." *European Journal of American Studies* 2 (2008): document 3, pp. 2–16. Online since 10 November 2008. Available: http://ejas.revues.org/3252. July 6, 2009.

Kanter, Rosabeth Moss. *Men and Women of the Corporation.* New York: Basic Books, 1977.

Katzman, David M. *Seven Days a Week: Women and Domestic Service in Industrializing America.* New York: Oxford University Press, 1978.

Kerber, Linda K. *No Constitutional Right to Be Ladies: Women and the Obligations of Citizenship.* New York: Hill and Wang, 1998.

Kessler-Harris, Alice. *Gendering Labor History.* Urbana: University of Illinois Press, 2006.

Keyssar, Alexander. *The Right to Vote: The Contested History of Democracy in the United States.* Rev. ed. New York: Basic Books, 2009.

Kibria, Nazli. *Becoming Asian Americans: Second-Generation Chinese and Korean American Identities.* Baltimore, MD: Johns Hopkins University Press, 2002.

Kloberdanz, Timothy J. "In the Land of Inyan Woslata: Plains Indian Influences on Reservation Whites." *Great Plains Quarterly* 7 (1987): 69–82.

Kohl, Seena B. *Working Together: Women and Family in Southwestern Saskatchewan.* Toronto, Ontario: Holt, Rinehart and Winston, 1976.

Krouse, Susan Applegate. *North American Indians in the Great War.* Lincoln: University of Nebraska Press, 2007.

Kuokkanen, Rauna. "Indigenous Economies, Theories of Subsistence, and Women: Exploring the Social Economy Model for Indigenous Governance." *American Indian Quarterly* 35 (2011): 215–40.

Lagerquist, L. DeAne. *In America the Men Milk the Cows: Factors of Gender, Ethnicity, and Religion in the Americanization of Norwegian-American Women.* Brooklyn, NY: Carlson Publishing, 1991.

Lahlum, Lori Ann. " 'Everything Was Changed and Looked Strange': Norwegian Women in South Dakota." *South Dakota History* 35 (Fall 2005): 189–216.

Lambert, Grace, and Cherry Monson. *Dakota Hoksiyopa Wan: "A Dakota Child."* Warwick, ND: privately published, 2001.

Lamont, Michèle, and Virág Molnár. "The Study of Boundaries in the Social Sciences." *Annual Review of Sociology* 28 (2002): 167–95.

Levorsen, Barbara. *The Quiet Conquest: A History of the Lives and Times of the First Settlers of Central North Dakota.* Hawley, MN: Hawley Herald, 1974.

Lillehaugen, Tosten Mikkelsen. "Tosten Mikkelsen Lillehaugen's Autobiography." In *Lillehaugen Family Treasures,* compiled by Theresse Lundby, trans. Selma Lillehaugen Moe, 9–19. 1917. Reprint, Greenbush, MN: privately published, 1988.

Limerick, Patricia Nelson. *Legacy of Conquest: The Unbroken Past of the American West.* New York: W. W. Norton, 1987.

Lindberg, Duane Rodell. *Men of the Cloth and the Social-Cultural Fabric of the Norwegian Ethnic Community in North Dakota.* New York: Arno Press, 1980.

Lindgren, H. Elaine. "Ethnic Women Homesteading on the Plains of North Dakota." *Great Plains Quarterly* 9, no. 3 (Summer 1989): 157–73.

———. *Land in Her Own Name: Women as Homesteaders in North Dakota.* Fargo: North Dakota Institute for Regional Studies, 1991.

Littlefield, Daniel F., Jr., and Lonnie E. Underhill. "Renaming the American Indian: 1890–1913." *American Studies* 12, no. 2 (Fall 1971): 33–45.

Lomawaima, K. Tsianina. *They Called It Prairie Light: The Story of Chilocco Indian School.* Lincoln: University of Nebraska Press, 1994.

Lovoll, Odd S., ed. *Cultural Pluralism Versus Assimilation: The Views of Waldemar Ager.* Northfield, MN: Norwegian-American Historical Association, 1977.

——. *Norwegian Newspapers in America: Connecting Norway and the New Land.* St. Paul: Minnesota Historical Society Press, 2010.

——. *Norwegians on the Prairie: Ethnicity and the Development of the Country Town.* St. Paul: Minnesota Historical Society Press, 2006.

——. *The Promise of America: A History of the Norwegian-American People.* Minneapolis: University of Minnesota Press, 1984.

Lowie, Robert H. "Dance Associations of the Eastern Dakota." *Anthropological Papers of the American Museum of Natural History* 11 (June 1913): 101–42.

——. *Robert H. Lowie, Ethnology: A Personal Record.* Berkeley: University of California Press, 1959.

Lundby, Theresse Nelson, Kristie Nelson-Neuhaus, and Ann Nordland Wallace, eds. *Live Well: The Letters of Sigrid Gjeldaker Lillehaugen.* Minneapolis, MN: Western Home Books, 2004.

Lynn-Sherow, Bonnie. *Red Earth: Race and Agriculture in Oklahoma Territory.* Lawrence: University of Kansas Press, 2004.

Maddox, Lucy. *Citizen Indians: Native American Intellectuals, Race, and Reform.* Ithaca, NY: Cornell University Press, 2005.

——. "Politics, Performance and Indian Identity." *American Studies International* 40, no. 2 (June 2002): 7–36.

Magel, Trevor M. "The Political Effect of the Ku Klux Klan in North Dakota." Master's thesis, University of Nebraska, 2011.

Mandell, Daniel R. *Tribe, Race, History: Native Americans in Southern New England, 1780–1880.* Baltimore, MD: Johns Hopkins University Press, 2008.

Martin, M. Kay, and Barbara Voorhies. *Female of the Species.* New York: Columbia University Press, 1975.

McCormack, J. Michael. "Soldiers and Sioux: Military Life among the Indians at Fort Totten." In *Fort Totten: Military Post and Indian School, 1867–1959,* ed. Larry Remele, 9–22. Bismarck: State Historical Society of North Dakota, 1986.

McLaughlin, James. *My Friend the Indian.* 1910. Reprint, Lincoln: University of Nebraska Press, 1989.

Medicine, Beatrice. *Learning to Be an Anthropologist and Remaining "Native."* Urbana: University of Illinois Press, 2001.

Mendelsohn, Daniel. *The Lost: A Search for Six of Six Million.* New York: Harper Perennial, 2006.

Meriam, Lewis. *The Problem of Indian Administration.* Baltimore, MD: Johns Hopkins University Press, 1928.

Meyer, Melissa L. *The White Earth Tragedy: Ethnicity and Dispossession at a Minnesota Anishinaabe Reservation.* Lincoln: University of Nebraska Press, 1994.

Monson, Cherry Wood. *Forde Acres.* Warwick, ND: Brenorsome Museum, 1975.

——, Betty Loe Westby, Cherrie Lane Monson Anderson, and Stella Rasmusson Papachek. *Warwick Memories.* Warwick, ND: privately published, 2002.

Morlan, Robert L. *Political Prairie Fire: The Nonpartisan League, 1915–1922.* 1955. Reprint, St. Paul: Minnesota Historical Society Press, 1985.

Moum, Kathleen. "The Social Origins of the Nonpartisan League." *North Dakota History* 53 (Winter 1986): 18–22.

Neth, Mary. *Preserving the Family Farm: Women, Community and the Foundations of Agribusiness in the Midwest, 1900–1940*. Baltimore, MD: Johns Hopkins University Press, 1995.

Ngai, Mae M. *Impossible Subjects: Illegal Aliens and the Making of Modern America*. Princeton, NJ: Princeton University Press, 2004.

Nicolisi, Ann Marie. "'We Do Not Want Our Girls to Marry Foreigners': Gender, Race, and American Citizenship." *National Women's Studies Association Journal* 13, no. 3 (Autumn 2001): 1–21.

Nielsen, Eugene. *Oberon, N.D., 1884–1990: "Echoes of the Past."* Fargo, ND: Richtman's Printing and Packaging, 1991.

Nielsen, Kim E. "'We All Leaguers by Our House': Women, Suffrage, and Red-Baiting in the National Nonpartisan League." *Journal of Women's History* 6, no. 1 (Spring 1994): 31–50.

Norton, L. J. "The Land Market and Farm Mortgage Debts, 1917–1921." *Journal of Farm Economics* 24, no. 1 (February 1942): 168–77.

Nugent, Walter. *Progressivism: A Very Short Introduction*. New York: Oxford University Press, 2010.

O'Brien, Jean M. *Dispossession by Degrees: Indian Land and Identity in Natick, Massachusetts, 1650–1790*. New York: Cambridge University Press, 1997.

———. *Firsting and Lasting: Writing Indians Out of Existence in New England*. Minneapolis: University of Minnesota Press, 2010.

Ödegaard, Örnulv. "Emigration and Insanity: A Study of Mental Disease among the Norwegianborn Population of Minnesota." *Acta Psychiatrica et Neurologica*, Supplementum I (1932): 11–190.

Olsen, Tillie. *Tell Me a Riddle*. New York: Dell Publishing, 1956.

———. *Yonnondio from the Thirties*. New York: Dell Publishing, 1974.

Olson, Daron W. "Norwegians, Socialism and the Nonpartisan League in North Dakota, 1904–1920: How Red Was Their Protest?" Master's thesis, University of North Dakota, 1993.

Omi, Michael, and Howard Winant. *Racial Formation in the United States: From the 1960s to the 1990s*. New York: Routledge, 1994.

Oneroad, Amos E., and Alanson B. Skinner. *Being Dakota: Tales and Traditions of the Sisseton and Wahpeton*, ed. Laura L. Anderson. St. Paul: Minnesota Historical Society Press, 2003.

Osterud, Grey. *Putting the Barn before the House: Women and Family Farming in Early Twentieth-Century New York*. Ithaca, NY: Cornell University Press, 2012.

———. Nancy Grey. *Bonds of Community: The Lives of Farm Women in Nineteenth-Century New York*. Ithaca, NY: Cornell University Press, 1991.

Østerud, Øyvind. *Agrarian Structure and Peasant Politics in Scandinavia: A Comparative Study of Rural Response to Economic Change*. Oslo, Norway: Universitetsforlaget, 1978.

Otis, D.S. *The Dawes Act and the Allotment of Indian Lands*. 1934. Reprint, Norman: University of Oklahoma Press, 1973.

Øverland, Orm. "Intruders on Native Ground: Troubling Silences and Memories of the Land-Taking in Norwegian Immigrant Letters." In *Transnational American Memories*, ed. Udo J. Hebel, 79–104. Berlin: Walter de Gruyter, 2009.

———. "Skandinaven and the Beginnings of Professional Publishing." *Norwegian-American Studies* 31 (1986): 187–214.

———. *The Western Home: A Literary History of Norwegian America*. Northfield, MN: Norwegian American Historical Association, 1996.

Paaverud, Merlan E., Jr. "Swimming with the Current: Education at the Fort Totten Indian School." In *Fort Totten: Military Post and Indian School, 1867–1959*, ed. Larry Remele, 43–56. Bismarck: State Historical Society of North Dakota, 1986.

Pederson, Jane Marie. *Between Memory and Reality: Family and Community in Rural Wisconsin, 1870–1970*. Madison: University of Wisconsin Press, 1992.

Perdue, Theda, ed. *Sifters: Native American Women's Lives*. New York: Oxford University Press, 2001.

Pfaller, Louis L. *James McLaughlin: The Man with an Indian Heart*. Richardton, ND: Assumption Abbey Press, 1992.

Pratt, Mary Louise. *Imperial Eyes: Travel Writing and Transculturation*. New York: Routledge, 1992.

Price, Monroe E. *Law and the American Indian*. Indianapolis, IN: Bobbs-Merrill, 1973.

Prucha, Francis Paul. *American Indian Policy in Crisis: Christian Reformers and the Indian, 1865–1900*. Norman: University of Oklahoma Press, 1976.

———. *The Great Father: The United States Government and the American Indians*. Lincoln: University of Nebraska Press, 1984.

———. *Indian Policy in the United States: Historical Essays*. Lincoln: University of Nebraska, 1981.

Qualey, Carlton C. *Norwegian Settlement in the United States*. New York: Arno Press and the New York Times, 1970.

Raaen, Aagot. *Grass of the Earth*. 1950. Reprint, St. Paul: Minnesota Historical Society Press, 1994.

Rabinow, Paul, and William M. Sullivan. "The Interpretive Turn: A Second Look." In *Interpretive Social Science: A Second Look*, ed. Paul Rabinow and William M. Sullivan, 1–30. Berkeley: University of California Press, 1987.

Raj, Dhooleka Sarhadi. "Ignorance, Forgetting, and Family Nostalgia: Partition, the Nation State, and Refugees in Delhi." *Social Analysis* 44, no. 2 (2000): 30–55.

Reifel, Nancy. "American Indian Views of Public Health Nursing." *American Indian Culture and Research Journal* 23, no. 3 (1999): 143–54.

Reyhner, Jon, and Jeanne Eder. *American Indian Education: A History*. Norman: University of Oklahoma Press, 2004.

Richardson, Heather Cox. *West from Appomattox: The Reconstruction of America after the Civil War*. New Haven, CT: Yale University Press, 2007.

Riggs, Stephen R. *A Dakota-English Dictionary*, ed. James Owen Dorsey. 1890. Reprint, St. Paul: Minnesota Historical Society Press, 1992.

Roach, Ellen Mattson. "The Early Days at Sheyenne." In *History of the Sheyenne Area, 1883–1976*, 4–5. Sheyenne, ND: Sheyenne Bicentennial Commission, [1976].

Robinson, Elwyn B. *History of North Dakota*. Lincoln: University of Nebraska Press, 1966.

Rogers, Elwin E. *For God and Land: Brown Earth, a Dakota Indian Community 1876–1892*. Sioux Falls, SD: Pine Hill Press, 2002.

Rogin, Michael Paul. *The Intellectuals and McCarthy: The Radical Specter*. Cambridge, MA: MIT Press, 1967.

Rølvaag, Ole E. *Concerning Our Heritage*. Trans. Solveig Zempel. Northfield, MN: Norwegian-American Historical Association, 1998.

———. *Giants in the Earth: A Saga of the Prairie*. Trans. Lincoln Colcord and the Author. New York: Harper & Brothers, 1927.

Rose, Arthur P. *An Illustrated History of Jackson County, Minnesota*. Jackson, MN: Northern History Publishing Company, 1910.

Ryan, Judy R. Peterson. "Chautauqua in Devils Lake, North Dakota: An Historical Study of the Organization, the Facilities, and the Programs." Master's thesis, University of North Dakota, 1990.

Sachs, Carolyn E. *The Invisible Farmers: Women in Agricultural Production*. Totowa, NJ: Rowman & Allanheld, 1983.

Salamon, Sonya. "Sibling Solidarity as an Operating Strategy in Illinois Agriculture." *Rural Sociology* 47, no. 2 (Summer 1982): 349–68.

———, and Ann Mackey Keim. "Land Ownership and Women's Power in a Midwestern Farming Community." *Journal of Marriage and the Family* 41, no. 1 (February 1979): 109–19.

———, and Vicki Lockhart. "Land Ownership and the Position of Elderly in Farm Families." *Human Organization* 39 (Winter 1980): 324–31.

———, and Shirley M. O'Reilly. "Family Land and Development Cycles among Illinois Farmers." *Rural Sociology* 44, no. 3 (Fall 1979): 525–42.

Salinger, Sharon V. *"To Serve Well and Faithfully": Labor and Indentured Servants in Pennsylvania, 1682–1800*. New York: Cambridge University Press, 1987.

Sandoz, Mari. *These Were the Sioux*. New York: Hastings House, 1961.

Sannes, Erling N. " 'Free Land for All': A Young Norwegian Woman Homesteads in North Dakota." *North Dakota History* 60, no. 2 (1993): 24–28.

Sanchez, George J. "Race, Nation, and Culture in Recent Immigration Studies." *Journal of American Ethnic History* 18 (Summer 1999): 66–84.

Satterlee, Marion P. *Outbreak and Massacre by the Dakota Indians in Minnesota in 1862*, ed. Don Heinrich Tolzmann. 1925. Reprint, Westminster, MD: Heritage Books, 2001.

Saunt, Claudio. *Black, White, and Indian: Race and the Unmaking of an American Family*. New York: Oxford University Press, 2005.

Schmeckebier, Laurence F. *The Office of Indian Affairs: Its History, Activities and Organization*. Baltimore, MD: Johns Hopkins University Press, 1927.

Schuetz, Alfred. "The Homecomer." *American Journal of Sociology* 50, no. 5 (March 1945): 369–76.

———. "The Stranger: An Essay in Social Psychology." *American Journal of Sociology* 49 (May 1944): 499–507.

Schultz, April R. *Ethnicity on Parade: Inventing the Norwegian American through Celebration*. Amherst: University of Massachusetts Press, 1994.

Semmingsen, Ingrid. *Norway to America: A History of the Migration*. Trans. Einar Haugen. Minneapolis: University of Minnesota Press, 1978.

Setten, Gunhild. "Farmers, Planners, and the Moral Message of Landscape and Nature." *Ethics, Place, and Environment* 4, no. 3 (2001): 220–25.

Sherman, William C. *Prairie Mosaic: An Ethnic Atlas of Rural North Dakota*. Fargo: North Dakota Institute for Regional Studies, 1983.

———, Playford V. Thorson, Warren A. Henke, Timothy J. Kloberdanz, Theodore B. Pedeliski, and Robert P. Wilkins, eds. *Plains Folk: North Dakota's Ethnic History*. Fargo: North Dakota Institute for Regional Studies, 1988.

Shoemaker, Nancy. "Introduction." In *Negotiators of Change: Historical Perspectives on Native American Women*, ed. Nancy Shoemaker, 1–25. New York: Routledge, 1995.

Simonsen, Jane E. *Making Home Work: Domesticity and Native American Assimilation in the American West, 1860–1919*. Chapel Hill: University of North Carolina Press, 2006.

Skowronek, Stephen. *Building a New American State: The Expansion of National Administrative Capacities, 1877–1920*. New York: Cambridge University Press, 1982.

Skurdall, James A. *Skurdall–Skurdell–Skurdahl: Emigrants from Sør-Fron to Dakota Territory: A Norwegian-American Family History*. Decorah, IA: Anundsen Publishing Co., 1999.

Smith, Sherry L. "Beyond Princess and Squaw: Army Officers' Perceptions of Indian Women." In *The Women's West*, ed. Susan Armitage and Elizabeth Jameson, 63–75. Norman: University of Oklahoma, 1987.

Snyder, Eldon E. "The Chautauqua Movement in Popular Culture: A Sociological Analysis." *Journal of American Culture* 8, no. 3 (1985): 79–90.

Stacey, Judith. "Can There Be a Feminist Ethnography?" In *Women's Words: The Feminist Practice of Oral History*, ed. Sherna Gluck and Daphne Patai, 111–19. New York: Routledge, 1991.

Starr, Karen. "Fighting for a Future: Farm Women of the Nonpartisan League." *Minnesota History* (Summer 1983): 255–62.

Stegner, Wallace. *The Sense of Place*. Madison, WI: Silver Buckle Press, 1986.

———. *Wolf Willow: A History, a Story, and a Memory of the Last Plains Frontier*. New York: Viking, 1962.

Stoler, Ann Laura, ed. *Haunted by Empire: Geographies of Intimacy in North American History*. Durham, NC: Duke University Press, 2006.

Strasser, Susan. *Never Done: A History of American Housework*. New York: Pantheon Books, 1982.

Stremlau, Rose. *Sustaining the Cherokee Family: Kinship and the Allotment of an Indigenous Nation*. Chapel Hill: University of North Carolina Press, 2011.

Szasz, Margaret Connell. *Education and the American Indian: The Road to Self-Determination since 1928*. 3rd ed. Albuquerque: University of New Mexico Press, 1999.

Thornton, Russell. *American Indian Holocaust and Survival: A Population History since 1492*. Norman: University of Oklahoma Press, 1987.

———. "Native American Demographic and Tribal Survival into the Twenty-First Century." *American Studies* 46, no. 3/4 (Fall–Winter 2005): 23–38.

Trachtenberg, Alan. *Shades of Hiawatha: Staging Indians, Making Americans, 1880–1930*. New York: Hill and Wang, 2004.

Trupin, Sophie. *Dakota Diaspora: Memoirs of a Jewish Homesteader*. Lincoln: University of Nebraska Press, 1984.

Underhill, Lonnie E., and Daniel F. Littlefield, Jr. *Hamlin Garland's Observations of the American Indian, 1895–1905*. Tucson: University of Arizona Press, 1976.

Van Kirk, Sylvia. *Many Tender Ties: Women in Fur-Trade Society, 1670–1870*. Norman: University of Oklahoma Press, 1980.

Vanek, Joanne. "Time Spent in Housework." *Scientific American* (November 1974): 116–20.

Vučković, Myriam. *Voices from Haskell: Indian Students between Two Worlds, 1884–1928*. Lawrence: University Press of Kansas, 2008.

Wall, Wendy. "Gender and the 'Citizen Indian.'" In *Writing the Range: Race, Class, and Culture in the Women's West*, ed. Elizabeth Jameson and Susan Armitage, 202–29. Norman: University of Oklahoma Press, 1997.

Warner, R. Stephen. "Work in Progress toward a New Paradigm for the Sociological Study of Religion in the United States." *American Journal of Sociology* 98 (March 1993): 1044–93.

Warren, Kim Cary. *The Quest for Citizenship: African American and Native American Education in Kansas, 1880–1935*. Chapel Hill: University of North Carolina Press, 2010.

Weist, Katherine M. "Beasts of Burden and Menial Slaves: Nineteenth Century Observations of Northern Plains Indian Women." In *The Hidden Half: Studies of Plains Indian Women*, ed. Patricia C. Albers and Beatrice Medicine, 29–52. Washington, DC: University Press of America, 1983.

Wenger, Tisa. "Indian Dances and the Politics of Religious Freedom, 1870–1930." *Journal of the American Academy of Religion* 79 (2011): 850–878.

———. *We Have a Religion: The 1920s Pueblo Indian Dance Controversy and American Religious Freedom*. Chapel Hill: University of North Carolina Press, 2009.

Whelan, Mary K. "Dakota Indian Economics and the Nineteenth-Century Fur Trade." *Ethnohistory* 40, no. 2 (1993): 246–76.

White, Richard. *Railroaded: The Transcontinentals and the Making of Modern America*. New York: W. W. Norton, 2011.

Willrich, Michael. *Pox: An American History*. New York: Penguin, 2012.

Wilson, Raymond. *Ohiyesa: Charles Eastman, Santee Sioux*. Urbana: University of Illinois Press, 1983.

Wilson, Waziyatawin Angela. *Remember This! Dakota Decolonization and the Eli Taylor Narratives*. Lincoln: University of Nebraska Press, 2005.

Wimmer, Andreas. "The Making and Unmaking of Ethnic Boundaries: A Multilevel Process Theory." *American Journal of Sociology* 113 (January 2008): 970–1022.

Wishart, David J. *An Unspeakable Sadness: The Dispossession of the Nebraska Indians*. Lincoln: University of Nebraska Press, 1994.

Witgen, Michael. *An Infinity of Nations: How the Native New World Shaped Early North America*. Philadelphia: University of Pennsylvania Press, 2012.

———. "Imagining Colonialism: The United States, the Native New World, and the Fantasy of an Unsettled Continent." Presented at the Native American and Indigenous Studies Association meetings, Uncaseville, CT, June 4–6, 2012.

Wold, Frances. "The Letters of Effie Hanson, 1917–1923: Farm Life in Troubled Times." *North Dakota History* 48, no. 1 (Winter 1981): 20–43.

Wolf, Eric R. *Europe and the People without a History*. Berkeley: University of California Press, 1982.

Wolfe, Patrick. "Settler Colonialism and the Elimination of the Native." *Journal of Genocide Research* 8 (December 2006): 387–409.

Wolfley, Jeanette. "Jim Crow, Indian Style: The Disenfranchisement of Native Americans." *American Indian Law Review* 16 (1991): 167–202.

Wood, Cherrie Lane, and Cherry Wood Monson. *Thanks for the Cornfield*. Warwick, ND: privately published, 1980.

Wood, W. Raymond. "An Introduction to the History of the Fur Trade on the Northern Plains." *North Dakota History* 61, no. 3 (1994): 2–6.

Wright, Myrtle. "A Ritual for Citizenship." *The National Magazine* (October 1916–March 1917): 331–33.

Wyman, Mark. *Round-Trip to America: The Immigrants Return to Europe, 1880–1930*. Ithaca, NY: Cornell University Press, 1993.

Young, Carrie. *Nothing to Do but Stay: My Pioneer Mother*. Iowa City: University of Iowa Press, 1991.

Zelizer, Viviana. *Pricing the Priceless Child: The Changing Social Value of Children*. New York: Basic Books, 1985.

Zitkala-Ša. *American Indian Stories*. 1921. Reprint, Lincoln: University of Nebraska Press, 2003.

Zolberg, Aristide R. "Immigration Control Policy: Law and Implementation." In *The New Americans: A Guide to Immigration since 1965*, ed. Mary C. Waters and Reed Ueda with Helen B. Marrow, 29–55. Cambridge, MA: Harvard University Press, 2007.

———. "Matters of State: Theorizing Immigration Policy." In *The Handbook of International Migration: The American Experience*, ed. Charles Hirschman, Philip Kasinitz and Josh DeWind, 71–93. New York: Russell Sage Foundation, 1999.

Index

Printed in the USA/Agawam, MA
January 13, 2020

747760.019